DO
is
GOD
Spelled
Backwards

Best Wishes, Clark

A Memoir

Clark Malcolm Greene

by Clark Malcolm Greene

PublishAmerica

Baltimore

© 2004 by Clark Malcolm Greene.
All rights reserved. No part of this book may be reproduced, stored in a retrieval system, or transmitted in any form or by any means without the prior written permission of the publishers, except by a reviewer who may quote brief passages in a review to be printed in a newspaper, magazine, or journal.

First printing

ISBN: 1-4137-8778-9
PUBLISHED BY PUBLISHAMERICA, LLLP
www.publishamerica.com
Baltimore

Printed in the United States of America

This book is dedicated to Paula Jean Matrosic Greene; for all the late night and early morning listening, the hand claps, and most of all for bringing me light when my thoughts grew dark.
Some people get no chances in life, some people get only one. You gave me two. You fill up my heart as well as my soul.

I'd like to acknowledge two other extraordinary women. Minus either one, this book might never have seen the daylight:

Phoebe Greene Linden – there is no measure adequate to you. I've loved you every minute. Thanks for being my sister.

Elaine Jordaan – without your keen eyes, the eternal cups of coffee and endless cigarettes, this book would still be rambling about.

Wait for Me

Pockets stuffed with memories, I run
back in time and place, trying to catch up with
a black and tan dog whose feet leave dusty detonations
on long ago country roads and old new sown fields.

Bounding dog, bouncing through tall marsh grass.
Vigilant to her boy, whose legs can't quite keep the pace.
Wooly Bear Dog chasing rabbits, or deer,
or butterflies, the same for one as another.

Big Dog, strong enough to carry us to other worlds,
and get back home in time for supper.
Rowdy Dog to strangers, man or beast, who get too close,
she lies quiet as I pull cockleburs and stickers who hitched our travels.

Sweating cheeks and panting tongue tell tall tales
far better than any boy words at dinner time when,
smells of Dog mixed with soap-scrubbed hands and meat-loaf
and bread pudding while she waits for Mom to look away.

Guarding Dog, on my bed lies in wait for dark dragons,
and dreaming of tomorrow's Indians and antelopes.
We sleep our way to sunrise,
knowing we have endless days to go.

One grows up, the other grows old,
while the man still runs to catch up.

Wait for me, Patch.

DOG Is GOD Spelled Backwards
Table of Contents

Chapter 1

First Breath

I wasn't really born on December 1, 1946. Despite the notice of Gerald and Dorothee's, "Little Tarzan"—9 pound, 10 ½ ounces—in the local paper, I drew my first real breath on March 2, 1950.

Our family hadn't yet reached its full compliment of four children; the additions of another brother and sister were still years away. In the spring of 1950, much of my energy was directed toward being me and it took every minute I had to do a good job. As the only boy in a family, I had several distinct advantages; one being that my parents were constantly trying to figure out how to keep me from pestering everyone else in the family.

We lived on the fringe of town and had a few animals: free roaming chickens kept for eggs, a few rabbits in cages kept for the meat they provided, and one goat kept for the heck of it. When I was tired of causing the chickens to stop laying eggs, wearing the goat to a frazzle or trampling up the garden, my energy could always be directed at my sister, Carole. About the best thing I could do was to make her holler. Carole, who'd be seven in September, called it being obnoxious.

I can still hear her piteous wails: "Mooooooooooooooooom, Clark's bothering meeeeeeeeeeeeee!!!!!!"

I had turned three that past December and we were still living in my hometown of Manchester, Michigan. When my father didn't have to work we sometimes went for rides on the weekends, so I wasn't too surprised when the order came for us to all "pile in" the car.

That Saturday would be one of those "let's take a ride days." Mom packed up a lunch of ham sandwiches and cold baked potatoes, an apple for each of us and a glass bottle of milk wrapped in a towel to share. Then off we went.

We piled into the family car, a Plymouth as I recall, and set off through the Irish Hills of Michigan. We stopped by the lighthouse at Big Silver Lake for lunch, enjoying the sweet spring air. Although still chilly, the trees around the lake had begun their transformation already and fringed the shores with that new pale green of spring. Set against the crystal blue of the lake from up on the hill, the view was a beautiful jeweled crown of colors.

Lunch was over quickly, just because I was three and a half. It was time to go when the only thing I could think of to do with my apple core was to put it down the back of Carole's blouse. Actions like this always worked to get the family moving and I thought we were going to head back to the house. Instead we started off in another direction, drove through a small village marked with a sign "Michigan Center." I was pretty surprised when we stopped by a farmhouse I didn't know.

I was already reading by then, early some said, but to me it almost came naturally and I read everything my eyes grabbed onto. As we turned into the dirt driveway, I saw nailed to one of the fence posts a sign that read, "PUPPIES FOR SALE" with the both the S's backwards. I read it out loud in case anybody had missed it.

"Puppies, Momma! Puppies, are you kiddin' me?" I almost shouted to the back of Momma and Dad's heads.

My mother turned in her seat as we pulled up and came to a stop, while Dad honked the horn. "Well Clark, do you think you'd like a puppy?" she asked. "Would you take really good care of one?"

"Yes! Yes!"

Before the dust had settled, our car was surrounded by two large dogs and what looked like about a hundred black and tan puppies. The big ones looked and sounded fearsome—deep and loud, hoarsely rasping in their warning barks. One of them put its paws on the car door to investigate through the quickly rolled up window and continued its loud announcement. Neither of my parents got out of the car until someone stuck their head out the back door of the house and hollered, "I'll be right there. You dogs! GIT! GIT!"

The two adult dogs did, but the puppies kept up their barking and woofing, roiling around the car like overgrown ants from a disturbed anthill.

An overalled man walked out to the car and Dad rolled down the window as if to ask a question, but the farmer was already saying, "It's okay, the big ones won't bother you now I'm out here."

What did he mean? What did "bother" mean? If he went inside, would we be "bothered"? I thought. Those two big dogs were gigantic.

We cautiously piled out (for some reason the Greene family always "piled" in or out whenever a car was concerned) and were immediately engulfed by the horde of squirming, prancing dancing, hind-end wriggling dogs.

"Where are their tails?" I asked, both enchanted and baffled.

Why, they had 'em, but they were really short! I remember being astonished about this, but I didn't have much time for more thinking. Slobber and spit, nails scratching, jumping up and down, couldn't hang on to them; they were dervishes, wild and careening all over the barnyard. Teeth and tugs pulled on jacket and pant legs. Nips and practice bites.

"Ouch! Ouch! Their teeth are sharp!" I hollered.

My mother laughed. "Oh Clark, you won't bleed to death."

They smelled of dog. Perfect. They were puppy breath and something sharp; a mix of puppy poop and pee, their mother's milk and straw and dust. Puppies and puppies have to be the two best smells God ever made. I was in heaven.

My Dad, meanwhile, was in deep negotiations with the farmer for what would be, in our family, a large purchase. Buying this dog would be akin to purchasing an appliance; it was expected to be of good value and to last a long time. My sister Carole put up with the chaos of the litter for a while but soon retreated to the car where she sat with the door open and her legs sticking out. She pulled her legs in and closed the door whenever one of the puppies went over to her and they soon got the message. She would like a puppy but it would always be on her terms.

Momma, good country girl that she was, had knelt down and was laughingly welcoming tongues to lick and noses to prod, her chin lifted to accept their kisses. Me too, me too! But these puppies were more than I could handle; up on hind legs, they knocked me this way and that, a shoving match among friends. They just wouldn't slow down long enough for me to latch on to one.

What bundles of energy! Whenever I could stroke a flank or pat a neck as they skyrocketed by, I would feel the mass of flesh and muscle, almost bursting through the silky black and tan curls. They were smooth, with soft ringlets of fur. I was later to find out that they had hair, a distinction that was important for some reason. They were Airedale Terriers and according to the adult examples that were keeping us under watchful eye, would get pretty big.

The adults had wiry, stiff curls and the male dog particularly was impressive. I was a pretty big boy for three and this dog was a lot bigger than me. Actually, at about 95 pounds, he was huge. The big dogs had come up and introduced themselves and after apparently finding no real threat, retired to the background. They didn't lie down but sat like sentinels, watching every move like guards, why, like a… guard dog! Heck, the big dogs were probably glad we were here, a puppy diversion to get rid of their offspring for a little while. These pups were wild! We had only been there about 15 minutes and I was tired already!

"Which one do you like, son?" Momma was asking.

How on earth could I tell? I hadn't had my hands on one for more than a few seconds. I did have at least nine teeth imprints to choose from but that wasn't much help. Mom and Dad were serious about this puppy thing! The pups were about ten weeks old and we could take one home today!

I was going to have to choose.

"Can I have them all?"

Everybody except Dad thought that was hilarious.

Momma said, "Choose one, son. We'll want a female."

Female, I thought? I was going to have to get even more help here. *How can I tell?* I could tell you basic stuff, like color and size and number of feet and ears. *Female?* There ought to be a label. I hadn't a clue.

It's a good thing puppies soon wear out. As their energy flagged, they would plop down randomly in the dust or rustle in several small wind-blown piles of old hay. Several took advantage of the watering trough, came over to give us a friendly swipe of their wet muzzles and then collapsed. One snuck up on Carole when she wasn't looking.

"Mooooooom," Carole keened from the car. "The puppies are getting my good dress all wet and slobbery."

"Oh honey," Mom soothed, "you're okay. Slobber will wash out and you won't melt."

Good, I thought. Now they were holding sort of still and I had the chance for study. They were all so much alike. Some were a bit bigger, but they were black and tan, with quick eyes and big feet. Momma and Dad were doing some figuring too. As Dad followed her, Momma picked up each puppy. *Wow, she looked right at their butts*! I would have gotten in trouble for that. Parents can surely be a puzzle sometimes. They even discussed each's butt briefly, either nodding or shaking their heads, before moving on to the next.

Suddenly, one of the puppies was through with its break and gamboled over to where I was kneeling in the dirt, grabbed firmly on to the cuff of my coat and gave a pull. It was one of the ones that got an affirmative nod. Nodding heads were always good in my book, though I didn't know for sure what it meant about puppies.

This pup growled in a language I understood perfectly. "Rrrrr, rrrrr." *Let's go.*

Momma asked, "It looks like you've been chosen, son. Do you want her?"

I got a little puppy rumble to tell me she wanted play, that I needn't be afraid, and an extra tug indicating my expected obedience.

"RRRRrrgh!" *Now!* She deepened her throaty growl for emphasis. "RRRRRRRRRrrGH!" *I said c'mon!*

Yes, yes, I understood! A second language and I'm only three!

She helped me to my feet and I followed the gyrating, on again, off again, punctuated pulls of her teeth. I allowed myself to be lead in whatever direction she chose, never mind about the coat.

Momma and Dad both laughed at me.

This puppy was the most beautiful one of the bunch: tan legs and feet, with a black saddle in the middle of her back. The black extended over top of her tail, but her sides and soft belly were a sandy tan. Her coat was soft, soft, soft as only a puppy's can be. She had the start of some whiskers on her muzzle, a wet nose and a wondering look on her face when she cocked her head to peer at me. She gave me some good long licks when I bent down to look in her eyes. I liked that, so I licked her back. She liked it, too! Mom said her tail had been docked.

"Like with a boat?" I asked.

"No son, in this case, docked means cut off. Airedales are supposed to have their tails cut short, although sometimes they're left long," Dad said knowingly. "Only idiots leave their Airedale's tail long."

"Ow! Does it hurt?" I asked, horrified at the thought of cutting, but glad I wasn't going to be considered an idiot.

"Son," my mother instructed me, "the animal doctor, a ve-tre-nar-i-un, always gives them shots in their tails to take the pain away before they get cut. Now you say: ve-tre-nar-i-un."

My mother seldom missed chances to introduce us to new words. I recited, "Ve-te-nary-man." Okay, got it; short tails means docked, animal doctors and no idiots here.

Dad gave the man some money, the puppy gave me the slip, dashed over and slathered several of her littermates with a lick and a bite goodbye, and she was off to the races once more. She did not say goodbye to the mommy and daddy dogs, but ran straight back to us, standing now by the car.

This pup knew something. I'd have to find out what it was.

"Take her out in the field and have her go potty. You'll have to get her away from the other puppies so she doesn't get distracted," my mother directed.

Boy *taking* puppy really means getting the puppy to chase the boy.

"Run away from her son. She'll follow you if you just run," Momma instructed. As I turned, the pup did too and soon we were moving in the same direction, side by side.

But more importantly, at the moment I didn't have a hint about this potty thing. *Was there a button?* I asked myself and secretly looked, but didn't see anything obvious. I'd find out later. I didn't have to wait very long, because the pup seemed to know what was required. Soon she squatted daintily and yep, went potty like a good girl. *Phheeww!* I hadn't pushed anything, and she did something, so I didn't have to sound dumb asking that question. Why, this was gonna be easy!

My puppy ran around in a couple of circles to indicate she was ready for something else and we headed back to the driveway.

She got in on my side, behind Dad, took to the car readily and wasn't scared or hesitant once we started off toward home. I think she even piled in just like the rest of us. She was, however, a real handful in the back seat. She investigated everything—Carole, the car seat, the picnic basket. She grabbed used napkins and waxed paper, licked mayonnaise from the paper plates and made a general mess of the picnic remnants.

"Moooooom, Clark's dog is chewing the napkins," Carole bleated.

"Carole Beth, instead of complaining, help your brother," Momma directed. "Besides, she's a family dog."

"Momma!" I yelled mightily. "I thought you said she's my dog!" I was righteously indignant. "I had to choose her and everything!"

"Don't forget Clark, she chose you," Momma stated as she looked right into my eyes. "Yes, she's your dog, because you're going to learn how to take care of her, but she is also a family dog and she needs to like everyone."

"Even Carole?"

"He's going to make his dog not like me," she wailed.

"She'll like you just fine if you're nice to her," Momma admonished. "Now Clark, don't let her chew those napkins. Carole, help him."

"Don't make me stop this car, you two," Dad menaced from the front seat as the commotion grew.

"Yes, honey, do stop the car and put the picnic basket in the trunk," Momma said patiently.

Dad finally had to stop. My puppy didn't have a collar on and was impossible to hold. Better the basket in the trunk than the dog. Dad grumbled, Momma just thought it was funny and Carole might have, too. My puppy then proceeded to get stuck, butt up, under the front seat. It looked like a passage and a place to crawl but it wasn't. Fortunately, she had really only lodged about halfway. This dog was hilarious! Carole managed to pull the puppy back out from under the seat, but then wouldn't give her back to me. I made pinching threats with my fingers until she finally handed her over.

Momma had noticed my pincers, too. "Let's see if we can figure out a name, you two." My mother's suggestion was more of a command. "Do you have any ideas?"

The puppy crawled up in my lap to hear the outcome.

All of the Greene family pets had names that began with "P." My Uncle Dave insisted that since the word pet begins with a "P," all pets' names had to as well and it had become a family tradition.

Momma had a canary named Piper, our goat was named Petunia, the chickens (yes the chickens, too) were Pete the rooster, while the hens were Pat, Polly, Pam, Priscilla, Penny, Priss, and Pot-luck. My Dad named the last chicken (you could tell where his thoughts were.) I never knew which chicken was which, but Momma did. Our rabbits were Peter Rabbit and Pollyanna, Prince and Princess, two breeding pairs, though sometimes Peter Rabbit was put with Princess and Prince was put with Pollyanna. Besides, the males were mostly kept in separate cages until some special day known only by Momma. Who can figure with rabbits? We never bothered to name any of their baby rabbits as they were destined for the freezer as soon as possible.

Okay, my puppy needed a name. Had to be a girl's name too. I suggested using Grandma's first name: Phoebe, but only Dad got a kick out of that idea. Mom thought not.

"Okay, let's see," I started naming. "Pepper, Panther, Paper, Pip, Penny, (nope that was a chicken) Paula, Pot, Potato. What about Pocket?" I thought and thought, but couldn't grab any more ideas. "Man, there just aren't that many good "P" names left." Old Carole couldn't come up with any either.

She and I started on names with "P" in them anywhere.

"Apple, Lippy, Sloppy..." No, those are dumb sounding.

"No," Mom interjected. "Her name has to start with the letter "P.""

I was stumped.

I think it was my mother who said, "Well, she does have a black patch on her back."

"Blackie!" I shouted.

"No silly, with a "P,"" she laughed. "How about Patch or Patches? Patch sounds pretty good to me."

Hey, Patch or Patches sounded *great* to me. I was way out of "P" names. The newest member of the family had been christened.

While we were working on names, Patch or Patches had fallen asleep again. All this new family stuff was exhausting. I thought a nap was a great idea and scrunched up on the big back seat with her in my lap. When I woke up, we were pulling into the driveway back in Manchester. I found her still there in my lap. Patch or Patches was home. We ended up calling her both.

I had no ideas about dogs. My mother, on the other hand, had plenty. Momma had all sorts of ideas about little boys, too. Training a puppy is really training a child, which in this instance, was a three-and-a-half-year-old boy. Oh, the puppy learns something for sure, but the knowledge that is required and must get transferred to the boy is staggering.

First rule: Animals come first. Always.

Second rule: Feed, water, take puppy outside. Puppy is up from the puppy's nap, take puppy outside. You're up from your nap, take puppy outside. Feed, water, the puppy goes outside. Take puppy outside, wait till puppy poops. Wait. Keep socks and shoes out of puppy's mouth. Take dirty clothes out of puppy's mouth. Don't let puppy chew father's slippers. Take puppy for walk. Don't let puppy jerk on leash. Don't let puppy chew on leash. Don't let puppy jump up. Don't let puppy bite Grandma. Don't *make* puppy bite Carole. Don't feed puppy from table. Don't let puppy lick your spoon. Teach puppy to sit. Teach puppy to lie down. Teach puppy to stop barking. Don't wait to take puppy outside. Come see what your puppy did. That's why! Take puppy outside!

Most rules started with "don't." All the words following "Animals Come First" are the second rule.

There were accidents and transgressions to be sure. Shoes were chewed, socks partially digested. A few times we didn't get outside fast enough. It didn't happen many times though, because I had to be the cleaner upper if she was the depositor. Nobody starts out perfect. I was a great example of that. Practice is required for all things and Patch was going to be an inside and outside dog, if… If meant that if she and I perfected her outside activities and timing she could stay inside until she had to go outside. We sometimes struggled to maintain her permanent residence in my room. She got swatted with the paper and I got swatted with the hand. We would do better. I promise, Momma.

I recall so very little else about our house in Manchester, except that the lessons for the boy and dog took place on the long front porch with pillars on either side of the steps leading up. Momma taught both boy and dog to come, sit and stay. Patch was much better at remembering the last two but I had had my butt swatted enough to look for who was calling me when "Claaark!" rang out. I knew about "stay" from being sent to my room, although I often got confused about how long it meant. Patch soon followed me around as if tethered, but the only strings we had were those we wanted.

Patch grew up lots faster than I did and a year later, in 1951, she was big, a really large dog. She had gotten her large size from her sire, and while still growing, now weighed in at 70 pounds or so, quite big for a female, and formidable in appearance. She had a large head, flat and broad across the top, with eyes and ears that perked when I called her. Her coat had turned from silky soft to coarse curls and had grown thicker. Her sharp little puppy teeth were replaced with wolf teeth, a set of canines that sported an extra one; doubles on each side. Patch was thick and heavily muscled in the chest and hindquarters and her strength was amazing. If she had a stick or rope in her mouth, you got it only if she wanted you to have it. Patch came equipped with an innate sense of territory, and learned to stay within the confines of our yard. She seldom crossed this invisible barrier unless we accompanied her. She stayed in the yard lots better than I did.

Patch possessed a knowing but wary disposition and was gentle with the family. If she had been introduced, you were considered okay. Visitors and people walking down the street were another matter, and if the family wasn't around she always viewed strangers with growling suspicion. Most folks walked on the other side of the street, even though they were never in harm's way. When salesmen, the postmen, meter readers and visitors came in the yard or to the door they always did so with a healthy portion of fear. I can't recall her ever biting an innocent visitor, but there would be times in the future when the not-so-innocent wished they were elsewhere.

Mother was a mainstay. A beauty to boot. Pretty enough to have been a movie star. Instead of going into films, Dorothee Phoebe chose directing the saga of us.

Mother was a singer and bringer of light to our lives and while there were a few times when I thought she would drive me nuts and once when I'm sure she did, she was an awesome molder of my character.

Her examples led and pushed and sometimes threw her family into the breach of life. She was destined to become first, second or even third mother to many more children than her own brood, yet she did a pretty good job with all. Mom made the rules up for the family, but enforced them equally with friends or neighbors, too, and monitored everyone's compliance. Mom modified her rules to suit the situation and on a few occasions threw them completely away, but I never saw her back away from a conflict. Her adversaries, occasionally including her children, quickly learned just how formidable her stature.

Our minimum number became six, two adults and four children. Five of us, my father included, continually revolved as satellites around the central core of my mother. The quantity of spinning children and adults varied as new lost souls were discovered or lead to salvation, but most changes increased rather than reduced our numbers.

My father would have been a tyrant if Mom had allowed. Even though she couldn't stop his continued attempts, Dad was mostly held in check whenever he got carried away. Gerald Godette Greene's face reflected the many frowns and quickly lit anger which sparked regular spankings. I spent a great deal of my early years being frightened of his fearsome temper. His laughter was often at someone's expense and he seemed too busy or caught up in something, almost as if he denied himself a complete good humor. Dad grew up during the Depression and that experience may have molded him into a fairly inflexible man. He inherited the disposition from his father and grew up to be a somewhat skewed version of the example set for him, but he always made himself available when I was more than I should have been or less than I could have been. He was a small man who always wanted to be bigger. When I got into or made trouble for myself, I pictured him as Goliath.

My sister, Carole Elizabeth, is four years older than me and lovely, though I didn't care to admit it then. When she was my mother's only child, Grandma Phoebe told her she was the most beautiful and perfect child in the world and Carole believed the description forever after. My mother spent Carole's entire life attempting to dissuade that notion, but never won the battle. Carole was musically gifted, playing piano and organ, and possessed the most perfect singing voice I had ever heard, head turning in its beauty. I sort of liked her when she sang in church; to be present when she sang was enough for any mortal. But Sunday was only one day a week and all other times we seemed to be in some sort of conflict with one another.

My brother, Gerald Godette II (actually Chip), is four years my junior and while I didn't think much of him initially, I did learn that having a little brother could be an advantage. It took Chip overlong to develop but I eventually managed to beat and tease and torment him until he became tolerable. As soon as he could keep up he followed me around just like a puppy, too.

Chip was my shadow and my constant companion if I couldn't figure out how to lose him. He could and would scream like a banshee at the slightest provocation, and sometimes even with none. We had a hundred adventures that other siblings only get to imagine. Chip was my confidant and confessor and more than a few times my betrayer as well. My brother got me into more trouble and conflicts and we had more fun together than five regular brothers were allotted. I loved him then as now with a ferocity reserved only for my brother.

The youngest Greene child was Phoebe Erma, "Peg," the object of my immediate affection and eternal devotion. Peg was born on Christmas Day when I was six, and from the first moment on I just knew she was related to Jesus. When my father carried her through the door I was smitten. She was blonde, brown eyed and cute as a button.

Peg was named after both grandmothers, although they had to pretend to spell Grandma I.G.'s first name with "E." Peg's initials wouldn't have been quite as charming with "I" for Irma and we sure couldn't have used them as her nickname. Mom kept her in pink and white dresses and her hair in fat sausage curls, just like Shirley Temple. As soon as Peg could talk she made up extraordinary tales of flying skunks and a boyfriend named Charge who dyed his hair a different color every day. She eternally enchanted every person she smiled at, for once graced by Peg's pleasantries, people were promised eternity. I pampered her and loved her, and as a boy who had just turned six, quickly knew it would be my privilege to die for her if the need arose.

I was just a mediocre kid who had a great place to grow up. Even with the extraordinary influences of parents and relatives I'd not have made it far without some other help.

Patch was the other real member of the family. It's a good thing she came along when she did.

We moved out of Manchester in the early summer of 1950, just as soon as Dad convinced my mother that life would be better in Monroe.

He told Mom the move was necessary because he was going to be transferred to another plant by the Ford Motor Company. I learned as a teenager that he'd asked for the transfer to escape Manchester and the close proximity of Grandma Phoebe, his mother-in-law.

We were moving to an area just north of the city of Monroe, Michigan, along

Lake Erie, a subdivision called Indian Trails. I hoped there were plenty Indian trails, because Patch and I had tons of important things to do.

We didn't stay in that house very long which was okay with me, because the name was a total fib. The street names were Indian sounding, like Cherokee and Sioux, but calling a road by a name didn't mean it was really Indian. Patch and I looked all over the place and we didn't find one single footprint left by one single Indian.

We did discover Mike Golden; a boy my age who had lived there really-really long, but he didn't know about any footpaths either. I figured the people who lived here were mostly a bunch of liars, a type of people my mother had already warned me about.

"You sure don't want to be known as a fibber."

I wondered out loud why we were living around a bunch of them then, but Momma said our neighbors didn't have anything to do with the name of the subdivision.

Somebody sure did though.

My brother came along when we were in that house, but at first he wasn't much to look at. I couldn't figure out why everybody else was so happy to see him. The most that little baby ever did was cause a ruckus and from his appearance it would be a really long time before he could do much more than cry and poop. His name was Gerald Godette, after my father, but we were going to call him Chip. As in, "Chip off the old block," my dad said, but I didn't get it. Where did my mother come up with the idea he'd ever be much use?

"You'll have so much fun together someday," she persuaded, but I had serious doubts.

I liked Mike lots better and besides, I couldn't find Someday on the calendar my mother kept on the refrigerator. Mom marked everything else important on that calendar.

Aside from the Christmas tree falling on me that year, not much else happened except the old lady who lived next door called all the time about Patch barking at night.

"We're renting," my mother explained.

I didn't know what that meant except Patch couldn't sleep with me, unless I snuck out, but I got in trouble for that. Mom just would not let me sleep outside with my dog, even though both of us fit inside her house. I liked my dog with me all the time. I didn't like Patch being outside any more than that old neighbor woman did. I was glad when we moved away from that fibbing place.

The packing up started in the spring, which none too soon for me, because when we went to see our new house, it had a fireplace just like Grandma Grace and Grandpa Clark's did, and a trapdoor and a big yard and a plum tree and all sorts of other good stuff, and Patch could sleep inside, Mom said.

Everything would be better when we moved. I just knew it would.

Chapter 2
House Rules

When we thought of any Greene family edicts we heard them in my mother's voice. Mother's directorial duties began with house rules.

The numerous sets of laws at our house were complex but readily understood; a pair of lens through which we viewed every day. Momma made sure we wore our spectacles and we were all convinced her directives were equal in weight to the laws Moses carried. They were similar, except many of my mother's decrees had her own reasons attached to their ends. Different rule types applied to different days of the week and as long as we remembered it was a Tuesday or a Friday or a Sunday, we knew which ones were being enforced. We were conditioned through constant repetition and my mother's excellent reflexes.

The Greene children learned to set and clear the table as soon as they could say the word spoon. We had rules for chewing and talking and sitting and wiping. Miss Manners might be invisible but we all knew she sat at our table every night. I personally thought she scooted her chair right in next to mine.

Table and Meal Laws were all made up of decrees:
"We will ALL sit down together EVERY night for dinner." No matter what. (Even if children were being banished with no dinner, we were required to say grace en masse before the offender's sentence started.)

"You will not take one single bite before saying Grace." (God will get you if you don't say thank You and I [Mom] will if He misses).

"Do not eat until everybody has food." (The vittles might not portion out at the first passing, you'll have to put some back and nobody [especially Mom] wants food with your spit on it.)

"No elbows on the table." (You'll get ugly calluses, a sign of apathy, and we are Christian in this house, remember what the Bible says about the lukewarm.) Although this was primarily a Carole rule, it applied to everyone else, too.

"Chew with your mouth closed." (Food on the plate is pretty, but it's ugly in your mouth.)

"Sit up straight." (Curved spines are signs of sloth too, remember the Christian thing.)

"Ask for the potatoes to be passed, don't reach." (The adjacent person might bite you, especially true when neighbor kids were invited and I [Mom] will crack your knuckles with my knife handle if you do.)

"Don't talk with your mouth full." (The words will be garbled through the peas and carrots and they might fall out, wasting the food.)

"Don't interrupt anyone else when they're talking." (Everybody will get a turn and if you don't stop you can go to your room.)

"Keep your mouth wiped clean, (Nobody wants to look at your sloppy mouth.) and keep napkins on your lap." (Once you've wiped your mouth, nobody wants to look at your dirty napkin either).

"Don't put the milk bottle on the table." (It looks uncouth and you aren't.)

"Do not blow bubbles in your milk." (Mom could never come up with a good reason for this rule. It was just a rule and it only applied to Chip.)

"Do not store food in your cheeks to spit out later." (Another Chip rule and we all knew it was because he regularly got caught spitting his peas into the bucket for the compost pile.)

"After dinner we will pray for every foreign missionary in the whole world who labors for Jesus in every jungle and slum and back street and gutter." (And you better remember the Indian Missionary School in Arizona.)

There were rules for Patch and meal times, too, and although they were continually quoted, they were seldom enforced.

"Don't feed Patch at the table." As long as we attempted to be furtive, this was an accepted activity and if the morsel was particularly attractive, even secrecy wasn't required. Everybody (even Mom and Dad) broke this rule.

"Don't let Patch drool in your lap while you eat." Each of us children ate most evening meals with wet crotches as she made her rounds, because Patch insisted on having her head as close as possible to any suggestion of available tidbits.

"Let the dog clean your plates before you take them to the kitchen." The incongruity of this allowance never registered on the family. I secretly believed it was Mom's strategy devised to save on dish washing soap.

"As soon as cooking pots and pans are cool enough, give them to Patch to clean first." During my childhood, I saw macaroni and cheese casserole dishes remain unwashed on the kitchen floor for days until Patch's tongue finally managed to wear away the baked on cheese.

We had other supper time decrees but they were vague and often surprising. Being at the Greene's dinner table was similar to a livestock judging at the county fair and equal to the requirements for church. We had to be at our absolute best or we might not win the blue ribbon prize of Mom's approval.

Personal hygiene came next and these credos started with bathing.
Baths were always in sequence, beginning with little to big sister, then the two boys, small to large, and then the parents had a turn. There was scientific reasoning that supported this progression.

First came the need for young female parts to be protected against all things imaginable and some that defied all manner of thought. Little girls, regardless of age, had to be defended from the onslaught of the germs and other things known to be hosted in the male body, so they bathed first.

The bathing sequence was also a circumstance of our hot water heater.

For one bath the water was hot enough for scrubbing and enjoyment. The second bather enjoyed a slightly less warm submersion while numbers three and four needed some of the original water held in the tub. (This same water rapidly getting colder while the sister got dry and I always thought Carole dawdled because she knew brothers were next.) Between bathers two and three the left over bath water needed supplements from the tea-kettle whistling on the stove. It was apparent that girls should be comfortable but with boys it didn't matter. Chip and I bathed in water that frequently had thermal layers and hot spots as the kettle came in. I still have scars from the occasional scalding.

In the summertime (the beginning and ending of which was a purely whimsical notion) our bathing took place at Lake Erie. My father always tried to push the early envelope by plunging in on St. Patrick's Day, but there were too many of those holidays when ice was still present. Once it melted, however, the lake was our tub and during the days between April and November our baths were a public spectacle.

My father's first yearly plunge always marked the ending of in-house tub baths for everyone else, too. There were plenty of early spring and late fall swims when no one could really distinguish between the dirt and our blue cold skins. We used Ivory soap, because it floats, and Fels-Naptha, because that was the only way to clean boys and dog properly.

If the towel wasn't dripping from the first user you had better be using the same one.

As the need arose, some bathers were also supposed to wash whatever undergarments were required for the next day. The scrubbed and wrung out underwear were then hung over the heat registers for use the next morning.

Teeth were brushed twice daily and Mom smelled our breath to check for quality.

Once a month or so she checked our gum-lines for buildup, something left over from her days as Michigan's first licensed female dental hygienist.

In secret she also randomly timed our brushings for duration, especially after she caught Carole putting toothpaste in her mouth instead of keeping the pearly whites cleaned.

Dentist visits were infrequent, because in our family there was no such thing as dental insurance.

Similar to bathing and tooth care, clothing rules varied with gender.

Two days were allowed for boy's underwear during the school year but we could wear them for longer periods of time during the summer. I thought this had something to do with the teacher finding dirty underwear when you got your butt paddled. Whacks were the measurement of kids, but clean Fruit of the Looms were judged to be parental qualities.

Girls got daily changes of undergarments. I was confused by this for many years, somehow believing my folks thought my sisters were more prone to school spankings.

School clothes were just for school and school included walking to and from the bus stop. If you dirtied or ripped or scuffed anything thus designated, "YouarebyGod" going to wear it every day that way until Mom or Dad thought you had learned a lesson (time greatly varied according on one's consequent behavior).

Until I was fourteen, I thought the only clothing able to be purchased new was underwear. Everything else was hand-me-down, either from relatives, Goodwill or the Salvation Army. My mother hemmed and hawed almost every stitch we wore and I can remember but few nights when she wasn't sewing or darning something. The older I got the more I "darned" my clothes too.

Room tidiness was one of few rule sets that weren't gender specific.

We all had to keep our rooms neat.

"Rooms will be kept picked up if you want to keep whatever you have." (I was often threatened with naked school attendance. I wanted to call their bluff but never did.)

"Beds are to be made every morning and there better not be any clothes other than pajamas under the pillow." (Other apparel under bedcovers fell into the same category as the floor.)

"Dirty clothes will be put in the clothes hamper in your closet and you boys will empty your pockets before they get put there." (This was a lesson for everyone, when Mom washed some of my frogs.)

"Boys, you may not take anything sharp to sleep with you." (This included the beaks attached to baby birds in addition to the obvious ones—scout knife, axe.)

"Clark, Patch is the only animal allowed in your bed." (No snakes, no bunnies, no muskrats, no opossums. No exceptions.)

Our regulations included a whole chapter about animals.

As we always had lots of animals, there were oodles of different policies to suit each species but one rule suited each. I learned it right away when Patch arrived.

"Son, the animals come first. Not second or third or when you get around to it—first."

"You will take care of your animals *every* day *before* breakfast." (A good way for us to go without breakfast was my mother noticing the animals weren't fed.)

"You will put fresh water every day in a clean bowl or bucket for every animal." (The fresh water rule frequency increased during severe hot or cold weather and you'd better know when the needs changed.)

"You will keep food bowls cleaned with soap and water and refilled." (If I see ants in their food dishes, guess what you're getting for supper?)

"You will pick up all dog and cat poop outside." (If I see dried poop anywhere it better not look like it came from the Greene menagerie.)

"You will pull fresh greens during the summer for the rabbits or feed the dried clover and alfalfa in the winter along with the feed pellets." (Remember that rabbit pellets cost money and the greens do not, so feed accordingly.)

"You will not let rabbit poop build up in the corner of their cage." (Their feet will rot off, and I will paddle your behind if they do.)

"You will keep brushed those animals that need brushing and will wash those that stink." (Your room smells bad enough already. You've got to do better, son.)

"You will remove burrs from your dog as soon as you come back from an adventure and you better not just pull them out. Be gentle." (If Patch whined in hurt, you could count on a lesson in how it felt to have your hair pulled, just so you knew.)

We had cats that were Mom's and a canary that she took care of, but we were expected to do our part with them also. This mostly meant watching the Siamese female cats when they were in heat, while being sneaky and ready to mate.

Female Siamese in the mating mood will remain silently hidden for hours. This is the only time they are quiet during the entire cycle. They are deliberate in their need to escape. Open doors without a foot blocking the bottom are an invitation for their flight. A constant howling and screeching and screaming accompanies their seasonal situation and encourages everyone to let them out, regardless of the consequences.

When we couldn't take any more yowling noise we allowed their escape but never said so. My father might have been the originator of this strategy. Anyway, kittens were later and far more enjoyable a circumstance than the racket.

All the rest of our zoo fell under the "Animal Rules." Our alligator, flying squirrel, fox kit, hamsters, all cocoons, guinea pig, seahorses, turtles, snakes (poisonous or non), spiders, butterflies, moths, gold fish and pike minnows, puppies, kittens, opossums, muskrats, wild ducklings, baby chicks, mice, baby birds stolen or fallen from nests, polliwogs, frogs, salamanders and the frequently undernourished next-door child better get tended every single day.

All these little pieces really made up only one edict. This caring for animals did not alter with the days of the week and punishment for our failures was as severe as any we received.

The final segment of the "Greene House Rules" was directed at injury and illness.

In the 1950s, the only health insurance we had was my father's wallet and the change purse my Mom kept the haircut and babysitting money in. Mom tended our childhood fevers and illnesses with a thermometer and Vicks Vapo-Rub. She doctored all injuries with cotton balls, torn up sheets, Mercurochrome and Bag-Balm, the latter a chief snake-oil treatment around our house. She did a great job with both health treatments. All of us and most of the other neighborhood kids lived to see adulthood.

We were given instructions to head home before blood loss made us faint and even if there wasn't anything sticking through the skin.

Other wounds could be dealt with later, unless you were the inflictor and then we were encouraged to rush the child to our house before their own parents found out. Neighbor kid's hurts healed faster through generous applications of milk and Mom's homemade cookies. Ours did too.

Bruises and scrapes weren't discussed, because they went away within a week.

Bloody noses and black eyes were questioned regarding the victor and then only once, followed by, "and I better not catch you fighting anymore, Clark Malcolm."

Temperatures were taken infrequently and pronouncements of well being varied with degree and gender. Girls stayed home at 98.8 but boys were okay until the red line reached past 103.9, and it was always harder for Chip and me because Mom kept our thermometer in the freezer.

The application of these many mandates made it easy to stay on the good side of the family, which in all ways meant Mom. There were other rules etched in stone but they branched out either from Mom's foundations or those of the church.

The only obedience school Patch ever went to was the same one I did.

We both attended Mom's School of Laws and Patch got the better grades. Mom did some teaching of us both but her focus was Clark. I really didn't train Patch. Her relationship with me was more of reaching an agreement than training. I agreed to listen to everything Patch told me to do.

Except for house training, none of her instruction was formal. "Sit, Stay, Lay Down, Come and Speak" were the only commands Patch needed. Once she understood the reason for doing her "business" outside, Patch told us when she needed to go out and we listened. She behaved through a knowing how to play her part in the games of our lives.

With the exception of fewer than a half dozen serious incidents involving other dogs or people, Patch was the most gentle of creatures imaginable. Visiting families with young babies had nothing to fear from her. The family across the street, the Hicks, had two boys and two younger daughters. All four of their kids were part of our extended family. Both baby girls in turn literally learned how to stand upright by using Patch's fur as a handhold. Any number of toddlers from the subdivision and church polished their walking skills with tiny fingers wrapped around a handful of her thick coat.

Patch took on the task of their faltering steps or struggling falls as if she knew of their importance. Her wisdom in discerning infants and their special needs came from some deep natural well and any other behavior on her part was unimaginable to us and to her. I never saw her look in the least bit miffed when she wore the additional adornment of a small hand or face nestled in her pelt. She treated every baby she ever met as if they were members of her own brood.

Patch possessed an intimate sense of boundaries and she expected all other of God's creatures to recognize the same lines she did. Demanded is probably a better word because she was free with her punishment of offending trespassers. But if they stayed out of her yard, she stayed out of their space. Although she ran free 98% of the time, Patch didn't have to be tied up to be confined to our yard. "Stay," whether it was at home or "here" with palm outstretched was as good as a written policy of compliance. I cannot recall a single breaking of the command sacraments given to her.

Every Sunday we stationed her on the front porch with, "Stay here girl, we'll be right back." When the car pulled into the driveway after church services we could count on Patch on the porch until one of us called her away from the front door. Her duty, of Sunday porches or our yard, was fulfilled until released every single time.

Patch also had an intrinsic sense of fairness. It could be prejudiced toward her family wards, but most often the offending party was of little importance.

I was once wrestling with a kid from the subdivision who was four years younger than me, my brother Chip's age. I was bigger, stronger and I reveled in the advantages of both. It wasn't much of a contest and he started to holler but I wouldn't let him up. Until then Patch had been joining in the playful fracas, rolling her body over and on both of us, shoving us off balance with her bulk. When I pinned his arms down with my knees, Bobby started to cry, but I held him there despite his wails.

Patch suddenly grabbed my upper arm in her mouth and held on firmly with a look that said, "Turn him loose." Not tugging as in play and not hard enough to hurt me, but as a reminder that fairness was required at all times. I was bigger and stronger than Bobby, and Patch was bigger and stronger than me. She didn't turn my arm loose until I moved to get off him.

Whenever I ran with Patch it was called catching up. She ran the legs off me and a host of subdivision kids. The only time we got ahead of her was when she didn't notice the start of a race and then our lead didn't last long. Her stamina was extraordinary and we spent hundreds of full days rushing toward real and make-believe places. She rested when we were worn out, never the other way around, and was first to her feet when time in was called again. If I walked she did too and was most happy when touching my leg, leaning on me every second or third step. Patch continually trotted by my right side and so I frequently walked in circular patterns from her irregular nudges. Under her guidance I always ended up back home.

Patch played with me during the day and slept with me at night. I should actually say I slept in Patch's bed, as there was little doubt who was the real owner at bedtime. No child who sleeps with a large dog can rightfully claim space except that which is allowed. Even as I grew bigger, the only changes to my allotment were of the shrinking variety. The rules of slumber were simple. I could have any part of the bed not already filled up with dog. The adage of a canine turning three around times before lying down was complicated by Patch's insistence of starting every night under the covers. Under the bedspread lasted just long enough for me to fall asleep, by which time she would be hot and panting from the warmth of fur and blanket and boy. It seemed that just as the deck of Squire Trelawney's *Hispaniola* appeared beneath my dreaming feet, Patch had to get out from under and duplicate the thrice around rule. The recurring commotion before or during sleep didn't alter our need to be together and I never imagined another way to go to sleep. If I spent the night elsewhere she slept with Chip, but when I was at home she was right beside me. Many midnight horrors were chased away by the great big dog lying close.

Chapter 3
No Kicking

I shared my very own bedroom in the new house with Patch.

Mom and Dad got pretty mad at me after I insisted on really red walls in my new bedroom and then was scared of the color. I even had to cry at night in order to get them to change it, but although Dad grumbled the whole time, he repainted it before sleep deprivation overcame him. Blue. There was nothing to be scared of now. The best part of the room was no Carole. Ha!

Chip was just a baby and still slept in Mom and Dad's bedroom. My new room contained a closet and a toy-box so I was "happy as a clam," even though I never saw one smiling. My Grandpa Clark said the clam-happy phrase all the time and that suited me perfectly because I was connected to Grandpa Clark big time. I was named after him! Except for my middle name, which I never told to anyone and didn't even use it to myself. The only time I even heard "Malcolm" was when I was in trouble or needed to pay close attention. Otherwise, I was Clark, just like my burly gruff grandpa.

The summer after we moved from Indian Trails, I really missed Mike Golden. But Mom said he could stay overnight just as soon as we got settled. He'd like this place way better than Indian Trails. We had a bigger beach with piers that I had to stay off them unless Mom and Dad were with me, but that rule would soon change. At first I had to be really careful around the lake, but if I promised not to even get my feet wet it was okay to play here. Mike and I could skip flat rocks on the water when he came. The beach had a million rocks, so I never had to hunt long to find one that was perfect. I practiced a lot because Mike might be a better thrower than me.

Patch went in the lake with everyday splashes because not even Mom's rules could keep her dry. Patch dove in the water like she was born to it. One of the marvels of Patch was her willingness to swim in any water, even if she had to break the ice of Lake Erie to do it. If I threw a stick way out she'd get it every time, no matter how far but most likely she wouldn't bring it back. I fooled her with stones for a while and she'd dive in looking all around for something that floated. My laughs probably gave her clues because she quickly figured out the sound of "kerplop" and soon she wouldn't even look at the lake when I threw a rock. Sticks were always chomped with a splash right out of the water. Quickly I realized that the bringing back part with Patch needed work but we had plenty of time to learn "Drop it, girl." Patch was smart, she'd catch on.

I needed to help Patch with another thing—the shaking off part when she got out of the water. She did a really good job, but that wasn't the point. She wanted to be close, like right next to me when she shook. Patch shook off twice too, and even if I was quick enough to dodge the first one she'd think I was playing and get really up close for the second. I thought if I could only combine the shaking off with the bringing back at least I'd have the stick. But the wet part was the problem. When Patch went swimming I got wet. Mom looked at me funny every time when I got home and told her why I was soaking sopping, but she knew I told the truth.

"I was just throwing stuff for her to fetch. Patch is all wet, Mom. Feel her."

"You'd better *not* be playing in the water, Clark Malcolm. I mean it."

The middle name event meant that Mom was serious.

Mike's dad dropped him off and he was going to spend a whole week! We'd be just like regular brothers but it was going to be crowded in the bed. Patch took up a lot of room.

I showed Mike all around the subdivision, but his father told him not to go down close to the lake without my mother or father going to supervise. I showed him from the road but that wasn't much fun so I made him wait while I ran to get some rocks to throw, but neither of us could make them reach the water. That was no fun either. Whew, well at least he doesn't throw better than me!

There were some great crab apple trees to climb so we did, way, way up to the skinny branches. We teased Patch the whole time and tossed crab apples at her but she could just not climb the trees. She tried! Ha!

She made us pay big time when we did clamber down. Which is just what she's supposed to do. At just a year and a half, Patch had surprising power, well beyond the muscles of any four-and-a-half-year-old boy. Lots of times she grabbed a pant leg to drag me across the living room floor and could knock me off my feet most anytime she wanted. Not hard and wildly, and she never jumped up but just pushed and pounced until you lost your balance. Patch could tackle too. With front legs splayed wide to capture, she'd charge and almost always put my butt on the ground. And that's what she did to Mike and me right now. Paybacks for all the teasing *and* the crabapples. She had more strength than both of us combined.

Barks! Dog slobber! Play growls! First chew on one then the other, back and forth, back and forth! Rolling us over and over with her bulk and she wouldn't let us up! Laughs! Growls! Laughs! Wild! How great was this! My pal! My dog!

I *was* as happy as a clam!

If weeks have wings this one surely owned a pair. Mom took us swimming to the sandy beach at Kress Park whenever we asked and we asked plenty. Johnny Kress pulled the big raft in closer to shore so we could cannonball into the water and jump up and down on the fat rubber sides like a trampoline.

We even got to eat hot dogs that we bought at the hot dog stand one day, a real treat because Mike was here. They were the best hot dogs in the whole wide world and we ate two apiece with everything slurping out the ends. Mike's hot dog squirted me and him when he took a really big bite, but that was okay 'cause we washed off the sandy catsup and mustard in the lake after our twenty minutes was up.

Mike and I wrestled Patch in the shallow water and each day we went to the beach, we came home with about five pounds of sand in our bathing suits. Mom laughed while we shivered as she rinsed us off with cold water from the hose. Mike said he liked Patch in the bed once we got situated, but I knew she took up a lot of space.

"Settle down now, boys," Mom and Dad alternately said from the living room where they sat; Dad reading in his recliner, Mom with some mending and her cat, Sun Yat Sen, in her lap. Settling down took a lot longer than normal since Mike was here, but Dad didn't even get mad about it.

Before we knew it Friday was here and that meant Mike's mom was going to pick him up in the afternoon. By late morning, I was really glad.

I'm in my room with the door closed tight. I guess you can't be any more surprised than me.

"You can just go to your room, Clark Malcolm, until you learn that fighting isn't nice. And close the door tight."

Which was okay with me because I didn't do anything bad. It was all because of bratty, sissy-baby Mike. He started it. I can't wait for his mother to come get him.

We were just playing down by the lake. Just fooling around and for no reason at all he kicked my dog.

We were both throwing sticks for Patch. Just as fast as we could find one to throw we pitched it in the water. I bet we had about ten in there and Patch couldn't figure out which one to get. Every time she'd get close to one, we threw another one behind her. It was funny, 'cause she swam back and forth each time she heard a new splash. It was really funny 'cause she got wore out swimming so much. Finally she headed back to shore and grabbed one floating close to shore on her way out. Prob'ly 'cause she just wanted to show us she could get something after all that paddling.

Patch huffed and puffed down by the water for a little bit and then ran up to show us her stick. And she shook off by Mike. He tried to get away but Patch got him with the second shake, too. Really soaked him, man, he was dripping by the time Patch got through!

I thought I was gonna die laughing. It was hilarious, him running away and Patch chasing after him, a game of follow the leader, just like she did to me.

And then he just kicked her. Afraid of a little water, the sissy baby Mike kicked my dog right in the side. She yelped pretty loud, too.

I ran right over to him and just got real close. That's all I did. Yeah okay, well, I shoved him a little bit but he had it coming. I told him something too.

"You can't kick my dog. Nobody kicks my dog."

Mike said he was gonna get in trouble for being wet and he wasn't supposed to go by the lake when grown-ups weren't there. I told him not to kick at my dog even if she got him double soaking sopping. He didn't listen to one single word.

He kicked at her again when Patch came over to apologize. She dodged him that time but he really tried even after I told him.

"You better not do that EVER AGAIN!" This time I screamed at him.

"Patch is just a dumb dog," he said, heretically. "A dumb stupid dog."

He said it like he didn't even like her.

"I don't like her in that crummy bed, either. And she's stinky, Clark. You got a stinky stinky stinky dog."

So I jumped right on him. And I was winning too until he got me in a headlock. And wouldn't let me up. And rubbed grass in my face. That's when I started crying and he let me up.

When I finally got loose, Patch and I went home. We followed our noses right up to our house. I told Patch not to worry. Mom would make that mean Mike sorry.

"My mom's gonna make you so, so sorry, Mike," I hollered that back to the scared-of-a-little water brat.

Mike followed even though I told him to take another street, but he wouldn't.

When I got home I told Mom all about it and how Mike started it, but she got mad at me.

Which is why I was in my room with the door closed tight.

But I don't care, 'cause Mike has to sit on the couch all by himself. I got my room. I got my books. I got my dog in here, too.

I knew Tarzan wouldn't put up with anyone doing dog kicking. He wouldn't even let anybody look cross-eyed at his apes. I knew kicking was definitely out. Jim Hawkins wouldn't put up with any dog kicking and he didn't even have a dog in *Treasure Island*, but I knew. I remember one time Tarzan even stabbed a few guys who tried to hurt an elephant.

I was just fine right where I was and I didn't even have to look at Mike 'cause my door was closed really tight. I wasn't going to go out to say goodbye to that bratty Mike, but Mom made me.

"Clark Malcolm," she said in her serious voice, "you come out here *right now* and say goodbye to your friend. Shake hands and make up like big boys."

Mom told Mike's mother we had probably had enough of one another. Maybe a week was a bit too long for little boys.

I didn't know about having enough. Way too much was more like it. I shook with him but I didn't mean it, and it didn't count either, 'cause I crossed my fingers behind my back. When I said goodbye to him I didn't mean the good part either, just the bye.

Mom really got after me when they left. I had to go back to my room 'cause I hadn't learned my lesson.

"Clark Malcolm," she said, still using my middle name, "you need to think about this some more. You don't want the last minutes of the last day to spoil all the fun you had with Mike. You need to act like the big boy here. You can call him later on the phone to apologize again and mean it."

So that's where I was. In my room. With the door closed tight. Again. But I didn't care.

Nobody kicks my dog.

Chapter 4

Pretty Good Place

The neighborhood was full of kids and dogs that all ran loose and my Patch could whip every one of them.

Our subdivision was about sixty miles south of Detroit, situated on the shores of Lake Erie. The original intent of the private community was summer living for those who could afford it, but we were there for the duration of every season. The other buildings we lived in left me no lasting marks beyond "that's where we used to live," but this was *the* place. Here I got scars of every kind, each a reminder of the green painted stucco house on Goddard Drive. The dwelling place in Pointe aux Peaux Farms my parents began to create in 1951 was my only real home. It would turn out just about the perfect place for the family. It was more than perfect for Patch and me.

Our house at 6169 Goddard Drive was a summer cottage converted to year–round use with three bedrooms. A sign stuck in the garden proclaimed "The Greene House" as our very own castle. It actually had four bedrooms, if you included the attic renovated to a sleeping space for my older sister. The house was heated by a smelly fuel oil furnace, which was afflicted with constant problems. A huge stone fireplace overlooked the living room and we used it continuously after the first frost for the extra heat. The crawl space under the house became the official birthing place for a succession of puppies and kittens and the trap door in the middle of the living room floor was used to rescue those litters. We were allowed to play on the roof until we caused leaks in the valleys and my father got tired of patching them up.

There was a water heater in the bathroom that couldn't heat fast enough and demanded baths spaced far apart for family members, a well with an often primed and finicky water pump and water pipes which were inclined to freeze each winter. The outside of the house was stucco and so uneven and mottled in texture my father waited until I was old enough to help him give it the only paint it ever got while we were there.

Even though the house appeared to be a normal structure with doors and windows, the inside space was tinged with the chatter and sometimes mayhem of our middle class mid-1950s family. A silent movie version of our home life is just not possible. The sights and smells of our house needed its built-in sound effects to attain the status of home.

While on Goddard Drive our family increased from five to six, with the addition of a baby sister, Phoebe Erma. She joined my older sister Carole Elizabeth, brother Chip and me as the always loved and often reined in products of my parents.

The resonance of the house began before souls were halfway through our front doorway. Suspended from ribbons and bows, Mom's bells chimed whenever the green painted door was opened, announcing each entry with pealing notes. For everyday entrances this greeting was a musical delight but for errant or late children the tolling of the bells could mark judgment and sentencing. "It's me, I'm home," must accompany the ringing music. While none of us were ever brave enough to test the result of silence, we all knew something terrible would happen if we didn't identify ourselves when we came home. No one went overlooked.

Our home was filled with doors of special meaning. Not only did they disguise personal objects but they could be associated with diverse activities as well. Much like the tale of the lady or the tiger, Carole, Chip, Peg and I could never be quite sure what we'd find as we turned knobs of revelation.

With the exception of some extraordinary mystical properties, our back door was identical to most doorways. Comparable to Ali Baba's opening, special words were required when it needed to liberate us into the enchanted worlds beyond. If left unsaid the threshold remained ordinary, but if properly pronounced and punctuated the portal permitted us to relocate to wherever we chose. Mom and Dad were the keepers of the incantation and they confirmed it each time we came in or went out.

"Don't bang...the door!" (The phrase wasn't as powerful without the interruption of the wooden screen door slamming shut while the last two words quietly fade to futile notion.)

From our impatience the screen had the protruding belly of a fat man facing out. From my father's intolerance it also sported b-b gun holes when he sent yowling cats elsewhere. Egress on one course presented all the possible adventures of marsh and lake and field. Access in the other direction might uncover the allure of my mother's knobby-buns, scones and chocolate chip cookies.

We used this rear access as if it was our divine right. So did every other child who set foot in our home. My mother once kept track of the comings and goings of children or pets for an entire summer day. On a scrap paper above the sink she created her "four lines with a diagonal slash" journal which marked our movements. The paper ended the day with eighty-three pencil-tick accounts of in or out and from that day forward she cherished the register as a weathervane of our activity. In complete disregard of the often ignored instructions, the house was comforted by the sound of the door slamming shut. She kept the journal thumb tacked to the wooden cabinet long after we children were grown, until my father retired and they sold the house in the late 1970s.

Directly outside the back door, a porch (or rather a stage) sat waiting for a succession of Greene family acts. Enough blood and tears were shed on the concrete stoop to satisfy the most dire of tales. Learning to carve wood can be a hazardous assignment for a boy and I sliced the palm of my hand one day badly enough to become blood brothers with half of Monroe County. My anguished cries were answered by Mom's usual acceptance of childhood injuries. While she Bag-Balmed and bandaged my hand she laughed that all my teardrops at least washed the red off.

My mother used the doorsteps as a summoning platform for us kids.

"WEEEEEHHOOOOOO!   CLAAAAAAAAARRRK! WEEEEEEHOOOOOO!"

I seldom heard her voice, but Patch usually raised her head and turned toward home. Patch's attentiveness was considered the same as if I'd recognized Mom's call and we'd scurry across whatever distance separated us from judgment or cookies. Mom's voice carried for miles and feigning ignorance of her call wasn't a valid reason not to show up. If you didn't hear her, you weren't paying close enough attention. Even if you didn't hear, someone else would and pass along the summons. Mom knew you would eventually get the messages to report in.

Bedroom doors could indicate school work, odor, tidiness status, punishment, or the privacy commandment for Mom and Dad liaisons on Sunday afternoon. Whatever the reason for closure, shut tight doors were considered sacred in our house.

My older sister's attic bedroom entrances and withdrawals were all enunciated with the *scrrrreeech* of springs as she pulled the fold up stairway down. Her bedroom was isolated from the rest of the family and I didn't consider her remoteness odd. Carole's four year seniority contributed to the fact that she was detached from the hubbub of my ramblings. On good days she reluctantly admitted kinship with the rest of us but most times Carole acted the stranger to me. She did grace our house with beautiful music and song, but I always got the impression she was a visiting impresario playing to a less than refined audience. I recall little about her bedroom except for the shrieks of her door.

My bedroom door was closed tight a lot of the time. While it was frequently closed for punishment it was also shut to keep the critters in. My brother eventually shared a bedroom with Patch and me. Notwithstanding Chip's habitation, the space was still mostly under Patch's control but we claimed some space, too. Aquariums, terrariums, fishbowls, snake bowls and turtle bowls, spider jars, butterfly-in-waiting cocoons, puppy maternity wards, squirrel, hamster, mouse and guinea pig cages, preying mantis egg cases, an alligator pond, baby bird and rabbit hospitals, forts and hideouts and kids from all around the subdivision at one time or another were crammed into a room about eight by fifteen feet. Our room smelled of boys and dog, interlaced with marsh and lake and the slightest odor of dead fish. Chip and I didn't have much in the way of purchased diversions except books, but we had everything else we could dream of.

My baby sister's room befitted her status and I cannot remember when she wasn't being attended by kittens or cats or little girl children of every size and shape. Siamese or tabby or calico or black and white kitties found places to purr in Peg's room, while little girls who I'd never seen before appeared to adorn her space. Peg would occasionally sneak one of our inhabited snake jars or turtle boxes into her room but for the most part she liked things pet-able. Dozens of kitten litters were nursed under her close supervision and I almost believed that the momma cats wouldn't have done a good job without her help. Peg believed it without question. Her room's extra spaces were taken up by Peg's pet skunks and her boyfriend, Charge.

Pink, frilly and lacy describes the space's colors but the sense of her bedroom was definitely royalty. Although her bedroom was the only access to Mom and Dad's room and they used it whenever sleep or romance called them, Peg's room never seemed a public place.

Except for the bathroom, where locking wasn't allowed, my parent's bedroom had the only other lockable door. The reason for the latch remained a mystery to me for years. The room bore windows on two sides but my mother only drew the curtains in summer. The glass was frosted opaque during winter weather. Their room was often off limits: most Sunday afternoons, days when my father worked the night shift and all early mornings. Mom and Dad's bedroom also lacked heat and became our logical choice for a food-locker in winter as well as a sleeping space. All of our Thanksgiving turkeys were reduced to skeletal remains in the frigid confines of their back room. We could fetch the food but every other admission needed special permission.

But our kitchen, living room, dining room and porch were as public as the great outdoors. More than places for the family, these rooms were open to every creature imaginable and some we had to get a second look at to verify origins. We learned early on to disguise our surprise when extra mouths to feed or heads to wash showed up.

The property, about a half-acre, included a large side yard to play in and a back yard where we couldn't, because of a septic tank and field that was too small for our family. A pear tree and a plum tree stood close to the house, and a rhubarb patch, forsythia and lilac bushes and pussy willow dotted the yard. Plenty of space existed for flower gardens. There was also a catalpa tree good at producing hard green beans and we used them for play and war with other members of the neighborhood. We hauled rocks and stones from the beach for years to fill in sidewalk, driveway, build a rock garden for Mom and cover the garage floor.

Pointe aux Peaux Subdivision had two stone pillars at its entrance with huge iron gates that were never closed. During the summer there was infrequently a guard at the gate, but he was just for show. If someone had really tried to force the issue, we all knew he'd wave them through. It was a bedroom community before the phrase was coined and originally came into being in the early 1900s as a summer vacation getaway for those city folk from Wayne and Macomb counties to the north.

It was filled up with kids my own age who were permanent and sprinkled every summer with dozens of families who sought respite from cities after school was out. The subdivision had a baseball field with a chain link backstop built by the neighborhood fathers, crumbling cement piers with steel cart tracks running between them for fishing at the lake and diving in, a boat ramp, vacant lots to build castles and battlefields in for all seasons, rocky beaches and marshes that held hideaways, quicksand, secrets and sins.

Many of the fathers were truck drivers, factory workers, salesmen and laborers. We had a dentist, several teachers and a few people living there who seemed to have money but no visible means of support. Most mothers stayed home but a few, like my own, provided babysitting and childcare. All the mothers owned a communication system superior to any the Army used; instead of dot, dot, dot, dash, dash, dot, dash, they watched and communicated every child's activities so fast they sometimes seemed instantaneous. Their messages were received by peering out a kitchen or bedroom window to confirm a child's passing, note his or her companions, whether they were drinking an unauthorized bottle of pop and if their coats were buttoned. If something looked amiss, more definitive methods were sent out in the right direction. The communication skills of the mothers were magic.

Adjacent to our community's border was Kress Park, a private, pay-to-swim beach with a jukebox, a bathhouse for changing clothes and a hot dog stand. We had two small grocery stores, one with gas pumps the Greene kids went to and one we weren't supposed to frequent because my mother didn't like the owner.

There were two other neighborhoods in the area in addition to mine. Stoney Pointe and Stoney Pointe Peninsula huddled together with our subdivision to cover the areas at the end of Pointe aux Peaux Road. All three mini-communities were bordered with either the marshes or fresh water of Lake Erie. I quickly explored and claimed one section of marshland for my very own.

Just north of my home. separated by farmland, lay tens of thousands of acres wilderness created with a boy and his dog in mind. Used by hunters for years and once the site of a gravel quarrying operation, it was open and inviting to me and Patch. Within a year of my family's move we scouted to every border and began to memorize trails and waterways.

Chapter 5
Not My Fault

I started school in the fall of 1951, while I was still four, going to Hurd Road Elementary School for kindergarten on the bus all by myself.

I almost didn't go by myself because the bus driver and Mom had a real hard time convincing Patch she wasn't supposed to go along, too. She just scrambled right on that old bus, just like she thought school was for her as well. Before anybody could react, she was standing on the seat next to me looking out the window. Once Patch was on, the driver couldn't get her off and Mom had to get on the bus and help, because I couldn't even pull her nose away from the glass. I thought she was pretty funny.

Even then she didn't go quickly. Patch was never good at backing up under any circumstances and especially so in the narrow aisle between the bus seats. With all three of us we still had a tussle; Patch was so determined to stay with me. It was always a problem to get her to do something she didn't want to do. Dad said she was the hard-headedest dog he ever saw. But she *was* always with me. It was already a joke at our house.

"If you're looking for Clark, find Patch," and, "If you want Patch, find Clark."

All the kids thought it was really funny that day but that bus driver sure didn't. And when Patch snuck back on after we got her off the first time he *really* got mad about being late. I heard him mutter "damn dog" but it was a good thing my mother didn't. Mom didn't allow anybody to use that kind of language around our house and she would have got after that bus driver for sure if he used that kind of language around us.

The bus ride was pretty boring after Patch got off, but I quit laughing when the bus driver looked mad at me in the mirror.

I liked school pretty well. Mrs. Lipp asked me to read a book in class and I did okay because the book was a really easy one about two kids and their dog. Art class was good too, and everything went just right until recess. Then I wished Patch had come to school with me. Maybe I wouldn't have got in that wrestling match with that kid, Bobby, who started everything. Mrs. Lipp, my teacher, wouldn't have been mad at me for fighting. Maybe I wouldn't even have broken my glasses if Patch were there. My teacher said she wasn't going to send a note home this time, but that "There'd better not be a *next*, young man." Except for the parts about Bobby and Mrs. Lipp and my glasses, I thought it went pretty well for the first day at school. I'd have to see how Mom and Dad felt about the glasses.

Patch was waiting with Mom for me at the bus stop. I didn't know Mom would be there. I needed to make up something quick about the glasses but I didn't think fast enough. She knew something was wrong right away when I got off the bus without those dumb glasses on my face. I had to tell her all about the wrestling.

"You know better than fighting, Clark. And you have to learn to be more careful with those glasses."

I got those stupid glasses last year right after my fourth birthday due to a "lazy eye" that I thought made me look like a halfwit. The weak left one aimed itself with an alarming constancy at the bridge of my nose. My eye would float inward at the worst of times, as when trying to face down a kid's challenge or reading. My crossed eye was obvious enough to elicit all sorts of giggles, cruel childhood name calling and taunts.

"Four Eyes, Specks, Geek, Cross-Eyes, Weirdo" all followed me around like a shadow.

The only sort of good thing the weak eye and double vision did was to let me read one book twice at the same time, but my kindergarten teacher said it didn't count as two. But I could retaliate with the best of them and on that first day of school I learned to let no slur go unpunished. Unfortunately, I needed to get better at the delivering part.

I needed to learn something more than schoolwork.

My father passed on his love of "the sweet science" to me very early in my life.

My dad had boxed a little during his high school years, as had his father before him. We watched Friday Night Fights together whenever they were on. I already knew the names of Sugar Ray Robinson, Rocky Marciano, Joe Louis

43

and Kid Gavilan and who they were. My father and I enjoyed watching those matches, slipping and throwing imaginary punches right along with the guys in the ring.

As soon as he saw those broken glasses, Dad knew the time was ripe for me to get tougher, so he taught me to box, to defend myself. To be a man. I had to be aggressive. I had to learn how to duck and bob and weave, how to throw a hook and a straight right hand. I had to learn footwork and to jab effectively, keeping opponents far, far away.

What I really had to do was stop getting my glasses broken. In addition to the necessity of correcting my vision, the maintenance costs of my glasses were continuous.

While the glasses did help me see better, I needed additional help to correct the errant eye. Along with the spectacles the eye doctor supplied a patch to be clipped over one lens, worn on the good eye in order to strengthen the bad one. This brought forth even more waves of mocking and heckling. The creativity of my schoolmates was astonishing.

Mom kept a detailed account of eyeglass costs, complete with pasted receipts from the optometrist, maintaining a running total. My baby book reads like a business ledger, but unfortunately all the monies were going out. I imagined she may have done this to prove parental care when people came by for a visit. "See how much we spend on him, Mrs. So and So. Yes, it is a shame we had a damaged child but we're still taking good care of him. We are good parents, even though he looks brain deficient with that eye."

While the pugilistic lessons slowly moved forward, glasses were broken with disheartening rapidity.

Dec. 5, 1950 – Clark fitted with glasses $44.00

April 9, 1951 – New lense (left) and frames $24.00 *Jon N. called me a name and hit me back.*

Aug. 23, 1951 – Polished lenses and repaired frame - $4.00 *Jon N. and I had a rematch.*

Sept. 3, 1951– Repair frame and ear hook rivets - $.50 *First day of school, Bobby at the swings.*

Sept. 15, 1951 – Broken ear frame $2.50 *Eddie E. and I were wrestling,*

Oct. 10, 1951 – New right lense - $4.56 *Another dispute with Bobby, this one over the teeter-totter.*

Nov. 30, 1951 – New frames and lenses - $18.54 *Big schoolyard fight, them versus us.*

Dec. 12, 1951 – Replace frames - $8.15 *Eddy E. and I for wrestling champion. He won.*

There are other entries for subsequent years, but the drain on my parents' finances was constant. These were terrible expenditures on family income in those years. My dad earned under $4,000 a year, less than $80 dollars a week. I already knew that "money doesn't grow on trees," another of my folks' oft-repeated dinner table lectures. Something would have to be done. It was doubtful they could find someone else to carry their burden because one look at the crossed eye and all prospective foster parents would be running. They were stuck with me.

Despite my dad's frequent application of what he called our "serious talks," but were really an application of his hand or his belt to my butt, I continued to woefully fail as a fighter for my honor or a protector of my glasses. The boxing gloves looked cheap by comparison.

In 1951 they called Santa direct. I got two pair for Christmas.

Mother voiced some concerns regarding my introduction to violence, which she also noted in my baby book. "He's so sweet."

"Always smiling and laughing."

"Good natured child. Hardly cries."

I think my father wanted to insure that my eye wasn't an indication of some more serious mental flaw. He wanted to check my reflexes and coordination, too. I *would* learn to box.

I'd have been happy to shut up those taunting mouths, and anything would be better than more spankings. The paddlings increased in their severity with each successive glasses tragedy.

"Show me. Show me."

The boxing gloves were huge, brown leather covered pillows, puffy with padding. They wouldn't have squashed a fly and had laces to tighten them up but couldn't squeeze small enough on my five-year-old wrists. It didn't matter, because my father was determined that I do something. He first put Patch out on the porch. Patch always watched closely whenever there was rambunctious behavior in our house and Dad didn't want to push his luck.

Dad made me take off my glasses before we began, ignoring my complaint of "I won't know where to hit." This was when he taught me about taking advantage of an opponent's weakness because when he popped me I couldn't tell which one to hit back. At first Dad patiently showed me proper stances for offense and defense, foot work and how to throw different punches, but then started just bopping me around. He didn't hit hard, but he didn't let me hit him back and just held me away with one hand while he pushed the other glove in my face.

The only thing he showed me at first was who was boss… and who could laugh the best.

Whether it was the punches that bothered me the most or the laughs that sparked the fuse, I quickly lost my temper. Flailing wildly, swinging with looping, arced punches, I only succeeded in moving air and I made myself madder when the cooling breeze from my hopeful fists failed to quench the hot temper. When I got close enough to see where he was, Dad put his hand on my head and held me away. That far away there was two of him.

"NOT fair!" I whined.

My temper turned to tears, something little children probably can't help. Only with Mom's intervention was the boxing match evened up a little. I went over to Mom and grabbed her around her legs and hid my wet cheeks.

"You've got to get on your knees and quit holding him away, Jerry," Mom instructed. "He'll never learn anything if he's crying."

My father, perhaps hearkening back to his father, called me a crybaby. I'm sure that his daddy probably called him names when he couldn't get through his young son's wall of tears. Later I was to excuse fatherly impatience as hereditary in the Greene family.

However, on that day when Dad called me a crybaby, I saw red. I put up with names in the schoolyard. I put up with names on the bus and walking home from the bus stop. Big people, neighbors and teachers, people in church snickered (so I thought) when my eyes crossed. I didn't need the same stuff at home.

Mom's orders got Dad down to my level. And just as soon as he had his hands on the floor, I got him good. I *was* a quick learner. While he still was in a horseback riding position, as if waiting for a rider, I exhibited his "take advantage" method of boxing.

I popped him right on the side of his head and knocked *his* glasses off. And then I took off. I shook the gloves off my skinny hands and I just ran away. Fast. Far away.

I was laughing inside and out.

There were lots of other tutoring sessions and my father continued to teach me boxing skills I would use throughout my young life. Fighting wasn't the greatest attribute for a boy to have but it was thought it wasn't all that bad, either. Parents then knew boys would peck at one another until feathers flew.

Boys were almost expected to exhibit some aggressive behavior, though mothers and fathers would all deny their acceptance of such conduct. Even as bigger boys, because they knew tempers would escape, fathers still taught their boys to fight and to defend themselves.

We didn't think of knives or sticks or guns then. The intent wasn't to kill or maim, only to establish some sort of order in our own little worlds. Fathers also made sure to instill fair play, and taught their sons "no dirty tactics, no hitting below the belt, no sneaking up, and don't start the fight—finish it." I liked the training mainly because he and I were doing something together as father and son. As much as I enjoyed all the other coaching I had a favorite session.

I liked the end of my first lesson.

In the meantime, Patch memorized school bus schedules.

Carole and I walked to the bus stop at Pointe aux Peaux's entrance each morning under escort. When I first began school, Mom accompanied us both to Jones' Market, where we were picked up, but soon the duty evolved. As soon as she determined that Patch had learned *not* to get on the bus and I had learned *to* get on the bus, Mom left the duty to my dog. Once again, Patch was the better learner, although two or three times, the bus driver closed the doors on her for reinforcement. She always insisted on standing next to the bus as the doors unfolded, but she quickly stopped climbing the three steps.

Not getting on the school bus did not stop her from talking me into skipping school. There were days, oddly enough, at the beginning and ending of my first school year when she was very successful. On those fresh spring or cool clear fall days, Patch was sometimes able to convince me there were better lessons than those to be found under the gaze of school teacher or at a blackboard. Her arguments were more than enough for me to forget the sure discovery of my absence and a number of times I stashed my books to spend the day at the lake or rambling around the neighborhood well away from the view of my house.

Although I was convinced that Patch was, in truth, the instigator of each one of these breaches, I was the one who bore the blame. No matter my attempts at pleading the irresistible nature of her temptations, I was the one who got punished.

Nevertheless, Patch took me to the bus stop every morning and was waiting to meet me when I got off. Rain or snow, hot or cold, Patch was as much a part of the subdivision entrance during the school year as the realtor's small office or the stone pillars that flanked the road. Her time-clock was infallible. With the exception of being in season or tending her puppies, she saw me off and met me every day for more than twelve years.

Chapter 6

Home Town

In spite of moving away from Manchester we went back to "The Farm" with a steady frequency.

The farm was ruled by my Grandma Phoebe Mabel, attended by her third or fourth husband, my Grandpa Teddy, the only one of her husbands I ever knew. Grandma was English through and through, her accent never changing, despite having escaped being put into "service" as a maid by her parents, secretly buying ship's passage and coming to America when she was twelve. Her commanding nature was the reason we'd moved from Manchester (Dad was not good with authority other than his) and her cultured speech was the reason she called me *Clock* in her British accent.

The first warm days of springtime meant muddy driveways, wooden doors swollen shut, Easter egg hunts and hard work at the farm. Just as soon as the budding greens first leaped, out went a clarion call to Grandma's children and their families. Uncle Don and Aunt Nance, Uncle Gik and Aunt Nita, their offspring, Mom and Dad and the Greene troop all reported for garden duty when warm days thawed the frozen earth. Memories of the Depression, World War II and "Victory Gardens" laid the seed-bed for home-growing much of what people ate. Although the garden was officially Grandma and Grandpa's, all our families benefitted from the cultivation of the three plots. It was a foregone fact that everyone would help.

The kids, no matter their ages, were counted on to labor right along side the grownups. Leaf and grass mulch that had protected tender roots during the bitterest of Michigan winter weather had to be raked and carted to composting piles. Old corn stalks, raspberry canes cautiously picked up after Grandpa's trimming, fruit tree prunings carted out to the brush pile were just as well done by small hands as by large. Our help also allowed the adults to prepare the huge areas for planting, something each of us aspired to do but had to graduate into. My grandparents' gardens covered more than two and one half acres, and every bit of ground was turned, hoed and smoothed by hand, a tremendous undertaking. We all learned at an early age to garden by the same method Pavlov used for his dogs. The tantalizing pies and cakes and cookies made by Grandma sent drool running down our chins and we were mindful of the equation "work equals food."

Grandpa planted by system. His system. One tradition at the farm was eating new potatoes on the July Independence/Birthday celebration we held every year and he had to plant early if he didn't want his spuds to be mistaken for tiny red peas. Grandpa Teddy saved and cut his own seed potatoes and he'd been planting generations of the same sliced and eyed and hardened off seed potatoes that his father, grandfather and great-grandfather had used. Grandpa believed the start of the tradition began before the Civil War and he treated those red potatoes just the same as any important family heirloom. No sense in spending money for store bought stuff when he had the tried and true variety passed on from grandfather to father to son. Grandpa used to laugh and say his first seed tuber came over on the *Nina, Pinta* or the *Santa Maria*. We believed him.

Everything else he planted, potted, picked, plucked or pruned was done according to the moon but not at night. Grandpa didn't carry an almanac in his pocket to tell him which lunar phase was in the night sky. He had every moon-slice and astral nuance down to memory. His was the absolute last word when any seed or seedling went into the sandy soil and in this nobody overruled him, not even Grandma Phoebe.

Grandma's spring gardens were adorned with crocus and daffodils and she unwrapped each one from its winter sleep the same way she did a baby. Grandma Phoebe's father had been a horticulturist responsible for a private manor in England and a huge berry farm in Michigan when they first came to America. Everyone helped in the flower gardens too, and if anything we were expected to be even more reverent to her blooms and buds than to Grandpa Teddy's vegetables and fruits. Pistils and stamens, grafting and bulbs, pollination, rooting and transplanting became not only vocabulary words but activities that little folk were required to master.

Despite her absolute love for blossoms, I never knew my Grandma to cut a flower for inside use. I believe she detested the withering part so much she couldn't cut the stem. Grandma believed in seeing the flowers where she and God grew them.

"Flowers belong outside," she said. "Gardens are places you go when everything else is topsy-turvy. All life's nuisance gets left at the gate when you're in a garden."

It was true about leaving problems behind when you were surrounded by her poppies, asters, roses, daisies, cornflowers and snapdragons. It was next to impossible to think of anything but flowers during the tours. Grandma tended her garden with the same exactness and demands she applied to her grandchildren. A careful planting, proper nourishment and water, pruning when needed and even the most stubborn of plants or children would burst forth in beauty. Despite what my mother said about God's part I was always convinced Grandma played the bigger part in the blossoming of both.

Patch played a part of spring time at the farm too, but in large part her labors weren't appreciated because the lawn looked terrible. Lawn maintenance wasn't her concern. She was disturbed about the gophers.

Grandpa was too, but they went about gopher control in different ways. After the ground had thawed sufficiently and those little rodents started burrowing in search of food, Grandpa went into action. Poison peanuts were placed at burrow openings and were accompanied by a warning about their arsenic potency.

"Don't eat the purple peanuts," Grandpa commanded to each of us.

Grandpa put guillotine type spiked traps straddling every tunneled trail and devised wind-driven wooden clackers that supposedly drove moles away from specific spots with noise. The farm's lawns were laced with enough poison, mole psychological deterioration devices and booby traps to satisfy any no-man's land, but it never worked to Grandpa's satisfaction. He never won the mole battles, but he never stopped trying.

Patch was more direct. She went after them where they lived.

There are few dogs equal to the earth moving capacity of the Airedale, a breed that could have been used for tunneling or digging to China. I personally thought that Patch believed some strange creatures other than moles lived underground, because she acted like she could hear them and wanted an up close look. A frenzied digger, her barks accompanied great plumes of dirt exiting between her rear legs, which she alternated with sticking her head in the cavern to sniff. Patch had a two front feet slinging dirt technique, using both front feet simultaneously to throw the dirt back away so new earth was exposed. Her whole head quickly became encrusted and she looked like a coal miner returning from a full day's work. Both of us boys had learned to avoid the behind part of her when she was digging.

It didn't matter that she found more moles in a single day than Grandpa could claim for the entire summer. If they would have just left her alone Patch could have exterminated every single mole that ever existed, but they didn't.

One look at the devastation of the yard was enough. Fruit trees with roots exposed, flower gardens torn asunder, lawns pockmarked as if land mines had exploded greeted Grandma when she peered out the front window one day as we visited. Under a pear tree, Patch was still in wild pursuit, but my English grandma was fearful for her tree.

"*Clock*," she stated flatly, "get that dog tied up."

By the time I got to her, she'd completed about a dozen fresh earthen craters. Each was more than a foot across and equally deep and had the excavated dirt and sod thrown about like irregular starbursts. After I pulled her away, we were joined by every disapproving adult that existed. Great holes in a gradual serpentine line marked the earthmoving attempts as Patch pursued some frantically burrowing mole. With rump wiggling enthusiasm, Patch indicated how proud she was of her efforts.

Nobody else was. The front yard was in shambles, its once well kept lawn now a grand example of bomb craters. I couldn't blame everyone for being upset, but I was smart enough not to mention that Patch's theme was only in keeping with Grandpa's tactics of mole warfare, even though I thought it. I wasn't too happy with her right then either. I knew darn well who was going to be filling all these blinking holes in, raking and scraping the loose dirt and replanting the sod.

Me. *Clock*.

All by myself.

As smart as Patch was she never learned to fill in a hole.

Chapter 7
Snakes and Snails

In the summer of 1952, Patch had her first litter of puppies, one of four she ultimately produced.

She had to be watched closely when she came in season, in "heat," and someone, probably me, hadn't been nearly attentive enough. Last spring she was gone like a shot, out the opened door and down the back steps looking for companionship. When she came back two days later all my folks could do was to hope that she hadn't been "caught." Puppies to me meant the roiling mass of prancing, wagging and barking creatures I had seen when we first picked out Patch. To my parents, puppies meant more food, more poop, lots of noise, inoculation shots they couldn't afford and finding homes for each of them. Patch came back, happy to see us again after her absence but looking contrite and slightly surprised with herself for running off.

Patch had definitely located a companion when she escaped. My folks were pretty upset when Patch got thicker in the belly early that summer but I was completely happy.

My father wished, "Let's just hope she doesn't have many."

Patch was going to have puppies.... Patch was going to have puppies! Patch having puppies meant I would have puppies, too. I hoped she had a hundred. She got so big it looked like she would. She got fatter and fatter and fatter. I started hoping she wouldn't burst.

Mom soothed, "Don't worry."

Twelve weeks or so after she originally got out Patch disappeared again and Mom said we'd have to look for her.

"She's probably gone somewhere to whelp her pups. Look in our garage, look in and behind Terry's garage and under the bushes out back, she won't go far." Mom went on, "Whelp means give birth to her babies, her puppies."

I've already told you about new words for my mother's children. Mom never missed an opportunity, not one.

We eventually found Patch under the house. She had squeezed her way through the crack in the wooden door enclosing the water pump. We heard little squeaks when we were in the kitchen or living room and rightly suspected her hideaway. Patch wasn't satisfied with just getting into the darkened space but continued crawling until she got all the way under the living room, a distance of about forty feet. Our living room wood floor was covered with just a rug but it was a real Oriental. A trapdoor in the center of the floor would allow access to Patch. I helped Mom move the couch, roll up the rug to get to it and lifted the door open.

Patch's eyes gleamed when we raised the trapdoor and she gave a woof of recognition and pride saying, *"Look what I did. Look! My puppies!"*

At her belly, lots of squirming, wiggling and squeaking dark little bodies nuzzled for her teats.

"She can't stay there, Clark," Mom said. "You'll have to go down there and pass them up one at a time. Wait a bit before you go down, we'll have to fix her a place on the porch or in your room."

"My room, my room! They can stay in my room!"

Mom gathered up newspapers, several of our pink woolen blankets and we created a little nook for Patch and the puppies in my room, right under the window. Mom went out to the garage and got a huge cardboard box and lined it with more newspapers. By the time Mom came back, Patch was standing up in the trapdoor opening woofing quietly to speak of her impatience. She barked loudly once, telling us while the dirt was fine for birthing when privacy was needed, but she now wanted her puppies to have a better place than beneath the house.

"Get down in there with her son, and hand them up one at a time, carefully, now," Mom admonished. "Watch out for their umbilical cords."

I knew of that concern from the baby rabbits.

I jumped down to the dirt and knew Patch was right; my room was a better place than this dusty, dark cobweb filled space. I picked the closest puppy and held it up for my mother but immediately pulled it back.

"Hey, they've got long tails!" I couldn't believe it. "These aren't Airedales!"

Mom laughed. "Remember the *docked* we talked about when Patch was a puppy?"

Oh yeah. Not like a boat and they got shots in their tails so it wouldn't hurt when the veterinarian cut them off.

I handed up the puppies one by one, keeping count. Patch sniffed each one as it passed, maybe not trusting or maybe keeping count herself. One, two, three, some were still wet and they all had a coating of the dirt from under the house. Mom said, "Wait a minute," and got a dishrag from the kitchen to wipe off each puppy when I handed it up.

"Seven, eight, man there are lots left yet! Ten, eleven. Eleven puppies, Mom, that's a big bunch of puppies, a real big bunch!" I was almost shouting.

"Did you get them all, son?" Mom questioned. "We don't want to leave any. Patch's puppies are called her litter. Puppies don't come in a bunch."

Sure looked like a bunch to me.

I lifted Patch up, too. Mostly I helped her scrabble out as she was full-grown by now and a bit too much for me to outright lift. I followed her up and inspected this box of black puppies. Patch gave the box of puppies a sniff and went back to the trapdoor, whining.

Mom asked me again, "Are you sure you got them all? Your dog seems to think something is still down there. You'd better look again. Take a flashlight this time."

I got one from the kitchen drawer, jumped back down to shine the light around. Sure enough there was one more. The biggest puppy had crawled away from the rest of the litter when Patch stood in the floor opening. There was one more! Patch could count!

Twelve! Twelve puppies!

"Are we going to get their tails docked?" I implored. "Can I keep the ends? Just like in the poem about little boys?"

Mom ignored my questions and instead concentrated on wiping off the last puppy and carrying the box into my bedroom to transfer the litter to their new spot. She knelt by the blankets and inspected each puppy's butt.

Mom finished her examination and told me, "Looks like seven males and five females. Two of the females and the big male have white spots on their chests."

As Patch seemed satisfied with the total, she lay down by the puppies and allowed them to swarm over her, where they found a good supply of milk.

Mom explained to me, "You'll have to give each puppy a turn nursing for a little bit, Clark. Patch only has eight nipples and there are twelve puppies. If you don't help the little ones they won't get enough milk. The big puppies will just shove the small ones out of the way."

Wow! There were rules for everything, even for puppies! And I hadn't heard them all yet, not by a half.

These puppies were noisy, grunting and making little noises all the time as they realized they weren't in the mommy's belly and kept searching, searching for the warmth they remembered. Their heads and tails shook with the effort of dragging themselves in searches, quivering as they called for food. When they weren't in motion they were asleep, but continued to whimper even as they slept.

They were great and they were mine, sleeping in my room. My puppies. Of course, they were Patch's puppies, too.

The big news at the dinner table was the puppies. All sorts of talk and plans about what we were going to do with them.

The rules were extensive: Patch would keep them cleaned up for a while, but once their business ends started working efficiently, I would have to; they were not to be allowed out of the enclosure unless Carole or I were playing with them; under no circumstances were they to leave the house for play; nobody could have one unless approved by Mom.

"Who's going to get one?" I asked, astonished at the thought. "We're going to keep all of them."

"Keeping them is out of the question. We are not keeping any," decreed my father when he came home, completely disregarding my offered opinion. "We'll have to find homes for all twelve."

We could only have one dog.

After some discussion we did decide one really good part. We were going to get their tails docked! Not wanting to spend any money on them, Dad said he would ask our family physician, Dr. Brezinski, if he would stray slightly away from human medicine just this once. Dad was pretty sure our doctor would perform the simple surgery. My father and he were good friends, as well as patient and physician. Dad would stop on the way home tomorrow and ask him. Yes, I could have the tails! Carole said it was disgusting. Mom thought it was cute. Dad didn't say anything, but I figured he'd want one too.

"I can keep the tails! I can keep the tails! I can keep the tails! I can keep the tails!"

"Snakes and snails and puppy dog tails.
That's what little boys are made of, made of."

It sounded ever so much better than the one for little girls.

Twelve tails! Why, I'd be the richest kid around.

We heard the plans the next night during dinner. Dad had stopped by his office and Dr. Brezinski said yes, he would dock the puppies' tails. We would take them over to the doctor's house in three weeks on a Saturday, when the doctor would perform the surgery. I could hardly wait. I was going to have twelve puppy dog tails all for my very own. I knew Carole wouldn't want any, because I had offered her one but was still confused about why anyone wouldn't want at least one of their very own. Oh well, all the more for me. I might eventually give Chip one, but wasn't sure he'd properly appreciate it yet. Not everybody could say they ever had a puppy's tail.

On the appointed Saturday we carried the box of pups into the doctor's kitchen. Mom and Mrs. Brezinski would be the nurses helping tend the puppies. Dad would watch along with me. Fascinated, I studied the procedure for every pup. Mom swabbed their tails with alcohol, making them squeal from the cold. The doctor gave each of them a shot in their tails and asked me how long each tail should be. He cut each one short and pulled the skin over the stump to stitch it closed and applied a styptic pencil to each shortened tail.

He wiped the first stub and handed it to me.

"Well, what do you think?" he asked.

I took it palm up and open, wanting to look at the first of my treasures. The little piece was about two inches long and so, so soft, and I whisked it lightly across my cheek. Only a few seconds ago, this was still attached to the puppy and wagging. I was keeping these tails for...EVER! He handed the rest of them to his wife as he cut them off and she placed each on a white cloth lying on the kitchen counter. I watched her close to make sure she didn't keep any but when Dr. B. was through there were twelve laid out in two rows. Mrs. Brezinski thought it was hilarious that I wanted the tails.

"Snakes and snails," sang Mom.

I inspected every pup as he finished, making sure the stumps met with my approval. It looked like Dr. B. had done a pretty good job, so good that maybe he had done it before. It looked like he cut every one exactly where I said. It hadn't bothered the puppies at all, many had fallen asleep, though several were getting hungry and making little throat noises to tell their momma it was time for nursing. Their momma wasn't here. We'd left Patch at home and needed to get the puppies back before too much longer.

"You've got to let the tails dry out for about a week. Keep them in a sunny window," Dr. B. instructed. "You don't want them to start smelling bad."

No, I surely did not. I had big plans for these tails. He covered the tails with another cloth and rolled them up before handing them to me.

"Don't forget, let them dry."

"Okay Dr. B. Thanks a lot. They all look like Airedale puppies now. You did a good job."

"Wait a minute," he said. "You owe me for the surgery."

"I thought my Dad.... You'd do it for.... I don't have any money."

My mind raced and I stuttered and stumbled through my thoughts, not expecting anything like this. What was I going to do?

Dr. Brezinski explained, "Well, you have to pay for the work I just did. Doctors are just like everybody else and they need to get paid for their work. Those tails are worth a lot and I could certainly sell them. How about I just keep half as payment?"

He must have seen my look of desolation as I thought of giving up my new treasures, but didn't prolong my anguish too much. I offered the bundle back to him but he shook his head and laughed. He continued laughing even louder and looked at my parents. I sure didn't want to give them up but I would. I didn't have any money.

"Okay then, how about I take one of the puppies when they're weaned?" He laughed again. "Those are pretty good looking puppies. I'll take this one."

He pointed to one of the pups, but in the wriggling squirming box, I couldn't tell which.

I thought for a bit and said, "Sure, when they're ready. Okay, Mom? Okay, Dad? Can he have one?"

They were both laughing as the doctor stuck out his hand to shake on it, a recognized method of agreement. I had shaken hands with kids in the neighborhood when we traded each other for something one of us couldn't live without. Now I'd made another deal.

Geezie Peezie! This only left me eleven puppies. Here only three weeks had gone by and they were dwindling fast. I resigned myself to fewer puppies. At least I still had their tails.

Chapter 8
Big People

Big people just don't pay much attention to kids.

Sometimes they don't even listen to kids, just like they jamb their fingers in their ears. I think when they get an idea in their heads it gets stuck in there and just won't come out. Almost like when Carole got a fishbone stuck in her throat. No matter what, Carole couldn't cough it out and Mom had to reach way down there and pull it out with her fingers.

Something killed one of Grandma's chickens, and every one of the big people wanted to lay the blame on Patch. We were at the farm and Grandma was mad because of her chicken, and her anger was almost like that bone, stuck right in her throat, 'cause no matter what I said, everybody was mad at me and Patch. That mad just wouldn't go away. No matter what.

Grandpa was mad because of the chicken. Mom was mad 'cause Grandma was mad. Dad was mad 'cause Mom was mad. And I was mad 'cause Grandpa tried to hit Patch with a stick. But Patch didn't even do it. Everybody thought I was lying when I said she didn't. No matter what I said, no matter how much I tried to tell them, in their eyes she was a chicken killer.

Grandma and Grandpa kept the chickens for the eggs. "Nothing like the yellow-orange of a farm fresh egg," Grandma said. "They lay lots of double-yolkers too and they're better for baking."

When Grandpa stalked into the house and said he found a dead chicken by the pen, all the grown-up eyes turned on me. He said it was all torn up, and he looked really mean at me.

"By some animal. Some dog, probably."

I knew he meant Patch.

I said it wasn't my dog and told them about that little black and white dog

I saw running out by the road, but Grandpa said there wasn't any dog like that around here. When we went down to look at the pen the hole was way too small for Patch to get in, but Grandpa said the chicken came out and then Patch got it. But I knew that didn't happen. No chicken would run out to any dog. Patch didn't even have any feathers or guts on her. The way that dead hen looked something sure should have stuff all over it. There were feathers scattered everywhere, just like it snowed when nobody was looking.

The grown-ups all acted just like they *wanted* to believe Patch did the killing. Grandma got even madder when I said they were trying to make a scapegoat out of my dog. I thought it was clever, but none of the grown-ups did. I knew Grandma was madder 'cause her lips got thin.

We sure were in trouble, such big trouble that we both got sent to the barn. Patch for killing that stupid chicken, which she didn't do, and me for lying about the little dog, which I didn't do either. It wasn't that the barn was a bad place. Heck, I played out here all the time when we came to the farm. It's just the way I got here, chased out by mean words and looks of disgust at what they thought. Just because she liked to sniff at those chickens through the wire mesh, the big people just knew she did it. Everyone calculated because there was a dead chicken and a dog, it meant that my dog did the killing. Their adding up was way wrong. All those smart big people didn't know anything about Patch if they thought she'd get one of those dumb flapping white birds.

Patch knew better even if they didn't.

But we were sure out there in the barn and couldn't come out. Probably no dinner either and Patch was wearing that stupid chicken around her neck too.

That was my grandfather's idea. He hollered at me right in my face. "I'll break that dog from killing my chickens!"

Even though I knew those hens were really Grandma's, I got the point. Grandpa said this was how they did it in the *old days* and it worked back then. They either tied the chicken around the dog's neck or they *shot the dog* back then.

"Worst thing in the world is a chicken–killing dog," he preached to the top of my head.

When I heard that last shooting part I didn't argue too much more, but I was worried about this bunch of people. They sure weren't acting like my parents and grandparents. More like strangers than people I knew, almost like those vigilantes in my Roy Rogers books; people who got revenge without thinking about who really did the bad thing.

This tying on thing was Grandpa's fix. He tied that tore-apart chicken right under Patch's chin with a piece of rope. He tied it pretty darn tight too.

"So she can't get at it," he said.

I think he tied it so tight 'cause he wanted to choke her a little. Like making it hard to breathe was good for anybody! Grandpa was just being mean. Just as soon as he closed the barn doors I loosened it up, but I couldn't take it off because Dad said I was in enough trouble already. I was afraid they'd come out here and check if I was minding them. Patch and I talked about the word enough but she couldn't figure it out either. The way it seemed to me, every time Mom or Dad said "Enough," they really meant "Way too much!" I sure had a lot to learn. I needed to get this barn thing right too. I'm in the barn with Patch 'cause my dog *had* to kill that chicken but she couldn't fit in the hole and only got feathers on her after Grandpa tied that dumb, dead, bloody bird on with a tight knot. I'm never supposed to be mean, but adults can if they want to be. I don't get it.

Patch and I talked about it for a long time, but neither of us could figure out how to make everybody believe us.

BANG! I really jumped when I heard the noise from Grandpa's shotgun. So did Patch.

BANG! The second shot really scared us.

I got even more panicked when Grandpa rolled the big door open. He still had his shotgun in his hand and at I first thought he'd changed his mind about punishing Patch. Maybe those two shots had been practice! I hugged Patch tight with both arms. Nobody's going to get my dog! I started crying and screaming at Grandpa as he walked toward us.

"Get away Grandpa! *GET AWAAAAY!* Patch didn't kill that chicken!"

Grandpa had rested his shotgun against the barn door before he walked up to the straw bale I'd been sitting on, but I thought he just wanted to grab my dog with both hands. He reached toward Patch and I hit his hand away.

"You get away from her!" I screamed at him again. "MOM! DAD! HELP ME! HELP!"

I wrapped my arms tighter around Patch, determined not to let go. I was frantic with fear, screeching and screaming.

"HELP! HELP ME, PLEASE! SOMEBODY!"

Grandpa finally grabbed both of my wrists and forced them away from Patch's neck. Even though I didn't have hold of her anymore I was still violently twisting, kicking at him and trying to jerk my arms away. It took me a long time to understand what he was saying, wildly fighting every second before my ears heard.

"Listen boy! Listen to me. I just shot the little dog you saw, shot 'im dead. The one you told us about came back and got another chicken from the pen. I heard the chickens squawking and took my gun with me when I went to look. I shot it just as soon as it scooted through the wire fence with a chicken in its mouth. That little *bastard* won't be killing anymore chickens. It wasn't your dog after all."

Grandpa reached over to untie the chicken from Patch's neck but I shoved his hands away.

"I'll do it. She's my dog, I'll do it. You leave her alone."

I untied that stupid dead chicken just as fast as I could, but just sat there hugging my dog, not talking and not looking at my grandfather. He turned around after a few moments without another word and walked back toward the open door, but stopped and turned around.

He looked back at me for a long minute and said, "I said she didn't do it, boy. Everything's okay now. You're not in trouble anymore. Bring that chicken up and bury it in the compost pile when you get it off her."

I didn't answer Grandpa, but just waited until he walked back to the house. I knew I was supposed to respond to every adult. Be polite. But I just couldn't call courtesy up right now. Grandpa still worried me a lot. I could only think that he hadn't known what he'd see when he rushed out to the chicken coop with his shotgun. Grandpa went out to the chicken pen with shooting in his heart. What if it would have been my dog out there? Grandpa didn't even say he was sorry and I figured he didn't think he'd done anything wrong.

I thought all these people, who were supposed to be so smart and so nice, even Mom and Dad, needed to know something more about dogs. My dog for sure.

Patch had chicken blood all over her chest from that dead bird and I needed to get her washed off. She shouldn't have to put up with this any longer. I lifted the bloody mass to look at the thing, but then let it fall to the plank floor and scooted the dead bird behind the straw bale pile.

Grandpa could find it later.

I worried about Grandpa for a long time after that.

Patch didn't act like she remembered the chicken thing at all when we went back to the farm that fall. But I couldn't forget the way Grandpa Teddy looked when he boasted of killing the small dog, and recalled just how frightened he'd made me feel. Maybe Patch forgave him, but I was still wary.

Patch and I always rambled when we went to the farm and especially when the leaves began to color and litter the forest floor. We loved the autumn the best. Beyond the fields, a great and grand section of woods waited to hear our tromping and we usually made sure the trees didn't wait in vain. The forested area had a small stream, a wonderful low marsh and was heavy at the fringes with underbrush. There were squirrels aplenty, quail and pheasant by the dozens, and Patch and I always enjoyed chasing one or the other through field and tree.

We got cussed by hundreds of squirrels when Patch caught one busy at its coming-to-winter gathering. She'd tear up the acorn strewn underbelly of the trees, trying to follow the frenetic zigzagging of their escape, when we happened to interrupt their work. They were sassy as could be and never passed up the chance to tell us just what they thought of us, bouncing stiff-legged and scolding on the safety of a high branch. Patch played the game to her best effort, but never managed to catch one. She couldn't climb a tree worth a hoot.

This time when we started out we flushed a pair of pheasants up next to the barn. The big birds frequently came close to the house in order to sneak loose corn from under the corn-crib and occasionally went into the barn where Grandpa stored the oats for his two horses. I'd surprised a young hen inside once and was almost startled off my feet when she made her whirring, flapping escape through the just opened barn doors. Often in the mornings, as I got wood for the stove, I'd see them marshalling about the yard and barn, in spite of Patch's persistent barking.

It wasn't unusual for our wanderings to be startled with their raucous calls as they flew toward the safety of the woods. Patch always chased them, until she figured out they weren't going to land and that she couldn't fly. Her joyous barking during the chase mixed up with the pheasants' high hooting made a sweet music, loud and happy. Autumn wouldn't have been the same without it.

Patch was such an exuberant hunter. She just wanted to smell everything—mice, moles, squirrels, gophers, raccoons, rabbits, frogs, turtles and game birds were held in equal esteem. She went everywhere their trails did, following the tantalizing scents through brambles and briars that would slow down a mosquito. I tried to keep up with her through this type of cover but on many attempts hit thorny, prickly spots that I just could not squeeze through without serious bodily damage. It didn't really matter, Patch waited for me to scoot backwards while I unstuck coat and pants from the spiky embrace of scrub locust or matted thistle. Part of every trekking day would be spent removing burrs from both of us, but that was just another pleasure in days already chock full of them. We both bragged of how this one or that one had become attached. Patch always had the more and better tales to tell.

We meandered snake-like back toward the woods, letting Patch's nose be our guide. The pheasants had flown to the edge of the wood, three hundred yards away, into an area thickly snarled with underbrush. I'd lost track of their flight path, but Patch had marked it well. Skirting a small copse of sumac trees, she plunged into the heavy cover with a triumphant woof. The wild fluttering that greeted her blended with the panicky chutter of pheasants and moments later Patch emerged with a cock pheasant clutched in her huge jaws. The tangle of growth prevented the birds from flying when she surprised them. She was so pleased with herself! Dancing and prancing and feinting in and out, now coming close for presentation, now hopping back to tease, all the while telling me what a great and powerful hunter she was, especially compared to me. She went on and on, growling to boast and soft wuffing for emphasis. Her eyes had the same shiny glint that the rooster's feathers held. It's a wonder she didn't puff up and burst.

I couldn't convince her to let me have it, although this was unusual. Normally after she'd had enough of her boasting she'd let me examine whatever prey she possessed. My examinations always had to be brief, because I never knew when she wanted to start the bragging again, but most times I at least got to hold her catches. Instead, she gave a muffled bark-bark and whirled away, trotting back toward the house. She ignored my calls, but stopped and whuffed again to tell me to hurry up. She was leaving, and I knew enough to follow when she called.

I hurried after her, following about fifty feet behind, over the sloping crest, past the barn and was intrigued to see her head over toward the north garden spot, where Grandpa was working. This garden held pumpkins, sweet and Indian corn, gourds and squash and other vine and root vegetables. Grandpa had been hoeing weeds when we left and was now stripping the colored ears of corn off the stalk for Grandma and Mom to use as fall decorations. He had his back to the barn and didn't see either of us approach.

Patch was silent as she walked up behind him, or maybe Grandpa was hard of hearing by then. She laid the dead pheasant behind him, took several steps backwards and sat down with it at her forepaws. I'd just walked up to join her when she gave a sharp and satisfied bark. Grandpa jumped, as much as a grandpa can jump, and turned around.

"Whaddya want, dog?" he asked, not too happy to have been startled.

Patch gave another bark, softer this time and walked toward the pheasant with her butt and tail doing the "I'm so wonderful" wag. She gave another half growl, half bark and nosed the pheasant closer to Grandpa, then backed away to peer up at his face.

Grandpa looked down at the iridescent, brown and black barred body and whistled long and slow, "Wheeeeet-wheeeeew. How about that! Pheasant for dinner tonight!"

"Rughhh! R-R-R-Rughhh!"

Grandpa didn't, but I heard the words *"Not a chicken!"* as loud and as clear as if she'd said them in English.

Patch further answered him with another proud dance, allowed him to pat her head, then turned around and walked back to me. She shoved her big snout under my hand and said it was time to get the burrs out.

"RRuuughhhh! *My burrs are better earned than yours, boy. Let's go!"*

Chapter 9
All I Want

Christmas was a-coming and Mom's already fat.

Grandma Phoebe was the boss of us, because Mom's going to have a baby, and she was lots tougher on us than Mom. Grandma sure petted Carole a lot, but she didn't put up with much from Chip and me. She didn't care that it was almost time for Santa, and we had to pay close attention to every one of her orders.

"Any day now, any moment now, your father might have to take your mother to the hospital," Grandma warned. "Don't pester your mother, don't be such a bother. You'll make the baby come before it's ready."

We even had to tiptoe when Mom was resting. Sometimes we had to "Get out of the house, Clock." We couldn't even be kids. No hollering. No running. No barking. No fooling.

Except for being really big in the front, Mom looked the same and almost acted the same. Except she took naps now too. But mostly she was still Mom.

The day before she forgot all about her big belly and helped Grandma bustle about in the kitchen. Cookies and pies for Christmas, the house smelled the best yet, peppermint sweet and full of cinnamon, all sugary-like. We could even smell the red and green icing that makes everybody's mouth water and we wanted some, please. Please? Glorious cookies a' baking, still hot from the oven we begged for one from each batch, but we had to wait until they were cooled and decorated. Wreathes iced with shiny sprinkles, bows and bells in dough silhouettes, gingerbread Santas with currant eyes that turned brown and yummy on cookie sheets. Piles and piles and piles of cookies, maybe enough even for us. Pies for after dinner that smelled so good we couldn't wait, but had to, says Gram. We've even got mincemeat made right here.

"Not out of a jar. Not while I'm here," Grandma pledged. She was the boss of the whole house, and that meant the food, kids, dog, Christmas, everything. Dad too.

We wondered out loud, "Won't Christmas ever come?"

Everybody helped decorate the house, but Mom mostly watched. Last week when we went to find the prettiest tree ever, Mom talked the tree-man into giving us extra, extra, extra boughs for the house. She had my father put up the pine branches just as soon as we got home and they made the house look Christmassy and smell great. Bells with mistletoe were hung in every door and you had to ring something or kiss someone when you caught them standing underneath. Mom and Grandma put colored candles in every room, but they were just for looking at, not for lighting then. Homemade Christmas stockings, red and green felt with decorations and our names stitched on, waited for the filling and we hoped there'd be no coal.

Just like every Christmas, Carole, Chip and I worried over what bad things we'd done during the year, hoping Mom and Dad wouldn't remember. Chip was only two and still in the "he's so cute" category, so he was okay. Carole was Carole, and as the oldest, to everyone except Grandma Phoebe, had moved into the "great expectations" realm. I fell under the "you know better" designation, and had heard it enough that I doubted I really belonged there. I'd had any number of swats and go to your rooms, but couldn't recall their basis, and secretly hoped Carole had done so much bad no one would notice mine. Maybe Santa had been busy elsewhere. I figured if I got any coal, it wouldn't be much. The day before Christmas was the longest day of the year.

"It's never gonna get here!" We lamented.

We brought the Christmas tree in the day before Saint Nick, early to open in the warm, and we decorated it! This was totally against everything we'd done so far. At our house, Santa usually had lots to do. Not only was he in charge of bringing the presents and filling the stockings, but he always had room for our decorated tree in his big sack, too. The surprise on previous Christmas mornings was boggling to a child's mind, but not this year. I somehow linked Mom's belly with us having to do some of Santa's work and wondered about it.

"Did Santa make Mom's belly big?" I asked my father.

He laughed, "You betcha."

Dad was in charge of the Christmas lights; untangling the cords (which were always mysteriously snarled beyond belief, no matter our care when putting them away), plugging them in, checking the fat glossy bulbs for tightness and grumbling about the ones that wouldn't light up. Putting them on the tree was his job too, but he wasn't in charge of that work. Mom directed the placement of every single light.

"Tuck that one in by the trunk, Jerry... You've got too many lights on that branch, Honey, it's drooping... There's a bare spot, move that light over there... Don't strip the needles off when you put the lights on, Dear... You need to hide the plugs, Jerry; they aren't pretty in the front... Turn the star just a bit more, Honey."

No wonder Santa wanted someone else to do it this year.

The fact was that we re-wrapped the ornaments and re-wound the strings of lights each year after the twelve days of Christmas, but it did nothing to change our belief that Santa normally did all the decorating. We didn't wonder how he got up into the attic for the Christmas ornaments any more than we did all the presents he brought. He was Santa; it was Magic.

When Dad was finished, it was our turn. We hung paper garlands and popcorn strings and mixed in ornaments unwrapped from their rustling and faded tissue papers. Each one was inspected and ooh'ed and aah'ed over as their origins were repeated. So may special ones; ancient blown-glass ornaments spotted with old candle wax, tin candle holders that used to have lighted tapers in them, feathered birds with clips to hold them in place, and shiny glass balls that nestled and softly tinkled against glass candles which bubbled when they got warm. Every one had a story. Then angel hair and more garlands of construction paper and shimmery, silvery icicles came next. We had a contest to see who put the icicles on best. Finally, candy canes in cellophane that we hooked on branches and real gingerbread men that we put way back in, but we couldn't eat these yet. We had to wait for these, too.

We had to wait for *everything*!

"It's the most beautiful tree ever!" All of us agreed.

"When does Santa get here? What time does he come?"

"Just wait, children."

When we finished the tree we stacked some of the presents underneath. There were boxes and packages to me; from Mom and Dad, from Grandma and Grandpa, but none yet from Santa.

That night we gathered around the living room. "Just in case," Mom said, and read us *Twas the Night before Christmas*, just like always.

"Everybody to bed now." Grandma made us get under the covers. We weren't going to sleep though. We wanted to hear the reindeers prancing and pawing of each little hoof. Even Patch was excited and turned around and around about twenty times instead of just three.

Santa came to our house and it had to be the first of his stops. Just in case was the middle of the night, Christmas morning still dark. Long before our eyes, which wanted to see Santa, had opened by themselves, Grandma was up and Mom and Dad too.

Grandma really bossed us now, "Hurry up children. Sit over there. Don't be so loud. Clock, put your dog away. No peeking at presents. Hurry up!"

'Cause Mom looked funny, sort of sitting on the couch, like her tummy was upset. Already in labor, she watched her children dump full to the brim stockings and eat our traditional oranges. Having an orange before candy eliminates the bad effects of sugar on teeth and bodies. It's a scientific fact and The Mom Law at Christmas.

"*Before* you have Christmas candy. You know the rules."

We had squirt wars with our oranges until Dad said, "Enough!" After stockings stuffed with hard candies, whistles and walnuts from the farm came the real treasures. Packages wrapped with ribbons and love for each and every one. We touched silky paper and fingered bows and peeked at labels to see whose was the biggest. From Santa to Clark. From Santa to Carole. From Grandpa and Grandma. To Chip and Clark. So many, so many, and all for us. I had five presents all my own. They were marvelous with glitter and we went one for each of us in turns until the living room was strewn with torn ribbons and sparkling paper remains, while Mom rose halfway off the couch, writhing every so often as we discovered what Santa brought. Gram was fidgety and nervous and anxious with my mother, but we un-wrapped every single one. Mom would not, could not go until finished.

One more, big, huge writhe on the couch and it was "Time to go, Dorothee."

Quick kisses and hugs.

"I'll see you soon, children. Mind your Grandma." As if there was a choice. Mom waved her goodbye. Then and only then was it time to go.

"You get back to bed now, children," Gram insisted. Now that Mom and Dad are gone, we don't even get to play with all the stuff. Can't even take it back to bed for dreaming.

"It's bad enough the dog sleeps with you," Grandma said. "Positively no toys."

Nobody went back to sleep, but we pretended, 'cause Grandma would get us if we were loud. Patch and I played "BITE!" under the covers, but we were quiet as mice. Well, we were quiet for us, 'cause Patch just growled softly.

We had almost a new Christmas when we did get up, except we didn't have to unwrap again. Then maybe we'd go to Grandpa Clark's house.

Carole and I were used to multiple Christmases, but Chip couldn't know yet. We got one at home and would get a second and third when we visited our different grandmas and grandpas. The trees were just as pretty and the gifts were just as shiny as our homegrown versions. We knew we would get more presents and just thought of them as a reward for our excellent behavior through the year.

That Christmas Day was great like always, but we got the very best package days later. Dad came home on Christmas afternoon with the news. My brand new baby sister was born on Christmas morning, just a little while after Santa's visit. I bet nobody else got one. How did Santa do *that*? How come he didn't just leave her at our house? Grandma wouldn't say and Dad just smiled.

I must have been really good. Of course, we had to wait to see her. No kids allowed in the hospital, unless they were sick. Absolutely, positively no germy little boys get to visit new babies. No Siree-Bob!

We didn't get any snow for Christmas that year, but three days later the flakes started coming down in the afternoon, just as Dad went to get Mom and our new baby. By the time he got them home it was really snowing and Grandma made me sweep off the front porch.

"We don't want your mother to slip," directed Gram.

Even though there was still just a powder of snow, I polished off all the flakes in feathery swirls. We turned on the porch light too, so they could see their way into the house and it wasn't even dark.

Dad came through the door, wearing his Navy pea coat and a young man's smile, the only time I ever remember him sporting both. He looked fresh as the snow, flushed with good thoughts and happy his wife and child were home again safe. Birthing wasn't such a given then as it is now and both he and Grandma shared relief when Mom and Baby Peg came into the house. Spotted with snowflakes, in his arms our really brand-new sister was all wrapped up so we couldn't see her, swaddled safe from the cold. Grandma was waiting. Holding his precious white bundle out to her, Dad hurried back to the car for Mom. Grandma sat on the couch with our covered up bundle on her knees while the merest of noses peeked out.

But we had to wait one more time Gram said, we couldn't see till Mom got here.

My father helped her to the couch and she sat next to Grandma.

"Wait till you see her, children." Mother gingerly spoke as she eased herself to the couch.

69

We gathered round to watch the unveiling, jostling each other and Dad for the best position. Dad acted so proud, looking at the white bundle. I peeked over Grandma's shoulder when she lifted the blanket off. She was tiny. And pink. And cute.

My Grandma exclaimed, "Oh Dorothee, she's so pretty."

I even got to touch her, this brand new Christmas baby. Chip is definitely going to get bumped to second in the cute category.

"Our new baby," Mom gleefully cooed.

Oh boy, she belongs to all of us.

I'm so glad we waited.

Each of us, including Carole, was well schooled regarding animals.
We were taught well and blessed with an affinity for all creatures, some that lived with us and some that only wished they could stay at our house. I certainly was in sync with my dog and the Greene kids' concern for animal health and happiness was reciprocal in every way, but no one was ever better at it than Peg. We soon coined the phrase "animal savant" in regard to her attraction to every animal she locked eyes with. Then again, Peg got an early start.

Well before Peg crawled, her favorite place was a pillow called Patch. Many were the naps both spent in that fashion. As soon as she learned to wobble upright and latch on, Peg moved through our house with an assurance that belied her age. Of course, Patch had a favorite in–house spot by then as well; anywhere my sister was had to be the best. Peg was the darling of the family and as a full fledged member with equal rights, my dog thought so too. If Mom would have fixed a way for Patch to get in the crib, I'd have probably lost my sleeping partner. When Patch was in the house, Peg had her fingers twined in her coat for comfort or stability.

In less than six months, a Peg–Patch partnership formed that rivaled even mine. Patch soon became as reluctant to leave Peg as Peg was to let go of her. Patch never whined or yelped, and ignored the wads of fur lost whenever Peg toppled. Patch only waited patiently, looking back until Peg pulled herself up with another two-handed grip. The bond grew so strong and evident that for several months my baby sister refused even to attempt a stand or step without Patch by her side. Despite Mom's adamant entreaties or extended fingers to help her walk, Peg's only move was a collapsing plop unless she had her plump fists buried in fur.

Walking progressed to riding, with Peg first draped over Patch's back, but soon she was upright and astraddle Patch's broad frame. Patch bore her burden as a constant pleasure and it was a common sight for "horse" and rider to gallop circle after circle around the rooms of our house. By the time Peg was three she thought herself an accomplished horse-woman and carried the notion into her teen years, when she rode her first real horse.

Chapter 10
Who Could Ask for Anything More

Other kids had monkey bars, swing sets, and toys that came from Sears and Hudson's.

Patch and I had a wilderness marsh.

We found an exclusive property area along the shores of Lake Erie which Chip and I called "The Marsh." While other kids came and went on our treks, every one of them just knew it was the Greene boys' private territory. I staked it out long before Chip ever set foot in it but he became part owner. As soon as he could keep up, Chip tagged along and we had five uninterrupted years of exploration before our land was invaded.

I first got parental permission to travel around the marsh when I was just six and a half years old. With the caution of "be careful son" from my mother, during the summer of 1953, Patch and I began to connect ourselves with the swampy wilds along Lake Erie.

Although the area had a multitude of uses at the turn of the 19th century, in the '30s or '40s, it had been allowed to revert to untamed wetlands. There were two abandoned steep sided quarries that had filled with water, another open expanse of a shallow man-made lake, four creeks and enough woods to get lost in; and so much marshland I would never traipse it all. Between Toll Road and the lake; east and west, and Pointe aux Peaux Road and Brancheau Road; north and south, I owned the most marvelous playground ever devised for a boy and his dog. Our spot on the map covered more than 10,000 magical acres.

Patch opened up the wild lands much more fearlessly than I did. I wasn't exactly scared but this was new in more ways than one for me and I was very young. I discovered much more than sights during that first trip although it only lasted several hours. I wore one of my father's old wristwatches and had promised to be back in several hours. Mom's approval also hinted at something much worse than carriage to pumpkin if I failed to honor that magic hour. The milestone of the trip marked my first real unaccompanied-by-an-adult outing and even though Patch was with me, my feelings of being disconnected from familiar faces and the safety of home was enormous. Our first excursion was limited to the lakeshore up and back, but it was so far away from any sign of people and houses, we might have been in Alaska.

At the end of the dusty road, a barricade warned "DEAD END" but that wood gate just marked a beginning for us. As we turned toward the lake and pushed through a tangle of wild raspberry bushes, the gentle curve of the beach appeared like a beckoning path. About forty feet wide, littered with mounds of brown water vegetation and driftwood, this sandy stretch didn't see much traffic. The houses along the lakeside of Long Road weren't able to view this out of the way playground and Patch and I were quite alone. Our original ramble led us to the first small creek that plunged to empty on the sandy beach and into the lake, a distance of little more than a mile north.

During this first expedition I couldn't quite work up the gumption to plunge through the heavy undergrowth by the beach but Patch was ever courageous and so I *allowed* her to be the first day's true explorer. She disappeared for long moments until my single-handed status triumphed in the battle of anxiety. I'd worriedly whistle or call until Patch came back to check that I was okay, but she'd quickly dive back in to renew her searches. After some time she had apparently checked and secured the area because she came and lay down where I sat under a small tree by the creek mouth. Another of many firsts that day included the attachment of hundreds of stickle burrs to her heavy coat. She'd attracted prickly seeds before but today Patch wore enough extra vegetation to blend in to the undergrowth. There would be some serious burr removal required when we got home.

The trek out had been one of wariness, but the way back was familiar with my own footprints. I noticed several paths cutting through the underbrush where animals came down for a drink or a splash. A re-examination of the beach revealed tangled treasures of fishermen's losses and I paused long enough to release several lures, hooks and sinkers from the snarls of string. By the time Patch and I regained the roadway I had claimed enough wealth to satisfy any boy's greed for "stuff." As we reached the roadway I was glad to see houses again, even if most of them were still empty of summer people. Despite not actually being *away* the evidence that other people still existed after so foreign a trek was comforting.

When we got back to the road sign, tucked in behind a heavy hedge of prickly bushes, I noticed the remnants of an old dock jutting away from an earthen peninsula opposite the lake at the end of Long Road. At a right angle to the road, a vague and shadowy trail beckoned my dog and me. Overgrown with trees, vines, thistle and burdock, it was obviously unused for a long time, but the spit of land might be an ideal observation post to the marsh. Unfortunately, this trail had to wait. My allotted time for the trip was almost up and I knew if I ever wanted to come back, I had to honor my promise. Mom was a great clock-watcher.

The very next day (no doubt a reward for being on time), Patch and I made sure to push our way through the stubborn brambles. The peninsula extended about two hundred feet into the marsh and at the tip we discovered a cat-tail ringed expanse of open water as far as we could see. This was great! There was only one way in, and it was brambly enough to make noise if some savage or wild animal was sneaking up on us, and water every where else. Perfect!

During that summer I found, re-floated and claimed a sunken flat-bottomed skiff. It was in such poor shape nobody else wanted to use it and I kept it tied up but it wouldn't have gone far on its own. The boat's sides were low enough to paddle with my hands but I had to keep several coffee cans for bailers or it sank within several hours. I bailed the boat before and during every voyage. No one ever disputed my claim to the leaky craft so finder's rights prevailed. For my brother, my dog and me that old holey boat was as good as any water craft ever made. It worked just fine.

The original intent of the old pier was anybody's guess. We kids thought booze was smuggled during Prohibition. This guess was supported by the thousands of broken brown bottles that were partly covered in the muck along both sides of the dirt extension. You could glimpse the pointed shards scattered about when the water cleared and we imagined the old dock was the site of some fierce gun battle and pictured Elliott Ness surprising smugglers on a dark night. We never went in the water here, knowing that no tennis shoe would stand up to the razor-like litter of broken bottles. We always entered at some other place whenever we set out spearing carp or hunting ducks or trapping.

Patch was flawless at finding the boggy quicksand spots. I think she managed to flounder into every one, sinking to her hocks before lunging about wildly to get back to firmer ground. Whenever I approached an already discovered sinkhole, she'd bark in warning. She was such an enormously strong animal, nothing as simple as a bit of quagmire could bother her tracking and trailing, but she was ever mindful of me. She was so protective of me when we went gallivanting I suspect Patch had entered into a confidential agreement with Mom.

I practiced and learned to build spring-set snares for rabbits, pheasant and squirrel. In colder weathers we camped out as often as I could manage to keep abreast of chores and schoolwork. My rudimentary woodcraft melded with Patch's natural instincts and we became wildly successful at living out, away from the comforts of home fires and family. Together as always, Patch and I became a familiar sight to any one or thing watching. We hunted, trapped and fished the area with a regularity that astonished yet pleased my folks. Both parents knew their son would find none of boyhood's customary trouble in our rough and wild country, but that I might find myself. During our years of tramping, Patch chased every animal known, and two men we didn't, through those marshes.

We spent that entire summer mapping out the remainder of our empire. Used seasonally by pheasant and duck hunters and once the site of a gravel quarrying operation, we now had it to ourselves. When hunting season was open we had to be extra cautious, but it was always irresistibly inviting to Patch and me. I had time limits to maintain, but I was allowed to explore as far as my spirit dared. With Patch along I learned to leave faint heart at home and delved deeper and deeper with each excursion. Within those warm months of summer 1953 we scouted to every border I could brave, and soon memorized trails and waterways. Patch and I waded and hiked and marched uncounted moments and miles through those wetlands and discovered two clear and cold bubbling springs which we used to refresh our thirst and refill canteens. The water in both natural fountains was so cold it hurt the back of my throat when I lowered my mouth to the rivulets. The springs served Patch and me for years.

We discovered isolated hillocks dotting the wetlands where we could dry out or I could recover from boyhood wounds of the spirit. The marsh became a sanctuary for me, a quick and secret seclusion of safety when parents or teachers or the world's spinning made me dizzy. Therein I discovered the marsh's power to diminish overwhelming issues and my own talent to release them when I was there. With tears in my eyes or blackness in my heart I found my way to solace many times in the marsh. I managed more easily to shed my problems with Patch as my confessor than acknowledge them to Jesus or family at our nightly devotions. I could have managed the trails blindfolded.

Chapter 11
Limits in Paradise

In 1953 Ralph was my best pal. We'd both read the really true-life accounts of Teddy Roosevelt and Alan Quartermain.

We knew Tarzan as if we had swung on vines together and practiced his animal-summoning yell, but not in the house. We could talk to animals just like Tarzan and the proof was Patch who came *almost* every time I called.

We watched for Cape Buffaloes to come bursting out of Mrs. Olsen's hedge at any moment and stayed ready for the charge of the lion we'd wounded but failed to find last week. We knew for sure of a leopard that lived in an old apple tree, but only prowled at night. There weren't any elephants in our neighborhood because we had never seen any and knew they were too large to keep out of sight, but everything else could have been in hiding and was fair game. Patch was omnipresent for protection and we were fearless.

Our Cub Scout canteens were filled with water, just in case we had to track some village threatening animal into the desert. We each had a knapsack to carry peanut butter sandwiches and an apple if we were on the trail for a long time. I had peanut butter and pickle while Ralph had his with jelly and mine were on homemade bread, but Ralph's were on Wonder Bread. I envied him his store-bought bread sandwiches and we swapped when we could talk one another into it. We shared pretty much everything; jokes and fears, likes and dislikes and hopes. We were destined to share more. That day we would spend by the Lake, exploring the shelves of rock and looking for some treasure swept to shore by the waves.

We knew of the dangers that Lake Erie held, had seen the huge whitecaps made by summer or winter storms and we had both seen remnants of shattered boats washed up on shore after the reckless fury. The lake was our friend, but it was one you had to watch closely all the time.

We started our expedition down by Ralph's house. His family owned a big home at the end of Pointe aux Peaux Road, right by the intake to our water station. There was a huge ditch that emptied into the lake from the station that always had six or eight inches of water in it as an effluent path of the water cleaning process. We waded through the warm water to get to the beach just as we'd done a hundred times before.

It was rocky here, with water rounded pebbles and sand which made the walking real slippery-slidey for feet. The shoreline formed a gentle "U" and we knew this to be a good place for fishing lures and floats from commercial fishing nets to be washed up. We both had a collection of each and hoped to add more, a continual treasure hunt. These floats were about 20" in diameter and much prized because they were perfect German mines when we played "submarine war," but we came up empty handed this time, no lures, no floats. Oh well, we knew we'd find something. We almost always did.

As we worked our way around the far side of shoreline, we walked up on a flat shelf of rock. It was about sixty feet long by about thirty feet wide, horizontal to the ground and overhung the water. It had depressions in it that held pools of water and in them we could find little crabs, water bugs and an occasional minnow that had been deposited by transporting waves. The ledge was dotted with fossilized clamshells and always slippery with seaweed, making for treacherous footing when wet. We stopped to inspect the pools, feeling with fingers under any jutting sections.

Experience had taught us that we sometimes got pinched fingers when we found a hiding crab, but we didn't care. The water came right up to the large shelf, had undercut the lake bed and there was no beach, none at all. The water at the jutting rock shelf was only about a foot deep and at one time or another we had both fallen in after sliding on the seaweed. It was no big deal except that the sandwiches got soggy, but we normally were wetted before each day was through anyway.

With a whoop, Ralph's feet went out from underneath him and he fell with a SPLAT! SPLASH! He slid right into the lake as if he planned it that way. I started to laugh, just as he had done the last time when it was I who was wet. My laughter stopped as Ralph started to scream in panic. Patch had run to the shelf edge before Ralph's screeches had much registered with me and was perched at the edge of the water, barking furiously, hopping up and down with each bark. I ran to her and looked over, about two feet above the water's surface. It looked like Ralph was wrestling with somebody, though at first I couldn't imagine who or what.

Ralph had fallen right onto some thing, some huge bloated body, something.... The waves were causing the thing's arm or tentacle, whateveritwas, whattheheckisit, to roll back and forth against Ralph's frantic struggles. The body was face up and had come to rest wedged in, halfway under the rocky ledge. It looked as if the monster-man was trying to hold Ralph down. We both thought that's what was happening and I added my screams to his, loud enough to wake this guy up even if he was dead. We were immediately both out of our minds with fright.

This was what the scary campfire stories were all about!

"Help! OhNo! Help! OhmyGod! Help! Crap-almighty! Help! Somebody! Help!"

I just knew this whateveritwas thing had Ralph in its clutches. Midnight spooky stories couldn't compare to this. Patch had jumped into the water and stood belly deep, barking, barking. Loud and angry barking.

I would like to tell you that I was brave and jumped right down there and freed Ralph from the clutches of this alive-but-dead-but-alive thing. I wish I could tell you that I reached down and pulled Ralph to safety with some superhuman effort. I wish I could tell you of some remotely brave thing I did that day. I want so much to say that I lived up to my credo of helping other people at all times. But I can't.

I was frozen rigid by the sight of my best friend being subdued by a zombie corpse and I couldn't do anything except scream and scream and scream. We both yelled ourselves out, hoarse and panting with the effort. Ralph finally struggled to his feet, and had gotten away but was yet standing in the water staring. I was still lying on the rock shelf on my belly, and neither of us could move or take our eyes off the body bobbing and moving with the waves. I finally stuck my hand out to Ralph and he grabbed it. I jerked him out of the water and we rolled over and lay on our backs panting with the horror. We were shaking so badly that any more movement beyond that was impossible, but at least we weren't looking at it any longer.

None of the details really registered until we borrowed each other's small courage to look again. It took us some time to do this and we lay silently quivering in our fear for five or ten minutes. The unspoken fear that it might rise up and get us eventually forced us to our knees. We crept back to the rocky edge and peered over but didn't look very long. It didn't have to be long. I saw everything all at once.

The body must have been in the water for a long time because the man's face was swollen and a sickly gray-blue-white. We couldn't see the eyes, only where they were supposed to be, because his face was so puffy. We could only tell it was a face because there was hair on top, waving back and forth in the water. His shirt and pants were torn, ripped up and his skin had bloodless gashes showing here and there through the tears in his clothing. The shirt ballooned out at the stomach, like someone had pumped it full of air despite the holes. At the time, this did not strike us as odd. We were still much too scared for reflection. Both his shoes and socks were gone and his feet were the same color as his face. We knew he was dead, but we did NOT know that he couldn't hurt us.

Patch was still barking desperately the whole time. I called to her with a quivering voice, but she stayed in the water. I didn't care. I figured she could stand guard if she wanted to, but not me. I'm leaving. So is Ralph. This would have to be reported to someone. We both took off toward home. I don't know that I ever ran faster in my whole life. The boogey man was real. I had just seen him. He might be right behind me. Close. I wanted my mother. I wanted my father. I wanted someone to convince me that that dead man wasn't going to get me.

Both our mothers called the sheriff's department within minutes of each other. Mom called Mrs. McKenzie after she hung up from the police to see how Ralph was. Mom turned her head away from the phone and said I would have to show the deputy where the body was.

I said Ralph could do it.

Mrs. McKenzie told my mother Ralph said again I could do it.

I said I thought the deputy might do without my help.

Mom sat with me on the couch while I told her the story over and over. I hoped it would be a good long while before I had to go back to that section of beach, but in about an hour the sheriff's car pulled up. Too soon for me. After answering some questions, Mom and I both got in and rode down to the beach with the officer. We stopped to get Ralph and his mother before venturing back along the lakeshore. Patch was still there marking the spot. Still barking. Like we were gonna forget! I pointed out the spot after we pulled up and the deputy walked over to the lake, motioning for me to come along.

I didn't want to but I went with him, and only then because he had a pistol.

Mom went too, followed by several other people that had trailed the deputy's car when he left our subdivision. A visit by police was big news around the beach, and they didn't come often unless there was trouble. The deputy only took one look over the ledge and went back to use his radio.

79

He didn't look long either.

A few adults in the small crowd went over for a look, but none of the other kids. Either their parents said, "No, you don't have to see that," or they were smart enough on their own. Everybody who looked wasn't smiling when they turned away.

The deputy told everybody, "Just go on home now folks. There's nothing for you to see."

Oh yes there was, there was plenty! I had seen more than enough, much too much. The deputy took Ralph's statement and then mine. He had a few minutes conversation with each mother and told both of us, "I'll be in touch if there are any more questions."

We didn't have to wait for the ambulance or coroner. Instead we walked back home. Mom explained about life, not death, the whole way.

Later I found out this body was that of a man lost the week before in a boating accident. No one ever said what he was doing on the water, fishing or hunting or just riding in a boat. I don't recall if I ever found out his name but I remembered the body vividly for a long time. It was my first introduction to a person's mortality. Although it wouldn't be the only time I got close to someone dying, this memory remained a stark and vivid meeting. I held Patch even closer by me at night for a long time. That body wasn't something I liked to think about.

I managed to almost tuck it away, but at night I was real glad Patch was there.

Although both Ralph and I avoided that spot for the remainder of the summer it didn't slow us down much.

I continued to have great freedoms given to me. Not because of my parents' indifference, but for the reason that they understood that many best lessons were learned by being on my own. Patch being my constant companion contributed to their loose reins as well, but several weeks later we were both put in jeopardy by one of those lessons.

Our plans that day included stopping by the fort before we went exploring. This camp was located on the southwest side of the marsh in a small clearing at the edge of the wood. There was a well-traveled path to the camp, more than a mile from the subdivision, and there were days when we made several trips.

Ralph and I had scrabbled together a hogan, much like the Mohican Indians constructed, and made from branches stuck big end deep in the ground in two straight lines. We bent them to overlap and tied opposing sides together in the middle, thus creating an open ended half round tube. On top of this we fastened and tied bunches of cattail fronds. It made a surprisingly waterproof structure. We were continually adding fronds as the original dried and disintegrated but it was a good shelter and when it collapsed under the accumulated weight we'd build another. That wasn't a problem; there were lots of willow trees and cattails at the swamp's edge for a new hogan.

We had a fire-pit off to one side at the front and we knew enough to wet, stomp and stir before leaving the ashes. We'd learned how to make spring snares and would infrequently catch a rabbit or two. We had devoured books of Indian lore and were proud of the fact that we knew how to make and maintain a camp.

We'd stocked the camp with several snitched, castaway or leftover items from our houses. We had an old wooden stool with the legs cut short and a ragged blanket we left hanging in a tree so it wouldn't mildew. One of us had sneaked away a pot for boiling water before we drank it, or cooking something we'd trapped. We were learning the rudiments of wood lore and had several merit badges to prove it.

That day we checked the snares we'd set, but while some were sprung, nothing was in them. It looked like we'd be going home for lunch. We whiled away the morning doing nothing important; straightening up the camp, making plans, being real outdoorsmen. Everything we thought critical to camping out was checked before we turned toward our houses. This evening, if we could come back, we'd see what had become of the raccoon family we'd seen several times in the spring.

We had tried in vain to catch one of the babies. Nothing would have been finer than a pet raccoon. But the mother was ferocious and more than a match for us when the kits were little and her snarls were warning enough. Now the young could run faster than we could. We could have set Patch on the momma but that seemed unfair, even wanton. We had a terrible time restraining Patch when we saw the family the first time and now every time we hunted for them we left her tied at home or the camp.

Later that summer, the family had grown smaller; the kits had grown fast but now the original six had been reduced to four. Some other animal, a fox or dog had gotten them or they had become victims of the road that bisected two halves of their woods.

One never knew in this life; I didn't need anyone to remind me of that. I was pretty sure the corpse Ralph and I found two weeks ago had been planning to go home when he was through at the lake. I was equally sure all those baby raccoons had been planning on growing up.

We each got the okay for a night excursion and got there early, but spent a lot of time convincing Patch she had to just hang around the campsite while we spied on them. She wanted to hunt them up right now.

I finally had to tie her up to a tree with some clothes-line Ralph pulled out of his pack and it's a good thing I did. We watched the sun trail down for a few more minutes before we set off toward the water's edge. We hadn't lit a fire but sat around the fire-pit with our backs to the bull-rushes and didn't hear a thing when Patch began a furious warning.

The big boar raccoon surprised us almost as much as that dead body had. With a garbled snarl it lunged out of the bushes about forty feet from our hogan. It must have been Patch's loud snarls that attracted him. The animal appeared as big as a bear cub but its fur was matted, dirty and unkempt and it was walking as if under some witch's spell, weaving and staggering off center. The black and brown head was twitching erratically, its mouth yawning wildly, trailing strands of spittle.

"RABIES!" Ralph and I both shrieked in unison.

All the kids in the neighborhood knew about rabies. A few of us had gone to the theater to watch "Old Yeller" and the horrors of the disease were as vivid now as on the movie screen. We'd also been pledged by our folks to run like the wind if we ever saw a dog acting strangely or "foaming at the mouth."

We didn't know for sure what the cause of this disease was, but we knew that people could get it. Something had to bite us or we had to bite something. The result would be that we would get shut up someplace with a stick tied between our teeth so we didn't bite our tongue off and if we survived that we'd still be crazy and thirsty all the time.

Patch was going wild, jerking fiercely against the skinny clothesline with such force it quivered like a bow-string. I ran back to her and threw myself over her neck in desperation just as the thin rope snapped. My frantic grab wouldn't have mattered one bit if Ralph hadn't helped.

Even in duo we almost couldn't control her furious strength. I later thought it was because she, in truth, had let herself be held back when she sensed the animal's terrible sickness. While I tried to calm her and watch the rabid animal Ralph tripled up the line and we snagged her close to the tree trunk.

The raccoon obviously heard Patch because he was now trying, circling slowly in his tracks, to find his way to the noise. It was fortunate his disease was in the advanced stages because if it hadn't been for losing the thread of its travels, the raccoon would have been on us before we secured my dog. Just as soon as we thought Patch couldn't get loose Ralph and I took off in different directions. It was a time for action, not for thought.

Although we were both badly frightened, we knew the animal had to be destroyed. Ralph went in search of a big branch and I played matador to turn the animal away from the tree where Patch furiously encouraged the raccoon to come over for a visit. There were several minutes when nothing I could do overcame the sick animal's attraction to Patch's barking and growling. I stomped and hollered, kicking dirt at the slavering creature and finally noticed a stick lying nearby. I made a grab for the branch when my foot stomping wouldn't keep it from the lure of Patch's noise.

I sure got its complete attention when I poked it. Up until now the poor filthy beast's movements had been jerky and erratic but when I jabbed it with the stick some open circuit closed just right. It whirled and leaped and almost got me, but only got my stick. Snap! The tree limb was now in two pieces. The branch I'd been using was only three feet long to begin with, but it got frighteningly shorter after that raccoon got done with it. At least the stub distracted it, because the animal treated its piece of the branch as if it were the worst enemy ever known. I couldn't risk another thrust with the little bit left to me. I cast about frantically for another branch to use.

With a yell of triumph Ralph leapt into the arena.

"HIYAHHHH! I got it!" He yelled.

He'd found a sturdy tree limb, nothing so puny as my measly twig. Ralph whacked it with a branch the size of a baseball bat right in the middle of its back.

THUMP!

"Hit it again!" I screamed when the raccoon gathered itself to spring at Ralph. "Hit it! Hit it!"

Spinning around to see the new antagonist, the raccoon presented its head to Ralph and he smashed down harder than before. Again, again, again! In frenzy, as vivid and vocal as my dog, he flailed and pounded the animal until long after it quit moving. Our yells of fear turned to triumph. When Ralph wore himself out, I took the club and gave the dead animal some whacks of my own. We were both shaking badly, but we managed to walk over to Patch and sat down.

We'd won!

After quieting Patch and ourselves, we gathered wood and threw it from a distance over the battered corpse until it was completely covered. Although the raccoon was dead we were still badly frightened by the specter of the disease and didn't want to get too close. We kindled a fire in another area, twenty feet from the body, and when it was burning, carried the flaming branches to the animal's pyre. Work usually quiets a racing mind and this was no exception. All types of questions and guesses floated between us.

"Can we catch rabies?"

"Will they have to shoot us like they did Old Yeller if we do?"

"What if we start foaming at the dinner table, someplace we can't get away?"

"How long does it take to show up if you do get sick?"

"Are you gonna tell anybody?"

"Are you?"

While Ralph and I watched upwind from the fire we made a pledge more strong than those we had to our parents.

"Don't tell. Swear it. Word of Honor." From and to each other. "Now you swear it. Word of Honor. Nobody can know."

We watched and fed the fire until nothing but ash marked the field. When Ralph and I parted for the evening, we vowed it all again. This fight belonged to us.

I was still flushed with fear when I got home but I convinced my mother it was due to the rambling we'd done that evening. I was still atremble so I busied myself with another task before I went in the house, knowing that it would take my mind further off the just won battle. Like all dog related duties, my parents expected me to determine when Patch needed a bath. I could only chalk up points if I did it without having to get Mom's "gentle" reminders. By the time I finished giving Patch a bath my jitters were gone.

Patch was single-minded in every one of her pursuits.

When she was searching for a buried bone, Patch never let a little dirt get in her way. If there had been a shift in the earth's crust, burying her treasure miles below ground, and she still needed the bone, the morsel would be found. If her nose indicated a living thing worth sniffing, the creature should hope there was a vast body of water close by to wet down the scent, or that it could out swim her. When another dog needed a whupping, Patch was resolute in making absolutely sure it got what was needed.

I followed her on my bike one day when she chased another dog all the way to Stoney Pointe, a distance of almost a mile, before she caught up. Though both animals were exhausted, my dog administered several well placed bites before she trotted back toward home. Once she had her mind made up it took phenomenal effort to convince her otherwise.

My father opinioned, "Your dog is the most bull-headed, pig-headed, stubborn, mind-of-her-own, balky, contrary'est dog that ever lived."

I thought her determination was her best attribute, except when it came to bath time.

Patch loved the water and I can't recall one single trip to the lake when she didn't get wet. She was a powerful swimmer, never seeming to get tired and loved cavorting with her brood. Fetching sticks, a leisurely paddle or chasing waterfowl were right down her alley. In weathers that would make us shiver and turn blue she plunged in time and time again.

Except when she needed a scrubbing.

My mother was usually the determiner of Patch cleansing frequency. No matter the weekly application of Murphy's Oil Soap, dog smell is magnetically pervasive and it soon soaks in and takes over all closed spaces, namely my room. The fusion of boy plus dog (or dog plus boy) aroma has a fascination all its own and as every true savage knows, it is a natural disguise. Because Chip and I smelled just like my dog we could sneak up on the wariest of wild game or neighborhood kids. Intrepid hunters, we three liked it just fine, but occasionally Mom wasn't quite so pleased.

Chip and I could tell when Patch was approaching the need for a good lathering. My mother made faces. She also made us keep our bedroom door closed and if we forgot she'd close it for us. Especially when some church member came over. Mom spouted "Cleanliness is next to Godliness" at us all the time, but I think she was actually concerned about a judgment of her own when the pastor came to call. Nevertheless, when Mom said it was time to scrub her down even Patch bowed to the commandment. Although God really lived in the marsh and He was the one who made Patch smell like she did, Mom won out in the house.

In warmer weather the task had unique strategies required to be successful. I have already indicated the marvelous ability of Patch's nose and her use of it wasn't limited to tracking other animals. Whenever we went to the lake for a swim, we had to pass two complete inspections. One was Mom's which included beach towel presentation and searches for contraband food. If Mom discovered food, the inspections included a recitation of the twenty minute rule. When Mom was through, Patch had her own singular examination. Once assembled outside the house and before we started the walk to the beach, Patch had to give each of us the once-over sniff test. No bloodhound or "trained to find drugs" canine was ever better than she was at locating her illegal substance. If we had it she found it. Patch learned through experience whenever her signature perfume was in jeopardy.

Patch could find Fels-Naptha soap at thirty paces. If she got even the slightest of whiffs, we could almost be sure that Patch wasn't coming with us. If you didn't have a tight hold, she was off like a shot in other directions, a sure sign that for today she and our room would continue to be unique in the universe. Patch would watch from another yard until we returned home and she felt secure. If the group only included Chip and me, she never wavered, but if everybody went swimming Patch became wary.

We even tried ploys. One person in the family would delay their starting off and be the bearer of the soap, thirty minutes behind the first group. On the rare occasions when we drove to the beach the soap had to be carried in the car's trunk and sometimes other kids would be asked to carry it for us. We ultimately resorted to wrapping a bar up in tin foil and keeping it stashed at the beach, but this was only moderately successful because she soon detected the spot and avoided the sites. She detested the Fels-Naptha, but it was the only one to use. Every other detergent wasn't strong enough to defeat the smell of Patch.

The bathing process itself was easy. Once resigned to her fate she was stoic, allowing lathering, scrubbing, sluicing, soaking, bubbling, cleaning, and scouring with eye closed patience. Patch accepted that she was in the presence of her lords and masters. She never fought or squirmed, she never whined or growled, and she never tried to get away.

Except when we were done. Until she was absolutely sparkling, glowing with clean, she never made a move. Rinsed with bucket or splash she was a statue. Fur brushed, groomed to perfection, show dog quality loveliness, Patch put up with the spic and span condition only long enough for our focus to fade. If we didn't restrain her or take her home, she'd bolt. When an outright dash didn't work she'd slink. Or she feigned nonchalance, knowing the limited attention span of two boys. Patch had her own ideas about proper grooming and ploys necessary to get it set right. None of them included the sharp tang of Fels-Naptha soap.

To Patch après-bath meant application of all sorts of beauty products. The first stop was a dusty road where she'd muzzle and roll for an abundant dose of her own powder. Grass would do in a pinch but she really preferred the dirt. The second stop on her makeover required a cream of just right dead fish, the more pungent the better and she was never happier than when her treasure was in its final stages of fermentation. Finally she'd pick up some stickle burrs for adornment, placing them ever so carefully in the most uncommon of areas. Dirt and mud and fish and burrs. Patch was good at finding every one. Then and only then did she feel ready to reappear before her distantly admiring audience.

Then we had to start all over again. Patch was only ever banned from the house when she found her perfect fish. The bathing and her own beautification was a never-ending summer cycle.

Colder weather wasn't quite so taxing. Once Lake Erie iced over we were better off. The dead fish froze right along with the lake and weren't so easily applied, but getting the inside shampoo started was just as much of a challenge. To begin we had to ambush her as she walked by the bathroom and we needed conspiracy to do it right the first time. If the first attempt failed Patch could not be dislodged from under my bed no matter who was doing the pulling.

Chip was the best hider in the family. From all his running away from Grandmas, Mom and especially me, he learned to be secretive with himself. It wasn't unusual for Chip to be under tables, behind chairs, up trees or stuffed under clothes and shoes in closets, and anybody's closet would do. Once we found him hiding under the car. The whipping he got for that hidey-hole location was worse than the one he was hiding from in the first place. But Chip could surely hide away.

Whenever Patch smelled ripe in the winter Mom set up the ruse. She'd call Patch and offer some leftover tidbit. While she was distracted, Chip would leap out from under the kitchen island and grab her. Coaxing and leading were not successful in getting Patch to the tub. We never lead Patch anywhere and when she was in season it sometimes took two. If she didn't want to go where you were headed, it was virtually impossible to get her there. Her four feet stiffly planted against your tugs only wore you out. Free outside and in, she mostly went where she wanted. With her tremendous powers of association she avoided the bathroom because she knew what happened each time she was there. We used Fels-Naptha in the winter, too.

Fortunately, eventually her great strength would wane, although it seemed to take forever. After Chip's initial leap from hiding and I had added my weight, she knew the end was near. By the time she had dragged us around several circuits of the house Patch usually tired and we could muscle her into the bathtub. Once we got started, she was resigned and the washing up was easy.

The finish was still the best part, even in the winter.

Outside it's not a problem, but inside sure is.

It is a scientific fact that an Airedale cannot be dried with a towel. Not even minimally mopped up. The towel gets wet and soaking, but the dog just will not lose moisture. The same fact holds true despite the invention of the electric hair-dryer. Unless you are president of your own generating station it's a waste of electricity. Their fur can hold moisture for days.

Airedales must be shaken dry.

Preferably in one of two places. Outdoors was next to someone and we had become accustomed to that. Inside was next to my father's red vinyl chair. Afterward she would occupy said now-wet-chair if he wasn't already there. If he was seated, so much the better, but just people-close was considered good. Her first choice would be visitors but any of us would do if only the family were home. No matter that we spent immeasurable time in our rubbing, discounting all the hollering and dodging, when she came from her house baths, something was going to get wet. Even Mom's pronouncements of, "Yes, she's dry," didn't stop water droplets from flying when we finished the job. We even pinned a towel around her middle, but after hours of wearing it, she still splashed when she shook. We soon just accepted that by the time Patch's bath was complete, the bathroom, kitchen and living room would look as sprinkled as if a summer shower had blown through.

My father grumbled about his wet chair because her water sprays trickled into the cushion seams and wouldn't dry out, unless soaked up by his gabardines. He could never figure out why we shouldn't be able to train her not to shake off or why we couldn't dry her completely. I really believe he thought Patch could learn anything she wanted and if she wouldn't learn this, it was for spite, and part of the reason she was "the most bull-headed, pig-headed, stubborn, mind-of-her-own, balky, contrary'est dog that ever lived."

By the time I finished this night-time scrubbing, Patch was clean, not really dry and I had calmed right down.

Patch's appetite for food equaled her appetite for life.

I never saw her get filled up on either. Patch may have drawn a few lines about food but I never saw them. She would eat anything. Leftover vegetables (raw or cooked), dried up and crunchy spaghetti, meat "gone bad," stale bread, the occasional piece of cat poop and whatever else looked interesting and edible. It's a wonder our compost pile got anything at all.

Patch's table manners belied her appetite. She was a dainty eater and never grabbed at food from pan or hand. She preferred to ease up to any proffered tidbits, always waiting for the spoken "okay girl" before taking food, including the dish that every one of God's other creatures recognized as hers alone. She'd defend her outside food bowl from stray and neighborhood dogs or cats vigorously but I never saw even a hint of dismay when we kids teased her with a pretense of taking food. She laid by my chair throughout virtually every one of my childhood meals, content to wait until an offering was handed down. She knew Mom's rule about waiting until the rest of us were done eating before plates were proffered for Patch to pre-wash.

But dainty didn't mean neat. Patch had to have her face washed after every meal. If you weren't quick to wash her shaggy whiskers for her, she'd do them on you. Several times at least or until she was sure she looked her best.

But I never saw Patch turn away when food was present.

We kids were chided and teased if we ate a lot of food or asked for a third (never on the second) helping. My father's favorite term was "you must have a hollow leg, because that's the only place that could hold all the food." If Patch hadn't weighed so much, I'd have thought all four of hers were hollow. Our entire family laughed at her ability to intake food.

One day, after Mom discovered an almost full cardboard container of oatmeal that had gotten "buggy," infested with weevils, she cooked them up. The homily "Waste not, want not," became an attempt to see how much "that dog can eat."

Saucepan after saucepan, full to the brim of oatmeal were cooked, cooled and swallowed. Mom and Peg did the first part, Chip and I did the middle part and Patch did the last part. Six or seven, four quart, pots full of weevil-ly Quaker Oats disappeared as quickly as we could get them cooled enough to prevent boiling the inside of her mouth. I think Patch especially liked the meat the bugs provided. Extra protein for strong bones and bodies. We ran out of spoiled breakfast cereal long before Patch got full. She did look like she was pregnant when she waddled out the door.

But she still looked hungry.

We were all astonished by the pan after pan of food and couldn't imagine where it all went. Chip and I tracked her when we put her outside, for about an hour after she was done eating. The three piles looked equal to the intake and we ran back to the house to report these important scientific findings to my mother.

Patch was at the back door looking for dessert.

Chapter 12
Treasures in Heaven and Earth

My father quoted three Bible verses incessantly:
"Jesus wept."
"It's better to sleep on a stoop than with a nagging woman."
"Spare the rod and spoil the child."

He never doubted the convenient wisdom contained in any of them, but he constantly quoted "Jesus wept" out of context. Dad recited those two words as if they referenced him. He also claimed we'd crossed the line, pushed our luck, were cruising for a bruising, or trying his patience, or got too big for our britches, or pushed him over the edge.

The list he kept for describing our many faults was mind-boggling. Although I'm sure I deserved many of the tantalizing phrases, I was often astonished when I'd earned one without recognizing I'd even been close to the invisible mark. Dad drew so many lines I had problems walking anywhere without crossing more than one on any endeavor. Too many cookies before dinner. A line. Not taking the garbage out. A Line. Boy behavior. A line. Not sitting still in the car. Another line. Being a smart aleck. A HUGE line that encircled me completely.

And another and another and another.

When he added the two word Bible verse to the one that started with "spare the rod....," I knew what came next. The part that hurt him more than me. Ha!

Dad didn't talk to us much when we were in trouble.

My father spanked. Often. Hard.

He had degrees of spanking, created especially for me and based on the severity of offense.

Something minor, like making my brother cry, might have earned me a bent-over-his-knees, open-handed swat or two.

More significant issues, as in fibbing or breaking my glasses, deserved his belt properly applied as I grabbed my jeans covered ankles.

For the real infractions; for me being a smart aleck, to him in particular, or sassing or deliberately ignoring previous warnings for even the minor offenses, earned the ultimate.

"Drop your drawers."

Belt on bare butt equals instant attention.

Instant sorrowfulness.

Instant compliance.

Instant fear.

I may have earned or deserved many spankings and probably did, but in my experience there is nothing quite as shocking as having a leather strap applied to regions best kept inside some article of clothing. While the anticipation of his homecoming was equally as worrisome as the spankings, the promise of his belt also brought something else with it.

Meanwhile, Mom relied on Holy lectures, lessons and learning to show us the error of our ways. She was inventive with punishments, choosing each tribulation's effect with a prescience that bordered on the amazing.

We stood in corners when we tormented one another with grimaces.

"The wall won't care what your face looks like."

We were sent to the bed with a pillow over our face when we were loud or sassy.

"Sass the pillow all you want. I don't have to listen."

Mom tied our arms, straight-jacket like, in one of my father's shirts.

"If you can't keep your hands to yourself, I'll keep them to you."

And taped our mouths with adhesive tape.

"You'll talk nice or you won't talk at all."

The last one was mostly for Carole. Her mouth was called potty so often she should have carried a roll of tissue. For several years she was taped up enough as if to appear she liked it. Maybe she did. She wore more adhesive-tape on her mouth than Mom ever thought of putting on our injuries.

When one of us (usually me) had hurt a sibling or other smaller child, often we were visited with a similar pinch, push or grab, just so we knew what our meanness had created for someone else. Any of Mom's physical lessons were surrounded with words of warning, pleas for Christian behavior and were often accompanied by a question as the sermon wound down.

"What would Jesus do?"

91

If we had been particularly horrid, sometimes Mom would finish her talk to us with words designed to cow us for the duration of time until it happened. It was always a sobering statement and the moments from utterance to occasion were dreaded every second.

"Wait till your father gets home."

I'd been playing outside with Chip and Dave Hicks and for some reason I cannot possibly fathom, we decided it would be just marvelous to play in the muddy gunk of our overloaded septic field. Our system was terribly undersized and was a large contributor to the reason for our bathing strategy. In addition to bathwater sharing, we were creative with all our liquid wastes and in order to relieve the tile field from too much water, we threw dishwater out the back door or poured it on flowers and didn't flush the toilet until someone deposited solid waste. Even more strange was that we considered all the water conservation efforts and the soggy, shiny black and sour smelling mud as equally normal in our family. The area was considered off limits, but we all knew it was a part of our life and where it was.

Despite Mom's many trips out to chase us away we didn't stop for long. As soon as she saw us scamper out of sight Mom went back inside but kept an eye peeled for repeat offenses. We came back time and again and her tolerance finally failed. More than likely it was also because of the mud-slinging fight we ended up in, but she soon decided it was time for the ultimate warning.

"If you boys don't stop, I'll tell your father."

The statement was more than enough for Chip and Dave. They took off, but not me. I could only think of how they'd both look after I'd pummeled each with a double handful. I stayed focused on my work.

I don't even think I heard Mom.

I was so busily involved in stockpiling beautiful black stinky mud-balls, I failed to notice her approach. When she grabbed my shoulder to get my attention, I thought it was my mud war buddies and I swung a handful around in offensive greeting.

Got Mom right in the apron.

It didn't help that it was a favorite apron she'd been given by her mother, but that really didn't have much bearing on the situation. It wouldn't have mattered what she'd been wearing.

My ears were close and the only handles not too muddy. She had my full focus when she latched on to one of them. There was tons of lecturing going on then, but the real problem began when she said the words that struck home fast.

"Wait till your father gets home."

After stripping me bare and washing me down with the hose, and although I thought the cold water was punishment enough, I was also sent to my room. With the door closed tight.

I could have told you exactly how the condemned man felt.

During the next several hours I worked myself into a real frenzy. When I heard my father's voice I panicked.

"Hi honey, I'm home," Dad called as he came through the door.

But I didn't hear any greeting. What I heard was "Pull your pants down."

I ran screaming out of my room, slammed through the back door and dove to sanctuary in Patch's dog house. She came right in with me.

In about five minutes Dad came out on the back porch.

"Buster, you better get your butt out of that dog house RIGHT NOW!"

I pretended I wasn't there, but I sent Patch out as a decoy.

"I'm telling you for the last time!"

Usually when we heard "for the last time," we caved in, knowing the inevitability of whatever came next, but I still pretended I wasn't there. I hoped he'd really believe it this time if I didn't answer.

"You're going to get just what's coming to you. Now get out here," he hollered. My father reached through the canvas strips over the doorway, grabbed my arm and dragged me out.

He stood me up and grabbed my chin in his hand, forcing my face up to lock my eyes with his.

"You listen when I talk to you. Don't EVER disobey me."

He punctuated each word with a jerk of my head.

"Now get in the house and get your pants off."

I was even more surprised than he was when I shook my head loose from his hand, crept away three or four feet and continued to shake it slowly back and forth.

I said a tiny and desperate, "No."

He was dumfounded and at first didn't know what to do, but it didn't take him long to remember. He made a lunge at me but pulled up short when Patch growled. I sidled even closer to Patch, crying and afraid, and put my arm around her neck.

"Get over here. Get away from that dog."

I shook my head.

Dad took another step forward.

Patch growled again, this time tensed and on her feet. Ready.

Dad was immobilized with rage, his words fighting one another to be first spit out, sputtering and wild with indignation.

I thought my father might explode. He made another step toward me and Patch really showed her teeth. I fearfully held onto my dog and if Mom hadn't been out on the porch Dad might have gone KABOOM! I think Mom was sometimes alarmed at his explosive temper and when she saw Patch's defensive posture, knew something had far exceeded the bounds of rational thought. Out of the corner of my eye I saw her hurry to Dad's side and try to pull him toward the house.

"Jerry," she softly called.

No response from red-faced Dad, who was still vibrating with anger and rocking forward on his toes.

"Jerry, come into the house," Mom insisted, laying her hand on his arm. "It was just an old apron anyway. Come in the house now. Dinner's almost ready."

Dad didn't want to give up the fight. I could see it in his clenched fists and I read it on his face. He stared me down for long minutes before he turned to go and then he did only after Mom stepped in front of him and blocked me from his view.

Of course Patch was focused on him as well the whole time, too, but I'd just been scared beyond anything I'd ever known.

I went back to the sanctuary of the dog house and skipped supper with the family that night. I wasn't yet seven years old but I was old enough to know not to be in the same room with him, despite the fact of the dinner table between us. Mom brought Patch and me out a plate of food to the dog house and waited while we had our exiled dinner.

"He's probably had a hard day, son," she explained. "I'm sorry now I said anything. Eat your dinner now. I'll come and get you in a while."

I didn't get the spanking I was supposed to that night, and in fact I never got whacked for that particular infraction. Spanking was a part of the 1950's culture and I almost expected them when I knew I'd earned one, but I never liked the humiliation or the hurt. I continued to hear "spare the rod" and still got spanked for any major or calculated errors.

But after that Dad made sure Patch was tied up before he started in on me.

Dad continued to quote all three Bible verses the whole time we were growing up, and reinforced the ones relating to children at every opportunity. I always thought the declamation about the nagging woman was just for show though. Mom told him pretty much what and when to do everything and stayed after him until it was done. I never saw him sleep on the stoop, either.

I told Patch she better quit it.
But she didn't.
Now she was really in trouble and I was too, 'cause…
"She's your dog," Mom reminded. "You know about minding when I tell you. And about lying."
Patch just wouldn't leave those dumb old sheets alone. I tried to get her interested in something else and we played tug of war with an old towel when Mom said it was okay, but that didn't work. I really scolded her, but it went in one ear and out the other, just like my Mom says for me. I whipped her pretty good with a rolled up newspaper but I didn't like that very much. I found out that whippings really do hurt the guy who's doing the whipping worse. Just like my father told me when I got spanked but I never believed it till then. But I whopped her anyway when Mom said to and it didn't even work either. Patch had sad eyes and looked like she was sorry, but she was just waiting till I wasn't looking anymore. Then she just snuck and got another one.

Everybody hung their washing out to dry around here. Even in the winter time when it's freezing cold, the moms clothes-pinned everything out. Shirts and socks and men's and lady's undies, too, all flapping in the breeze. Mom always said they smell better, so good "you can smell the sunshine in them."

It was kind of funny at first, but I didn't dare say so. Patch wouldn't fool around with Mom's laundry; she knew better than to mess around with our stuff. She didn't bother with Mrs. Terry's either, even though it was right next door and she could have gotten it real easy. She had sheets out to dry at least once a week just like everybody else. Patch could have gotten the Hemry's stuff too, 'cause there sure was a lot of laundry for all their kids. Mrs. Hemry always had rows of clothes pinned up on her clotheslines. Everybody else's was hanging right on the path Patch took to get Mrs. Edwards's sheets but she just passed the other stuff up, like it wasn't even there.

Patch sure did like those white sheets Bolie's mom hung out.

We didn't know where the first one came from. Nobody did and in particular I sure didn't. Of course it didn't look much like clean laundry when Patch dragged it home. Brown dirt and mud, smeared with green streaks, with just a teeny bit of sorta white left. It looked more like a big animal's skin from Patch's dragging and chewing and rolling. I figured it must have washed up on the beach 'cause it was pretty wet too, so I just let her play with it. We used it for lots of things. I twisted it all up and tied it around the maple tree to play circle. Patch could really grab hold to run around the tree. She played the circle game real good. I hung it over a limb for Tarzan swinging and hollering stuff and Patch tried the swinging too but she couldn't growl very well with her mouth full of sheet. She was sure good at chewing it though. Mom told us to burn it in the trash barrel when it got really shredded and stinky from all that pulling and swinging. And that was that.

Until a week later when she brought home another one.

The second one made Mom suspicious. Mom used the same figuring for Patch she did for me. How do Moms figure these things out?

"Once is chance. Twice is trouble."

Patch carried this one right home. She probably remembered all those circle and swinging games we played and wanted to hurry up and find me. This one was hardly dirty at all and didn't even look bad except for that big rip where Patch tugged it a little probably. But it was somebody's. 'Cause it had gold and red embroidery on it. Mom said it was somebody's really good sheet and she wanted to know whose it was.

Mom made me go looking. Patch had to go looking with me, too.

But I just pretended. I wasn't going to go up and ask everybody if they were missing laundry.

Jiminy Crickets! Who did Mom think I was? Sherlock Holmes? J. Edgar Hoover? I can't just go up and knock on Hemry's door or something and tell on Patch. That'd be snitching on my best buddy, my pal.

So I only made up that I asked everybody. Patch and I played by the ball park so Mom couldn't see us until I figured enough minutes were up for me to do all that knocking and asking. Then we went home and said nobody was missing any laundry. That's when I got in the same trouble as Patch.

Mom did her own knocking and asking. Well, she didn't do the knocking part, 'cause she used the telephone. Mom found out where that stupid sheet came from.

That's when I had to do all the scolding and hollering and whupping with Patch. That's when Mom did all the same stuff with me, but just the scolding and swatting, not the hollering. I danced around a little (almost like the circle game) so the swatting didn't really hurt but I acted like it did. When I made up some fake tears Mom quit smacking me but she wasn't finished with both of us yet. So I got soap in the mouth for lying and Patch got tied up for snatching. I had to go in my room too 'cause I'd been sneaky and Patch couldn't even come in.

And I got in even more trouble when Dad came home. He didn't care that

I already got swatted cause he gave me some hard ones of his own. Carole thought my spanking was funny, but Dad made Chip and Peg cry, too, 'cause I was crying for real this time. And he sent me back to my room with the door closed tight. He didn't even care that I already whapped Patch. He took his own newspaper out there and just whacked her for a long time. She had to stay tied up for two whole days when he was through.

Just 'cause he was gonna have to buy Mrs. Edwards some stupid sheets.

But that was nothing. A week after she got free again, it got really, really bad.

You should'a seen how mad everybody got with the third one.

It's a good thing I was listening when Mrs. Edwards called to tell on my dog. I could tell right away from the sound of Mom's voice. Dad wasn't home yet, but I could already hear him when I listened to my mother. There was going to be a whole lot of sorry around here.

Mom told me to get Patch.

"You get out there right now Clark Malcolm, and find your dog. She took another one of Joyce's sheets. She's going to have to have a real whipping this time. You bring Patch right back home when you find her. Do you hear me?"

I nodded like I was gonna do it.

But I knew right away I wasn't. I wasn't sticking around for this, not me, and not my dog. I didn't want to look at my Dad's red face when he got home. It had been bad enough watching my Mom when she was on the phone and got even worse when she hung up. Now Mom said she was gonna whip my dog again.

Oh no, she wasn't.

And I wasn't gonna whip my dog ever again just 'cause they say to. I'm not even staying around this spanking mad place.

We ran off. Away from home. Far away where nobody could ever find us. Patch and I walked down the side of the road and I was crying again. Just imagining the whopping Patch was gonna get made me cry. Lots of cars streaked by us and a few beeped their horns but I didn't even look up or wave. I didn't care about those dummies; I just wanted everybody to leave us alone. Patch and I were gonna live someplace else. Maybe even a foreign land, like Africa.

But Mom must have called people when I didn't come: Right. Back. Home. She and Mrs. Terry caught up with us out on the paved road.

Man… now Mrs. Terry knows! Everybody was gonna know pretty soon! When her old green car pulled up along side of us with the window rolled down and I saw Mom, but at first I pretended she wasn't there. I was really mad. Then I yelled at her, too.

"You're not hittin' my dog anymore! I hate you all! Get away from us! We're never comin' back home!"

We were gonna run into the woods but Mom's voice made me stop.

"Of course you're coming home, Clark sweetie," Mom soothed. "Come here dear, you're not going to get a spanking."

"What about Patch?"

"She won't get a whipping either. We'll have to figure out something else."

"You promise? Dad will want to smack her really hard. I'm not lettin' that happen any more."

"Nobody will spank anybody. I promise son. Now you and Patch get in the back seat before somebody runs into the back end of the car and kills us all. Come on now. We'll figure out what to do."

I was still pretty worried about Dad, but I didn't want anybody running into the back of the car and killing Mom. Or Mrs. Terry.

Patch just jumped in when Mom opened the door, but I hung back until a big old car whizzed by blowing its horn.

"BEEEEEEEEEEEP! BEEEEEEEEEEEEEEEEP!"

"See what I mean, son. The cars go fast out here. Not like in the subdivision."

I followed my dog quick after that.

We didn't get any whippings either. Not from anybody. My Dad sure wanted to but Mom wouldn't let him. He got really red in the face and his eyes kinda bugged out but there wasn't any hitting going on.

He did some stomping though, like he was trying to leave his foot prints in the floor. Mom didn't get after him like she would have if I'd been stomping but she did tell him to go outside. I would have got a swat for the very first loud foot. I watched him to make sure he didn't whack Patch, but he didn't even look at her, just sort of walked around the back yard stomping for a while.

We had a family council at dinner to figure it all out. But everybody acted like it was my fault because everybody came up with something for me to do. Just me, nobody else.

"Watch Patch closer."

"Don't let her run free anymore."

"Whip her harder."

"Have Mrs. Edwards call when she's doing her washing."

I thought up the best idea. Well, I sort of borrowed it.

Mom thought it might work and Carole did, too. But Chip and Peg couldn't figure out how it would. My Dad didn't think it was a good way to teach her, but that was because he really just wanted to whop her. He was probably worried about having to buy another stupid sheet.

Mom called Mrs. Edwards and said we were going to keep the last sheet, but we'd give her some money.

I tied that old sheet around her neck, just like Grandpa Teddy did with the dead chicken; with lots of wraps so she looked stupid, with a big puffy white collar on, really dumb. I tied the ends of the sheet together with some tough string so it wouldn't come undone either. Patch couldn't even get it off with her paws.

At first it looked like it wasn't gonna work very well, 'cause Patch thought it was a game. When it was new Patch liked it. Wore it proudly. Like a reward. But she scraped and bit at it as soon as she figured out I wasn't playing anything. Then she just wanted to get it off. She tried to chew it whenever it worked a little loose but I just fixed the ends again when she got some in her mouth. Mom said Patch had to wear it until she was cured and I couldn't take it off for swimming either.

Mom's *cured* meant Patch had to wear it until she said "Take it off."

Until took the whole dang summer.

It got really nasty. Dirty. Stinky. Yucky. Fishy.

Mom said I couldn't even take it off to wash it and I had to close my door every night when I brought her in. I didn't care. Patch could have smelled like anything and I'd still want her in my room. Chip was even a little wiener about it until I made him "give," but that was easy and pretty good fun, anyway. It usually only took me about three Dutch rubs to make him give up.

My Dad stayed mad about it a long time but Patch never even looked at any flapping clothes while she wore it.

One day it just disappeared, gone for good.

Mom first suspected me and I had to swear on the Bible I was telling the truth.

I didn't take it off and Patch didn't mess with Mrs. Edwards' laundry anymore after it disappeared.

I figured Patch just had enough of that sh-ee-t to last her, but I wasn't dumb enough to say it out loud.

It's not easy having an obsessive person in the family.
My folks had another issue to deal with beyond "not really" stealing. No,

the person wasn't me.

Addiction puts a terrible strain on everyone, watching for signs of recurrent behavior, looking for clues to indicate the addict's return to the source of the compulsion. Our family had gone through the usual denial period, not wanting to believe the obvious. Grandma Phoebe knew it from the very first, although she had a hard time convincing Mom and Dad. Grandma was particularly interested in curing him, though everyone was getting tired of the difficulties he caused.

My baby brother, little Chip, was infatuated with ivory.

More specifically he pried the thin strips from Grandma's piano keys every time he wasn't watched closely. Like any good addict he tried to keep it a secret and had several stashes hidden around the farm. Mostly he liked to slide them between the pages of books and magazines where they would surprise an unsuspecting reader, but Gram had found several underneath cushions of her couch and living room chairs. A number of times Chip got a "good talking to," administered by whoever found the ivory or caught him in the act. The condemnations became more severe as the acts went on and on despite Gram's closing the lid whenever we were there. She would have locked it up if she could have found the key. His four year-old fingers always managed to open it up, ignoring the pain of getting them pinched badly when she caught him in the act and the lid crashed down.

Gram said, "Maybe that will teach him, Dorothee."

It did not.

Mom tried slapping his hands. No success. She tried tying mittens on his hands. No good unless she tied them on tight enough to stop the circulation. Gram wanted to use the Chinese method of theft prevention and lop the offending hands off. Mom said no. Chip would take the keys off. Grandma would glue the keys back on. Chip would take them off. The supply and demand system was in full blossom. Chip would not be denied.

This autumn day everything came to a head. Chip required watching, and both Mom and Grandma made rounds to see what devilment he had created during his forays through the house. He could sneak pretty well for a four-year-old.

This time he got caught with the evidence clutched tight in his thieving little hands. This time he got a spanking. He was first really surprised, then shocked and finally hurt and angry. We kids did get spanked, but these punishments were reserved for acts we knew better than to do or repetitions of the same sin over and over. Dad was called into service, as most often he was the administrator. I think the tactic of the male role as spanker was created to insure that boys especially, didn't grow up to hate women in general and their mothers specifically.

Wise women long ago knew that even absent a father's punishment, boys would automatically go through a period where they didn't have any use for Dad. Boys would already be mad at their fathers for being their fathers, so the mothers might as well have the fathers be the ones who did the spanking.

Chip was really light on his feet and slippery as an eel. Though Dad had him by one wrist, he danced and hopped around in a circle while my father turned in order to keep Chip's butt in range. They circled round and round, Chip giving extra spurts of speed and a hop every time a hand made contact. Chip's wailing accompanied this swing-your-partner dance but the noise would never be confused with music. When he was little, few sounds could compete with Chip when he believed himself suffering. He could hoot right along with the biggest, loudest train that ever existed, only at much higher octaves. To say that his screams were piercing only diminishes their impact on ear and heart.

Dad wore out before Chip did and he bolted for the back door as soon as Dad let him go. Screaming all the way, he slammed through the door with a crash and must have run down by the barn, because the noise got a little softer. Not much, but the glasses in the cupboard weren't clinking together, now that we could hear other noise. Peg stopped her sympathy wails and the house was much, much better now that he had gone. Dad followed him to the door and called after him once.

"Let him go, Jerry," my Mom wearily said. "He'll be back when he cries himself out."

I could see from Gram's look that she hoped Chip had an unlimited supply of tears. She had been waiting for Chip to get a comeuppance for a long time and was not so secretly pleased to finally see it happen. Grandma didn't like Chip for a long time due to the piano thing. She thought it was evidence of either a weak character or defiance on his part. She liked neither trait in anybody, especially family and wasn't shy about showing her distaste.

Sometimes my grandma scared even me.

But I had to admit the quiet in the house was pleasant. Everyone also knew that with Chip outside he couldn't get to the piano and we could let our guard down and be less vigilant. Now that it was over, we all got a reprieve. We resumed our pre-screaming activities but it wasn't long before my mother told me to go find Chip.

Grandma whispered, "Go the long way." Mom didn't hear her.

"Chiiii-up! Chiiii-up!"

I whistled for Patch, headed out toward the barn, hollering, and fully expected to find him in the straw and hay piled on the upper level of the barn. We had both retreated there singly and in pairs when we caught the dickens, something not new to me. It was not only a good place to play but you could lick your wounds there when you needed to. Surprised that he wasn't up there, Patch and I headed down to the lower level of the barn. Grandpa kept the horses and pigs down there and all the grandchildren had been cautioned about not bothering the animals, but I thought Chip might have gone just down to watch them.

I called and called and called. Where was Chip? I called some more, trying to make a game out of it so he'd show himself. I looked back on the barn's first floor. Not there. I went all around the barn several times calling his name. No response. Patch and I headed back to the house by way of the orchard, the garden, Grandpa's workshop, by the Concord grapes, the lower garden and the swings, trees and bushes in the front yard. No Chip. Patch's excellent nose didn't notice a thing. It looked like Gram's suggestion was coming true. I thought he might have snuck around me and went back into the house when I was in the barn or orchard. My calls of "Chiiii-up!" had sounded more fed up as they progressed. Maybe he thought I was mad at him, too, and ran back to his Mommy.

"The big sissy baby, just wait till I got hold of him!"

I fully expected to see him sitting in the house playing with something or with Mom and was really surprised when she asked me where my little brother was. I gave chapter and verse of where I'd looked and started to get really mad when Mom said to go look again. Carole had to help this time, too, but we weren't any more successful together than I had been by myself. No Chip.

We went back to the house and reported.

Mom said, "Everybody out! Chip's scared and hiding. I knew you spanked him too much Jerry."

I saw my father with an, "it was your idea" look on his face, but he didn't say anything. Grandpa Teddy asked me if I had looked by the pigpen. I said yes and he asked me if I had seen anything down there, anything at all.

"Nope. I looked by Pete and Pat, too."

These were Grandpa's big draft horses, although he didn't work them any more. But I knew what the unasked question of pigs was about and so did everybody else. Big people got worried looks on their faces.

Grandpa Teddy raised and butchered his own pigs. Normally this happened every fall when the weather turned cool and would chill the pork quickly, so the meat wouldn't be tainted during cutting and wrapping. Last fall Grandpa decided he didn't want to do any more butchering despite the fact that he had two ready to be done. These pigs Grandpa now just kept and each one now weighed close to three hundred pounds. Even Grandpa seldom went into their pen for the pigs were bossy and demanding, pushing each other and Grandpa about in their search for something to eat. Grandpa had teased us with "the pigs will get you" and "I might put you in the pen so the pigs'll eat you."

We kids believed.

Apparently the adults did as well.

Mom told my father to get down by the pigs "right now" and take another look. Dorothee also told everybody else to get outside and find her baby boy.

Two aunts, two uncles, one grandma, one grandpa and four cousins obeyed as if the orders had come from Above. It had been more than an hour since Chip got his spanking and had run out the door. A four-year old wouldn't stay hidden this long. Dad and Gik and I were to go out to the fields and woods. I went because I knew my way around out there and had Patch for the snuffing, Dad and Uncle Gik along for extra eyes and authority. Uncle Don and Aunt Nance were to each take one direction along the road and far boundaries of the upper and lower gardens.

Carole, with cousins Greg and Henry, Don and Nance's two sons, would redo the original barn and workshop search as well as the small copse of sumac trees beyond the upper garden and orchard. We had a lot of ground to cover, sixty acres and it would be dark before much longer. There was talk of the sheriff, but Mom thought it was too early to resort to that. Grandma and Grandpa would drive slowly up and down Grossman Road in case Chip had decided to really run away. We searched in the woods, mostly along the edges between the fields and trees, and had spent another hour out there finding lots of burrs but no brother.

We could just hear someone faintly 'Halloooo'ing, halloooo'ing', us from the direction of the farm, but it was a long walk back and dark by the time we reached the house.

Chip had been in the corncrib the whole time, burrowed under the dried ears for camouflage.

Dad started to get all worked up until Mom said, "No, Jerry, no more. He's been through enough."

When we got back home Mom took Chip by the hand and walked him over to our piano, a big upright Story & Clark in the dining room. She pried off a single piece of the ivory and handed it to Chip.

"If you lose that one sweetie let me know, there are plenty left."

He never needed another of Grandma's. I'll bet he still has it.

Peg was a collector, too.

Not quite as compulsive as Chip but edging up to and toeing the borderline. Peg was a great grabber of cats. If she had only been able to keep them from mewling she'd have been able to keep them longer.

Although we had our own cats that belonged in our house, every other cat Peg saw belonged to her. Phoebe Erma might have learned to stand and walk by grabbing a handful of Patch's fur but as soon as she could toddle, her pinafores wore kitty-cats. Cats or kittens living in our subdivision got more than one visit to our house. If Peg managed to sneak by Mom and Dad those felines saw the inside of her closet or a box under her bed too.

We children were all expected to be out ramming around. When the sun was shining, outside. When the snow was falling, outside. Freezing cold or boiling hot, windy or sweltering, we played outside. If it was only sprinkling, "A little rain won't hurt you," or, "You're not sugar; you won't melt" and we were outside. We were told to "Go outside and play" virtually every day of our lives. The outdoor behavior was considered a measure of good health, identical to strong muscles and bones and white teeth. If we were inside at any time when it wasn't raining buckets or tornados hadn't been sighted, we'd better be sick.

Peg never figured out why she got caught when she'd snitched a kitty, but I knew. Unlike the perfection of Chip and I, Peg was never real good at sneaking. All of the actual owners quickly learned the Greene house was the most likely place to find their missing pets because Mom made her take them back. Peg made her kidnappings a dead giveaway. She stayed inside to pet and play. Even though Peg soon wised up and secreted herself in her closet when she swiped one, Mom's sixth (or how many ever it was) sense always knew something was not right. There was a child inside.

Peg borrowed kittens or cats despite every other girl's tears and justified her possessions.

Standing with hands on hips, she'd proudly announce, "I'm giving her (or him) a better home." Her argument remained the same regardless who the real owner was or how loud they bawled.

Peg had dolls to play with, but the reason for them was more for the clothing than for the dolls. Most of the time these doll-babies wore nothing. Peg kept the pretty costumes laid out and ready for her catnapped victims. If Peg handled a cat, no matter its gender, it was going to wear something frilly. She loved to dress those kitties up. If it was daytime and Peg's door was closed you could bet she had another. When the milk got used at more than its normal alarming rate, check Peg's room for extra occupants and if there was an extra noise added to the cacophony of our house, we figured Peg was just dressing another one.

Peg dolled them up regardless of how they felt about it and despite their scratching protests. Peg might not have been good at sneaking like Chip or I, but her determination was better. She probably learned her single-mindedness from Patch. Mom learned to listen at the closet every time she passed through Peg's room and Peg's behavior laid down another knowledge morsel around our house. Peg's absence most likely signaled a new possession. If you couldn't find Peg, listen for the cat's meows. It never failed.

Peg never got over her little girl love of a kitty.

In addition to all of our fortune hunting, Mom had her own ideas about treasures and they weren't for "laying up" here.

Mom was determined we prepare ourselves for the likelihood of leaving.

As in departing, "this mortal coil," just another of her favorite churchy phrases.

We were raised in the Church. I mean *in* the Church.

To say that we were a church going family didn't come close to the description of our actual God related activities. Our family attended... no, we participated in Church. We were involved in every aspect, from cleaning floors to cleansing souls, from washing windows to being washed in the Blood of the Lamb.

Mom kept copies of Baptist pamphlets, flash cards that asked people if they were saved, and small volumes of the King James New Testament in a drawer in the dining room sideboard, just in case she could bring home some backsliding former Christian or out of the gutter, and wanting to be better drunk that she met on a trip to the Salvation Army. We always blessed this food to our bodies and pledged our bodies to the service of the Lord. Mom demanded that her children be as white inside as she scrubbed and combed and washed us on the outside. We operated under the restrictions of the Ten Commandments and at least two dozen more created by Mom. Her gifts of love or food or baths to the unwashed neighborhood kids had so many strings attached they resembled spider webs.

There were extra laws for Church even though God had plenty of His own. Mom paraphrased a Bible verse substituting the words "attend church" for the word "pray" to read, "attend Church unceasing," as though she thought we should offer our supplications that way, too. Mom believed that if we were full of the Holy Spirit there simply would not be room for a sin to get in. Transgressions wouldn't be able to squeeze in anywhere.

My indoctrination began early. My mother made me swear a pledge before I reached the age of awareness, and while she still held sway over my thoughts. I was mustered into Youth Groups, Youth Chorales, the YMCA and every Bible Camp my parents or current church could afford to send me to. Mom made sure I was carefully but thoroughly indoctrinated into the wonders of salvation. I was supposed to act holy at all times. Mom knew the only way to make that happen was to soak her children in as much sanctimony of church as our young bodies could absorb. By the time she realized how badly my vessel leaked it was too late.

We went to church regularly. Sunday morning services were not just expected, it was a condition of regularly spaced meals. We went to church three times on Sunday if you counted Sunday school and I marked every minute. After Sunday dinner we prayed for understanding of the day's sermon. Sunday evening services were slightly less mandatory but could only be skipped if there was definite proof of homework that must be done before bed. We went to Wednesday night Prayer meeting and Youth Group on Fridays. As I grew older and wiser, I learned to cache away certain schoolwork that had no looming deadline and reveal it on Wednesday nights, thus exempting myself. There was talk of a Tuesday and Thursday "Kids for Christ" reinforcement class, but no one besides my mother was interested.

This was not just your run of the mill, lip service only, from the sidelines, church attendance either. We participated in all the Holy activities. We were expected to sing, confess, witness for the Lord, speak up when asked questions in Sunday School, memorize the Bible "chapter and verse" and were encouraged to push others out of the way when it was time to recite them. We got attendance pins that looked like battle awards for never missing a Sunday and hung one below the other so that everyone knew what good little Christians we were.

We were expected to "take Jesus as our personal Savior, Dedicate Our Lives to the Lord," and go up to the front of the church when an invitational such as "Ye Who Are Weary, Come Home" was sung. We were also commanded to set examples for every blinkin' child we ever met or had the most remote chance of meeting in the future.

I was baptized numerous times, being submerged once by every pastor of each Baptist Church we ever attended. I started to believe that baptism would wear off and had to be renewed like some hyena or male lion scent marking their territory. All the Baptists I knew believed that you had to get dunked, sprinkles weren't worth the effort, because all the sins didn't get wet and therefore weren't really washed away. Besides, we knew some sprinkled people who only thought they had been baptized because by their example it surely didn't take.

I once found myself at the beach preparing for a very public baptism in front of every sneering heathen that lived at Stoney Pointe. The wait for others in line before me allowed me to realize this baptism act as something more as an exhibition than of professing some faith. I made a solemn vow that it would be the very last time I allowed anyone to tell me how I was supposed to demonstrate a belief in God.

According to my mother, except for unsaved, the worst title we could bear was hypocrite. The third most despicable was lukewarm, for we would end up being spat from (or spitted, according to a different king's version) if we weren't on fire for the Lord. In complete disregard of the very fact we were constantly being told we were sinners we had to behave as if we were not. I never quite figured this dichotomy out, forever puzzled by the futility of my actions according to the tenants of the church.

Bible School started the day after regular school let out and everything I remember about it revolves around the fact that those two weeks were equal in length to a year's normal education. Worse yet, we were expected to scour the neighborhood for others to be shanghaied into the Lord's service. The pastor considered it testifying. I considered it strong-arming. The methods we used weren't important, short of ropes and tethers. We only had to persuade other kids to attend and I could be convincing. I head-locked many a kid to experience the company of Jesus and invited so many kids one year that I got a prize Bible for bringing the most new kids, but I think I cheated. We got purple ribbons pinned to our shirts for attending every day of the two-week long Vacation Bible School. The purple awards should have gone to the kids I injured when I asked them to attend.

The last and final church edicts were Bible Camps. We learned how to associate with other Christian children in an outdoor environment, enjoying God's creation, playing games of redemption and bearing witness to our faith all the while under a supervision modeled after a maximum-security prison.

The preferred child-to-counselor ratio was three counselors for each kid, but all the God-loving adults didn't want to waste their vacations and they had a hard time maintaining that quota.

Boys and girls were incarcerated well separate from one another after their sixth birthday, which oddly enough was the minimum age required to attend camp. The largest portion of the counselor's time was spent patrolling the "No Christian's Land" between the barracks. The only things lacking were the minefields and German shepherds and I heard rumors they were looking for them. We were made to wait in segregated lines (couldn't chance an accidental close encounter) for every meal and had to sing a ludicrous ditty announcing how holy, happy and hungry we were while we waited. Our attendance was obligatory, but my parent's finances didn't stretch to allow each of us to go every year. I was reluctant to forfeit one of my turns but every so often could convince my mother to let Chip or Peg go instead of me.

I expressed a true Christian virtue: it's better to give than to receive.

Chapter 13

Keep One

We'd worn a path to the straw bale target.

We got bows and arrows for Christmas, and in spite of a cold winter, Chip and I practiced our archery for hours. Not only had the grass died, but the path was worn enough to collect water when it rained or the snow melted. We were serious about archery practice. We each had about six or eight arrows and had marked them with our secret Indian signs in order to tell who hit the target (Clark) and who shot their arrow in Mrs. Holler's back yard (Chip). Patch added her teeth imprints when we weren't quick enough to retrieve the arrows. Although Chip slowly became better, his little boy fingers and arms still weren't quite strong enough to accurately hit the target every time. I had to give it to him though, he no longer cried when the bowstring twanged against his forearm. He was getting tough, just like his big brother.

We each received target arrows at Christmas along with some bird arrows. The bird arrows were regular except that the head was a Hershey Kiss shape made out of wood. I suppose the theory was the arrow would stun, not go clear through whatever small rabbit or pheasant body we managed to hit. At this point the stunning was still conjecture because the blunt bird arrows flight was erratic and despite hunting feverishly in the winter snow we had been largely unsuccessful. The new target arrows had better metal heads, ones that tapered to a less blunt point and they looked deadlier than the old ones.

One exception was that I had bagged a rabbit one winter day with a target arrow but it was purely luck, because the rabbit ran into the arrow instead of the other way around. Patch brought it back with the arrow still in it. I never admitted the rabbit's zig versus zag and instead chose to enjoy my brother's admiration for the tremendous shot. He was hard to convince at first, but with some persuasive comments and by vigorously rubbing his face with snow I helped him see the truth.

Our hunting was pretty poor, due largely to the fact we needed more practice and better arrows to hit what we were aiming at. In truth, even once in a while would have been great. We had pretty much demolished all of the arrows we'd got for Christmas. The bows were powerful, and both of us were getting stronger and had learned to fully draw the bow. We shot at anything that vaguely suggested animal shapes. Trees that moved, rocks that jumped, and even some houses managed to get in the way. They were all pretty hard on our arrows.

We tried gluing cracked shafts, taping with scotch and electrical and masking tape, wrapping the cracks with thread and even thin copper wire. We soon learned that once an arrow got cracked its flight days were coming to an end despite anything we tried. Those which snapped off close to the head and were shorter than usual, we tried to shoot after reaffixing the metal tip, but they didn't work real well at short distances and not at all on long shots.

Our parents were going broke and getting tired of keeping us in store-bought arrows and several times we went without. In our Christmas stockings we got "Arrow Rules," chapter and verse. Mom and Dad tried to say Santa made up the rules. I knew better, but Chip believed.

1. Don't shoot rocks.
2. Don't shoot trees.
3. Don't shoot houses and garages.
4. Don't shoot cars, mailboxes, and dogs.
5. Don't shoot the road or the road signs.
6. Don't shoot over water.
7. Don't shoot the neighbors.

For infractions of #1, #2, #3, #4, and #5, our arrows would break or be taken away if Mom or Dad or Carole (she was such a tattletale) saw us. If we violated #6, we wouldn't have the arrows taken away, they would just be gone unless we went swimming or could get Patch to retrieve them. Rule #6 was pretty unlikely to be broken. Once an object was thrown, tossed or pitched for Patch, the thrower most likely was seeing the last of it. My mother was fond of saying, "The Lord giveth and the Lord taketh away."

Patch just taketh.

So did Mom and Dad.

Rule #7 meant that the bows would be used for kindling wood.

In keeping with the spirit of these rules we determined to only shoot at the target. It was then early spring and lawn mowing wasn't necessary yet, so there were no extra quarters in my pocket. We sure couldn't buy too many arrows on my weekly twenty-five cents allowance and Chip didn't even get one yet. So the target it would be, aiming at bulls-eyes or hand drawn silhouettes unless something completely irresistible came along.

As part of my big brother role, I tried to teach Chip things like running and throwing, being tough, swimming, riding a two-wheeler and not acting retarded. These essential life skills were necessary for any little kid and my brother in particular. After all, I had a reputation to uphold, an image to maintain. I was an Indian, a trapper, a Marine, a mountain man, a Viking. I'd vowed early on not to be followed around by a drooler. I admitted Chip had made some great improvements, but he still had a long ways to go. I also knew that without my constant attention he would backslide. I continually reinforced the importance of my considerable knowledge with Dutch rubs, full nelsons, head-locks, Indian knuckle gouges, arm-twisting and running off and leaving him. He was a pretty good learner, but he learned every one of his lessons loud.

I had to be really careful with any learning experience. If I had to teach him within a half mile of our house I had to be sitting on him with one hand free to cover his mouth. Chip could WAIL, he could SCREAM, he could HOLLER, he could SHREIK and BELLOW, and he did all of them well.

But as an Indian wannabe, Chip had to learn the Indian ways, like tracking, building traps and snares and looking for signs of the enemy. He already learned Indian dances and playing the tom-tom and he looked pretty good once Mom gave him a Mohawk. I'd been concentrating on the relationship between the white man and the Indian: the scalping and raiding and torture parts.

I'd once staked him out in the ball field and smeared honey on his belly, but Mom rescued him before the ants got to him. I was thinking about the burning at the stake thing but was sure he'd start screaming before I got the match lit. He was learning through the secret torture method but it was slow work. Scalping would come next but not for real, but he wouldn't know the not for real part. He'd scream.

Patch got worried at the shrieking, too. She'd run back and forth in short spurts, almost as if she couldn't make up her mind to help me or run tell Mom what I'd done. Patch switched sides quickly though. Every so often she laid on Chip, smushing his head with her body, but even that wouldn't quiet him for long.

I tried to explain my strategy to Mom, and that this was all part of Chip's training, but her comments stifled my efforts. I thought it was Chip who needed stifling.

Mom picked up mysterious vibrations even when she was out of range. She would home in like a sound-seeking missile on her poor baby boy and showed up within seconds of the alarm being sounded. The impact of her arrival was just about as devastating as well, vaporizing my lessons like smoke. I could hardly get started when she'd arrive out of nowhere, like the Lone Ranger or Hopalong Cassidy. Just in the nick of time.

"You better be nice to Chip."

"He's just a little boy, don't be a bully."

"I'm ashamed of you Clark, you know better than that."

"If you can't be nice to your brother, you'll have to go to your room."

"Can't the two of you do anything without making him cry?"

It was a wonder Chip learned anything.

As usual, on that spring day we had an audience during target practice. Dave and Steve Hicks, the brothers across the vacant lot were watching us shoot and would retrieve the arrows for us. I also taught Chip about how Indians protected themselves, by keeping their weapons in good order and being aware of their surroundings.

Watching. Listening. Keeping still. Keeping quiet. Never shoot all your arrows.

"Keep one." I told him.

I knew we needed to retain one arrow: the Indian way. Just in case another tribe attacked or someone was after you on a blood hunt. There was often warring between tribes and I told Chip it happened all the time. Tribes fought amongst themselves over horses, the division of booty from the last raid or women, though about the last I didn't know why. There were soldiers, those Blue Coats and Long Knives who invaded our lands or even the black-hearted cowboy who wanted to graze his cattle on our ancestral burial plots. A real Indian could never be too careful, too cautious.

"Keep one arrow." I taught.

Chip had a difficult time with that. He figured if he had to go pull the arrows out of the target (getting his brother's arrows was a part of his Indian training too), he would shoot every arrow every time. I could not get it through his head, although I had tried sitting on him, grabbing his arm for a knuckle gouge and tickling him. He hadn't screamed yet, a clear indication that my tactics had to intensify in order to be effective, but I was reluctant. We were across the street from our house and nothing would prevent Mom from hearing his slightest whimper. She'd have to be in a coma and even then I wasn't so sure she wouldn't hear him.

I ragged him and called him names; sissy, baby, spoiled brat, dink, or retard (the last one softly in case Mom was listening). I told him he'd never be an Indian.

"No matter what, no matter how hard I try, despite all I've done already, you'll NEVER be an Indian. Never. NEVER!"

That did it; he started whining just like the baby he was and said he wasn't playing anymore. He also said he wasn't going to get my arrows. He quit.

"Okay you big sissy, you big baby, I'll go get them myself," I told him. "See if I care. You'll never be an Indian. I don't CARE!"

I stalked to the target, I pulled my arrows out and left his there. He could get his own arrows. I sure as Heck wouldn't, not in a million, not in a billion years! Never!

I turned around just in time to glimpse the arrow before it stuck in my chest with ffffft! and thwak! The shaft struck me, solidly penetrating. Astonished, I looked down at the feathered shaft hanging from my body.

I had an arrow stuck out of my chest. Just like in the movies! It stayed there! Right in there!

He'd kept one.

"Owwww!"

Dave Hicks hollered, "Chip shot Clark! Just shot him! He's gonna die!"

I saw Dave and Steve take off like racehorses. I supposed they weren't sticking around to see if Chip had any more arrows.

"Owwww! Ouch! Owwww! You shot me you little turd!" I borrowed a word from my father.

"I'm gonna beat your butt soooo bad," I screamed as I charged at him. "I'm gonna murder you! I'm gonna kill you!"

He started hollering, "Mom, Mommy, Mommmmm, Clark's getting me!!! He's getting me!"

I chased him around the field a couple of times, but he eluded me every time I got close, twisting and turning to duck away. The shouting and hollering and screaming grew louder as the little baby ran toward our house looking for the safety of my mother. He was really shrieking now because I was getting close and he knew it. I was going to kill that kid. I was.

Mom stepped out on the porch just in time to see the arrow jiggle loose from my chest and fall to the ground. I had just about grabbed Chip when he dodged around behind Mom, who had stepped off the porch.

"He shot me! The little twerp!" I yelled. "He shot me for no reason. Look!"

Mom liked the word twerp just as much as she liked retard so instead of inspecting my sure to be fatal wound, she grabbed my arm. Hard.

"What have I told you about your mouth, Clark Malcolm? I've told you again and again and again."

Mom looked forbidding right now.

"You just better get in this house!"

"Chip shot me! Mom, he shot me with an arrow! Look! I'm bleeding!"

"I've told you and told you and told you what would happen if you didn't learn to watch your mouth. You're going to learn if it kills me to make you."

It wasn't her dying I was worried about just then. I'd been shot.

"I am NOT going to tell you again. Get in the bathroom."

"Mom, Chip shot me," I tried reason. "He shot me in the chest and then ran in here screaming just like a little sissy baby."

I should have left off the last part. Mom had started to listen when I calmed down, but when she heard little sissy baby, it set her off again.

"There you go with your mouth. This is exactly what I mean, young man. Now get in the bathroom!"

There were multitudinous uses for our bathroom. First were the obvious ones, baths and toilet, brushing teeth, combing hair, shaving chins for my father or legs for Mom. The medicine cabinet had band-aids, toothpaste, Bag-Balm, Mercurochrome and iodine for cuts, just regular articles. I'd practiced many a sorrowful look in the bathroom mirror. We did the usual stuff that everyone does in a bathroom.

But our bathroom was also used as a site for discipline.

That's where Mom kept the Fels-Naptha Soap. That's where she used it on kids, but not to wash grass or blood stains out of clothing or clean a face.

That's where she washed the bad right out of our mouths.

Mom did not let go of my arm. I had been known to escape if the opportunity presented itself and where punishment was concerned my mother was swift and sure. Mom looked at the blood soaking the front of my shirt and lifted it so she could look at the puncture.

"It's not deep." She pronounced. "You'll live. We'll get some Bag-Balm and a gauze pad on it. You'll be just fine."

I was consoled a little by her promise of attention. Mom reserved store bought band-aids for *very serious* wounds.

I remember thinking, "That's better Mom, I need some attention."

"But I want to see you take a good lick of that soap first. Put it right in your mouth, right in that nasty talking mouth of yours. I will not have my boys talking that way. Not at all! And don't you forget it!"

Yuck! That stuff tasted bad, but I always made sure I got enough to produce a few bubbles. Mom had been known to take over the application if she thought you weren't doing a good job and her soaping was always the more vigorous. While I was soaping up with bubbles and making sure she saw evidence, Mom got the Bag-Balm tin down and put a good glop of it on the puncture. She tore open one, precious, Johnson & Johnson gauze for a bandage and taped it across my chest with adhesive tape.

There. Good as new.

"You can't see it if you put another shirt on." Out of sight, out of mind, was another of her favorite homilies. "Give the shirt to me and I'll wash the blood out and sew up the hole."

"Now I want to know," she began. "What did you do to your brother to make him shoot you?"

I'd get Chip later. But I didn't hold the grudge after the snake.

Chapter 14
Tails and Tales

August in Michigan and hot, so hot even the dust smelled peppery. "Let's go Patch!"

There's something out there that needs us, I was sure of it. She and I headed down Pointe aux Peaux Road, into the south side of the marsh today, and skirted the wet edges until we were well past the water. There, we turned back to the beach beyond Long Road's ending. Patch and I had made this circuit all the time, in order to check special places like the quicksand area, and where we always looked for something to rescue. There were the two "forts" I had built waaaaay back in that needed attention. I always checked the tin cans strategically placed for signs of disturbance and Patch would sniff about, ever wary for interlopers.

"Marking" our territory like all wild animals, we had to make sure everything was just the way we'd left it. After all this was our marsh, we were in charge of it and had to make sure of any trespasser's intention. This navigation would take us about six hours, but I asked/told Mom where we were going, so "we won't be back for lunch." Mom knew how important these security marches were.

The first segment went well enough, though I had to call Patch off the rabbit she flushed. We stopped for a drink from my canteen when we got to my fort, Patch first, panting hard yet from the bunny chase. I held my cupped hand for a bowl under the spout to pour her drink and then had mine.

The fort really was just a natural opening before the bigger trees marked the woods' edge. I'd strung a piece of clothesline between two trees, draped a piece of oilcloth over the rope and anchored the other end with two pieces of sharpened branch. My work produced just enough room underneath for

Patch and me, which was perfect because we were the only ones who knew of its existence, now that Ralph had moved away. No one else in the whole wide world knew where it was or where we were, not even Chip. We lay in our campsite, me listening to the whirr of the grasshoppers and Patch's short panting breaths. The day was so hot we had to close our eyes against the sun. It was a perfect place for a nap and we didn't have anyplace we were expected.

Patch woke up and I felt her stiffen, felt her growl under my hand. We had both fallen asleep. We'd have to hurry or we'd catch it for being late. We weren't a third of the way through the march and from the sun it looked like we'd slept an hour or so. We'd have to hump it. Nine year-old boys sometimes take a little waking up, especially if they've been baking a while in the sun. Six year-old dogs do not, which is why Patch growled me awake. When the sleep finally fell out of my eyes I saw why she rumbled in her throat.

While we slept we had a visitor. A small two-toned brown snake had parked itself in front of the makeshift tent before it decided to nap with us or watch our slumbers. When Patch winded the scent, she raised her head quick and the snake, not really asleep, raised to its defensive posture. I heard it too, soft like BB's rolling in the kitchen drawer. When I looked closely I could see the small button-tail trembling, making the noise against the grass, sounding the warning. At the end closest, a little arrow shaped head taste-tested the air for my intentions.

I grabbed Patch by the collar. I didn't want her to get bit. Worse to my mind, she might kill the snake and it was a treasure. I told her, "Sit! Lay Down!" She did, but my loud voice agitated the snake and it decided this was not the place it wanted to be.

A rattlesnake! Hot Ziggity! I knew it was a Massasauga or Swamp rattler because they were the only species that could be here and I'd read about these smallish poisonous snakes. This one was young, less than twelve inches long. I thought I had seen one last summer, but my science teacher said they were up north, not down here. I couldn't wait to let her know that good old Monroe County had at least one. She'd be so excited. I was so excited. Better yet, I'd catch it and take it to school in the fall.

I'd have the best "What I Did On My Summer Vacation" that ever was. I'd be the famous-est in the school. Everybody would want to see this.

I'd already caught plenty of snakes in my day. I was a veteran, a pro. Garter snakes, corn snakes, milk snakes and one blue racer had fallen prey to my quick eyes and hands. I knew this was different, a venomous snake, and even this small variety would still be a problem if it bit me or my dog.

I told Patch again, "Stay!"

Knowing dog that she was, she did, leaving me free to catch this quick little bugger. I looked around for a stick to trap its head and found a suitable piece. I grabbed the branch, fully expecting the snake to continue to slither away, but was surprised when it coiled back up. Its tail protested my interruption and the snake scooted around to face me as I circled for better position. Hmmm, this snake wasn't trying to get away. It was defending something.

I teased it with the stick and jumped back when it struck even though the distance between us was three times the strike length. The strike was just a blur and return, fast both ways to resume the buzzing coil.

Wow. This snake was quick! I teased it again to get the same result even though I was ready this time. Whit-whit, there and back, the motion was almost too fast to see! This time I noticed that when the snake struck, its whole body lay for an instant in the short grass before it pulled itself back to recoil and ready. There was the opening I needed. I could trap its head with my stick when it lay outstretched. Hah!

Once again I teased it to strike. Once again and once again and again. I couldn't get the stick in position fast enough after I used it to provoke the strike. I couldn't control the long stick. It was much too long. I snapped it in half, all the while preventing the snake from gliding away, something it seemed to be trying more and more as my teasing continued. It recoiled anew every time I intercepted the break away attempt. My new plan included teasing the snake, stick held left-handed and waiting poised with my free hand to pin the brown arrow against the dirt. As soon as the snake was extended, I'd pounce.

No problem.

Whit!

I grabbed for the head just as soon as the snake's head hit the dirt and was surprised to feel only grass and dirt under my hand. Before I could pull my hand back I felt something else. The snake struck quickly one more time and it hit on the edge of my palm in the meaty part of my right hand. I looked at my hand, really surprised and saw two little red holes.

"Huh! That little sucker got me."

I don't know whether I'd have tried that XX and suck thing, but I didn't have a knife, so I got back to the task at hand. I did suck and spit a number of times but I don't know if it did any good. I couldn't taste anything over the blood, so I quit. The bite didn't hurt and I was *gonna* catch that snake. Besides I already had the bite, the harm was done.

Either the repeated strikes or biting me tired that snake out, because it slowed down, but it still took several more minutes before I managed to catch it. I finally trapped the head when it wasn't quick enough to elude the slap! in the grass.

"Ha! Haaah! Gotcha!" I held up my captive. Patch had joined me as soon as I grabbed the snake.

My hand began to feel a little funny. I'd expected that, although funny wasn't the word for what it was feeling. Fat was a good word. Puffy was another good word. I had to transfer the snake's head to my left hand to hold it. Numb was a good word, too.

"Come on Patch!"

It was about a mile to get back to my house but almost forty minutes of walking because of the route. All the while my hand increased its uncomfortable feeling and size, but I wasn't overly concerned. I had read enough about the snake to know its bite was serious, but usually wasn't fatal if you weren't allergic. If I'd been overly sensitive to the venom, I figured I'd have been dead thirty minutes ago. I remained pretty detached about the bite although I wasn't so sure how indifferent Mom would be when I got home. I'd probably catch the dickens in addition to this snake. Patch kept jumping up to my snake bearing arm and bumping the snake with her nose. I had to order her away again and again during our walk back.

The snake had coiled itself around my arm and relaxed a bit but I didn't loosen my grip on the head. I didn't squeeze tight. I certainly wouldn't want to hurt the poor little guy. I wanted to show him off. My arm began to swell up more, first at the wrist and then to my forearm. The two little punctures grew angry red and turned white to ring the holes. I kept checking my hand and was starting to wonder it the books were right. Well, I was almost home; just a bit more now.

I started hollering just as soon as my foot touched home ground, but I went into the garage to get a jar or box for the snake. It had been hanging limply from my left hand during the last half of the walk, stressed at the capture and the times when Patch had a mind of her own. Mom followed the sounds out to the garage and gave a little squeak when I held up my right arm. I didn't raise it very high because I couldn't.

"What have you got? What on earth have you done to your arm?" she asked.

"It's a rattlesnake, Mom. A Massasauga swamp rattler. They're not even supposed to be around here. I'm keeping it."

119

"How nice, son," she told me and meant it. "Now let's take a look at your arm."

First she helped me find a big two-gallon canning jar with a lid and I slipped the snake tail first down. Mom understood priorities and she realized this capture was well up on my list. The lid already had holes punched in it, so had obviously been used for critters before. We went in the house for close arm inspection. My arm was bloated like a sausage by now, my wrist no longer distinguishable from the rest, all of it swollen big enough to prevent flexing at the elbow. It hurt, too, and the arm had changed from numb to ache to pain on the way home. The bite area was now a purplish sort of yellowish dark meat. All right!

Mom called the doctor. He must have said it couldn't have been a poisonous snake, because they weren't found in this area.

Mom said in response, "Well, my son found something poisonous that bit him and his arm's swollen terribly."

Mom hung up moments later to say we better get in and let him take a look, but the doctor wouldn't have any anti-venom. More than likely, there wasn't any around here because there was no reason for it. Mom paused to put some ice cubes in a plastic bag and told me to hold it on my swollen arm, rubbing it gently with the cold.

"Bring the snake, son. He'll want to see it," Mom instructed and then told Carole. "We've got to go. You watch your little brother. I'll take the baby [referring to Peg] with me."

I sat in the back with my snake but Peg went up front with Mom. She wasn't taking any chances with her daughter. Before car seats nobody thought the real danger lay in unrestrained toddlers.

The doctor was amazed. He also couldn't do anything more than what we were already doing. He first asked how long it had been since the bite and said it probably wouldn't get any worse.

"Keep the swelling down with ice, keep it elevated. No, there wouldn't be any charge. I'm glad I got to see the rattlesnake, I didn't know there were any around here. You're lucky it's just a baby, but that arm is going to hurt for a good while yet. Take aspirin."

That was it. Go home and rest.

On the way home Mom said the snake couldn't stay. Despite my protests, it was too dangerous to keep at home. I argued a little, but my heart wasn't in it. *The poison was probably affecting my ability to sound convincing*, I thought. But it was Mom's reasoning that won out. I had a baby brother and a baby sister, a big sister, a dog and a mother and father, all of whom would be at risk with a poisonous snake around the house.

"It definitely has to go. What if it somehow got loose and bit someone else? As soon as your arm is a little better, you have to set it free."

I didn't get much sleep for the next four days. My arm burned and ached something fierce, but eventually it subsided. My mother kept enough ice packs on it that I started to worry about frostbite, but she said I was being silly. I looked at that cool little snake a lot. I wanted to catch him a mouse or a frog but Mom said I had done enough catching for a while and the snake would be just fine until I let him go, but I wasn't through trying. I really didn't want to let him go and kept up pleading long enough to get a warning about the snake's immediate release if I didn't hush.

I hushed.

Mom came up with the idea of the Monroe County Zoo, a small private animal habitat just outside the city limits. I had been there two or three times, and they had a few animals of interest but not many, although they did have some other reptiles.

I wondered if they really would like to have my snake. It was a pretty uncommon snake around here as near as I could determine and maybe they would like to have it. When I called them, they first thought I was playing a prank and I had to let Mom talk. She even spent a little while before they believed what I caught. But they sure would like to have it if it was a Massasauga rattlesnake. They surely would. They asked Mom if we wanted them to come and get it, but I shook my head no when she asked. She told them we'd bring it out when I was feeling better and then she had to tell them the whole story.

I went out to talk to my snake. He shook his tail just like he always did when I tapped on the jar. He might like it at the zoo. They'd feed him regularly and he probably wouldn't have to look very far for his next mouse meal. He'd be better. So would the zoo. They'd have an oddity for this area. And nobody other than a few rodents or frogs would be punctured by those small fangs. Okay, that's where he'd go.

We didn't take him for more than another week and I ended up catching two or three small frogs for the snake. It struck them within seconds of them being placed in the large jar. The frogs only made one or two hops before they stopped moving. Some didn't move at all.

Yes, and that's just how my arm felt.

I watched as he walked his jaws over a frog, swallowing it headfirst until the feet disappeared too. This was one cool snake!

When we took him to the zoo the people were extremely excited. They examined the snake closely through the big jar and agreed that it was a Massasauga rattler, but like they didn't believe it. Some people just have to see to believe. I had to tell them where I found it, if I'd seen any more and how I'd caught it. But I only told them little bitty pieces. I thought they might try catching more if I told them really where. So I kinda faked them a bit. My marsh was my marsh, after all. No trespassing! I changed the subject.

I said I wanted to see where he was going to live and they took me out to the reptile area. The enclosures were huge, about four feet by six feet and had branches sticking at angles out of the sand on the bottom. There was a depression for water and a small shelf in each enclosure that the snake could go under for privacy. The places looked pretty good; a heck of a lot better than the big jar he'd been living in. Okay, he could stay. I tilted the jar and slid him into his new home. He lay coiled up, taste testing the new air. I looked at him a long time before we said goodbye.

We went back to the zoo well into the fall that year, whenever I could talk Mom into taking us. We always got in for free because I was a contributor and I told the ticket person every time we went. They also put a plaque on the cage that gave his common and scientific names and my name was there, too, right after Donated By.

I had a great time telling everyone at school but lots of the kids didn't believe it at first. My teacher organized a field trip and the whole class went to the zoo. The snake recognized me on every occasion and buzzed his tail just like the first time, even after he got bigger. I *was* in the same category as Frank Buck, me, the famous wild animal collector.

"See the CHRISTMAS RABBITS! See the REINDEER DOG!"

That's what the sign said and we were packing them in at five cents a head. Big Money!

Making money for the Cub Scouts was even more difficult than making a few dollars for ourselves. You had to make money the Cub Scout way and all sorts of restrictions applied. Plus the whole Den had to do something together so that ruled out the eleven boys mowing the same lawn.

"Besides," Mom said, "you'd cut each other's feet off."

We could do nothing so mundane as grass cutting. We would have a Cub Scout Fair.

My mother was a great Den Mother. She thought of all sorts of wonderful things for Cub Scouts to do. At one meeting she paired us up and set the task of making fire with a bow and stick. We kept busy for a month until tired of the trying. It was pretty smart on her part, because all she had to do after the Pledge was hand out the equipment and re-offer the prize of cookies. We desperately sawed back and forth, the bow's thong making the stick twirl round and round for the entire meeting. Whenever a wisp of smoke appeared, we'd stop to inspect for the sure to follow flames. Almost didn't count. We never made more than a slightly hot stick out of that challenge but we still got the cookies and milk.

Once we got to make moccasins out of real leather just like the Indians but the cutting out and stitching parts caused us problems. The footwear mysteriously moved forward, seemingly worked on just like in the Shoemaker and the Elves storybook. One boy or another wouldn't remember that he had progressed quite that far at the last meeting. But he must have. My mother ended up sewing each and every one of them for us, but we thought we'd done the whole of it. All her efforts didn't inhibit the Indians running around the house one bit when they were done.

She was really great at hiking, too, and once we got the first burst of running out of our systems we followed her like she was the Pied Piper. Mom could spot stuff; she'd see treasures only Cub Scouts could love. We were always astonished with the discoveries we made when we followed close behind. Arrowheads and magnifying glasses and slingshots and yo-yos were always turning up. We never suspected she "salted" each trail well in advance.

For this project though, all of the parents had to be involved. No exceptions. Mom couldn't handle this alone. We had a special Cub Scout meeting with all the moms and dads to parcel out the jobs. We made them swear the Scout oath, just for this time. There would be terrific amounts of work for boys and adults. The Fair would be even better if other sisters and brothers got involved. Advertisement posters needed to be made and posted on tree trunks, telephone poles and put up in Orleans' and Jones's store windows. Tables and tents and folding chairs must be gathered up. Pies and cakes to bake and sell were a must. Everybody liked them and they'd make tons of money. We needed help with balloons and prizes and grab bags and pots full of fake terrible stuff for the blindfolded challenge. We wouldn't turn any help away.

Oh man, was this going to be something! We were going to have a song and dance play put on by Tanya, Bobby's older sister. Their daddy would put together the stage with a curtain that really worked. There would be a Big Top Tent just like a real circus. Stan's father was going to get the tent but we had to figure out what to do with it.

"Who wants to be in charge of acrobats and clowns? Dave and Steve? Okay with you, Beverly [their mother]? Okay then, you're them, boys."

A Midway with water-balloons and a ring toss and a baseball throw all with prizes. We would have a Side Show with secret surprises (like our Christmas rabbits) and Andy's mother was going to be The Bearded Lady and we'd have a Strongman in a leopard skin (don't tell, but it's Mr. Edwards). Cub Scout Honor, we'd never let on about the Side Show attractions. This was going to be the best.

"Who's going to bake? Gloria, Pat, Joyce? Cookies, cakes and pies. Okay? Good."

"Who can get a truck for transportation to and from the Newport Church parking lot for the fair? Mickey? Wonderful! Ken, Bud, both of you and Jerry can help with that."

"Who'll help with the cleanup? Bud? Good! Mickey? Andy? Good! Oh, I *know* you will honey, thank you."

Everybody was doing something.

"Carole, you're in charge of the posters, making and getting them up."

Mom got volunteer help like an army sergeant. And she kept a list.

Cub Scouts, families and even neighbors were busy for a month. Mom kept track of progress almost every day. Posters were colored and painted bright with "Circus!" or "Side Show!" or "Games and Prizes!" and we made a million I bet. We even put notices up at Shorty's gas station and Detroit Beach and the church bulletin board. I bet that was a first! Everything else thumb-tacked up there was Holy.

We were even going to have a Snake Lady.

Just before school the last weekend in August everybody showed up at the church. Even those people who didn't go there pulled right in, just like they were regular Baptists. Work to do and Mom was orchestrating the whole thing. People stopped their cars to see what we were doing and they all got invited to "come back tomorrow." The firemen came down from the station to help us set up all the tents. More volunteers. A beehive couldn't have been busier.

"The Big Tent? Right there at the end."

"Blindfolds go over there in that tent."

"The hose for the water balloons is in the shed, right there."

"Let's get those barbells over by the Snake Lady's platform."

"The pies and cakes will get sold from that table."

"And put up the signs. Just tape them on."

"The ring toss is too close to the line, we'll run out of prizes."

"Good!"

"Good!"

"*Now* we're getting somewhere!"

It took all the dads a whole day to set up the Fair at the church and it really, really, really looked just like a traveling show. And only in town for the weekend.

We got home late that night and we still had to make the Christmas Rabbits and a Reindeer Dog. Our two white ones, Prince and Princess, (same names, different rabbits) both big New Zealand Giants, got a dye job. They didn't think too much of being on the kitchen counter but I held them down one at a time. The rabbits didn't take long once they figured out they couldn't squirm away. One green. One red; well mostly red, we ran out of food coloring, so Princess only got half dyed. Mom said it didn't matter; white was a color of Christmas, too, like snow. Princess did look pretty cool. We started at the back so she was bisected front and back, white and red. I thought she'd pass. I couldn't get the red and green off my hands but Mom said it looked okay.

We had some serious trouble with the reindeer horns even though they looked just great. It only took Patch about five seconds to paw them off her head. Every single time. And she wouldn't listen. On the head, off the head, again and again. No matter how much I tried to convince her to keep them on she didn't like the elastic around her neck. The hardest headed dog that ever was. Well at least she was consistent.

Mom said not to worry about that either.

"I'll think of something."

I went to bed but Mom stayed up to iron my uniform.

It was really early when Mom got us up and we had lots to do getting the car loaded up with rabbits and kids and paraphernalia. In the morning I still thought my colored hands looked really funny with the blue uniform, but everything else was spiffed up just right and my new Wolf Pack necktie ring was ferocious. My yellow sash was covered with badges Mom had been sewing on. Twenty-six now and I was counting on more. I looked cool. Yeah, Wolf Pack!

THE CIRCUS WAS IN TOWN!

The crowds of people were enormous. Moms with kids. Dads with kids. Moms with dads and dads with moms. Old people and babies in carriages being pushed. Kids with kids. All sorts of people combinations who just couldn't wait for the Fair to be open. 10:00 a.m. the posters said and when we started taking tickets, they spread out fast, kids running to see everything all at once.

Boley's dad looked just like a Strong Man even though the dumbbells were fake. He and Boley had painted the hollow floats all black and a broom handle between with 1000 pounds lettered in white on each end. A great big black cardboard box marked 10,000 pounds with a ring on top was the heaviest of all. His skinny legs made him look a little bit funny but the big belly looked just right under his leopard skin costume. He wore a fake moustache made out of mop strings and he grunted and groaned red-faced with every lift. Everybody was laughing and pointing and yelling.

"More!"

"More!"

So heavy he needed a break.

"Next show in fifteen minutes."

Our Snake Lady looked really exotic and far away, too. More leopard-skin but hers looked much better and lots of the dads stopped to watch. She slunk up the stairs and looked through the boxes marked "LIVE SNAKES," but not choosing right away. She presented one snake to the crowd, being ever so carefully tenderly cautious and writhing in time to a record she'd found. With a long stringy wig and snakes made from socks Molly sure played her part. When she guided that serpent back and forth on display every eye had to follow but they weren't just looking at snake.

"More!"

"More!"

Snake handling was dangerous and she needed some time to stay brave.

"Next show in fifteen minutes."

Even the Bearded Lady could be charming although she just sat, but everyone came up to see. She told them a tale of how come she was hairy. Her mother had much more hair and you should have seen grandmamma, too. She never, no never, would she shave this beard off!

"More!" "We want more stories!"

But she had to go. Beards are itchy, hot work.

"Next time in ten minutes."

"See right next door, a REALLY GREAT SHOW!"

Tanya and Bobby put on real talent business because she could tap dance and sing pretty great. She looked cute, "adorable" someone said, in her frilly short skirt and shoes that went clickety-click, tappety-tap. Bobby changed records, but that was enough, the people just looked to see her. She twirled two batons while she tapped to the crowd and everyone clapped when she stopped.

She sang several songs that everyone knew and gave them another when one and all shouted, "More!" "More!"

Dancing and singing sure was hard work, so...

"Next show in thirty minutes."

The big tent was marvelous but it was so hot inside. There weren't any seats but the crowds sure packed in at ten cents a head and you had to have a ticket. Dave was the acrobat and Steve was the clown but they both swung back and forth by their knees from the swings. Headstands and handstands that weren't very good mixed up with leapfrog, piggybacks and tumbles that were. Steve had a horn that he borrowed from my bike and he honked it whenever he walked. Honk, honk with each step, honk, honk! The crowds clapped the same no matter what.

"More!" "We want MORE!"

But death defying and tumbling tires one out.

"Next show in thirty minutes."

The Midway was maybe the best place of all. No one had ever seen green and red rabbits and it cost everybody, even little kids, a whole nickel to look. The Reindeer Dog only made one appearance and she wasn't too happy with that. It didn't last so long either because when she scraped the horns off this time she ran off with them. She dashed through Mom's legs to freedom and Fair with branches in mouth and bells on her collar a jingling. That didn't matter because everyone laughed when she ran away and they really just wanted to see the Christmas Rabbits!

The ring toss and water balloons and baseball throw had kids standing three and four deep to take their turns. Three tries for a nickel and the change boxes were filling up. Brown grab bags full of candy and peanuts were won even if they didn't get a ring on. The water balloons were a huge hit in spite of the fact that many kids, who weren't scheduled to be, got sopping wet. We ran out of balloons pretty quick.

"None too soon," Boley's Mom said.

Kid after kid went through the Blindfold Challenge and nobody guessed what the pig guts and monster brains really were unless they peeked.

The Shows and Acts went on all day long and most folks came right back for seconds. Extra helpings of song and dance and kids who wanted to make sure the rabbit was still green and just one more look at the Strong Man, Mom.

"Please."

Peanuts and Popcorn and Kool-aid and Lemonade if you still had nickels left after the shows. Pies and cakes and cookies went fast at one dollar for a pie and two whole dollars for a cake. The moms should have baked more goodies. Prince and Princess did what all rabbits do and all the kids at the booth laughed until tears came rolling down their faces. I could have made even more money taking bets on different colored babies if Mom hadn't made me separate them. Too bad.

Patch put on a grand finale when a big male collie came sniffing around the rabbit cage and I didn't even have to say sic'em. They raised clouds of dust as they roiled about and lots of folks ran over to see. Her bells jingled through the whole fracas. It took her a while but she whipped that dog good and he finally ran away howling. Everybody crowded around to see that battle.

"Good girl!"

If I'd only sold tickets for that we'd have made more of a fortune.

The cleaning up was the hardest part of the whole day but none of the Cub Scouts or the dads could go before it was done. The Den Mother said. Church tomorrow and people had to park here. We'd all get the Mom Blessing if it looked good.

"Can I have one more look at the Strong Man, Mom please?"

Chapter 15

On Thin Ice

"I'm gon-na stay at the Far-r-rem, Ha-ha-ha, haha haaaa! You do-en't get to. Ha-ha-ha, haha haaaa! Gram-maaaa loves me bet-ter! So do-es Grand-Paaaa."

I loved making Carole mad and when Mom said I could stay longer at the farm after we went out there for our second Christmas I couldn't resist rubbing it right in her scowly old nasty face. It wasn't often I could wreak any vengeance on my older sister. Carole mostly bossed me around and told on me when I wasn't even doing bad stuff. When the opportunity for payback arose I tried to take advantage with every fiber of my just turned nine-year-old body. I knew how much Carole enjoyed the pampering and attention Grandpa Teddy and Grandma Phoebe lavished on her when we were there. This time, Surprise! Clark would get petted far beyond the normal one day holiday gathering. I was going to stay a whole week.

As we grew old enough to recognize its importance every one of us competed with each other and cousins for the honor of being blessed by a stay at the farm and the rivalry was fierce. The entire family recognized the importance of entrance into the throne room of Grandma's home.

"I'm gon-na stay at the Far-rem, Nanny-nanny moo-moo, I'm gon-na stay at the Far-rem. Gram-maaaa loves me bet-ter! So do-es Grand-Paaaa, Haha-ha, haha haaaa!"

Carole's down-turned mouth was reward aplenty for my taunts.

"If you don't stop, Clark Malcolm, you won't get to stay either," wafted Mom's voice from the kitchen. "What have I said to you about teasing?"

"I dunno," I fibbed.

"Yes, you do," Mom corrected. "I've told you time and time again it's not nice to tease your sister."

I personally thought it was lots better than nice. It was great. I remembered the time and time again part, but I was smart enough not to mention either thought. I knew what came next.

"I'm sorry, Carole." I made one nice face for Mom and when she turned away, satisfied with my exhibition of remorse, made another for Carole.

"He's making faces at me Mom."

See what I mean about the telling stuff?

I had to make a whole brand new face for Mom.

Innocent.

Two days after Christmas we piled in the car to celebrate with all the Fowler side of the family relatives. Mom's brothers and wives, my cousins and Grandma and Grandpa. A Christmas at the farm was special in many ways. Because I would stay through my whole holiday vacation, it was even more of a festivity. Grandma and Grandpa said I could bring Patch for the whole stay.

"Wow, Patch is getting a stay over too!"

Carole didn't talk to me the whole way out.

She's fit to be tied, I thought. *Which is just what I'd like to do with her. And push her out the car window. And not go back to get her. Ever.*

But I knew how hard Carole could pinch. Patch's bulk and Chip between us wouldn't prevent her twisting talons. The thought of the pinch and Dad driving, sitting only an arm's length away, kept my mouth quiet. Zipped. Dad's knife blade temper had put dampers and brakes on trips before.

"Don't MAKE me stop this car."

I'd heard his warning enough by now to be wary on trips. It wouldn't do to further jinx my stay.

Winter at the farm was fashioned with snow and ice and fires in the fireplace. Situated on the fringes of the Irish Hills of Michigan, the town of Manchester was accustomed to large accumulations of winter weather snowfalls. Snow meant snowmen and snow ladies, while ice meant getting stuck in the driveway. The best cold weather picture I see of the farm consists of the two snowy ruts for a driveway, when the house and barn wore a quilting of white and smoke puffed out of the chimney.

Sometimes Grandpa would have a path cleared through the yard's heaps of snow.

Sometimes not.

If the only pathways clear were the driveway's two deep grooves, we walked to the house with a tightrope balancer's act. When Grandma's voice did shove Grandpa out the door, he made a semi-green and frosted trail exactly one shovelful wide which led to the back door. Either course was perfect because they both ended up inside.

As soon as the back door opened we were greeted by grandparents and the wood cook-stove, with each as warm and welcome a reception as the other. Both warmed your heart, while only one thawed your hands. Winter fires were constant in the farm's fireplace and old cook-stove. Our wet mittens and leggings were hung across close by chairs to get ready for the next "go outside you boys." Large logs split for the fireplace and smaller sticks were chopped for the cook-stove. Bringing in the wood was everyone's job except Grandpa's when the family came to call. Everyone meant the grandchildren.

When we piled out of the car the snow was perfect. Me first, then my dog. My mittens knew how to do their work.

I whacked everybody I could with wonderful, marvelous, spectacular snowballs. I concentrated on Dad's back, Chip's stocking cap and Carole's butt. I got some missiles in return from Dad and Chip, although my brother couldn't yet throw worth a hooey. I earned the highest glory, Carole's complaints, for one shot in particular. Perfect. Mom carried Peg from the car, but they were safe. I considered both of them off limits.

Just to show freedom of choice I got Patch with two big ol' honking ones too. Those first two took her off guard.

"Rowr-rowr!" Patch said she'd join the game and asked if I knew the rules. "Rwor-rwor!"

I got her with another one.

The last one was the mistake.

She muscled me into the snow bank Grandpa had piled along the path and decided I needed some rolling and squashing to go along with the cold. Patch pressed her advantage when I tilted backwards over the mound and used her weight to keep me captive. Mouthing my jacketed arm, Patch created just enough havoc to keep me down and off my feet. Patch wasn't reluctant to reinforce her standing in the family order and whenever I managed to get one up on her, it was never up for long. Patch loved seeing the piper paid in full.

All these rules were hers.

Instant retribution and then move on; just like Mom.

Snow-boy and snow-dog climbed the steps to the door. I got to go in.

Patch did not.

Once inside Grandma escorted us to the living room. The first item we had to see was the second-most perfect tree in the world (number one was back at our house), and all the aunts and uncles and cousins and presents and food and Christmas cookies and pies. Wow! We honored Gram's presentation of the dining table with oohs and ahhs and noted her hand-written place tags. The folded cards might announce a child's graduation to the big table or told us whose elbows we had to avoid during dinner. Each family member went through her welcoming ritual with a sense of awe and appreciation. We all knew everything here was indirectly or actually Grandma's creation. These family gatherings re-established her right to claim the family design. Once the family homage was complete I was allowed to dry Patch with an old towel and bring her inside.

Patch was the only creature I ever saw, including Dad, who wasn't cowed by Grandma's presence.

She'd have to learn about Christmas at Grandma's. Later.

Right then she was much too busy with inspections.

First Patch had to sniff, sniff, sniff, sniff, sniff, sniff, sniff, sniff, everything and everybody. She liked the kitchen and people, especially the cousins and Uncle Gik, all the cupboards full of promise, pans on the stove and the fireplace. She didn't care much for Grandpa's pipe rack, Uncle Don's clouds of pipe smoke and Grandma's words of warning when she got into the kitchen.

My dog jumped right in on those presents when the gift giving started. I really didn't need the help but she did it nevertheless. It took me twice the effort to open the gifts with her there but it was all part of the fun. She tried to assist everyone else with their wrapped packages as well.

My dog did the sniffing routine again, for one and all, in case she missed something at first. The repeated twitching nose was the second one. Patch's desire to further develop new friendships and special locations was more than Grandma could bear. Her views on dogs consisted solely of outside locations, with the rest of the animals. I was sometimes included in that group. It was only with the greatest of reluctance that Patch was ever allowed inside her house. The season probably influenced her initial decision, but Grandma's goodwill only went so far.

"Put her on the porch, Clock." Grandma instructed. "She's underfoot all the time. I can't move without stepping around her."

Grandma's cultured English accent pronounced my first name "Clock." I spent many fearful childhood years hoping none of my friends ever heard her pronunciation. My eyeglasses had already earned enough nickname slurs to suit anyone. I had the broken spectacles to prove it.

I didn't blame Patch for hanging around there because it smelled wonderful in Grandma's kitchen. I'd have been in the kitchen, too, but had already learned the wisdom of being scarce when women were bustling about with dinner.

Patch on the porch was a mistake.

I had heard "three strikes and you're out" during more than just baseball games. Dad used it whenever I tried his patience beyond six seconds. It never took me long at two seconds at a time.

When I opened the door onto the porch for Patch's temporary exile, she went willingly, almost as if it were the best idea in the world. I should have known when her rump began wagging excitedly as she hurried out to the porch but I didn't. Had I looked closely I'd have seen the immediate saliva glistening her chops when she brushed me aside but I just closed the door.

During the winter their porch wasn't included in the heat scheme of the house. It was a sun porch and not really meant for all seasons and in winter the glass doors and windows were opaque with frosty patterns. Identical to my parent's bedroom, it also became a cold storage for food. Thanksgiving's turkey skeleton still awaiting the soup pot, numbers two, three and four homemade bread loaves and casseroles ready for Christmas dinner re-heating, all chilled before their final destination.

Despite the cold weather, it was the best place in the world.

For Patch.

I was busily involved in a game of Chinese checkers with my cousin Greg when the alarm went off.

"CLOOOOOOOOOCK! CLOOOOOOOOOOCK! YOUR DOG!"

It was more of a drawn out, one breath shriek than a series of alarms, but it summoned everyone from the living room quick enough to have been fire bells. Grandma stood in the doorway with her hands planted on either side of her hips. Mom, Aunt Nita and Aunt Nance stood behind her and peered over her shoulders, dismay coming off them in such waves I could almost see them.

When I ducked through and under various female bodies and arms, I saw that Patch looked quite content.

Sated.

Lying under the porch windows, Patch cocked her head in question at Grandma's screech.

"Was there a problem we wanted her to deal with? Monsters about?"

I thought it was funny because the four-week-old Thanksgiving turkey carcass was clutched firmly in her mouth. But immediately after I laughed I wished I hadn't. The glares my laughter produced were only the beginning.

Big turkey.

Big dog.

Big Trouble.

Three strikes: You're out.

Between her forelegs lay her appetizer's scattered crumbs of evidence and from the appearance, she'd already enjoyed two loaves of bread. The third one lay close by and was clearly punctured with her teeth marks, as if she'd deliberately placed it within easy reach. That way Patch could have it when she finished the bird without getting up from her dining spot.

During my nine years, I'd already become familiar with ear grabbing as a deterrent and as a punishment. My attention was immediately focused when being lead or directed in this way and I was frequently the guinea pig for new techniques and tactics. My mom was an expert in the field because Grandma had been her teacher. They both did it very well. I didn't like it when my ears became handles but I had stopped being surprised by the application. I tried to look on the bright side. Once they're released, the grabbed ear or ears feel warm, almost a nice feeling after the pain subsides.

But up until now Patch had not been so privileged.

Patch's ear status altered as Grandma marched up and snatched the turkey out of Patch's mouth. Patch surrendered it without moving a muscle and watched her toss the carcass onto the platter where it belonged, but she shifted everything into high gear when Grandma grabbed one of her ears and hoisted. With a whine, Patch got on her feet, stood at attention and quick marched out through the bathroom, through the back room and out the door. Grandma didn't turn loose of her brown ear until Patch was halfway through the door and still moving to get away. When Grandma turned away from the door, I ducked behind her and quickly followed my disgraced dog. I knew when to try to avoid any notice, but I might as well have walked right in front of Grandma. Despite the door her words came through loud and clear.

"You tie that animal in the shed or out in the barn," Grandma commanded. "Don't think she's ever coming back in *this* house."

Grandma's displeasure was seldom made vocal. She didn't need words to get her point across. Under normal circumstances we recognized her thin lips and stern eyes as an indication of some line we'd disregarded. Her expressions were fearsome and so evident that no one could mistake her mood. I had seldom heard her speak above a normal tone, but when her annoyance did break the sound barrier, despite the soft volume of voice, her words had the identical effect as a sonic boom. Everyone turned toward the source.

Patch, however, had already forgotten her part in the stolen meal. Outside was as good as in, it made little difference to her. Now that she had food in her, she was ready to play. She jumped and leapt in the snow, stopping to grab a mouthful before dashing away. I trudged behind her to the barn, knowing farther away from the house was the best place for my dog.

"C'mon girl." I patted my leg. "You've done it now."

Once secured in the barn Patch made the best of the situation. After the turkey, a nap is called for. After her requisite spins, she lay down in the loose straw Grandpa kept for the horses. She *would* be able to relax. Patch didn't have to go back to face anyone's wrath, but I needed to show up for dinner before someone came after me. I knew there'd be no sense in compounding existing problems.

I didn't have much fun at dinner. Most of the conversation alluded to the despicable guilt of "your dog" and I knew they weren't talking to anybody but me. Although the Christmas ham was tasty enough for anyone, the atmosphere around the table got real bad when we ran out of bread. In addition to the heaps already on Patch, some blame had jumped over to me and stuck fast. Grandma kept her family audience in head bobbing agreement with my failure to have a well trained dog.

I skipped dessert, got dressed in my winter wear and walked back to join Patch.

"I hope you enjoyed the food, you dog. You." I grabbed her neck in both hands. "Grandma is pretty mad at you girl. We've got to figure out how to apologize."

Patch didn't seem to know what wrong she'd possibly done. She got extra food from us all the time. Patch got chicken and turkey carcasses, as well as beef and pork bones. With the specialized canines of the Airedale she crunched poultry bones like stick candy. Patch was pot and plate licker, leftover eater and compost pile tender at the Greene House. In addition to all blatant food offerings, she got tasty morsels slipped to her whenever Mom and Dad weren't looking and sometimes even when they were.

Patch and I idled away the time with serious conversation but neither of us could come up with a method to attract Grandma's good graces again. Maybe she'd just forget.

Some hours later, after the sky started to turn dusk, Chip wandered out to the barn.

"Mommy said to tell you we're going home soon. You better come in and say goodbye to us. You're supposed to bring Patch up with you."

I lagged behind my brother for a few minutes. I knew in my heart Patch's summons would not indicate her forgiveness and I was right.

When I reached the door, the rest of the family was saying their goodbyes with hugs and "Merry Christmas!" Dad started out to bring the car along side the house for easier loading of people and presents while everyone got second helpings of the good cheer. Mom told me that Grandma had *requested* they take Patch back to Monroe with them.

I ran to both grandparents in the living room and asked. "Patch can stay, can't she Grandma? She'll be good, I promise."

Mom followed me into the room.

"No Clock, Patch has to go home. I'll not have to worry about what she's getting into the whole time you're here. You can get along without her for a week."

"Please Grandma," I begged, but I knew the futility of the plea. "I'll make her behave."

"You can choose, Clock." She ordered. "You can stay, but not the dog."

I turned to face Mom.

"Wait for me okay?" I asked her. "I've got to get my clothes from upstairs. I'll be right back."

When I turned again to face my grandparents, Grandpa appeared amused, but Grandma's face, normally serene, was momentarily washed in surprise. The look quickly faded from astonished disbelief to studied and deliberate indifference in the space of mere moments. Grandma walked back into the kitchen as I scooted up the stairway to gather my clothes from the attic bedroom.

I sat on the bed for just a moment and thought through all the special treatment I'd be giving up. Bacon and eggs, pancakes and waffles, homemade jams and jellies on home baked bread for breakfast! Free access to books Mom still considered too old for me to read. No real chores except firewood and those I wished to do. The attic bedroom, always considered a special place, would be mine if I stayed. No Carole while I was here. Every splendor I could imagine would be mine.

Easy choice…I rode all the way home with Patch curled at my feet.

I had goals.

At nine years old I was after merit badges. I had a Cub Scout sash adorned already with emblems for archery, Indian lore, athletics, lifesaving, nature, camping, community citizenship, dog care, reading, swimming and woodcarving. Dad always said if there were merit badges for getting in Dutch, hounding parents, pushing my luck, cruising for a bruising, or trying his patience, my sash wouldn't have room for anything else. My sister Carole suggested giving badges for being a pain, bothering and being a snot, but as far as I knew, none of these were even being considered.

I was chasing badges for hiking and wilderness survival. The activities had to be witnessed by parents or the Den Mother and I was pretty sure Mom wasn't going to take a hike with me in the middle of January, dead winter. I asked Dad.

His first response was, "What?"

I gave him a complete description of how long for the hike (2 miles, at least), what we had to do during (note flora and fauna, keep a log), had to do in the middle (build a fire and cook a meal), and what we had to do at the end (prove survival by showing up at the next Scout meeting).

Dad's next comment was, "When?"

I said, "Right now."

When he got his laughing under control, he said. "Sure we will, when the weather warms up."

"In the summer when sane people take hikes."

"When there would be flora and fauna to see while hiking."

"Not when the branches are bare, animals are hibernating and when every campsite would be buried under four feet of snow."

Then he'd be delighted.

"No Dad, I really want to do it in the winter, because nobody else does."

Despite my, argument, he stuck to his guns.

"Why do think that is?" he asked, but didn't let me answer. "I'll tell you why. Because it's cold and they're smarter than you," Dad continued. "Son, it's winter and bad enough I have to drive in it every day."

Besides trips to get firewood off the woodpile or scraping car windshields, my father kept his outdoor activities to the barest of minimums. My father argued that he fell in that category of smarter people, too.

"There is no way I am going on a two mile hike during the winter, Clark, and that's final."

My father ended many conversations this way, mostly when it was something he didn't want to do or something we were going to.

My dad could have earned a merit badge for "That's Final" years ago, if Scouting had one. Fortunately for me he had made that bold statement without figuring on Mom.

Somewhere between dinner that night and dinner the next, my father decided to take his son on a winter hike. Somewhere under the blankets of the bed in the coldest bedroom on the planet a choice more suitable to global goodwill was made. Whatever the strategy employed, it worked splendidly. We were going hiking. In the winter.

That's what was final.

Lake Erie had frozen solidly that year, as it did most years. The ice was thick enough for fishing shanties and fishermen and even cars to be driven on it. Many people just drove out, chopped a hole in the ice and dropped a line in for perch or the occasional pike. They often sat in their cars keeping warm with the fishing pole stuck through the window. We brave kids scoffed at this tactic. We knew that in order to really ice fish, you had to get cold, and had to actually be freezing if you wanted to catch fish. Those softies, those city people weren't really ice-fishing, they were just pretending. Besides, we had seen the holes created by automobiles when their owners had been just a little premature in trusting the thickness of the ice. Despite the not infrequent loss of someone's car, people continued to drive out for fishing.

Dad and I planned our route and destination. We would start at our house (uh-huh) and walk out through Stoney Pointe, walk across the ice of Brest Bay to Stoney Creek, build a fire and cook, and then reverse our course and be back home. Dad said it was almost four miles there and back, but if we were going to go on a hike it might as well be a proper one. Anybody could do two miles but we would do more.

We made lists of supplies to take: two canteens full of water, hotdogs and a raw potato wrapped in tin foil for each of us for lunch, a small pot, toilet paper (Be Prepared), some kitchen light-anywhere matches, some newspaper and a little bit of dry kindling wood to start the fire, my scout hatchet, Dad's pocket knife, dry socks if our feet got wet and extra gloves if the same thing happened to our hands. We packed small scissors to cut the ice from between Patch's toes which was sure to form during the hike. If left unattended, the ice would dig into the soft spaces between each toe and cause bleeding. We wanted no lame dogs on this trip. A notebook and pencil was included for documenting flora and fauna although Dad still insisted we'd be lucky to see anything except snow and ice. And Bag-Balm. Everything was rolled up in woolen blankets lashed at each end with heavy cord looped and knotted for arms. We didn't own backpacks, and didn't know anyone who did.

We would be as prepared as possible for winter: long-john underwear of course, leather gloves, flannel shirts and wool sweaters and the kind-of red and sort-of green scarves and mittens Grandma Phoebe knit for everyone. Mittens went over gloves. Wool, Navy watch caps, with another earflap hat tied over, earmuffs and the homemade snow goggles I had made in Cub Scouts, but none for Dad. Leather boots for hiking with wool socks, also knit by Gram, two pair on each. Dad would have his Navy pea coat and I had my new for Christmas winter coat. Patch wore what she always wore, a heavy coat with fine water repellant hair underneath. The troop was set.

We would leave the next Saturday morning, early Dad said, so there would be plenty of daylight for lunch and hiking back.

On Wednesday or Thursday or one of those middle days, Mom decided Chip should go, in order for Dad to spread the goodwill further, so to speak. He was five and a half years old, she reasoned, a sturdy child and the experience of spending a winter adventure with his big brother and father was one he would remember for the rest of his life. My father put up a considerable dispute with this: Chip would get tired, he was too young, his legs were too short, the ice was likely to be treacherous and uneven, it would be cold, and we'd have to carry more food, more extra gear.

No, Dad didn't think Chip should go.

"Maybe next year we'll do it again and then he can go. Next year," my Dad promised.

He sounded just a little like us when we were pleading for something we knew we weren't going to get. Same results, too.

My mother probably recognized that a repeat performance of a winter hike next year was as chancy as sainthood for Dad, or a pig flying by. And the pig would be carrying a horse for the beggar to ride. She wasn't going to say it wouldn't happen, just that the likelihood was slim.

"I really think Chip should get to go," Mom repeated.

And that's what was final.

That Saturday was overcast and Mom commented, "I sure hope it doesn't snow while you're out."

"Of course it won't, the clouds are sure to clear, and leave nothing but blue skies for our hike," Dad predicted. "Why, it'll probably warm up too, a January thaw most likely."

My father in particular possessed a belief that he could forecast the weather unerringly, far better than any TV newsman.

"Ok Jerry, just watch the weather. Have fun boys." Mom sent us packing. Hiking…. in the winter.

The Greene "men" set out across the beach. Patch ran ahead to scout and came back to report.

"The way is clear," she woofed. *"No ice goblins about. Follow me!"*
And off she'd go for another look ahead.

The hike really began when we left the roads in Stoney Pointe and ventured out onto the lake ice, where the area for hundreds of yards surrounding the shore was a jumble of ice pushed and stacked by the wind. Huge blue-green chunks of ice in piles six and eight feet tall were laid pell-mell around the snow covered shore. It took us some real hunting, some inventive twisting and turning and doubling back to finally find a way onto fairly smooth ice. Dad carried Chip for much of the way and pulled me over or through the ice maze several times.

Patch was invaluable once she got the hang of the game and saw that we were heading out on the ice. We followed her lead.

It began to snow.

Not more than a few flurries, nothing but a dusting. When we reached smooth ice the going was easier and the walking took much less effort. Far off, the shoreline of Brest Bay curved away from the straight line we followed to the mouth of the creek. It looked far away to me, way far off if someone would have asked me, but the fever of the adventure was on us, even Dad, as he turned and pointed back.

"Look how far we've come, boys."

Where we'd started looked farther away than where we were going and we'd been walking almost two hours.

I asked, "How far have we walked Dad?"

My father looked back toward Stoney Pointe.

"Looks to be about two miles and we've still got a ways to go. Must be a bit further than I thought."

Every once in a while we came to clear ice, slick and shiny, free of snow. Looking down, everything was deep blue and transparent, no bottom. Chip and I looked for fish while the wind at our backs, pushed us along, helping. Chip and I ran and slid across the smooth areas. I had never been out on the ice this far. Because the shoreline curved away from us as we walked, we were almost ¾ mile off shore, really far out, and the line of the land was distant. Soon we realized it was snowing harder, too, and starting to accumulate. We had to stop and get the frozen snow out from between Patch's toes. I noticed her whimper a little as we walked. After another half hour there wasn't much sliding and playing going on, because Chip and I for sure, and maybe Dad, were getting a bit tired. It sure would be good to get there, get a roaring fire going and have lunch. Even though we were closer now, we still had to skirt some piles of ice, with more ahead of us before we got to shore.

Even Patch reduced her scouting distance, patrolling ever and ever closer. In fact, she was walking at our sides, tongue lolling this side and that, panting. Either she was sure there weren't sea or regular monsters about or she wanted to be close if there were.

The ice at the creek was even more of a jumble than at the Pointe. Great slabs two feet thick stood on edges or atop one another. It wasn't piled as high, but there were fewer clear spaces to walk between. Chip and I got pulled and pushed most of the last hundred yards to the shore. Dad was definitely in a contest with Patch for panting champ by the time we got there, although his tongue wasn't lolling. But we made it!

Halfway.

With lots of help from Patch, though we didn't ask her, Chip and I gathered driftwood. Patch found new energy as she tried to take the wood away from us before we got it over to the site we had chosen. Two are better than one. We eventually got more to my father than Patch could cart off. Dad got a fire going with the kindling we had carried and we piled the driftwood on the small flames. The dry wood began to burn and quickly put off a great and welcome heat.

As soon as Dad got the fire going, he took the potatoes out of my blanket and stuck them close to the fire's edge.

"You boys want your hotdogs now," my Dad asked, "or you want to wait until the potatoes are done?"

Silly question, Dad.

"Now, now!"

"I'm starving."

"I'm famished."

"Let's eat NOW!"

"Hey, we forgot the hotdog forks."

"Okay, Cub Scout boy, go cut us some sticks to use."

Dad handed me his opened knife. I did not have a knife of my own yet, but hoped to soon. It would all depend on me doing some sort of demonstration, my father said, but I didn't know what he was talking about. Yet.

Those three hot dogs didn't stay in the flames long enough to get warm through. Mine was gone in about a flash, and I sure could have eaten another. I gave the last bite of my hotdog to Patch. She didn't fool around with her taste either; it just disappeared.... vanished. We'd stopped out on the ice several times for water breaks and we had to refill the canteens. I made a bowl out of my hands for Patch to drink from and Chip poured water for her. I got up and packed the small saucepan with the cleanest snow I could find and set it on two rocks to melt by the fire. Oh man, this was living. This was wilderness survival. The walk to get here had definitely been a hike. I could envision the new merit badges on my sash.

We all sat at the fire, hands outstretched to the flames, as if to store the warmth for the trip home. Patch laid nose first, close enough to make her sneeze from the heat, but she kept her nose right there, soaking it up. Dad kept turning and poking those potatoes. We were ready for more food just as soon as they were done. The spot we had chosen was sheltered from the wind. A small hassock of grass and sand made a good backstop for the fire and radiated the heat out to us where it belonged. The snow now fell heavily enough to make little hissing, spitting noises, but the fire was warm and the potatoes were cooking. We didn't care.

We sat by the fire a long time and my father said he couldn't understand why the potatoes weren't done, that maybe the fire wasn't hot enough. Chip and I got more wood, really got the fire going, a blaze. We'd get them cooked all right. We had been in our little camp about two hours now, it was well after noon, and my father said we were going to have to eat those spuds now and head back. I was hungry enough to eat them raw. I didn't care if they weren't done. I'd eat them. My belly was empty.

My Dad must have felt that way, too, because he rolled them out of the fire and juggled the scorched tin foil wrapped balls until they were cool enough to remove the covering.

"Here," he said. "Catch."

I peeled the foil back and was pretty amazed to see the potato black, like charcoal and showed my father, who had discovered the same of his and Chip's.

"They're just a little burned on the outside, peel that burned stuff off."

Okay, but mine was black on the inside too, charred through to the center. The potatoes may have still felt raw when he poked them with his knife but they were burnt crispy. My potato was junk. I offered a chunk to Patch, a non-choosy eater if ever there was, but even she turned it down. I thought if she had eaten her bite, I would have tried it, too. Chip said he was real hungry and began to whine. I could have told him that whining was a bad idea.

Chip hushed when Dad said, "Enough now."

No food for anyone. All of the potatoes were burnt black.

One of my father's rare "dammits" slipped out, and this time there was definitely a "God" in front of it.

"Okay boys," said General Dad, now mustering his troops for a forced march. "The sooner we get back home the sooner we can get something to eat. We've got a ways to go."

We put out the fire by piling snow on top of the burning wood. Hungry flames hissed and steamed in their protest. I was going to get good marks for fire safety, too. I'd be sure to bring it up at the next Scout Meeting.

The wind, which had been friendly on the way out, was against us on the way back. Instead of gently nudging us along it now shoved us back heartily, stinging our faces with the snow. We wound our way around, over and through the ice piles once again. The snow and wind continued to pick up and it wasn't long before I saw that my Dad had picked up Chip to carry him piggyback. The wind increased enough to make the ice begin to move and it cracked and groaned by the time we got past the jumbled piles.

We didn't talk much after that.

Dad said only once or twice, "We've got to get a move on son, no dawdling now."

I knew that. I'd seen the ice really moving in the winter, relentlessly climbing the stony beach as if it was alive. As young as I was I recognized the awesome power it had. My father had seen all that as well. We silently acknowledged that a problem might be ahead.

We made good time on the way back despite the wind and snow. We weren't enjoying this walk and so were deliberately trying to get back, no wandering here. The wind continued to blow hard and steady. Our whole walk was accompanied by noise underneath our feet, grinding like teeth. We didn't see any cracks or open water yet, but the ice seemed to be talking to itself, as if making up its mind about these four animals treading along.

My father kept saying, "Got to go son, got to go."

I had grabbed Patch by the scruff of her neck and allowed her to pull me along. Patch whined every time the ice made a loud noise. I felt like whining, too. It began to get dark.

I sure didn't want to be out here at night. Dad wasn't talking anymore. He was just putting one foot in front of the other and carrying Chip piggy-back, who had fallen asleep. Dad woke him up several times but a few minutes later Chip's head would fall over and he'd be fast asleep again. Dad had to work harder to keep him in place. He ended up shoving Chip's feet into the pockets of the pea coat.

The wind in our faces slowed a bit as we approached Stoney Pointe but the ice noise got louder, really popping loudly by the time we got within several hundred yards of the shore. The land acted as a dam against the wind and the walking was definitely easier, but the noise was scary and getting worse. It was mostly dark now. Despite the effort we had made to race back, darkness won. The footing became worse as we approached the shore and picked our way through the ice piles. There were large patches of open water between us and the shore.

"Clark, you watch your step."

My father sounded worried.

"You too, Dad. I've got Patch. I'll be alright. She can see good in the dark."

Dad was in the lead as we approached to shore and I heard him say, "Damn it! Open water, of all the…," and his voice trailed away. "We'll have to walk along the shoreline and see if there's still a bridge through. Be careful son, the ice is moving, be really careful now."

I heard him talking to Chip, telling him to wake up now. Making him wake up, demanding. I could see a space of about fifteen feet between the edge of the ice and the shore. We probably could have waded ashore, but the wet wouldn't have done us any good. We still had almost a mile to walk before we got back home once we got on shore. I had never been swimming on this side of Stoney Point either, and didn't know how deep the water was or how steep the lakebed sloped down.

I told Dad that Patch and I would go on ahead.

"Patch can see really well. She'll be able to find us a way."

My father said to go ahead, but to wait for him if we found a passage.

"Don't get too far ahead. I want to be able to see you," He added.

I could definitely feel the ice cracking, not exactly breaking up under our feet, but with a sense of movement like that of a raft on the water. Patch and I walked another hundred yards to a jut of land just south of Stoney Pointe before she suddenly pulled from my grasp. She was on shore before I knew it.

"Here, over here!" Barking, barking, barking, insistent. *"Come on, right here!"*

Dad hollered, "Clark, you okay? Clark!"

"Over here Dad! Here's a place! Patch is already across."

I waited for him to catch up. We stepped ashore like stepping from a boat, just a little step between ice and shore and didn't even get our feet wet. Piece of cake. My father eased Chip off his shoulders with a groan. We started back home walking down the street, everybody walking now, Chip too.

"We can stop by Jackie's or Dennis' house, Dad. They're in my scout troop and they just live over there," I said, pointing at some nearby homes. "We can call Mom and she can come get us."

My father reached over and ruffled Patch, giving her a good petting. He grabbed my hand and Chip's, too.

"Boys," my father said. "I think we'll finish this hike just like we started."

Chapter 16

A Fortune in Furs

"Make Big Money with Furs!"

Hey, I liked the sound of "Big Money." I liked big and I liked money and when they were used together, I liked them even better. That's what the ad in the back of *Boy's Life* magazine said. It said the same thing in the Cub Scouting magazine that came every month. I knew if it was in the scouting magazine it had to be true. It was the Scout's Bible, though I couldn't make the comparison at home, fearing accusations of blasphemy. Now all I had to do was figure out how to get furs and thereby get the big money. I was pretty sure they weren't talking about the few furs I had managed to tan when butchering the rabbits my family raised for food. It would have to be another animal's fur.

Having seen Davy Crockett at the theater, a hero in the movies, I was inspired to be a frontiersman in all ways. I saw no incongruity in switching between Indian or mountain-man or cavalry soldier, changing with favorite reading at the time. I knew about traps and snares and had caught rabbits and pheasants in snares just like the Indians had done. I read stories of mountain-men, their exploits in hunting grizzly bear, buffalo and cougar.

I'd read enough to know that beaver trapping was wet and cold, hard work, placing and setting and running the trap-line, and using scent to attract the beavers. I knew that the best pelts were winter pelts when the animals, just like us, were interested in keeping themselves warm. There weren't any beaver in southern Michigan, but the marsh was full of the domed shaped houses of the muskrat. The swim-ways they cut through the cattail rushes crisscrossed and made the marsh look like an abstract diagram. Every time Patch and I went to the marsh I would see the silvery "V" their heads cut in

146

the still waters as they swam. The marsh was full of them; hundreds of their houses dotted the expanse. Patch had dug up a few of their mounds in frenzies of barking, and continually plunged in the water to catch one but never had.

I'd written to the fur trading company last summer and printed just as neatly as Mom.

Dear Sirs,   August 12, 1956
I am an experienced trapper and have accumulated several hundred muskrat pelts. They are green, not tanned, but excellent prime skins. Is your company interested in purchasing these pelts?
Sincerely,

And I signed my name. Okay, I knew that there were two fibs, maybe three, in the letter, and one omission for sure. I was "almost" an experienced trapper. I had read enough to know the lingo like, "green" and "prime" pelts. That would be enough to convince anyone. There was also the part about several hundred pelts, but I thought I could put that to rights quick enough once I got started. I also didn't tell them I was going to be ten.

While I waited for an answer I did a little research. I asked Walt.

"Sure," he said, "I ran a trap-line myself when I was a boy, right on them marshes, too. There's a bunch of old traps in the barn at my brother's farm, but I can't get them." Walt went on, "If you go ask him he might sell 'em or give 'em to you, though."

I didn't know his brother Simon as well as I knew Walt. I had seen him a few times at Jones's Market, but if I wanted those traps I would have to get to know him better.

By the time I'd worked up enough courage to approach Walt's brother, school had started. I asked the bus driver to drop me at the farm on the way home from school and he did, though he asked me if it was okay with my parents. I said sure, which was sort of true, but only because I wouldn't be in trouble after I told my folks what I was doing.

I stepped up on the back porch door and knocked. A woman, who I quickly found out, was the housekeeper, answered.

I thought she was his wife and said, "Hi, Mrs. Nadeau..."

But she interrupted with a harsh laugh and a statement or question of, "You think I'd marry that nasty old man?" She added, "I just cook and clean."

From where I was standing with a view into the kitchen, people could dispute the last part. Pots and pans, old newspapers, boxes, burlap bags, a jumble so large, I couldn't see how she had managed to answer the door. It didn't even look like there was a way through the untidy heaps, but she had to have come from somewhere.

I started again, "Is Mr. Nadeau, Simon, Walt's brother, here? My name is Clark and I need to see him about some traps. Walt told me to come see him."

She opened the door, but whispered conspiratorially as I passed, "You better not tell him Walt sent you. Si and Walt haven't spoken since their Momma died. He'll probably run you off if you even say Walt's name."

Whew, not only was the kitchen dirty, but it or she didn't smell all that good either.

There was a path after all and I followed several steps behind, still not figuring out where the odor was coming from. We went in to the parlor or living room or the front room, whatever it was. It looked just like the kitchen, littered and stacked and stuffed and piled and jammed full of boxes and newspaper. One old chair held Simon, Si, the housekeeper called him. He looked just like Walter, younger, but not much. He was a lot scruffier. Dirty. Filthy. I told him who I was and what I wanted.

He thought a minute and said, "They might be in the barn, but I ain't seen 'em in years. If you kin' find 'em, you kin' have 'em."

"Really? Thanks a lot. Thanks a whole lot, Mr. Nadeau, thanks." I said as I followed the track back the way I thought I had come in.

My sense of direction was pretty good, because I was out on the back porch. The housekeeper followed me out on the porch. It wasn't the kitchen that smelled; it was her. It was probably him, too.

Walking to the barn, getting closer, it looked like misshapen animals were trying to evacuate through every available opening. Through the one open door and out holes made by missing siding, all sorts of cast off machinery, more burlap bags, feed and grain sacks, straw, egg cartons and vegetable crates spilled out into the yard. The barn didn't look like it was really bulging, but the spillage gave it the appearance of doing so. It looked like everything that was in wanted to be out and everything that was out needed to be in. I wanted in. How to get there? The one small door was stacked full.

I tried to get the big barn doors open but neither one would slide in its tracks. I tried the smaller door and managed to squeeze in, stepping around another pile of rubbish. Every space looked full, shutting out any view of the interior walls or planking. The second level had hay mows on both sides which dripped cobwebs and straw. I walked around stacks of broken crates and coops, stepping up on piles of lumber, disturbing dust in clouds. Ancient hay and straw bales lined both sides, so old the twine had broken on much of it and allowed the bales to accordion out of shape. There was a patch of sky open in one corner of the barn where the roof had failed, directly over an untidy stack of hay. In the middle of the barn sat a huge steam-powered threshing machine and an old wooden-sided manure spreader that was full of car fenders, bumpers and several seats.

I had seen pictures of threshers in history books and watched similar working models at the county fair. "Rumsfeld Oil Pull" was printed in faded red and gold letters on the open cab's sides. It had huge steel-cleat wheels in the back and smaller ones in the front. It was mammoth. I stepped up on the operator's platform and pulled a few levers. *I could run this thing*, I thought. I crawled over other piles indistinguishable in nature except that they were numerous and hugely filthy. Everywhere was stuff. I made a circuit of the barn, not seeing anything that looked like muskrat traps.

How ever was I to find these traps?

This barn was going to take a lot more searching before it coughed up any treasure. I would have to come back.

I walked up to the house again, slapping my pants and shirtsleeves as I went, trailing, billowing, dust. *Oh, Oh. School clothes*, I worried. *I was going to catch it for this. I'd think of a good story. Hey! This was a good story. I'd stick to the truth.*

The housekeeper answered the door but didn't open it.

"I'll have to come back, if that's okay with Mr. Nadeau," I said. "It might not be until Saturday, when I can wear old clothes. My mom's going to give me what for when I show up looking like this."

I stuck out my still grimy sleeve as proof.

"Umph" was the only response I got and I convinced myself this meant okay.

"I'll be back later to look some more."

I walked out to the road and started home. I hadn't walked far when our neighbor, Mrs. Terry, stopped her car and asked me if I wanted a ride.

Mom did give me the dickens for my school clothes, but when I explained how they got dirty and what I was doing when they did she seemed okay with dirty son and clothes. I told the story of my imminent riches at dinner that night. Dad asked me if I really knew what I was doing.

"Sure," I said. "I'm gonna be a trapper and make lots of money. I'll share it with all of you."

Nobody much believed me when I recounted all of the junk that was there, but Mom did comment on all of the dirt I brought home with me. Chip said he was going to be a trapper, too.

Mom said. "We'll see."

I didn't get to go back to Nadeau's farm for some weeks and had to walk this time. No rides were available.

"Yes Mom, I have old clothes on," I said in response as I walked out of the door.

Patch went too as long as I was walking.

When I knocked on the farmhouse door I had to start the whole story all over again for the housekeeper.

"Helen, just call me Helen," she said.

I went over the traps I wanted with her and was led once again to the front room through teetering piles of accumulation for Mr. Nadeau to hear the reiteration.

"Stay here girl. Sit." I instructed Patch even though she didn't appear in a hurry to follow me in.

I introduced myself again to Mr. Nadeau and politely listened once more.

"I ain't seen 'em in years…. might be in the barn. Maybe. Go ahead if you want."

Helen walked me back to the door and told me the reason Simon hadn't seen the traps in years was that he hadn't been out to the barn in that long. She said since he ran out of room for storage he didn't have much call to go out there.

"Watch for snakes," a parting word from Helen.

The barn hadn't lost any of its clutter; in fact, I thought it might have looked worse than the first time I dared the space, but Patch plunged right in. I followed her.

There was a small, enclosed room in the back, an attachment to the barn structure with an open doorway. I wound my way through old fruit crates and baskets. It looked like chickens had lived in the small room once upon a time, but this place hadn't heard a cluck in a long time. Of mice or rat droppings there were plenty and as I kicked the piles of junk apart, I exposed their shredded and feathery nesting materials. I tried to keep the kicking to a minimum so that I could continue breathing. The dust was terrible, old and stale, burned eyes and nose, sneezing, sneezing and coughing. I should have brought a kerchief to cover my nose and mouth.

Patch, meanwhile, was having a grand time raising even more dust.

I looked and lifted, finding old birds nests, more mouse evidence, some desiccated furry bodies of them when piles of garbage had fallen, crushing them and nest.

Patch was a huge help. At least she thought so.

I wandered around the barn, re-inspecting places my impatience had previously missed or overlooked. There was so much junk here I was starting to lose hope. I sat down on an overturned section of log. Attached to one end of the log was an anvil that had crashed through several crates when it fell over. I grabbed my dog and sat down on the log and waited long enough for the dust to settle. This wasn't working out like I had imagined.

"Whaddya think girl?" I asked Patch. "Want to say the heck with it?"

"Rwwwwfff."

No, she did not. There was too much more to look at in here.

Along the walls where junk piles had fallen I could see harnesses, old ropes and log chains hanging on nails and hooks. The thought occurred that any pictures of spring traps I had seen all showed a short chain attached. Maybe they had been hung up when someone cared about the condition of the barn, before Simon had become a collector, a hoarder of junk and a slob. I had to squeeze between stacks and piles to see along the walls, where old shovel handles leaned against the barn's framing and a lantern with broken glass lay on the floor.

A burlap bag bulging with something hung off a nail. Whatever was in the bag was heavy enough to have bent the nail down and the bag was hanging by the heavy material caught on the spike's head. It looked promising and sounded a dull clank when I reached through the junk to poke it with an old shovel handle. Too bad when I poked the bag because the old fabric surrendered and it fell behind all those fruit crates. I would have to move the whole blinking stack if I wanted to confirm the contents of the bag, but I suddenly had a good feeling about this.

After an hour of shuttling boxes full of old shoes, clothing, papers, dishes, everything imaginable, I could just reach through to grab the burlap. I'd had a hard time finding a place for the stuff I moved; it was almost impossible to add to the existing mess without toppling everything over. A thrill of excitement washed over me as I felt the curve of the trap's jaws and I dragged the bag to me and lifted it to shake the dust loose.

Oh yeah, there were traps here. I took the bag outside and dumped it on the ground. One, two, three…., here were twelve rusty traps with chains attached, a big ring through the ends of each chain. I already envisioned catching twelve muskrats every time I checked my traps! Why, I'd have those several hundred pelts in…. seventeen days! No time at all. All right!

Patch had followed me out of the barn and I ordered her back when I put one trap on the ground and set it by stepping on the spring catch to open the smooth jaws. The trigger made a satisfying but ominous click as it set. Looked like it would go off. I stepped back inside the barn and grabbed the broken shovel handle I had used to poke the bag. I just touched the round pad of the trigger, just barely grazed it and jumped back startled. Snap! The jaws snapped shut.

Patch ran up at the noise and I hoisted the handle. The trap's jaws had bitten into the old, but still hard wood, about a ¼ inch on either side. It wouldn't do to put a finger in there. Or my dog's insistent nose.

They would need some cleanup and rust removal, some oiling, but I knew how to do that. No problem. I went back into the barn and got a bag that wasn't quite so flimsy, loaded the traps in and listened as the chains slithered in after each one. I could hardly wait. I put the old bag back in the barn (three parts to every job) but knew no one would notice if I didn't. I ambled up to the porch and knocked, wanting to say thank you before I started walking home.

At my knock, "Helen, just call me Helen" asked what I wanted. Rather than go through the whole story and endure the resident odor again, I held up the bag, rattled it for sound effects and said.

"Traps."

"Oh, yeah," said Helen. "Wait a minute. Got something"

She came back in a few moments and thrust an old bottle toward me.

"Si says there's scent in this, but it's all dried up. Put some water in it and it'll be good as new." Helen made a face. "If you ask me it smells bad enough already."

I wondered how she could know.

I started to say thank you, but the door had banged shut and she was making her way back into the trails through the kitchen.

I hollered, "Thanks Mr. Nadeau! Thanks a lot!" and headed home with my treasures.

I shook the bottle to confirm its dryness as I walked, unscrewed the top and gave a tentative sniff. Helen was right; this smelled bad. Nasty.

I offered the open bottle to Patch and almost wasn't quick enough to keep her from grabbing it out of my hand.

She thought it was great, but then again she liked rotten fish.

I thought it wasn't going to attract anything. I almost threw the bottle in the ditch, but knew Patch would go get it. Instead I stuffed it in my coat pocket.

I walked all the way to Walt's shack, bypassing my house. I wanted to show him the traps, but he wasn't home. Dang! I wrote him a brief note on the pad he kept by the door. Subdivision residents would do this when ditches and lots needed mowing or branches hauled off, so I knew he'd get it. I tossed the bag down by his door and headed back home. It didn't make sense to haul them home and just have to bring them back again. I had already determined that I would ask Walt to help me get them cleaned up. I was pretty sure he would.

The next morning after chores and breakfast I untied Patch and I rode my bike down to Walt's. Patch must have thought my mission unimportant, as she headed off to the beach, in search of dead fish or something else more interesting than muskrat traps. How did she know what I was up to?

Walt was up puttering with the tractor, and said, "Got your note. That them?" he asked, motioning to the bag.

"Yeah, and your brother just gave them to me, too, no charge. I couldn't believe it," I told him.

"Well," Walt frowned and spat. "That's a goddamnsight more'n he ever give me, the sonofabitch. Let's see 'em, bring me one. These are *my* traps, by damn. That sonofabitch! Simon had 'em all the time. I trapped them marshes when I was fourteen, let's see, must'a been 1901 or '02," Walter muttered as I handed him one. "They're pretty poor boy, you're gonna have to get 'em cleaned up a lot before you get any 'rats in 'em," Walter claimed. "You need to scrub 'em with a wire brush, scrub 'em again in really hot soapy water and then do it all over again. Then you need to find some rotten fish and rub the traps in the skin. Carp is best. They're oily. I ain't takin' any time with this. Boy, you're on your own. My trappin' days'r done."

I guess I *was* taking the traps home.

I found a wire brush in the jumble of Dad's workbench and set to the traps. It took me the rest of the day to get them reasonably free of rust and I worked through lunchtime, saying I wasn't hungry when Mom called. More important stuff to do. Patch came home smelling of dead fish, I thought probably because I hadn't given her any of the scent. Although I knew I'd be the one bathing her, at least her gucky attraction would be a benefit this time. Later she could lead me to the fish I needed for the traps.

I asked Mom if I could boil the traps in soapy water and she said of course I could, but when I started bringing them into the kitchen she also said:

"Outside is where that kind of work goes on, not in. You can build a fire over by the burning barrel. Get that big old pot out of the garage. It's sitting right on the shelf in the back."

Our burning barrel was a 55 gallon drum with the top cut out and air holes punched around the bottom. It was the site of all paper trash burning and had also been used as a crematory for dead animals and the skins which used to cover rabbits. The area around the barrel was covered with shiny black specks and flakes of ash. A perfect place. Scorched earth.

I scrubbed and scoured for several days straight. About a week later I heard the tractor pull up in the front and stop and wasn't too surprised when Walt walked around to the backyard. He picked up the traps one by one, nodding slightly in an almost approval. He said that they could be better but because I was just a boy, they'd do alright. I remembered the bottle of dried scent the housekeeper had given me.

Walt unscrewed the top took a sniff and another, "Yup, that smells like 'em, dried up though. Put some water in it, it'll smell even better. If you ever catch any 'rats, I'll show you how to cut their glands out. Keep the bottle full, 'cuz you won't catch many without scenting up the trap stakes. You got a while to go yet anyways. You can't set any traps till after the marsh ices over."

At dinner that night Mom told Dad, "A letter mistakenly came here for your father today, Jerry. From a fur company. Must be a business interest."

"No, no, that's me!" I hollered. "That's me. It's the company that's going to buy all my muskrat pelts."

"All what pelts?" Dad laughed. "You haven't set trap one yet."

Yeah.

I rushed into the kitchen and retrieved my "official' response," and came back to the table holding it outstretched like a holy book. I was grinning so big, I thought I'd split. I ripped the envelope open.

Dear Mr. Greene, it began. All right! They thought I was a Mister. That had to mean they thought I was a trapper too.

The fur company said they were buying muskrat pelts right and left. Well, that's not the way they put it, but that's how I read it. They told me that they would grade the pelts once they received them and the current price they were paying, 22 cents per prime green pelt, with lesser prices for firsts and seconds. I didn't pay any attention to the other prices; all I saw was the 22 cents.

Other than prime was something I wouldn't have to worry about because all of mine would be the best they'd ever seen. Let's see, how did it go.... twelve pelts per day at 22 cents per pelt, that's a lot of money. Why, I'd be making $2.64 every day for the rest of the winter. My Dad probably didn't make *that* kind of money. I'd be wealthy, I'd become a fur magnate, and I'd buy everything for everybody. Who'd be laughing then?

They also said I had to pay freight and something about return freight. I didn't know what that meant, but who cares about little things like freight. Everybody look! I was in business. I was a *fur trapper*.

The marsh finally froze toward the middle of December that year, right after my tenth birthday. Walt had stopped by several times to talk about choosing proper locations, staking the traps and scenting the stakes to attract the muskrats. The last part was important because the muskrat was territorial and would investigate the strange smell of another muskrat. They just couldn't resist finding out what or who was new in the neighborhood.

"Just like people." Walt laughed. "There are traps for people too, just different kinds. Some trap's got fur on 'em already. If you know what I mean."

I didn't. Walt could be mysterious.

Saturday was clear and biting cold, perfect for work. After chores I set the traps, all twelve, in the swim-ways and raceways close to muskrat huts. It was easy to set them but wet work and cold. I had to take my mittens off for each trap and place them properly, right side up, carefully on the mud so they didn't sink in. The ice wasn't thick by the reed beds and the muck the cattails grew in wasn't frozen so the stakes I'd cut pushed into place pretty easily. I sprinkled a few drops of the scent on each stake. It took me about four or five hours to set and scent all twelve traps and my hands were numb by the time I was through. As soon as the last one was set though, I went back to the first one to check for muskrats. Nothing, nothing at all in traps one through five. I was frozen through. I'd come back tomorrow.

I had to beg and plead to check them on Sunday, a "Day of Rest" at our house. "And on the seventh day He rested," Mom was fond of saying. "God built the whole world in six days; we should be able to take care of our meager work in six, too."

Yeah, I thought, *but did God have a trap-line?* I kept up long enough for Mom to have to choose between letting me go and some Biblical punishment, crucifixion or pillar of salt. Fortunately, Mom regarded lessons including work as holy as church, and that I was likely to mope all day with my thoughts on the traps. If I was going to be a pain in the butt for the rest of the day, she was able to choose regardless of Sunday's intent.

"Change out of church clothes first," she insisted.

We always had to get out of our good clothes as soon as we came home on Sundays. I figured those duds still had Jesus on them.

I coaxed Patch out the back door and had a hard time getting her away from the fireplace, but as soon as she was outside Patch got into the spirit of the trek. The present moment was always her method of operation.

As we walked back to the marsh, I reviewed the trap layout, tracing the path I would take to check each, one through twelve. The ice had reformed over the holes created when I first set the traps and I had to chop new access at each station. First trap, nothing, second trap same way, empty. I should have had two by now. Something was not right. As I replaced the traps, I sprinkled a few more drops of the scent on each stake. Maybe I'd been too stingy the first time or the scent was no good. It sure smelled no good; terrible to me. It had gained an awesome potency when water was added. Walt said it was fine.

As we approached the location, I saw a dark shape struggling and leaping, becoming more frantic as we closed in. A muskrat caught fast by a front leg, squeaking, squealing in pain and fright.

I thought they died in the traps. I hadn't planned on live and injured animals. I had to restrain Patch with a "SIT" before I approached the struggling animal. I had been lectured on animals enough to know that they could feel pain. Suffering by any creature was to be avoided at all costs; not allowed. I felt terrible that this one had been trapped still alive for who knew how long, but there was nothing to do but step on its neck and kill the animal with the side-axe I carried for the ice. I held the animal up, away from Patch, for inspection and saw how the foreleg was twisted and shattered. Dang!

I tried to convince myself that the animal had only been there a few minutes, but saw how it had been chewing at the trapped limb. Not good, not good at all. I'd have to check traps frequently if this was going to happen. I wasn't going to like this if I had to kill each one.

I tucked the body in the canvas sack Mom had sewn for me and finished the run, checking each trap with ever-colder fingers, but celebrating each of the six muskrats I took that day. The other muskrats had been killed outright by the traps, had died quickly with no pain, jaws sprung tight over necks. Patch was a good one to celebrate with, leaping and barking with the enthusiasm only a dog could develop. Maybe the first muskrat was unusual. I'd been raised to believe that some animals were put on earth to supply man and didn't have a problem taking their lives. I'd been helping Mom butcher domestic rabbits for three or four years already, but made sure the killing part was swift and sure. *The first one had to be a quirk*, I thought as I headed for home. Patch kept her nose almost stuck to the bag, and tried to snatch it when she thought my attention wandered, making a game.

I was chilled to the bone by the time I got home and was going to go in, have my Sunday's rest and skin the muskrats tomorrow after school, but Mom said:

"You get out there right now and finish the job."

Oh yeah, the "Three Parts to Every Job" rule. How had I forgotten?

I had heard this three parts thing since I had ears. "Preparation."

"Doing."

"Cleaning Up After." No exceptions. "This is the way we do our work, do our work, do our work, this is the way we do our work, so early in the morning." Mom made a song of it when I was just a baby.

I skinned out the pelts and stretched them over wire coat hangers formed into an oval. I carefully scraped each pelt to remove any fat still clinging, not wanting to cut through the skin. I rubbed them down with salt and hung them one by one on the clothesline, out of the reach of Patch, who wouldn't be able to resist them. We had all learned this lesson when we discovered several rabbit skins she'd shredded. If I was to sell these pelts, Patch must be denied. The winter weather would first freeze and then dry the pelts quickly, freeze-drying, further preparation for sending them to the fur company when I had enough to be considered a good cache.

The dark meat was very good; tasty, if you removed the scent glands. I wrapped each in freezer paper or put it in a pan of water if Mom wanted fresh. We used the muskrat trapping results just like we did the rabbit. We had a freezer full in the spring despite my family's ability to consume vast amounts of food. I was putting food on the table and so my activities were praised when we had it for dinner.

I was pretty proud.

That night I boasted of the muskrats and how I had to dispatch one myself. I talked about it a lot easier than I had done the deed and didn't let anyone know how the muskrat had sounded when it squealed, but I could still hear it. The talk moved around the dinner table, each their own turn. Carole said she had heard that a man from our neighborhood was sleeping with another man's wife and got caught. My mother told her to hush, it wasn't our business, hush, but she went right on. It was all the talk. Gossip was flying around like birds before a storm.

I wondered if that was the trap Walt was talking about last week.

At first I hung them in the garage when the cold wind had finished its work, but they ended up in Mom and Dad's room. Some dog, but not mine, got into the garage when the big door was left open. Patch's barking woke me and I rushed outside to chase the dog away, before it got to more than a few pelts. After that I made such a pain of myself, worrying and griping about the loss of those few pelts, Mom said I could put them in their bedroom. Under the bed, hanging on window latches, stacked in stiff piles, my cache grew. I worked the trap line all winter, checked them every, or every other day and had accumulated about 150 pelts during the freezing weather, a pretty good bundle. I dressed and stretched each one with the same care as the first. They were good pelts.

They hardly smelled at all.

By early March the weather had gone through several freeze/thaw cycles making the trap line too difficult to keep going, treacherous walking on the rotten ice. I gathered the traps up one final time, knowing I would do this again next winter and took them home and washed the mud off. I finished by wiping them down with cooking oil I had begged from my mother and hung them up in the garage. Third part of that job.

Now all I had to do was get them sent off for Big Money. I asked Mom to get me some stout cardboard boxes from the grocery store the next time she went shopping. I'd written to the fur company again, several weeks prior. Yes, they were still buying pelts, Mr. Greene and gave me shipping instructions again. I counted the pelts as I packed them in the boxes. One hundred and forty-three, not counting the four slightly dog-chewed. I calculated my earnings, figuring they wouldn't give me much for the chewed up pelts. I kept them out of the equation, hmmm, 143 at 22 cents makes $31.40, a vast amount of money to me. Thirty dollars was a lot of money to anybody in 1957, and even my Dad had to admit that I had done a good job.

I was always wary of his quick flash temper, but he did a good job of holding us up or out or down as the situation called for. Up or out was good, down was to be avoided if possible. This time it was up for admiration. Mostly it was down in my case. I felt pretty good about his acknowledgement.

I would have to pay for the shipping by U.S. Mail, but that wouldn't be much. I'd get an advance from Mom. Everything else was profit.

I was proud when I took the big boxes, all five of them at once, to the post office in Newport. The United States Mail. The boxes filled the back end of the station wagon full. I'd sent thank-you notes for birthday and Christmas gifts, Valentines Day and birthday cards myself of course, but this was different by a bunch. I was shipping something, like the businessman I thought I was. The postmaster even looked impressed when I told him what the boxes held and that I had spent the entire winter to get them filled up. The shipping came to almost ten dollars, severely cutting into my profits and I was disappointed when the mailman told me the amount. There is a cheaper way to send them but they won't get there as fast, he said.

"How much cheaper?" I asked, trying to save any money I could.

I had worked hard and desired as much money for my labor as possible.

"You can save almost half by sending it economy mail, but it might take longer. They'll still get them in two weeks or so. The boxes just have be stored in Chicago until there's enough for a truckload."

I didn't see anything wrong with that, but asked Mom if it would be okay to wait that long to pay her back.

"Sure it is son," she replied, "and look at all the money you'll save."

The wait was interminable. I hung around the mailbox every day for my Big Money. Every day I was sure it would arrive and when it didn't was sure it would the next. By the end of April, I was getting worried. Where was my big money? Mom said I should write a letter to find out if there was a problem. I wrote.

Today we think nothing of long distance. We place phone calls all over the world, holding long discussions for hours with people in other states, even on the other side of the planet. But in the 1950s, long distance phone calls were reserved for birth and death announcements, strictly for critical issues and weren't something we considered often. This wasn't important enough to spend long-distance money on.

I got an answer in about two weeks. The fur traders had never received the boxes, they said, never got them, Mr. Greene, and didn't know what happened.

Never got them? How could that be?

"Call the post office, Mom, call them, please! Please!"

It's a good thing the post office wasn't long distance. She called, spoke to someone and hung up the phone, "They'll have to look for them Clark, sometimes packages get delayed and sometimes they get lost. It's too bad we didn't insure the pelts. Maybe we should have."

We called every other day or so, but the boxes were still missing. We heard nothing for weeks, well into June, after school finished up and summer was here.

"There was nothing anyone can do," the postmaster said when I or Mother would call. "They are still looking for the boxes and will eventually find them. Don't give up hope."

Easy for him to say. He didn't have to listen to my father every single night.

"Great white hunter. Professional trapper. Daniel who?"

I did give up. Either the stuff was lost and gone forever or my attention span wouldn't allow the continued grief. I stopped calling, no more hounding Mom and the post office, and stopped lamenting my lost fortune. Didn't mope much either. Too busy to mope.

Summer was here!

The post office called sometime in July. They had found the boxes! They found the boxes! They! Found! The! Boxes! They were forwarding them to the fur company, express, the Postmaster said, because they had contributed to the problem. He went on to say I had, too, because the address wasn't exactly right, I had printed the address wrong. Part their fault, part my fault, nobody's fault really. I remember thinking it wasn't his money.

I got a registered letter from the fur trading company in about a week. All right, my Big Money at last. I could pay my folks back for the postage, have money to spend for the rest of the summer, be a big man, and have money to prove I really was a trapper. I was so excited when I got the letter that I ran around the house waving it triumphantly. BIG MONEY!

Dear Mr. Greene, July 12, 1956

We are returning the five boxes of pelts. We opened two of the boxes and regrettably found that the green furs had all begun to decay and are of no value. We are sending them back postage collect as is company policy. We regret the problem with delivery, however we cannot be responsible for the situation. We look forward to doing business in the future.

Sincerely...

"What?"

The post office called and talked to my mother about a week later and told her to please come get the five boxes. Postage was due in the amount of twelve dollars. The fur trading company hadn't been concerned about economy.

The postmaster said he wanted us to get the boxes right the heck out of his post office. He wasn't having these boxes lying around.

"You need to get them tomorrow! They STINK! They stink really terrible!"

There was some serious discussion about the pelts around the dinner table. Mom relayed the talk with the Post Office and that she or my Dad would have to go get them tomorrow, that the boxes were smelling up the whole place. Mom also mentioned the postage due, something I didn't have the money to pay for.

My Dad wanted to know, "'JustwhatinHeck' are you planning on doing with a whole bunch of rotten furs, and 'WhointheHeck' is going to pay the postage for something he 'SureintheHeck' didn't have anything to do with, except unfortunately, to be the father of." Good thing he had to take a breath.

"What a waste," he went on. "Looks like there won't be any *Big Money* coming our way. I know, maybe we'll put them in your bedroom for a while."

He laughed, but it wasn't a funny, ha-ha laugh. I'd hear about this for a long time. He wasn't going to be really mad, but he would be teasing and goading for a long while. The long while began right then and there and continued during the ride to pick up the pelts.

A man helped me and Dad put the boxes in the car and asked, "Why would anybody want whatever's in these cartons? Who sent you this stuff? I'd sure be telling somebody not to send me any more." He laughed, "Damn, that stinks!"

Dad laughed along with him, but that was just for show.

The post office guy should have ridden home with us. Dad stopped laughing before we got out of the parking lot. The trip from the post office was a whole lot quicker than the trip to. Dad held his head out the window, broke every speed limit on every road, squealed the tires when he turned the corners and muttered the whole way. I couldn't make out most of the words, but I knew he wasn't singing from the church hymnal. Those pelts did smell rotten with decay, and had reached a point of foulness that soaked through the bottoms of several boxes. We drove down Long Road, straight back to the marsh and Dad helped take the boxes out of the car.

"Drag them down there," He directed with a pointed finger. "I'll wait for you in the car."

Usually it was dead fish she'd rolled in.

Patch was always bringing stuff home. Every once in a while she would bamboozle some dog out of their bone and bring it home to bury for later. She could chew in leisure when the new theft had grown old, when the heat was off. Our backyard was testament to her snatching ability, dotted with small mounds to mark her treasures. The lawn frequently sprouted some ball she'd seen and just couldn't live without. Pilfered beach towels became part of our linen collection and kids followed her home every so often so I guess you could say she even brought them home.

But this was a first. This time Patch brought us a baby.

Mom heard her impatient woofing at the back door, summoning someone, anyone. Mom said when she opened the door to let her in Patch just sat down and woofed again. Patch didn't want to come in, she wanted to show and tell. When Mom looked closely she saw the baby. Pink and tiny, teeny-tiny. A newborn baby rabbit, barely two inches long, and so new that it was only covered in pale fuzz. Eyes still closed, ears laid back tight to its head, with a belly so thinly covered you could see dark where the innards were located. And wet. Patch had carried this baby rabbit home in her mouth. When my mother bent down to get a closer look, the bunny twitched. Still alive!

"Clark, you'd better come see what your dog brought home this time. You need to hurry son, we've got to help if we can."

I didn't hurry 'cause I was thinking of those dead smelly fish when Mom said Patch brought something home and by the time I got to the kitchen Chip and Peg were already standing next to Mom. I had to look over their heads to see. With Patch too, there wasn't much room, but I squeezed in. Mom had bundled the baby rabbit up with a tea towel for a nest and was drying dog slobber off its teeny body. Every time she stroked the towel down its flanks the little animal gave a squeak and twitched its head from side to side.

"Where'd that come from? Patch brought *that* home? That's funny."

"This little one needs some milk, get some warming up on the stove. Don't heat too much, because the baby's stomach is really tiny. Why the whole thing's no bigger than a minute. It won't take much to fill this mite up."

After the milk was warm and Mom had tested its temperature, she dipped a toothpick in the warm milk and held it in front of the bunny's nose. As soon as the baby smelled the milk, the little head raised up and it's tongue lapped the droplet right up. Mom kept at it until the baby wouldn't take any more. She loosely wrapped the towel over the baby and told Chip to take it into our room.

"Clark, you take Patch back outside. Try to find out where this baby came from. There have to be more babies; you know rabbits have more than one at a time. Patch had to dig this one up from somewhere and she probably destroyed the nest. It's important you be quick. If there are any out there they won't live long. The momma rabbit won't come back to a dug up nest."

I looked all over, spending more than an hour in fruitless search, but Patch wouldn't help. She didn't seem to be paying attention. She was always interested every other time we went looking. I don't know why but she just refused to find that nest and I eventually gave up. I sure couldn't sniff it out by myself and if she wasn't going to get involved there was nothing for me to do. No matter how I encouraged her, she wouldn't trail anything.

But Patch picked her head up quick enough when I said, "C'mon girl, if you're not gonna help, let's go home."

She started trotting back to the house and I had to run to keep up with her. She was waiting at the front door when I reached the porch but she wasn't happy about the delay. She couldn't believe it had taken me so long, a very poor showing on my part. What Patch wanted to do was get back and check on her baby rabbit. As if I should have known that. Just as soon as we got inside the door that's what she did. Went right into our bedroom and lay down next to it. Mom had fed the baby again while we were looking for the nest. When she finished Chip put the nesting towel on his bed and stayed to watch. Patch walked in, shoved him away with her head and got right up on his bed and curled around the bundle. She thought this baby was hers! Ha!

Mom came in to smile over the unlikely puppy Patch thought she found. We had our own "Ugly Dog-ling" story. Patch had claimed that baby as soon as she snatched it from the nest. Mom said Patch would soon get tired of playing mother to a rabbit, but I wasn't so sure. I thought it a little funny Patch was making such a fuss over a rabbit, but Mom said it was just her mothering instinct taking over. Oh well, at least this baby's tail didn't need to be cut off.

When the story got around the neighborhood, kids started lining up at the door to see Patch and her new "pup." Some adults came, too. Patch slept with that baby every night and watched us carefully every time we fed it until we had to put it in a cage. But once that little sucker started hopping around Mom made us keep it confined. No rabbit poop allowed in this house. Even then Patch lay down by the cage. Within several more weeks we had to put it outside with the rest of our rabbits. Patch mostly stood with her nose up against the wire mesh and so did her baby. After the move outside if I was looking for my dog I just looked by the cages.

We took Puppy out of the cage and let Patch and him chase each other around the yard. They played the game for years and Puppy never once tried to run away. They enjoyed the game no matter when and in all weather and Puppy was one of the only rabbits that ever reached old age at our house. He may have been the only one. Patch loved that orphan until it died four or five years later.

There was a gone-to-ruin brick farm house inhabited by goats on the outskirts of town, facing the main thoroughfare M-50, slightly east of US-23.

Just behind the house in a pale green and shabby mobile home lived their landlady and more goats. Lots and lots of goats. The yard, the field behind the house and trailer, the neighbors' yards and more often than not the highway too was the goat's pasture.

We'd been driving through Dundee to get to and from Grandma and

Grandpa's farm since we moved to Pointe aux Peaux. In the middle of singing "On our way to Grandma's Farm" we'd pester my father to pull over. Every time we got to the further side of town every one of us kids begged and pleaded to stop and see the goats.

"Please Dad, just for a minute? Look at all those cute little goats. Please Mom, make him stop!"

Several times we slowed down because one had darted in front of the car but we'd never met them up close and personal.

On the way home this Saturday afternoon Dad surprised us all. On the way to the farm we got his, "Enough is enough!" edict regarding our entreaties and we were still remembering his reddened face when we drove the homeward leg. We hadn't said a word this time, but he was obviously in a benevolent mood now because he pulled off the side of the road in front of the goat house. As soon as the car stopped I was sure Dad was wishing we hadn't. We had a Toggenburg on the hood, a pair of Alpines on the roof and two half and half's with their hooves tapping on the car windows. On again-off again, up again-down again, round again-round again. They were like monkeys in their antics, peering upside down from the roof or right-side up from the hood, first at the front then at the back windows, curious to see who these new people were.

Dad got spitting mad.

"Damn goats, they'll ruin the car. Get off!"

He thumped the headliner and windows at them but his noise seemed to make them all the more inquisitive. He honked the horn and they loved that too, jumping down with each blat, but leapt right back up in between. They were having such a grand time, seeming to dance over the Ford's paint job and Dad got horrifically angry. He started the car's engine with another curse but my mother stopped him with her hand on his arm.

"We're here now Jerry. Let the children get out and at least pet one or two."

"Look at what they're doing to the paint job!" my father protested.

"You children get out and lead them away from the car," Mom instructed. "Clark, you hold on to Peg's hand. Don't let the goats knock her down."

My baby sister was a beautiful child. She had long blond hair, fat ringlets and curls past her shoulders. Inventive and outgoing, I never saw a child or adult who wasn't immediately taken by her pretty face and saucy wit. She was this family's princess for sure and I loved her fiercely. I would absolutely not let anything happen to Peg.

As soon as I opened the door we had a goat in with us. It jumped in, astraddle my legs, and began nuzzling Peg's face with its lips, delighting my baby sister, but certainly not Dad. That really set my father going but Mom thought it was funny.

"Jeez, Dorothee, look at the…. Damn does that thing stink! Get that goat outta here! Dorothee, come on, for Pete's sake!"

Mom laughed but she was holding her nose while she chuckled.

"Push it back out. Carole, help your brother. Push harder, it'll go. Push son!"

Patch thought the new addition to our family was great and as soon as the goat noticed Patch they went overboard in becoming acquainted with each other. Goat and dog wrestling became a quick spectator sport for the rest of us, but Dad's voice put the contest on hold.

"Clark, get that damned goat out of there."

I was surprised Mom didn't get after him for the language, but I shoved it, held Patch back, wrestled it all at the same time and finally got it in a headlock and manhandled it outside. I instantly learned three truths about the goats.

First, it is awfully hard to get a goat to do anything it doesn't want to do, especially if it means moving backwards.

Second, these goats smelled really bad.

Third, the bad smell comes off on everything and everybody.

My father instructed, "Get out on the other side of the car. Maybe they'll get run over if they go out into the street."

Mom laughed again. "Jerry, they're just goats. They're cute. Don't you remember our Petunia?"

"I didn't think those goats were ever cute and we've driven by them for years. I didn't think they were cute when we stopped and now that I got a whiff of them I can absolutely, positively say they smell bad enough to cover up all the cute in the world."

We four scrambled out as their discussion progressed and Patch followed us before I could grab her. No sense in getting embroiled in this adult stuff, the car was stopped and none of us thought Mom would let Dad just drive off and leave us. When we four talked like that it was argument and if left unchecked always resulted in reprimands but it was a discussion when Mom and Dad did it. It really didn't matter what it was called. Mom won all of the discussions around our house. Our discussions or theirs, one way or the other, there was only ever one winner.

The goats, meanwhile, had lost all interest in the car. It wasn't moving and giggling like we were.

The goats now had different kids to play with. And a dog. The honking horn had enticed the old woman to come out of her trailer, and she waddled toward the car.

But the goats got to us first. Like antelope or deer or…. goats. Up on their hind legs in mock attack, plunging stiff-legged in play, cavorting about as if we were long lost relatives, gamboling playfully to nudge and shove us and each other about. Patch woofing, smelling, chasing each and every one, over and over again. A frenzy of goats of all sizes, rough-housing us as if we'd played together for years. Chip butted heads with some, keeping it up until a bigger one put him on his rump. I kept an eye on Peg. These animals were pretty rambunctious for a little girl of four and I shoved several away when they bumped her too hard.

Patch was embroiled in a game of "tag you're it" with all of them. She'd crouch down with forelegs splayed until one of them would charge, then dash away before they got there. We thought they were great. They were all tearing up the close cropped grass of the yard. I thought that maybe we should take one home so Patch had a whirling dervish to play with. I'd ask before we left.

Peg was enchanted. Whenever one of them slowed down a little, she'd latch on with both arms until the goat had enough quiet time and broke free. She'd wait with arms outstretched until another one ran in to fill the embrace back up. When she hugged the goat, they appeared to sprout a golden mane as her tresses flared when she pressed her face to their flanks. Peg didn't wait long for new goats. Like the rest of us kids, Peg had a real affinity for all animals and the goats sensed the kindred spirit in her. Within ten minutes she'd had her arms around a dozen different animals and some were coming back for seconds. The old woman finally made it to the flock of goats.

When she walked up to us my first thought was of my dad. If he thought the goats smelled bad he should be here with me. The fresh air had lessened the animals' odor as compared to the confines of the car, but this woman sucked the fresh out of everything. This had to be where the goats picked up their rank stench.

She smelled old and looked old. Bent over with age in a filthy blue dress, her face and neck were crusted with oily grime in all the creases, wattles and crevasses. I imagined I could see the waves of odor rising off of her like a cartoon of Limburger cheese. The woman's hair, greasy yellowish-white, was stringy, snarled and appeared not to have been combed or brushed. Ever. Her feet were sort of shoved into black slippers and I almost couldn't tell where slipper left off and her grimy skin began. I held back a gag when she moved in to admire my baby sister and moved us upwind just as soon as I could. Carole retreated to the car in a blink. Even Patch made short work of her usual sniffing routine. When I looked closely I thought I saw some movement in the woman's greasy hair but at first believed it was my imagination. I looked again, holding Peg away while getting just as close as I dared, upwind or not.

It looked like her scalp was *moving*!

It was moving! Jeezie Peezie! Crawling! Creeping! *Bugs!*

"Oh My God!" I hollered, knowing I'd have to pay later for the cuss.

I scooped up Peg, gave my brother a shove in the direction of the car, whistled for Patch and backpedaled, one arm around my sister's waist, the other out defensively in case that filthy woman got closer. She followed me right to the car, but as soon as I tossed Peg into the back seat, I shut the door. I rolled down the window and kept whistling for Patch. She was having too much fun with these new playmates. The woman took up a position by Dad's open window. I saw him swallow an urp and I couldn't believe it, but he didn't roll the window up. The old woman started talking to Dad.

I was mortified.

"Mom, she's got *BUGS* in her hair!" I hissed between my teeth.

My mother must not have believed me or misunderstood me.

"What'd you say son?"

"SHE'S GOT SOMETHING CRAWLING ALL OVER HER HEAD!"

My teeth were clenched as I hissed the loudest stage whisper ever heard.

"She's got what son?" my mother asked.

Mom still wasn't hearing or believing. But Carole heard me and gave a shriek.

"BUGS!"

I couldn't stand it.

I yelled, "She's got Goddamn bugs, Mom! All over her head! BUGS!"

My mother reached over the seat and slapped my face.

"You don't *ever* need to talk like that. I heard you." But in another second she'd said all in one breathe: "Goodbye. Thanks for letting us look at your goats. Clark, get your dog in here. We have to go now. Roll the window up, Jerry. Let's go home. I said roll the window up, Jerry! Pass Peg up here to me. You three take your clothes off. Right down to the underwear! No arguments, thank you. Clark, you check Chip. Carole, you check Clark. Then Clark switch and check Carole. Let's go Jerry. The traffic's clear on this side. For land sakes go, Jerry! Go!"

I was lucky I finally got Patch's attention. We were in a rush like never before. She came up to the car, but she was followed by the entire herd, and

Patch didn't want to go just yet. I eased the door open, grabbed Patch by the scruff and squeezed her through the door while I fended off her new friends with my foot. Patch smelled like Airedale and goat. The goat was far worse. I shoved her over the back seat into the back end of the station wagon.

My family wouldn't have considered themselves modest. I had seen both parents and all my siblings naked on several occasions. After a bath Mom would dash through the house with a towel on her head and another around her waist. Chip loved to run naked and had escaped out into the subdivision on any number of days. We took baths in the lake and were expected to get bodies and privates well scrubbed. We kids held conversations with one another while seated on the toilet. But today we set new heights in baring it all.

Mom stripped Peg down to bare-nitchey in about three seconds flat. While she was getting Peg's clothes off she somehow got her own blouse off, too, so she could track any wanderers who might migrate. It didn't take the rest of us much longer to get our skivvies exposed, even though three in the back seat doesn't lend well to disrobing. Despite complaints and elbows, I soon started back ruffling Chips hair and Carole did the same for me.

"I got one! Chip's got a hundred!" I cried. "What do I do with it Mom?"

"Just flick them out the window," my mother ordered. "Make Patch lay down and throw that old blanket over her, son. Keep looking."

Mom had draped Peg's legs over the back of the seat laying her down face up on the front seat. Peg's toes wiggled in protest but Mom's determination won that battle just like all the rest. The car was filled with Ughs! and Yuks!, all sorts of noises of dismay and disgust. I saw my father open the vent window wide so the wind would blow all the critters away from him and edge closer to the door. Everybody was scratching and itching either for reason or imagination. It seemed contagious. I scratched Chip, Chip scratched Carole. Carole scratched me and I scratched me. Mom tweaked, picked and tweezed Peg all over, turning her over this way and that, but gave a more horrified gasp when she started looking through her hair.

"Oh no!"

Mom held up and pulled apart Peg's Shirley Temple golden sausage curls, opening up a view of her scalp.

"Jerry, she's got hundreds of lice all over her! You've got to stop at the drug store. The closest one, I don't care which one."

The entire trip home and the wait in the drug store parking lot was spent busily picking vermin off one another and trying to crawl out of our skins. Us three in the back seat had done well enough so that more searching than picking was going on now although we were still finding some. Mom's arm was still sailing out the window with regularity and from those actions and her facial expressions it appeared she wasn't gaining much ground.

When Dad climbed into the car with the bag of chemical defenses from the pharmacy, Mom said, "What took you so long? Did you see anyone we know?"

Not one of her finer moments.

The drug store was only ten minutes from the house and when we got home my mother really went into action. "Go tie your dog up this minute," Mom commanded before the car stopped moving.

Mom and Dad, everybody got right down to their birthday suits in the side yard, buck naked, and despite the screening of lilac bushes, this was a definite first for the family. Probably for the neighbors as well. Carole, almost fourteen and already busty like Mom, complained bitterly, but nobody faced down my mother when she was like this. Clothes were thrown in a pile to be burned later, another very radical move on this group's part.

We didn't get rid of clothing in this house and I had my father's pants to prove it. Adults, teenage daughter and all the rest made believe we were invisible, but we weren't. My mother carried Peg through the door like some soldier wounded in battle or some little lost lamb.

Water on the stove to boil in every existing pot and pan we owned. Fine toothed store-bought combs handed out with instructions about dipping them in the bowls of alcohol between every stroke. Carefully reading aloud the instructions for the special shampoo and repeating in case somebody missed something the first time.

Mom stationed herself at the bathroom door while we lathered, scrubbed, lathered, scrubbed, lathered, and scrubbed again until I was sure the top of my head had turned soft and mushy. Then combing, this way, that way, the other way, creating and destroying dozens of new hair styles with every repetition. Start all over, check in and around groins, butt cracks and armpits, lather with soap in all crevices and cracks, swab ear and nose openings too. Check your navel. Every one is still naked. Nobody cares and nobody notices. Do all the first parts and second parts again. There will be no further contamination in this house.

"They've laid eggs already!" Mom shrieked. "Her hair, it's full of lice eggs! My God, Jerry we'll have to shave her head!"

With a shriek, Peg tried to get away. If Mom hadn't stopped her she'd have run down the street naked as a jaybird. She started to wail. It took both my parents several long moments to assure her they wouldn't cut her hair off but

I couldn't do anything to comfort Peg.

I was too stunned. My mother said *God* and she wasn't praying.

I was also having a difficult time imagining my younger sister being bald.

Our infestations were nothing compared to Peg's. She had been doing all the goat hugging and nuzzling. I figured those pests were tired of tough old goat and literally jumped at the chance for a nice tender four-year-old. I thought they probably called to one another as they leaped.

"Hey you guys! Look over here! Fresh meat! Not goat!"

The rest of us were rid fairly quickly of the parasites. There was a desperate battle for Peg and it took a long time for Mom to finally declaim her lice-less. As it turned out my sister got to keep her long golden tresses, but I don't think anybody ever took them for granted again. Mom scrubbed and combed Peg's hair two or three times a day for a week before she was sure the lice were defeated.

Patch took some heavy labor too. We didn't usually trim Patch's curly coat. Our everyday grooming practice was limited to burr and mud removal, currying her thoroughly to remove any possible hitch-hiker.

Not this time. The day after our infestation, Mom got out her hair cutting shears and gave Patch a Butch. All over. I thought she looked like an Army recruit, a Marine. Patch wasn't too happy about it either, but nobody crossed Mom at our house. Not even my dog. After the haircut we spent the entire day bathing her. Over and over and over again.

All four of us kids were sworn to secrecy regarding our pestilence; it would never do to let the world know we'd been plagued with lice.

Cleanliness and Godliness. And of course public opinion.

When the episode's disgust had faded a little, we kids all decided it was all Dad's fault. It surely was his idea.

We didn't ask him to stop that time.

Chapter 17

Traditions

We had candles for each evening meal.

And every night Dad said, "And they're delicious, too."

We gathered nightly around the dining room table, a mandate, either of Mom's wishes to allocate time for all of her children or to check us for signs of new injury. Fuel intake was the primary reason of course, but five of the family used the time for story telling, recounts of close calls or the opportunity to listen to the variation of a newly modified rule. Our meal times were important as a solidifier of family discourse and as an opportunity of listening to Peg's newest imaginary travels. Unfortunately, with the exception of Dad's nightly repetitious humor, he was largely an observer of the clatter that accompanied our meals.

Dad stayed at the sidelines, I think, because he often appeared slightly surprised and overwhelmed at the uproar which seemed to accompany dinner. I also believe he enjoyed his chosen role of being the sternly disciplined and loved-from-a-distance father, and deliberately perpetuated this feeling of seclusion even as we sat at the same table. His reluctance may have stemmed from many things, but whatever it was, Dad wore it like a suit of impregnable armor. My father had forgotten how to have fun.

One night while we were finishing up the three-thousand, eight-hundred and twenty-second or so around the table dinner, with a generous helping of Peg's flying skunks, we were interrupted. In jerky and uncertain flight, a small pale green insect fluttered into the room and made a circuit of the table. No one identified the blurring tiny wings until it settled on the table cloth.

"Baby Preying Mantises!" Peg, Chip and I shouted simultaneously.

We didn't ask to be excused, although the request was definitely a part of

Miss Manners training. Three chairs scooted back, ten feet (remember Patch) jammed though the dining room doorway and we pounded through the kitchen to my bedroom.

Chip and Peg and I continually brought home amphibian eggs and insect larvae of all types. Cocoons, chrysalis, egg cases, pupae, frog and spider eggs, pollywogs, and ichneumon wasp egg infested caterpillars all found places or leaning spots in our bedroom. Mom encouraged and taught us how and where to look, marked her calendar with likely dates of transformation and when we couldn't be quieted in any other way, frequently tricked us into watching for the "it'll be any-time-now" emergences of folded wings or pinhead-sized bugs. We had an ant farm we made ourselves complete with ant-lions, because we liked the ferocity of their attacks on the ant population. We had butterfly and moth collections, knew the difference between "good and bad" bugs and could identify every insect in Michigan at distance of twenty paces.

Right now we had hundreds of baby preying mantises all over the bedroom and living room, and hundreds more oozing out of three ruptured brown egg cases. Walls, floors, bedclothes, turtle bowl (which he was certainly enjoying) and closet were alive with the quarter inch long babies. Perfect miniature replicas of the adults, each equipped with extended forelegs, transparent wings and the look of tiny green assassins. A small wave of them had escaped out the open top of the converted aquarium in which we normally kept our "I hope I'm there to watch" hatchings, and had crawled or flown through the bedroom door. The one that flew to the dining room must have been an advance scout because dozens had followed it through the house.

Preying mantises headed up the category of GOOD BUGS because they were so cool in their ferocity and eating methods. We'd been called by Mom to watch one devour a BAD BUG on many occasions and were always on the lookout to discover one of our own. Being the first to see one in the wild was almost a rite of passage for the Greene kids and we gathered their eggs cases with a devotion bordering on mania.

Mom thought this preying-mantis's excursion was delightful. She quickly joined us in the bedroom and finger-herded several onto a sheet of paper and carried them into the kitchen. We examined them under a magnifying glass, gently lifting their forelegs with a toothpick for closer study. Mom pointed out the abdomen, leg joints and attachment and we all watched as the tiny heads swiveled to take in all the giants surrounding it. We were enthralled.

My father was not.

"Geez, Dorothee!" he complained. "They're all over my chair! They're in MY house!"

172

"Yeah Dad, aren't they great!" I exclaimed from the kitchen. "They are so neat."

"We'll take care of them, Jerry," Mom soothed. "Why don't you sit down and read the paper."

It wasn't a question, but Dad didn't need any encouragement. Usually when he was in the living room, his body was completely hidden behind a newspaper or his eyes narrowed out from over a book. Although I don't recall ever having a book discussion with him, Dad was an avid reader but I think there was more to it than just a love of literature. Another of our family's Miss Manners rules of etiquette disallowed interruption when another person was engrossed in reading material and my dad used this as an additional layer to his armor.

My father sat down in HIS chair and picked up HIS paper.

WHOP! His hand made a hollow sound as he slapped the chair's arm.

"There's one you don't have to worry about," he flatly stated.

"Jerry, this is good for the children. I told you we'll take care of them all," Mom charmed. "This is how they learn. A few baby bugs won't bother you. Read your paper, dear. We'll get them all."

Instead my father launched himself out of the chair and began swatting them with the newspaper he'd rolled up. *THWAK, THWAK.*

"They're in MY house!" Dad roared, sounding offended. *THWAK.* Methodically he began inspecting the walls and floors as he walked to our still insect-issuing bedroom door. *THWAK.* He closed it with a slam. *THWAK.*

"That'll keep them in there at least," Dad triumphed. *THWAK.*

From the kitchen I saw him swatting at bugs and at bugs that weren't there, just for effect. *THWAK.*

THWAK.

THWAK. THWAK, THWAK.

"Jerry, just sit back down dear," Mom cajoled. "Come on children. Let's get them gathered up and put outside where they'll only have to worry about natural predators."

Mom wasn't above a little sarcasm, but she floated out of the kitchen and led Dad back to his chair, while she unrolled the newspaper she'd secreted from his hand.

My father, satisfied now with his re-affirmation as household head and contented that Mom had at least momentarily abandoned us to tend to him, sat back down and re-erected his newspaper shield.

We stayed up late that night catching the babies and carefully escorting them under cupped hands to release in freedom. Dozens of trips. Mom insisted we put them in garden spots, hidden from birds.

"So they'll have a chance to grow up and kill BAD BUGS," Mom explained.

Dad eventually went to bed while we carried hundreds of individuals or small groups outside and watched them scamper to bushes or tree trunks, scattering the fragile babies about our yard. As the clock struck midnight Mom called a halt to our bug catching.

"We'll look again in the morning," Mom bed-timed us. "We've got most of them, I think. Clark Malcolm, you make sure that screen stays on the aquarium."

We found a few more the next morning and liberated those as well, but when we looked outside for the ones we'd released in the dark, we found none at all. All gone.

My father continued to inspect HIS house for weeks after the episode, repeatedly hoping for some more babies to swat, but he didn't find any. Including us. Each of us learned at a young age to tread lightly when Dad was brooding. My father stalked the house whenever he felt threatened, especially when he had a captive audience and we knew the results of a failure to watch him closely.

We continued to gather eggs and pupae of every conceivable type, but were much more careful about their confinement. Our bedrooms were filled with every conceivable item or animal we were strong enough or brave enough or secretive enough to drag home. We loved each birthing and each creation.

Dad did not.

Dad went first. My Uncle Dave went next.

Now it was my turn for duty. I was going for two whole weeks all by myself, my first real experience at staying away from home. I had been to other kids' houses for a night over and stayed with grandmas and grandpas at either the Farm or 22022 Indian Trails in Detroit, depending on which side got me, but this was going to be very different.

Camp Birkett was a YMCA camp located in Pinckney, Michigan.

I thought I'd have to pack up enough gear to survive in the wilderness. Live on my own in the wild. My mother said she'd help.

Dad still had the footlocker he used when he went, his name and address printed inside the lid. My Uncle Dave's name was there too, with his particulars printed right along side my father's. I got to print my name and stuff with a china marker so it wouldn't wash off.

174

"This is what a tradition is," my father explained. "Maybe some day you'll send your son here too."

I didn't know what son he was referring to. I wasn't sure how a person went about getting one and didn't even know if I would ever want one of my own. There were sure times when I thought my father was sorry he had me. I remembered several times when he said he should have sold me to the slavers. Why, he said it just last week when I made Chip, the little sissy, cry so bad.

Dad wasn't saying sell him now though. I was going camping. This would be high adventure, full of boys my own age, with counselors to organize activities. They'd help me build character. This was a bit confusing, too. Both of my parents called me a character, lots of times and when they said it they weren't always happy. Why would I want to build another one? Why would they want me to? I was going to have to find out a whole lot at this camp.

Mom packed the trunk. I didn't even have to worry about it and she made a diagram of what was where and how many so I didn't have to search when I needed a clean pair of underwear or new socks. Sweater and sweatshirt, toothbrush and paste, jeans and more jeans, t-shirts and one "good" shirt "just in case" and my old nasty tennis shoes "in case you go to a marsh" and towels and my bathing suit, a little jar of Bag-Balm and some band-aids.

"I put a bar of Fels-Naptha soap in there too, son. If you have any tracks in your undies, you be sure to scrub them clean."

I wondered if all mothers were as concerned about underwear as mine was. I figured I could ask some of those kids at camp. My mom seemed fixated on the cleanliness of my underwear and my soul. Her aim was for them to remain lily-white and she kept close tabs on both. I thought I kept the pair up pretty well, although I wasn't yet sure what my soul was. I figured they were equally important 'cause Mom never let up on either. I always checked my underwear at night. Being a good Christian son I already learned the wisdom of hiding any uncertainty from Mom about God stuff. I kept my ignorance to myself, but I worked on it with "Now I lay me down to sleep…"

We drove way past Manchester to the camp. Man, this was really far. The entrance to the camp had a big wooden sign that arched over the road into it.

CAMP BIRKETT, with *YMCA* underneath.

We had to park waaaay down the road there were so many cars at the front. Dad and I had to carry my trunk all the way from the car, switching sides when my arms got tired, up to a table marked REGISTRATION.

There were boys just like me running everywhere. Mom, Dad and I stood behind a man and a redheaded kid who turned around and said he was Samuel Thomas Knight Junior, but to call him Sammy. When I told him my name, his father turned too. My dad stretched out to shake hands and said, "Did you go here too?" to the kid's father. He answered, "Yes I did" and before I knew it his dad and my dad were hugging one another! What?

"Sammy?"

"Jerry?"

"It can't be."

"I don't believe it!"

"How many years?"

"Twenty-five or twenty-six now, it must be."

"Imagine that."

"Twenty-five years ago."

They tossed the words back and forth so fast I almost couldn't follow, my head wagging, trying to stay with this. Sammy (now Mister) Knight and Jerry (now Dad) Greene went to this camp at the same time! They were flabbergasted. So were the moms who introduced themselves to each other. Nobody was more amazed than I. It was the first time I ever considered that my dad was once a kid, just like me.

My dad had been a kid. Amazing.

I shook hands with his dad and Sammy shook hands with mine. Everybody was laughing and grinning, looking at faces all over again. We were suddenly all old friends. In an instant. This was what tradition must mean.

Sammy now Samuel said, "Let's try to get the boys in the same cabin" and Jerry now Dad thought that was a great idea. The guys at the registration table put us in Wolverine, just fine with me. Wolverines were tough. We got nametags for our shirts and Mom pinned mine on. Robert, our counselor, was standing at the cabin door when Dad and I carried my footlocker up.

"Hi...Clark? You got a nickname?

I shook my head.

"We'll have to do something about that. Nice to meet you."

He shook hands with Dad and Mom and they came in to look at the cabin. Six bunk beds lined each side of the cabin. Some already had boys sitting on them or clothes lying across the blankets.

"Pick one out son; we're going to go now." My father said.

I couldn't help thinking, already?

They said goodbye, be good and have fun. "We'll see you in two weeks."

When they left I got a big lump in my throat. Mom and Dad were leaving and I was staying here. What if they didn't come back? What if this was really a slaver's camp in disguise? What if…?

"Let's Go!" Sammy grabbed me by the arm and hollered, "We got to muster up! Down by the flag pole!"

We took off, running as only we could do.

"WOLVERINES!" We screamed, wind-milling our arms like propellers. No Mom! No Dad! Freeeeeeeeeeeeeeeeeee!

"YOU BOYS GET IN LINE BEHIND YOUR COUNSELLERS!" blasted a loudspeaker.

Our counselor, Robert, was waving his arms. Pushing and jostling and shoving and laughing all in a row we stood behind.

"Straighten it up now boys, get in a straight line. Does that look straight? C'mon, c'mon. That's better now, a little more. There. Good."

A man with a megaphone got on a wooden platform and told us what the camp was all about. Swimming and canoeing and archery (oh boy!) and "Capture the Flag" and making fires and reptiles and wildlife and hiking and games and everything else. There was so much boy noise the megaphone didn't help very much, but then he really hollered.

"YOU WOLVERINES! DINNER DUTY TONIGHT AND TOMORROW! If you boys can't keep quiet and listen, you can serve and clean up the mess hall!"

Everybody had been yelling, but nobody was now. Why did we get picked?

"Don't worry about it guys, we're just the example. He does it to one cabin on every first day at camp. It's just to show you who the boss is," our counselor laughed. "It's our turn in the barrel." He laughed again. "I might even tell you what that means if you guys are good."

Everybody was pointing at the Wolverines. Laughing at our group. The man on the platform began again.

"Everyone back to their cabins." A huge groan rose from boy mouths. "Get your suits on and report down at the lake."

The moan turned to a cheer. "Yee-hah!"

We marched back to our cabin. Where do we change?

"Strip it off right here boys." Robert said. "Don't worry, you all look the same. You want to hurry here boys. First cabin at the beach gets to start first."

"Start what? I thought we were going swimming," I said to Robert.

He told us that first there would be a test to see which areas each of us could swim.

"Some of you will swim shallow, some will swim mid point and for those who can swim well enough there's a raft pretty far out," he continued as the group quick walked to the lake. "And if you want to be able to go on the canoe trip next week, you have to swim four lengths of the dock without touching, the same distance to the raft."

Ok, I could swim. I learned how to swim two years ago, right at Kress Park, jumping off the big raft. No problem, I went swimming all the time at the beach. Swimming was easy.

We weren't the first ones back but everybody got to go in the water anyway and soon enough we were all splashing and fooling around. Robert told us to listen for the whistle, that we would be next. We couldn't go out of the area marked by white floats and it wasn't deep enough to swim here but who cared. We were playing catch and ball tag, throwing the rubber ball to hit someone "it." This was fun enough for anyone.

A whistle shrilled and the Wolverines all trooped out to the dock. It was all white with one board standing out, painted red, about twenty feet from the shoreline. The swimming instructor, Jim, told us the water at the red starting line was about four feet deep but got deeper quickly. Two times the length of the dock meant you could swim in the second area marked by rope-connected buoys, and four times meant unlimited swimming out to the raft for the diving board and you were automatically allowed to go on the overnight canoe trip next week. Those boys who could not make the two lengths were confined to the shallow area until they were able to swim better. There would be swimming lessons for all those who wanted them and lifesaving lessons for those boys who could already swim well.

Wow, this wasn't like swimming at all. This was more like school for swimming.

Lessons were starting. We had to jump feet first off the dock. It was the last time we could touch the bottom while the test went on. I jumped. I started swimming along the length of the dock and Jim walked alongside while I splashed and stroked. I made it to the end and panicked just a little when there was no bottom under me.

"You're okay, keep swimming."

I swam some more, but my swimming technique began to falter. The "no bottom" kept floating to my mind. It was deep here. What if I had to rest? At our beach, I could always put my feet on the bottom. Never even thought about no bottom before. There had always been a bottom. When I got back to the starting line, I grabbed the side of the dock.

"Okay, you did good. Who's next?"

I started to protest even though I was tired and a little unnerved about deep water.

"No, the rule is no touching anything. That means the bottom and the dock too. I think you need a little practice anyhow. Swimming lessons are every day, you'll get better."

Nobody else in our cabin made all four laps either, but it was far. About half made two and some of the boys couldn't swim well enough to get that far. When we were through Jim said we had all done very well, even those who hadn't completed two laps.

"The distance is 75 feet to the end of the dock, boys. If you could have made all four laps, you'd have swum 300 feet. That's a long way for ten and eleven year olds."

"Hah! I'm only nine and a half!" I cheered to myself.

"In the morning we'll have lots of instructors to help you. You'll all get better before you go home. Some of you may even make lifeguard, but you'll have to work really hard to do it." Jim handed out colored tags with pins. "Whites have to stay in the shallow water and Reds can swim the middle area. Nobody here gets blue. Yet. You better not get caught in an area you haven't qualified for. I'll take away your swimming privileges for the rest of your stay. No exceptions. You can all go back and swim some more now. Stay where you belong."

We all ran back and played. We played in the shallow area with Robert, not wanting to separate from our new cabin-mates. We were having so much fun it didn't matter where we were. Jim said we could lose privileges if we were caught only once. Rules just like those at home, no second chances. Maybe this is where Dad learned that. Did Mom come here too? Nope, this was a Young Men's Christian Association camp. I was surprised they even let Mom stand in line to register me. I'd ask somebody about that.

Robert called us out of the water, but we were the only ones who had to leave.

"Dinner duty guys, you remember?" he said first and then to our immediate groans. "Our turn where?"

"IN THE BARREL!" We screamed back.

"Let's go boys, you're about to become waiters and busboys. No sneaking bites either," Robert told us. "I'll be watching."

Dinner duty meant lots of things. We had to carry platters of food to the tables. We had to pour milk and water from pitchers. We had to run back and forth, refill and re-carry more platters and pitchers and refill and re-carry. Kids can eat. Kids can eat a lot. Dinner duty also meant two more things. We had to clean up after everybody and scrape the plates into a big galvanized trashcan. We didn't eat until everyone else was done and everything was cleaned up.

When we finally got all the plates cleared someone in the kitchen staff brought food out for us. Watching others eat is a sure fire appetite stimulator. We were famished and that food got crammed and stuffed and chewed and swallowed, really hogging it down. We hollered good-naturedly to the kitchen, "More food. More!" They came running with more. I thought dinner duty was pretty good. Look at all the food we got. Maybe we could do it every day. We were stuffed plumb full. No room. Robert told us there was a small benefit for this duty. In exchange for the work, we get unlimited desserts.

"YAHOO!"

When another person from the kitchen brought us six whole banana cream pies, I was sure we should. I'd do this for a living. We each didn't get pieces of pie either. We all just dug right in, Robert too. This was living! Yeah!

After dinner there was a canoeing safety movie and a campfire with scary ghost stories after that. We got more rules at the campfire too, about demerits for kids and cabins. There were plenty of rules. By the time we got to bed it was late, but most of us were too excited to go right to sleep. Robert said any talking after lights out was demerits. Oh, okay.

"Goodnight Sammy."

"Night, Clark."

"RISE AND SHINE! RISE AND SHINE! Last one dressed and out has to sweep!"

I just managed to beat one kid out the door. Hah!

We were up first for dinner duty, and it apparently included breakfast and lunch too.

"Extra desserts now too?" someone asked.

Robert told him. "Just at dinner, don't push your luck."

Before anybody ate, we got announcements for the day's activities. Canoe safety held in the shallow area. Michigan wildlife with a Department of Natural Resources officer down by the fire pit. Swimming lessons at 10:30 for those interested. Archery and volleyball and baseball and horseshoes after lunch and a rest period. There would be another campfire at night and the counselors were going to put on a skit. Our counselors would be awarding us points for our play, a grading system that could qualify us for a "Secret Society" which we could join if we did good stuff and amassed enough points.

Breakfast was crazy. There were stacks of French toast and pancakes that looked three feet tall and syrup in gigantic containers. Bacon and sausages heaped on greasy napkin covered plates and big pitchers of milk. The kids ate breakfast much faster than dinner, laughing and hollering and shouting for the Wolverines to "Hey! Hurry up, we're staaaarrrrving over here!" I'd have liked to bonk a couple of them with an empty platter, but it really was fun. It wasn't going to be our turn forever. We hurried to clean up and bolted our food when we ate. There was a whole day to do here. Let's not waste any time.

The Wolverines went back to change into our swimsuits. Everybody stripped down and changed quickly. Robert was right. Everybody looked the same. Public disrobing was old stuff the second time around and two kids started a towel fight when they were butt naked. Robert threatened demerits but everybody knew we'd try that again when he wasn't around. We were sure a few demerits never hurt anybody. The canoe safety was interesting. We learned to get in and out safely and what to do if it capsized. Everybody had to take several turns and it took a long time for everybody to finish. Some of the kids were pretty funny getting out. I was one of them when I went right over the other side with a splash. We didn't do any paddling or steering stuff. There'd be more tomorrow.

I loved the lecture on snakes and turtles. The D.N.R. officer had a leatherback turtle, a huge snapping turtle that he held high by the tail, several painted turtles and a box turtle, too. I identified each turtle at the same time he did. He touched the snapper's nose with a pretty thick branch and crunch! That hooked jaw snapped it right in two.

"They can bite a finger off the same way."

I knew that.

He put the turtles away and started with the snakes and I moved closer still. He had two or three fox snakes, a blue racer, some regular old garter snakes and a hognose snake. He said people sometimes mistake the hognose for a rattlesnake. Then he uncovered a timber rattlesnake and most everybody stepped waaaay back. Not me. I told everyone of my encounter with the Massasauga rattlesnake. I showed the ranger where I had been bitten and held up my hand so others could see but most of the boys were too far away. The punctures had faded to tiny white spots long ago: you could still see them but you had to look close. I'd show 'em later. The officer seemed pretty impressed with my scars.

I helped him milk the rattlesnake, holding a jar with rubber over the mouth while he pressed the snake's venom sacs against the rim. Two streams of yellowish liquid pooled at the bottom. "Who wants a taste? It tastes just like orange juice"

"Me, me. I do, I do!" He asked me if I had any cuts or sores in my mouth and I said no. I took a little sip, unsure.

He laughed, "Go ahead, it won't hurt you.

I took some more and when no one else wanted any, I drank the rest. He was right. It tasted just like the "extra can of water-added" orange juice I got at home. Weak. The officer told me I was a regular "little professor" when I inquired about how they made anti-venom.

Robert, my counselor laughed. "That's it, Clark. That's your camp name. You're now the Professor."

The officer had a hawk that couldn't fly, a raggedy old beaver and a red fox in a carrying case that snapped when your hand got close. This guy was cool and he wore a gun. Cooler.

Swimming lessons went okay, but I didn't get to do much swimming. I learned instead how to put my face in the water turning it to the side for a breath, pretending to swim, all the while bending over in waist deep water. Stroke, stroke, breathe, stroke, stroke and breathe. Over and Over. I swallowed a lot of water before I got that part right. I didn't swim much and didn't even try for distance, but my instructor, Fred, said it was all a part of swimming. I needed more practice. We had plenty of time to qualify for the raft and the canoe trip.

"Don't worry."

My cabin served lunch and I had never seen so many peanut butter and jelly sandwiches in my life. Great towers of white bread with jelly oozing out and pitchers and more pitchers of milk. Everything was easy to hand out and we got to eat right along with all the rest. This group was noisy now that we were eating with them, but I hadn't heard a thing when I was serving. Lots of kids talked with their mouths full at these tables, and it was pretty fun when I tried it, too. Mom wouldn't be pleased but nobody here would tell. After lunch and a twenty minute rest period, there was another rule. We had a designated letter writing time.

"Buddy boys, you better be writing a letter home. Hand them in to me. Demerits if you don't."

Baseball was great and we whipped the Raccoon cabin by a million runs. I had the best score in archery, way far ahead of everybody else. Robert said that winning at archery would go toward secret society stuff. We were done with dinner duty at last, but the spaghetti we had that night must have been the dickens to keep up with. The skit was funny, all about this crazy doctor operating on different people behind a sheet. This Wolverine was just about wiped out by that time. The day had been full to the brim. They were keeping us so busy there was no time that wasn't filled right up, no time for mischief. It was all mischief, I thought as we marched back to the cabin. Sammy threw his arm over my shoulder as we walked back to our cabin. I just wanted the bed.

"RISE AND SHINE! RISE AND SHINE! Last one dressed and out has to sweep!"

When we got outside all the other cabins except the Fox cabin were standing in the road to mess hall. Fox had the dinner duty. All right! One of those kids had the biggest mouth. Turn about is fair play. I ragged him good when he carried us a plate of scrambled eggs. His ears turned really red. Turn about is fun, too.

New rules today. There would be an Honor Table at each meal. The cabin that had done the best for the day got to sit there for all meals on the following day. They got served first and dinner duty had to really be nice to them too. The Camp Commander told us the camp looked like a pigsty and we all laughed but he wasn't fooling. Everybody was going on a hike today but we were going to dress the whole camp first. We would rake roads, pick up trash, clean cabins, even spruce up the small wooded areas along the paths and behind the cabins. There would be an inspection and the hiking would be lead off by the cabin that did the best job the first time. Everybody else would have to continue working until their areas were judged spick and span. Only when our Camp Commander, Mr. Wilson, was satisfied would we be able to set off on the excursion.

It took a long time to make that man happy.

We were going to march along the lake, find a treasure designated for our cabin and bring it back. We weren't supposed to open the small chests when we found them but carry them back to campfire tonight. There were maps and clues for us to follow and find. The cabin with the best time got to sit at the Honor Table in the dining hall. We would be timed the whole way there and back and there were extra points for cabins and boys that could be earned by spotting wildlife or naming plants and trees. We would win this one and the Wolverines took off running, leaving Robert behind to holler, "STOP, WAIT, NO RUNNING!"

We didn't win and we didn't care. We had a ball.

At swim practice after the hike, I swam three laps before I gave up. That breathing stuff really did help. I could swim almost as good as Tarzan. Sammy made all four. I was going to have to do better if I wanted to keep up.

Sammy and I were becoming real close, completely disregarding our friendship's young age. Sammy had a nickname, too. Everybody got one in our cabin. Sammy's new surname was Red. It just couldn't have been anything else with the brilliant red crew cut he had. I could spot him a mile away, but there was seldom more than a few feet between us. Our counselor Robert already referred to us as the Bobbsy Twins even though we didn't look anything alike. The Professor and Red. Red and the Professor. Even the other cabin captains knew we were buddies. Red could run faster than me but I was better at archery. He waited for me to catch up lots, because we ran everywhere. I showed him how to draw and shoot the bow better and he got extra points for archery. He was better at swimming but we were about the same when it came to falling out of the canoe.

We swapped shirts and stories. I had a dog and he didn't but his folks kept promising him one someday. He didn't have any brothers or sisters and I said there were a few extra at my house and I'd give him one of each if he wanted. We told each other lies and wished we could be brothers, which wasn't a fib. I told Sammy, Red, my twin, I knew a way for us to become better than brothers but I didn't have a knife. He told me he'd brought one even though it was against the rules and his parents didn't know. Perfect. We would be blood brothers, in a solemn ceremony only for the true of heart. Indian style. I told him all about it and he couldn't wait.

"Tonight, right after Robert falls asleep," I whispered. "Tonight."

I said I was going to ask his dad if he'd take Chip in trade and he thought that'd be just great.

That night after lights out, we snuck through the cabin door and walked down by the lake. Our counselor was fast asleep, mouth wide open and making funny growling noises. The camp was asleep, no sounds, no lights in Camp Command or the dining hall. There was a light at the end of the dock and we sat Indian fashion on our haunches facing one another. Sammy handed me his knife and his hand, extended palm up for the cut. He didn't say ouch when I cut him and I was just as brave when it was my turn for slicing. It sure did burn though. We gripped each other's hands and pledged lives and deaths and I tied them together with a loop from one of my shoestrings. Brothers. Better than that. We remained on the dock for a long time not talking any more until we knew our blood had mixed enough. We snuck back to the cabin and I fell fast asleep.

184

Robert saw the cuts on both our palms in the morning and asked first Red and then me what had happened. We both said, "I don't know," and acted surprised to see the cuts ourselves, but he let it drop and didn't insist on an answer. He looked at us both and laughed a little, looked at our hands again and we all marched to breakfast.

The days all twirled together, mixing and merging into one long adventure. I managed to make four laps by the first Saturday but it was a struggle and Fred said I really should practice some more before I swam out to the dock. The cabins played battle-ball elimination and the Antelopes had this kid who could throw really hard. He got everybody out and they won. I showed my cabin how to make fire with a bow and stick and Robert was astonished. Extra points! The Wolverines were on the Blue Team in Capture the Flag, the camp divided even-steven for the game. We got on old school buses to travel out to a hilly area and set up our Blue flag to be defended and their Red one to capture. We flew up and down, running between hills tearing off the enemy's red arm ribbons when we could and they did the same to us. Somebody snatched that Red flag when they weren't looking and screamed the whole way back to our hill. We ran interference for him, keeping red ribbons away. Blue Team won! Wolverines! Yeah! Blue Team! More points. Everybody slept good that night and I bet nobody even got up to pee.

Midway into the second week, on Wednesday night some counselors snuck into our cabin in the middle of the night. They were good at it too, cause I didn't hear a thing until it was too late. A hand went over my mouth and I was lifted out of my bunk. I squirmed and struggled and I would have screamed too but for almost getting smothered.

Oh No! I knew It! My parents had sold me!

When the monster carried me out of the cabin I saw Red and another kid Billy, who was really great at canoeing and baseball standing out in the moonlight with blindfolds on. Oh. I knew what this was. Those big guys were really good. I didn't hear a thing when they snatched Red and Billy either.

Someone slipped a blindfold around my eyes too and whispered, "one sound Professor and you're out. Understand?"

I nodded.

"Turn to your right and put your arm out. Don't let go of that shoulder. Got it?"

I nodded again. This was Secret Society stuff. Undercover in our underwear. We'd never tell.

We were led blind for a long time, stumbling and falling over stuff. Pillows

185

and boxes and a canoe turned over one time, an obstacle course for Pete's sake. Somebody had rigged this trail, for sure about that. Counselors were constantly telling us to "be quiet, be quiet, no noise, that's your last warning, Professor or Red or Eddy or Tommy," but it never was. They lead us way past the dock and we had to "Swear to God and Camp Birkett" before they took our blindfolds off. There was a bonfire and I blinked in the fire's glow. We weren't even in the camp! We went "Off Limits" beyond the fence where we weren't even supposed to go!

There were eleven boys standing around the fire, eleven kids in boxers and briefs wondering what came next. Once the swearing in and on was done we had to hold oars outstretched until our arms fell off, go under the water with someone holding us down until we almost drowned and then stand on one leg not falling when the waves or our judges pushed us. They put our blindfolds back on us and we had to squish through pig guts they said, until we found a sacred medallion. We sat around the campfire still blindfolded and got up one by one groping in the dark until we identified somebody through touch.

One of the counselors walked around the circle and painted our faces black with poster paints, the kind that dries all cracked up, and we swore another oath never to tell. We were Shadows now, only eleven strong but we were powerful. We were the only ones who could have withstood the initiation. Secret Society, no one could ever know. No one. Ever.

"Wash that paint off on the way back. Don't make any noise when you get back to your cabins. Remember your oath."

The canoe trip started the next day, but not everybody got to go. Red and I both did. Everyone had to take canoeing lessons but some of the boys couldn't get the hang of the swimming, or paddling and steering. It didn't really matter because the other boys were going to rowboat around the lake with the counselors and staff who weren't canoeing. I'd made it to the raft the day before, the day after we won our Capture the Flag. Red swam beside me the whole way out and we dove off the really high diving board again and again, but not head first.

About fifteen boys and seven counselors, one man to a vessel with two boys each and two guys with two bigger craft holding the tents and supplies pushed off into the Huron River. We were going to paddle all day, pitch camp, sleep in tents and come back the next day. Gone from Birkett for two whole days, wilderness style. Way far. There would be no phones or conveniences out here, peeing and pooping in the woods. Great! I hoped they remembered the toilet paper.

186

What a trip. We saw blue heron fishing along the banks and a man who was fishing pulled up this huge fish, a muskellunge he'd landed just as our boats glided by. He held it up for us to see. Gigantic! And we gave him a cheer as we passed. All the other time was quiet except for breathing. The river did all of the talking and said everything worth saying. We saw a fox one time and a deer, too, both drinking from the river. Quiet was good. We did the listening and paddling. This trip was hard work and we stopped to rest twice before we got to the campsite but we didn't get lunch.

"Push on boys. Time to push on," was what we heard when somebody asked about food.

Some other people from Camp Birkett were waiting for us when we got to our new encampment site. Half the kids unpacked the canoes and set up tents and others gathered firewood, "only deadwood, boys," and got two cooking fires going. We got steaks from the staff people to roast over the fire once we had cut suitable sticks to use. The people who were waiting brought us Kool-aid and potato salad and ear corn to roast in the fire's coals, too. I cooked my steak just long enough to get it warm because I had a hole where my stomach was.

Famished. I was famished, had never been hungrier in my life, not even on one of those "go to your room" nights. We all tore chunks off the steak while it was on the stick and swiped our mouths with arms across to get the juice and we had a common big spoon that we used and passed around for the potato salad. We ouched! ouched! the corn out of the fire and it didn't need butter and salt. This was the best eatin' I ever had. This was the best livin' I'd ever had. Red and I shared a pup tent that night and we brother-talked our way to sleep.

The trip back was slower, because lots of us had grown blisters during the night, but I didn't. Red and I were in a canoe with no counselor this time, him in the front and me behind steering. During outward-bound leg, we got graded too but we didn't know it. When we shoved the canoes in this morning one of the men asked who'd like to try it alone and both he and I said we would. We didn't talk much. All the sights filled us up so much there wasn't room for words. Except for "a little right" or "a little left" when Red saw a log or a stone to avoid, no talking fit just right. We got back in time for dinner and again we didn't get lunch so there was lots of eating going on but it didn't taste as good as last night's. I think most of the kids were glad when campfire was over. The boys who didn't go canoeing rowed to the other side of the lake both days, and they got to play a game called water polo. They all said it was fun but hard to do, you had to swim the whole time. Sleep came easy for me and there wasn't much talking as I drifted off.

"Night Red."

"Night Professor."

Friday was the last day before our folks picked us up. I was going to have a shoot out in archery with a kid from the Eagle cabin to determine the champion archer and a volleyball tournament for the four best cabins who had won the most games so far. After the two events there would be free time until the closing ceremony that night, our last night at camp. Everybody was a little subdued that day, kids and counselors too. Something pretty wonderful was coming to an end.

Robbie (nicknamed Buster), the kid from Eagle cabin and I shot six arrows each at two different distances. When the judge added up our scores we were tied dead even. We had to have a shoot-off, best arrow out of three, further away than we previously shot. Buster shot first and the judge told someone to run and get a ruler when he went to look. It looked so close to dead center that he had to measure.

He announced. "Perfect shot, exactly in the center. Perfect!"

Then he walked back to the shooting line and said I didn't have to shoot if I didn't want to. I couldn't do better than perfect so it might be a waste of time.

I asked him to let me try anyhow and although he looked dubious, he did. Buster's arrows were left sticking in the target, evidence of his perfect shot. My first two arrows were good, both in the center but nowhere near good enough, not close to perfect. I drew my last arrow back as far as I could. My third arrow flawlessly struck the notched end of his perfect arrow and bounced back to fall on the ground. Nobody believed it, certainly not me.

The judge let out a "Whooooeeee! If I hadn't seen it I wouldn't have believed it! A tie, you're both PERFECT! We'll have to award medals to both of you. It's never happened before! I can't believe it."

All the Wolverines hooted and hollered, slapping me on the back in congratulation. Extra cabin points for sure tonight.

Red walked up and said, "Amazing, just like in Robin Hood. Just a little harder and it'd split his!"

After the volleyball tournament we all went back to the cabin with nothing particular to do. Robert told us we were on our own.

"There're horseshoes and volleyball and football if you guys want to start some pick up games, there are plenty of other boys already playing."

He had a new group starting to arrive tomorrow afternoon and he had activities to get ready.

"You boys figure out what to do now, I've got to get ready for tonight and tomorrow. I'll come get you later before we go to Ceremony. I think we might be close to having the best cabin in camp. The camp commander is adding up the scores but nobody will know until the ceremony. That was really great shooting out there, Professor. We needed those points and they might have made the difference. Maybe we should have called you William Tell. Hah! See you in a little while."

Wow, what to do, what to do?

For the first time in two weeks there wasn't something scheduled, nothing planned to occupy us. Someone suggested Indian leg wrestling and we did, then breaking out of full-nelson wrestling holds and we did that, too. Then Red said arm wrestling for the champion of the cabin and we selected adversaries for one another. Red started with Billy and whipped him easy. T.C. (we called him Top Cat because of his initials) pinned Crazy Charlie with a smack. I had trouble with Ted (Ted-Bear) but managed to force his hand down. It went one pin and out until there were only two left, Red and me.

Two weeks of being buddies, of being more than pals and brothers didn't matter a whit. Our blood was up from the wrestling and we both wanted to be champion. Red pinned my arm back good, but I thought he lifted his elbow off the table we were using.

"No fair, your elbow came off!" I accused. "That's not fair! I get another chance!"

"No I did NOT!" he said. "It was fair and square. I'm the Champ of the whole cabin."

"That's cheating and you know it. You're a cheater."

He called me names and I called him some more. He said I was a poor loser. I said he was a cheating rat. I hollered at him.

"You're not a Champ you're a Cheater! Cheater, CHEATER, CHEATER!"

He dove across the table and we really were fighting, all mad and hollering, end of the world mad, but he got me in a headlock I couldn't get out of and I gave up.

"Give?" He jeered.

"Yeah, I quit. I give. I give up."

We glared at each other when we got untangled, little boy proud, unable to be first to say sorry.

Some of the boys patted him on the back.

"Way to go."

"Really good."

Others told me they saw him cheat.

"I saw his elbow."

"He did cheat, I saw it."

Sammy went and sat on his bunk. I walked outside down by the lake to watch a horseshoe game.

Robert gathered us up for dinner. Sammy walked to the mess hall with another kid and I messed around with our counselor on the way. Hamburgers and French fries with Cokes! I never got Cokes at home, Mom wouldn't allow them and I sucked down as many as I could. We had a special cake that said Camp Birkett on it. The ceremony was fabulous. I went up and got my medal when Robbie got his and everybody applauded and whistled and stamped their feet.

Commander Wilson said, "Buster and the Professor made history here today boys. Two perfect shots! That's never been done before and probably never will again. If you come here for a hundred years, it just won't happen again. Let's give them both a big hand."

We hammed it up on stage, bowing and raising our hands together. We got whistles and raspberries and hoots. Robbie and I loved every second of it. Celebrity! Mr. Wilson awarded the volleyball ribbons, horseshoe championship and the baseball blue ribbons to each team member. He told us there would never be a bunch of boys here just like us, we were all great.

Our cabin lost out to the Eagle cabin but only by a few points and we groaned in losing. No award for second. The Eagles got to sit at the Honor Table and all the other boys had to shake their hands and tell them how great they were. They got the biggest pieces of the cake and the largest scoops of ice cream and we all made a big deal out of it.

After the ceremony I went right to bed. I was ready to go home now. So much fun was tiring and I wanted to get away from the Cheater anyway.

After breakfast the next morning, we had to dress the camp, this time stripping the beds and rolling the mattresses up when they were bare. Cabins all got swept clean, roads raked smooth and all the trash picked up by 9 o'clock when the parents would start arriving to take us home. The Wolverines had the beach duty and we raked the sand smooth right to the waterline. Sammy worked one side of the beach and I stayed at the other. Mr. Wilson walked around and said the camp looked great, but now it's time to get all of your stuff checked out. Don't leave anything behind. It was soon time for us to vacate the cabins. Two by two, in pairs we helped carry each other's gear to the front of the camp but I didn't help Sammy and he didn't help me. Quits.

I was really glad to see Mom and Dad.

"How was it? Did you have a good time? Tell us all about it. What did you do? What was your favorite? We got your letters. Where's that nice boy Sammy?"

I said I'd tell them all about it in the car, on the way home.

We had only gone about a half mile down the road, when in the telling of the good times, I blurted out about the fight with Sammy, that rat, that cheater. I hated him. He was a cheater. I started crying, blubbering over betrayal, loss, disappointment, leaving camp, everything I guess.

I wouldn't say my father was a good laugher. He laughed when something was funny. He just laughed quick like he wanted to get through as fast as possible. I was really surprised when my Dad began to first chuckle and didn't stop. His amusement grew and grew until it seemed he couldn't stop. He laughed louder until he was laughing so hard my mother told him to pull off the road if he couldn't stop. He never laughed this long, even at Red Skelton who he thought was hilarious. When my Mom told him to pull over, that made him laugh even louder and I started to get mad.

"Sammy cheated!" I screamed.

My father turned in his seat after he stopped the car on the shoulder. Tears were streaming down his face and he took off his glasses to clear his eyes. He started laughing again and couldn't talk. His loud merriment was scary, I didn't see what was so funny, and felt nothing could be that amusing. I was so mad I had to close my eyes. He was making fun of me, but at least I could make him disappear.

When he finally quieted some he said. "Son, I'm not laughing at you. Let me tell you a little story. Mr. Knight, Sammy's father and I got in to a terrible fight when we were at camp all those years ago. A dreadful fight, so bad our cabin got demerits and we had bathroom cleanup for a whole week when we got caught. Over something stupid, I'm sure but I don't even remember what it was. We called each other names the whole time we were cleaning and mopping too, we were so determined to stay mad. The only reason we didn't fight again was that the counselor said he'd send us home if we did. We ruined so many days being angry at each other we couldn't find a way back to having fun. When we left camp after two weeks, we still hated one another."

"Who won your fight?" I asked him, hoping that at least maybe he beat up Sammy's dad, some small redemption.

"You know Clark, I'm not sure I remember that either," Dad said softly.

"It wouldn't matter now anyway, would it? You'll learn that someday."

Sammy's treachery mattered. He cheated on me. But my dad had hugged the guy he got in a fight with! Is all this supposed to be a tradition, too? I sure would be glad to get home. I sure would be glad to see Patch.

Just before we got back to our house I remembered to ask Dad about having a turn in the barrel.

"Robert wouldn't tell us," I inquired. "What does it mean?"

My ex-Navy Dad said, "You'll have to wait a while before you're ready to learn about that, too."

Chapter 18

Displaced People

When I got back from Camp Birkett I was convinced my first duty lay within the marsh.

Although Mom and Dad wanted me to stick around the house and recount camp stories for several days, the two week lapse in my patrols was a much stronger responsibility. Patch was more than ready, too. She knew the importance of re-establishing our presence even if nobody else did. Despite being somewhat homesick while I was away, what I really needed was to get back into my routine tours of duty. While Mom wasn't real keen on me leaving again after such a brief stay at home she did say I could spend several days and nights out, something I had started doing last year without serious mishap. Anytime I didn't come home with something bloody, bruised or missing was considered a minor triumph around our house.

Mom especially operated from a principle which encouraged her children to discover their own limits. Added to her additional belief of our capability to accomplish anything that we truly wanted, she allowed all of us uncommon freedoms. If anything my small successes at camp further cemented her faith in this notion and my camping out was halfheartedly approved. I guess she'd rather disappoint herself rather than her kids because regardless of her true wishes, Patch and I were allowed to head out to our marsh the day after my return home. I packed up my bedroll and woodcraft tools, several cans of pork and beans, and a paper bag of dog food for Patch before going to bed. I left at first light, after quietly filling my canteen in the kitchen, then as now enjoying the stillness and unique nature each day's sunrise created.

As soon as we entered the woods Patch ruffled the hackles on the back of her neck and uttered a low growl. Lifting her nose high, scenting the airs, she took off like a bullet through the woods, not stopping or waiting when I first called and whistled. Barking, barking, barking, marked her progress and I trailed further and further behind until her voice was distant and faint. I struggled to catch up to her, knowing fully her disregard of my summons was out of the ordinary. After a chase of about ten minutes I realized where she was most likely headed and I turned toward the campsite we'd established on the border of grasslands between the marsh and the old quarry.

She'd apparently stopped, because now as I stumbled through the trees and overgrowth, her voice was getting louder.

Patch stood stiff legged and snarling just inside the cleared perimeter of the camp. By our lean-to stood an older Negro man with graying hair, a stranger. Dressed in faded bib-overalls and a ragged jacket, he was waving a crooked stick in Patch's direction, warning her off. He hollered at me as soon as I parted the chest high grass.

"You call thet dog off, boy!" He shouted again. "Get 'em back right now! NOW!"

"You need to throw that stick down mister." I told him. "As long as you've got a club in your hand she won't listen, but she won't bother you unless she thinks you're gonna hurt me. Easy girl, easy now."

He looked pretty doubtful, but when I walked up next to Patch and put my hand on her ruff she did quiet down. When Patch relaxed the man did as well and lowered his threatening arm. It still took him several more moments of convincing himself of the wisest choice, but he eventually let the stick fall from his hand. A small fire was burning in the ring of stones I'd laid out when we built the campsite and he edged the branch with his foot toward the flames with a smile.

"Boy, she scare de whiz out'ta me! Boyoboy," he said, still grinning. "I'se jest settin' here thinkin' 'bout coffee an' she run thru dem bushes like dis's her place. Growlin' and snappin' and actin' all bad-nasty. Where yuh frum?"

Now that he stopped shouting his accent was so thick I had to struggle to understand him. Patch and I stayed at the edge of the grasses but the man limped over and sat down on the big log I had rolled from the woods last fall. He slumped, leaning forward with his arms on his knees. I hunkered down next to Patch, both of us still wary of the stranger, but he kept up a patter of voice that belied his strange appearance. He appeared much older than my folks, with wrinkled face and hands and wild, great white eyebrows that crawled between his eyes and a striped engineer's cap. His clothing was pretty old too, especially his farmers bib-overalls. They had patches of repair attached everywhere. I studied him for several more minutes, finally concluding he looked old enough to outrun if I had to. Besides, Patch was here and although instinct told me of caution, I wasn't brought up to be a fearful child.

"Yup, one minnit it's all nice an' quiet lake, de next minnit I'se wishin' I'se sum'weres else. M'name's Tobias, but you kin call me Tobe."

I remained silent yet, studying both him and my next move. I felt somewhat invaded in my campsite but the man appeared friendly and my Miss Manners-Christian upbringing won out.

"I'm Clark and this is my dog Patch," I told and warned him at the same time. "She won't hurt you unless you try to hurt me or I tell her to. She's really a good dog but she really likes me better than anything. She's got wolf teeth."

"Yeh, an' I seen ever' one of 'em too. Dey looks woffy alright." He smiled again. "I wan't put here ta hurt no body. I'se jest here, jest passin' thru."

"Well, this is my camp. I made it. This is kinda my marsh, too," I said. "Patch and I come here almost every day. I made that lean-to and everything. That fire pit. You have to be really careful with fires around here."

"You Daddy own dis marsh an trees?" Tobe asked as he limped toward the fire.

"No, but it's ours, Patch and me," I answered. "Nobody else ever comes here except me and a couple of other kids. I know all about this place, how to get everywhere, all the way up to the creek," I pointed to the north and continued. "I got an old boat and I know where to catch rabbits in a snare and catch fish, too."

"Somebody sho makin' de big noises en yo marsh den boy. Did yuh tell em s'okay?" He laughed, a genuine sound. "Out dat way dere's a pile of sumpin' going on."

He pointed.

"Big engine all clankin' and groanin'." Tobe laughed again. "I guess yuh know enough ta lead a real huntin' party doan yuh, Scout? I'se not staying here long, be headed south, all the way ta Alabama. Too many winters up here done frost me right through. I reckon I had enuff ice'n snow ta last me a while. I'se headed home now."

I got up from my crouch and walked toward the fire, keeping my hand tight on Patch's collar the whole time. I kept the fire between Tobe and me, still hesitant, yet on the other hand feeling more comfortable with each of his smiles. Tobe was my first actual exposure to an adult black man and our meeting didn't come with the added safety of a well known grownup in attendance. Tobe looked friendly but guarded, and kept his eyes glued to Patch as we approached.

"Sure she not gonna bite'n snap me?" he asked. "She look bigger'n ever when she close up. Pleez don' turn her loose at me."

"No, just hold your hand out real slow," I instructed. "Don't touch her, let her touch you and let her smell you real good. Don't pull your hand back until she quits sniffing. She just needs to meet you."

Although he didn't look much like he wanted to, Tobe slowly extended his arm. His wrinkled hand trembled as Patch gave him her ultimate test, but when her rump began its friendly wriggle his shoulders relaxed in relief. I relaxed too. If Patch thought somebody was okay I certainly had nothing to fear. I squatted down next to the fire and Tobe resumed the task of coffee making Patch had interrupted several minutes ago. Patch lay down by one of the trees making up the lean-to supports, so satisfied with Tobe's passing grade she was completely at ease.

He kept up a running banter while he puttered with a banged up aluminum pot.

"Where yuh live? Roun' here? What kine thet dog? How old is yuh boy? Yuh said yuh knows where I kin ketch sum fishes?"

He opened a twist of brown paper lying by the log and sprinkled some ground coffee into the top of the pot.

"Yo Momma let yuh drink coffee, boy? It all I got." Tobe laughed when I shook my head no. "Yuh a'bit young but I'll share if'n yuh want."

"I've got some pork and beans if you're hungry," I offered. "I'm going to stay out in the marsh a couple of nights, so I've got food for me and my dog."

"Pork'n beans be bout de best brek-fast I ever had. Yuh sure yuh got nuff ef I eat'em too?"

"I can get more from home."

Shrugging off my blanket roll I reached in and pulled out one of the Campbell cans.

"I've got my Scout knife to open it with."

I handed him the can and started to dig in my pants pocket but stopped as an open blade mysteriously appeared with a 'whhtt' in his hand.

"I got one'll do jes' fine." He smiled again when I startled at the sight of his switchblade. "Don't worry none boy, jest fer cookin' an stuff in de woods. I use it fer ever thing. I bin livin' out ruff since I left Musss-keegan. I bin up at dat place since de first big war."

He sat the can on the ground and forced the knife tip through one end with hands familiar enough he could look at me the entire time he see-sawed the top open. Tobe nestled the can next to the coffeepot at the edge of the fire. After the red, gold and white label burned off, Tobe and I watched the beans start to bubble on one side of the can. He turned the now blackened can with an ouch and a grin to heat it through.

"Beans bes'be hot for ya kin eat em."

While we ate Tobe told me of his trip south. He had worked in Muskegon since World War I in a munitions plant, "running de machines." Now he wanted to go home to the small town where he was born and raised. I found out he was hopping trains, but had hurt an ankle when he got on the last one outside Detroit, the reason for his limp. That's why he'd ended up in the marsh to let the stiffness and soreness ease before he continued. He pulled up his pant leg to show me a dark bruise, swollen badly, showing blue-black through his skin.

"It sho' hurt fierce. I cain't try no mo' trains til it get some better, I might' haf'ta run some. Dem railroad folk don't much lak you riding on dey trains wiffout a ticket." He laughed and continued. "Dey act lak you slowin' d'em big engines down er sumthin'. Some mens jes' got de mean heart, I guess."

Tobe handed me a tin cup of coffee and I rightfully couldn't refuse. I had beans, he had coffee; an even exchange. I took a sip. Oh man, this is bad, but I smiled through the taste. The coffee tasted so bitterly horrid I hoped Mom never thought of it as a form of punishment. I swallowed it down anyhow, more of a show of equality with this strange man than anything. The beans were great. I had a spoon from my pack and Tobe had one stashed in a coat pocket but we used the can for a bowl between us. After we finished passing the blackened can back and forth until it was empty, I told Tobe that Patch and I had to get moving along. I related my two weeks away at the YMCA camp and we had a lot of checking to do before we bedded down for the night. I told him we might come back here to sleep but not to be surprised if we stayed at another of our spots. He patted Patch before we left.

"I sure be glad we friends now, dog." Tobe soberly chuckled. "I wan't sure ef yuh wanta eat *me* fer breakfast when yuh first show up. Mayhap I see yuh t'morrow. Mayhap not. I might move on ef my foot feel better. Yuh got be careful out'n dat marsh, Scout. Ain' ever body all smiley lak me."

"Don't worry, we know our way around here. Come on girl, let's see what's out there." I shouldered my pack and turned to wave when Patch and I got to the edge of the camp's clearing. "See you Tobe."

We walked further north in the direction Tobe had pointed, toward the second quarry, a half mile distant. I needed to see what he was talking about, but I only half believed his story. I was dumbfounded to see a mass of huge construction machinery parked along the old gravel road. I couldn't believe it! What was going on here? Invasion in my marsh!

First Tobe shows up and as if one stranger isn't enough, someone or something else had been real busy bringing all this earthmoving equipment in here while I was at camp. I was immediately sorry to have gone away, leaving my wilderness open to foreigners of all sorts.

I didn't see anyone around the trucks and bulldozers so I crouched and walked closer to see the big yellow machinery, calling Patch as I crept up. The number of machines was astounding. Dozens and dozens of pieces, all ready to chew up everything in their way. I ran my hands over the tracks and blade of one of the dozers. It even felt ominous lying still, but I still couldn't imagine what all this stuff was doing here. I'd been coming back here for more than three years and had only seen just a few people in all that time. There'd be lots of men required to run this stuff, but it still hadn't dawned on me what it was here for. I wandered in and out of the machinery, idling my hands over each piece as I passed row upon row upon row. I was stunned by the alien nature of the scene before me. It all looked so out of place.

I was so engrossed in thoughts of the equipment I didn't hear the truck until it was almost right in front of me. Startled again, I froze, like an animal caught in the headlights. The word FERMI was painted on the door of the blue truck and a man stuck his head out the open window and yelled at me.

"Hey kid! Get over here!"

That cured my paralysis. I took off like a rabbit. Away through the rows of trucks and bulldozers, darting right and left past this one and that. I called to Patch as I ran.

"Patch! Patch! Come on girl!"

I ran low to the ground stooped over at the waist, peeking back as I put some distance between the man's voice and myself. He'd jumped out of the truck when he saw me bolt, chasing me several hundred feet, twisting and dodging through the parked vehicles, while he continued to holler. The more I ran the more he yelled. He lost track of me when instead of continuing through the rows I jig-jagged into the grass along the far side the parking area. I could just make out his shape through the rushes as he stalked along the back end of the line of trucks, shouting to the wind, but he didn't see me.

Once I reached the cover of the grass I crawled well away from the sound of his voice. Good thing there was heavy vegetation here, with saw and marsh grasses almost abutting the parking area. As I lay in hiding I couldn't help but wonder if big people thought all kids were morons. His thoughts had to read something like, "Let's see, the best way I can think of to get a kid to approach a stranger is to holler and scream at him." Mrs. Greene's kids might be sneaky, but we weren't dolts. His big angry voice had just made me run the faster. I wondered where my chicken-dog Patch (who was supposed to warn me about this kind of stuff) was or if she knew enough to remain concealed.

After a while I heard the truck's door slam and its engine noise eventually faded, but I remained motionless until I was sure the man had driven far away. I thought of the phrase I'd heard from Tobe this morning, "scared the whiz out of me." It wasn't quite as bad as that, but close to it. Everything I'd seen startled me: the machinery and the man. I knew I'd have to work my way far roundabout this activity, back to the campsite where Tobe was. He'd need to know about the guy in the truck, even though the spot where I'd left him was distanced far from any vehicle access. After I was sure the guard had gone, I resumed creeping and reached the bank of the small stream emptying into the quarry basin, another fifty yards away from the chase scene.

I stood cautiously, inching upward until I could peer over and through the whispery stalks and reeds. No sign or noise of the truck as I turned in a full circle. The guy had given up, but it wouldn't have mattered anyway. Once I had reached the grasses I didn't think there were many people who could have found me if I didn't want to be discovered. I whistled for Patch and she surprised me too, thrusting her head through the rushes at my back with a soft woof. I whirled to face her and grabbed her big head in my hands.

She softly growled in pleasure, doing her dog-talk, wondering about the new games we'd played with strangers today.

"Where you been?" I demanded. "What, did that guy scare you? Come on you big chicken, let's get outta here."

Patch and I walked toward the lake, avoiding the boggy wastes which paralleled the shoreline at a distance of forty yards. To get to the beach line I had to cross a slash of exposed dirt and as I looked both ways could see the scars a bulldozer had made in the soft sandy soil, every tree, bush and scrub pushed up alongside the bare earth. They were building a perimeter road for patrols! Dang, dang, dang!

Cleared ground, now I had another area to avoid, but I knew it would be impossible for me to be surprised by anyone if I stayed in the marshy spots. I knew they sure wouldn't be driving their trucks in the soft mucky ground and if they had to walk, couldn't know their way around as well as I did. I had so many hidey-holes and vantage points in this swamp I didn't think Mom could find me. And, her tracking skills were astonishing.

It took me more than three hours to work my way back to the lean-to, because I had to stay well at the perimeter of the marsh. I approached the secluded spot from the identical direction I had this morning and startled Tobe when I parted the bushes.

"Scout, I bin lookin' fer ya, but you snukked around de back o'me." The old man grinned hugely. "Yuh sure look lak yuh bin rollin' round en de dirt an muck dis here day. Yo momma gonna give yuh what fer when yuh gets en de house. Ha! She be slappin' yo haid so much yuh'll think it'sa drum."

"Nah, I mostly come home looking like this when I've been out here. Mom just thinks I look like I've had a good time." I smiled too. "Mom's great."

"Ha! Dat she is. Hey dog!" he said as he reached toward Patch. "Yuh 'members Tobe?"

Patch welcomed his petting as if she'd known him for years. I was always amazed at the here and now of Patch. This morning she'd been ready to eat him up and now she almost knocked him over with happiness at the reunion.

I shrugged off my pack and slumped to the log seat, suddenly tired by the day's revelations, confused and worried by the evidence of construction I'd seen. I recounted my fright and flight to Tobe, who listened carefully, and interjected "M'Gods" and "sheeeeit's" when I paused for breath or recall. I told him of FERMI's big open-house two years ago when they explained the power plant they would build. Mom and Dad took the bunch of us to hear the presentation about all the good they'd do for the community and schools, new paved roads and all sorts of improvements. They'd cooked hot dogs and popcorn for the community in an unheard of and amazing microwave oven and freely handed them out to families and kids. Nuclear power, the wave of the future, was going to take place right here in our community.

They sure didn't say anything about wrecking my marsh though.

Tobe came over and sat next to me on the log, still hobbling from the ankle injury. I pulled my canteen out of its canvas cover and handed it to Tobe. He looked at me closely, studying my face before he unscrewed the lid and tilted it to his mouth.

When he handed it back he asked, "Wha' yo momma'n'daddy say if'n dey know'd I be drinkin' fum yo bottle?"

I took a swallow and poured some in my hand for Patch, who slurped and lapped as noisily as she possibly could.

"Why would they say anything? You're thirsty, aren't you?"

Tobe didn't answer my question but I hadn't answered his either. I went on, now spitting out my frustration and fear about the morning's encounter, getting myself worked up, and agitating myself to tears. Patch laid her head on my lap and I absently stroked her fur, imagining myself running through the parked equipment wreaking destruction as I went, fantasizing loudly to myself and Tobe. I'd find some dynamite, blow up the machinery, set fire to the stuff and run the whole bunch of them off. Tobe listened to my ravings and slid his arm around my shoulders, offering some comfort for the terror I'd had.

"Scout, yuh gotta lissen ta ol' Tobe now a minnit. Dis de guvmint, prob'lly. Dis a big companee an' dey doan care 'bout no lil' fella an' he dog. Yuh an' all yo' folks cain't stand en de way of dis. It called Pro-*gress*. It wuk lak dis. Sum peeples got big moneys, but dey ain' happy wif' jes' big. Dey tryin' make more'n big. All de time. Dey take dey money to Un-kle Sams an' says let's do dis an' let's do dat. Dis is good. Un-kle Sams says okay, cause'e doan' wan' stan' en de way o' Pro-*gress* neether."

"But this is my marsh!" I said between hiccups. "We were here first. I'm not leaving."

Tobe snorted, "I din't say yuh hasta leave. Yuh just gottabe smar-teh den dem. Yuh gotta figgah where dey be at, an' yuh gottabe sumplace else. Dat's all. Dey cain't be ever place an' yuh got away once a'ready, din't yuh? It gonna be a long time for dey gets ta de place where dey done nuff to keep you en they mind. Dey be too busy ta fool wid' a lil' boy. 'Sides, yuh dun told me yuh's a scout, din't yuh?"

I nodded slowly, still upset over what I considered a serious trespass, and still not convinced of my continued freedom in an area I considered mine. I was struggling to understand what Tobe was saying, but not doing a good job of shrugging off the terrible feeling that had settled over me.

"They can't do this Tobe. It's not fair! This is MY marsh!"

"An dey cain't take it away fum yuh if'n yuh's smarter den dem," Tobe told me seriously. "Yuh jes' gotta wuk around dem peeples. Jus' cause dey gots money doan mean nuffin', if'n yuh doan let em."

Tobe and I had settled into a quick familiarity I'd not before known with another adult. While I still had some trouble understanding his words, I didn't have any problem telling him how I felt. He didn't tell me or indicate with his words he thought me beneath the thoughts I'd been expressing. Tobe instead, through his attentions, offered suggestions to allay my fears, to bolster my own confidences regarding retaining the freedoms I sought in the marsh. My folks would have sympathized, but would probably insist I cut down or even curtail my campouts completely. All I had to do now, according to this adult, was be sneaky and keep out of their way. I could do the sneaky part.

Tobe steered the conversation away from the problems of the day with tales of "Musss-Keeegan" and he spent the remainder of the day and evening doing a very good job of cheering me up. By the time dusk had fallen, I'd been solaced enough to think better of myself and not so much about the enormity of the construction project and its impact on my beloved marsh.

I'd unrolled my blanket and with Patch beside me watched darkness settle over the fields and wood. The sounds of the night started slowly, frogs and crickets singing, Tobe still bantering soft sounding words from the other side of the fire pit, and Patch's long breaths melded together in a sound almost as familiar as my mother's voice. I was pretty sure there was no better place on earth. I managed a "Night, Tobe," but only half heard his reply before I fell asleep.

Patch had us a rabbit when I woke up in the morning. She was sitting next to me, pleased with herself, looking down when I creaked my eyes open. I reached up to pat her head and saw the rabbit. Patch gave a sharp bark to tell me she deserved much higher admiration than a still sleepy rub or two. Her loud woof woke Tobe with a start and I sat upright to work her over, scrubbing my hands up and down her heavy neck as just payment for breakfast. She danced away, jousting back and forth at me in play, just what she needed as compensation for the meal she'd brought.

"What a good girl!" I laughed. "What a dog! You aren't a chicken scaredy dog after all. Good girl!"

Tobe hobbled over to us and praised Patch, too.

"Whatta dog! She do dat regular fer you boy? I be hongry e-nuff to eat de hop and jump of dat bunny." He laughed. He bent over and chuckled again. "Dog could come wid me an keep me en meat for de res' of my trip. Dat sum dog!"

"Patch stays right here with me," I joked back. "We've got too many things to do."

Tobe smiled. "Yep, an I bee-leve yuh gonna get em all done, too. Dat sure sum dog."

He reached down to pick up the rabbit, but pulled his hand back when Patch growled. I grabbed her scruff and laughed.

"It okay, girl."

I scooped the fat rabbit up and handed it to Tobe, walked over and took the old sauce pan from the back of the lean-to.

"I'll go over to the spring and get some water to wash it off if you skin it out." There's a great fresh water spring right over there. It won't take me but a few minutes. I'll pick up some fire wood when I get back."

I picked up the battered bucket I kept at the camp and whistled to Patch. Instead she lay down to watch Tobe. I shrugged my shoulders and set off. I thought she probably wanted to make sure the skinning was done properly. She could find me if she needed to.

Tobe had the rabbit dressed in the few moments it took me to fetch the water. I'd filled my canteen while I was at the spring and let Patch have a long drink from the bucket before I handed it to Tobe so he could wash off the rabbit carcass. I walked back into the woods and used my hatchet to cut a pair of heavy forked branches and one long one for a spit and carried them back to the camp. Tobe had started a fire when I went to get the water. When I returned with the branches, he sharpened an end of the long one and impaled the rabbit while I cut the others to length and forced them into the ground for supports. He'd thrown the pelt to Patch when he finished the skinning and she was racing around the lean-to reliving her capture. Tobe and I both hooted at her antics.

Patch flipped her head, released the pelt and then dashed over to snap it up again, repeating the exploit over and over again. Running up to the scrub brush, she'd whirl to scamper back across the grass, head held high and proud, again and again. She feinted at us, offering the pelt, then growl and spin away. She worked harder in the play than she did when she caught the rabbit and we couldn't contain ourselves. She kept it up until she'd exhausted herself and us.

The toasty-tasty smell of roasting rabbit soon rose up from the browning carcass and all three of us sat down, watching it drip juices into the fire. Patch looked at me scornfully when I offered her some of the dry dog food I carried. She wanted what we wanted, don't bother about any distractions, nothing else but bunny would do. She had moved close to the stick Tobe was slowly twirling, her muzzle and nose almost right over the fire. I didn't blame her a bit. I was drooling just as much as she was.

When the rabbit was done Tobe lifted the stick off the supports and gingerly slid it off the skewer. He yelped with the heat, but we both were too hungry to wait for cooling. He broke the roasted body expertly in half, handed me a dripping hot leg and then further tore the back out and also handed it to me.

"Yuh kin give yo dog thet. She oughta get de first piece. T'hout her we just be thinkin' 'bout sumthin' t'eat."

Patch gently took the proffered meat and Tobe was surprised with her docile manners, but Patch had never snatched food when it was offered. Heck, she wouldn't even eat unless you told her it was okay. A natural trait on her part, as if she knew her proper behavior was expected, her mouth was always light when hand feeding came about. Patch lay down and began crunching her share. Tobe and I did our own version, smacking our lips with the complete pleasure of the meat.

"Dat dog doan even grab?" Tobe exclaimed. "I'da give it, but I membered dem toofs and den I heard somebody sayin' no. Ha! Musta bin me doin' de sayin'! Dat sure some dog! Yuh lucky Scout, yuh one lucky boy." He bit off a piece of meat from the leg he'd kept. "Man, dis be bout de best I chew en'a long time!"

I could only silently agree with everything he said, because my mouth was busy with roast rabbit. No time or space for words, so I just nodded.

After we'd finished, we tossed the remnants into the fire and watched the bones char and burn, I told my new friend I would be back later. I was heading home for a wrap and some Bag-Balm for his ankle but I didn't tell him of my real reason. I somehow knew he'd protest, so I just said I had to check in, let my folks know nothing bad had happened, even though it wasn't exactly true in my opinion. Plenty of bad had happened right here in my marsh. I was still anxious about the power plant and road work taking place. I would need to make some specific changes if I was going to continue using this as my own personal wilderness.

I'd have to relocate two of my three campsites. The one we'd used last night, would be the only one secluded enough to escape detection. In fact, as I thought of it, I was surprised Tobe had been able to find it in the first place. I wasn't concerned about this one because it was virtually surrounded by swamp. If someone was unfamiliar with the terrain they could get bogged badly enough to stay there forever unless outside rescue appeared.

Patch and I had already found the remains of a hunting dog held fast in the muck. From the look of the thinly covered bog the poor animal had struggled furiously for a long time before exhaustion and the sticky mud claimed its life. I knew where all the soft spots were and so did Patch and our explorations were safe enough, but any stranger in the area needed to exercise a great deal of caution. Through my boyish blundering I'd already recognized being in the marsh demanded my complete attention.

I slipped the lead on Patch when we got to the backyard.

"I'll be right back girl. Just a minute."

Mom, Chip and Peg were slightly surprised when I came through the back door but I told my mother I was going back out for at least the rest of today and would probably spend another night. I grabbed a couple of cookies, motioned to my brother and talked to Chip in our room for a short while, letting him know what had happened. He wanted to go back with me but I convinced him I needed to further scout out what was happening with all the machinery. After I swore him to secrecy and told him about my narrow escape yesterday, he believed me when I said I needed to make sure it was safe enough for him to go with me. I didn't tell him about Tobe; that part was too much of a secret to share just yet. I furiously did chores before leaving, in order to reduce any possible arguments about my leaving again right away, but I didn't get any serious urging to stay home.

I took the time to comb and brush the stickers out of Patch, because she was so thick with them I had to. Even though I spent more than a half hour unsnarling the cockle burrs with Chip's and Peg's help, they were the only voices that wanted me to stay. Mom was accustomed to me staying in the marsh, thoroughly accepted my affection for the place and just kissed me before I set out again. I tucked the Bag-Balm tin, elastic bandage and stuffed the extra cookies into my pack before I said, "Bye, see you sometime tomorrow," and slipped out the door.

Tobe appeared extremely worried when I handed him the wrapping and salve.

"Yuh went home? Yuh tell yo momma 'bout ol' Tobe out here?" he asked with a grim look. When I shook my head in reply he resumed his normal smile. "Well, dat be alright den. I doan be thinkin' dey feel real good 'bout dey boy if'n dey know I's out here wid yuh."

I didn't think it would matter but with my parents but who knew for sure? Tobe being in my campsite fell into one of those pieces of information which would be best served held close, away from any scrutiny. He sure did like the Ace bandage and the Bag-Balm though and after he smeared his ankle I showed him how to wrap it so the bandage provided support. He said it felt better as soon as I finished and although I was a believer in the magical qualities of the stuff, even I didn't think it worked that fast. He assured me of the improvement and limped several steps as proof but he walked the same to my eyes. I didn't stay. I wanted to look around north of yesterday's excursion and I told Tobe I might not see him tonight.

"I'll most likely sleep on the beach tonight. We'll be above the construction by a mile or more," I told Tobe just before Patch and I set off.

"Yuh need to keep yuh eyes sharp, Scout. De words prob'lly out on yuh by now. Dat firs' man tells some other mans an' dey all be lookin' fer yuh. Kid'en a dog, ever one be a lookin'."

I laughed out loud, but I heard the truth in what he said.

"I'm a scout, Tobe. Don't worry about me."

In my mind I knew I'd have to be more than cautious all the time now. Most adults I knew would take something akin to my escape yesterday as a personal insult and want to pay me back for the act. I hoped the guard hadn't seen Patch yesterday when he surprised me. She was so distinctive I was sure her identity and home would be revealed as soon as big, black and tan rushed out of somebody's questioning mouth. Just have to wait and see if someone came to our door, I guessed. Meanwhile I had places to go.

I skirted all possible contact by sticking to the beach area, but even as I approached the northernmost marsh I could see evidence of construction. The perimeter road they had begun on the south end looked complete at this extreme. I stayed well hidden and soon heard the sounds of a vehicle approaching. I pulled Patch to a crouching position along side me and as I watched a blue truck drove slowly by the screening of bushes where we lay. I thought the driver was the same guy who had put up such a fuss yesterday. The cover was heavy in this quadrant of the marsh with sumac and hickory and the truck quickly disappeared around a bend in the gravel roadway. My spirits descended further still as I saw roll upon roll of chain link fencing and posts in a mountainous pile.

The construction was going to include chain fencing?! I knew this stuff wasn't given away for free and the miles needed to encompass the vast region would be enormous. I couldn't believe it. What was the possible need for this extent of exclusion? I waited by the road, still concealed for three more circuits of the truck. Its reappearance varied a little but every hour plus the blue truck nose emerged from the south and slowly vanished to the north. Maybe Tobe was right. I was at least this smart. Every hour or so a circuit. Even a dumb kid could figure out this schedule.

Patch and I made a cold camp just off the beach that night within hearing of the roadway but well out of sight. I didn't risk the flickering glow of a fire but it was summertime warm anyhow so I certainly didn't need one for heat. I missed not having one though. A fire was comforting whether you needed the heat or not. I bet there was one going in the other camp. Tobe would know the reason for a fire beyond my young thoughts. He knew about something else but I'd never paid much attention until he said it.

Beans taste better hot.

I continued to time the security circuits until I fell asleep and the regularity was within ten minutes every time. The truck's noise brought me to half wakefulness with each passing, but it was somehow comforting. I knew I would be able to enter my marsh at any point and time I chose if their patrols were limited to this recurrent riding around in a truck. All I had to do was get through or over any future fence, cross about fifty yards of cleared area adjacent to their graveled lane and slip into heavier cover. Easy as pie. Piece of cake. I pulled Patch's big body closer and her throaty dog-talk whispers sent me to sleep.

In the morning, they almost caught me while I was peeing. Definitely not fair. A guy's just gotta go when he wakes up.

I should have heard them but just emerging from sleep sometimes dulled my senses. One minute they weren't making any noise, but the next instant I heard voices. Two men with a stick and sort of a telescope stood no more than fifty feet from my sprinkles. I dropped to the earth looking frantically for my dog. Patch could be friendly enough to want an introduction but I was against that thought and she might need to be restrained if she thought a visit was necessary. I turned my head to peer behind me and saw her watching them from a crouch. No noise of suspicion or warning, but she'd sensed my reserve and mimicked my desire to remain concealed and separate. I crept back to the beach and hurriedly rolled my pack together. Giving a soft whistle to Patch, who'd remained behind watchfully hunkered down, we trotted quickly back toward the southern limits of the marsh.

And ran smack dab, plumb into, right on top of, a group of men putting up that stinking dumb chain link fence all the way to the waterline. They saw me the same second I saw them. This was the only way back. The area to my right was already cordoned with the eight foot high mesh and the area to my left was water. One of them hollered at me. I stood stock still, anxiously searching for the best action to take. I thought of running back toward last night's spot but the fact remained I'd have to get past these guys somehow unless I was willing to stay on the beach forever. Besides I knew if I ran there were enough of them to catch me. "Face it up big boy, you're trapped," I told myself out loud.

Tobe's words, "Yuh jus' gotta be smar'tah den dem," came to my mind. I sure hadn't done that. Although the thought of these men scared the dickens out of me there was no other way around. I sauntered toward the group of workmen trying to act as innocently as possible, but I sure didn't feel confident in my "sma'tah" right then. Every one of them, arms crossed or hands on hips, was looking at me and Patch as we walked up.

"What are you doing son?" a hard-hatted man asked. "You're not supposed to be back here. Didn't you see the NO TRESSPASSING signs?"

"No sir," hoping the lie wasn't evident.

I doubly hoped these guys weren't as good at lie detecting as my mother. I pointed south along the beach.

"I came all the way along the water, early this morning, down the beach from Pointe aux Peaux. You guys weren't here yet, I guess"

"Well, you need to stay out of here. This is private property now, a big construction project. You need to find some other place to ramble round." He looked at Patch. "You best take yourself and that dog out of here before you get hurt." He added meaningfully, "Or in trouble."

"Okay mister."

I could hardly contain my delight. I might get away with this!

"I get in trouble enough by accident. I sure don't want any on purpose."

Those hours of practicing my sorry faces in the bathroom mirror must have worked because he dismissed me down the beach.

"I'll just bet you do son, I'll bet you do." Several men laughed at his sarcasm. "You remember to find someplace else to play," he repeated as I walked through the knot of men. "I'm not kidding now. This is no place for a kid."

"I said I would mister. C'mon Patch let's go."

My voice pulled her away from her inspection of the men. I waved my hand in response as I left the group and didn't look back at them until I was almost a hundred feet beyond, but thought I could feel every eye still on us. Those guys *were* still watching us! I waved again but they didn't return the goodbye, and I was too relieved to do much of anything except walk. That guy was pretty good, at least he didn't holler at me and demand to take me home but he missed the boat on one thing. This was just the place for a kid, and I knew who.

We soon reached the end of the sand beach and scrambled through the bushes to Long Road. Instead of going toward home or to the spot where Tobe was, Patch and I walked out on the wide spit of land that ran into the water west of the road. My sorry little skiff was here, sunk to the edges just like usual but I wasn't interested in paddling around right now anyway. I sat at the end of the short peninsula and had a good long think-talk with my dog, Patch leaning into me when she sat down. This wasn't going to be good, the aftermath of this invasion. I knew as soon as I saw all the stuff and those guys I'd wind up in trouble over this, because right now I wasn't even considering any giving up. I could almost taste the problems coming my way, imagine the groundings and punishments but I didn't care. This spot was too much of me, too much of my dog, too much of everything I treasured. I couldn't just hand over and forget its allure so easily. I'd figure out how to steer clear of them.

Patch agreed with every word I said.

It was early afternoon by the time I'd emptied my head and heart of the disappointment, fear and anger I'd felt. Together Patch and I could continue moving about in our private preserve, but I would just have to do so in great secrecy. I got up, dusting myself off in more ways than one and started around the western edge toward Tobe. As I walked along the boggy reaches of the marsh I couldn't help but wonder how those people were going to be able to enclose all of this property. The task was enormous as well as not suited to being fenced in. With the evidence I'd seen so far they seemed serious enough, but I couldn't fathom the need to make it so exclusive as to prevent my use.

Tobe was cooking when I got to the clearing. At the edge of the woods white feathers were strewn about caught on stalks and stems of the reeds and bushes. Smelled pretty good even before I got there.

"Hey, der's de big Scout hissef an he dog too." He waved happily as soon as I walked through the brush. "You slep' out last night?" I nodded but he must have noticed my sad-sack look because he asked immediately, "Wha'sa matta boy, yuh best friend run off? Nope, she right there." He laughed as Patch followed me into the clearing seconds later.

I recounted this morning's discovery as well as the lengths and lies I resorted to when I was cut off along the beach. Tobe thought I'd done well. I wasn't so sure.

He continued to turn the spitted chicken and said. "Sorta lak dis here bird. It wasn't 'zactly mine but it wuz all just runnin' around a farm house ov' dere, lookin' fer sumthin' ta do and I give it sumthin' real fine ta do. Makin' de best outta de sitsi-ashun. You gotta do dat. Make de best yuh kin outen dis. De world ain't come to no end, it jest be changin'. It allus doin' dat. Yuh just don't be catchin' it changin' b'fore dis."

"Doan dat smell grand?" he chuckled. "Dat almos' as grand as dat bunny hoppeh yo dog snatch us. C'mon here and sat y'self down awhile."

When I sat on the log next to him he continued talking me through this upset.

"Dey goan be a day right round de cor'ner when you doan even be thinkin' bout dis place. Right now it be the best spot fer yuh, but fore yuh blink yo eye dis all be past an' gone. You must keep de good pieces an' let the bad parts slip by de way. Unnerstan Scout, dis ain't de end, es just' different."

"Why are they trying to keep me out?" I asked, but thinking I'd never forget my marsh.

"Jest cause dey ken," he replied. "Membeh when I says some mens just be mean heart'd? Dey jus be dat way cause dey kin be. Dey do dat cause dey figgah it be fine an' all, mak'em look big. Dem mens think big, make no never-mine bout no lil' boy an' a dog."

Tobe finished up. "Nuff now. C'mon boy, c'mon dog, lets eat."

Our meal together was completed in silence. I didn't come close to understanding what he was telling me but I was too shy to admit it. My eyes kept wandering to the horizon over the marsh, wondering and questioning.

"I think I be leavin' in de mawnin' boy. My foot be better, dat stuff yuh brung do me some kinda good. I prob'ly kin catch me a slow train if'n I get close by de track. Yuh an' yo dog bin makin' me laff plenty much roun' heah, an' feedin' Tobe too. I be better in lots'a ways now n'when I get here. I doan think I be fergettin' de Scout. Gimme yo hand boy, shake wid' ol' Tobe."

I couldn't help the tears that went along with my outstretched hand and Tobe turned the handshake into an embrace.

"Yuh goan be jest fine, boy." His words floated down on top of me. "Sheeee-it boy, yuh already fine nuff fer me. Yuh dog a good'n too, neveh seen nuthin quite so as dat dog."

He shooed me away from the camp after he released the hug, knowing something about long goodbyes I had yet to learn. Reluctantly Patch and I pushed through the shrubbery and I stopped to wave but he was turned away, busy with his own farewell feelings. As we walked home I thought there was a great deal I still needed to figure out and didn't know about. I might not even want to know about some things. Only two real thoughts came to my mind.

I knew I'd be alright, just fine, like Tobe said. I also knew I'd keep going in the marsh.

I slapped the side of my leg, calling Patch.

"Come on girl, let's get the burrs out of you."

Chapter 19
Slip Sliding Away

It was one of those perfect winter Michigan mornings.

A day clear and cold. It was identical to thousands before, but different because my brother and I had finally convinced Dad to pull us on the sled behind the car.

We were at breakfast, a weekend ritual for the family, when we all sat down at the same time in order to send and receive snippets of our collective lives. The windows in the dining room were etched with frost, in feathery patterns of ice. Patch, finished with her morning business, was standing outside her house at the base of the elm tree, woofing and wondering where in heck everybody was. Her muzzle glistened with frozen whiskers and her front legs gave a little hop every time she'd bark, as if to convey just how anxious she was, too. She knew something was up.

Chip and I were ready; we had been all winter, in fact. We imagined ourselves sliding down a never ending mountain, higher than Mount Everest, slicking our way through the subdivision to our hearts' content. Breakfast this morning was intolerable, almost like waiting for Christmas. Long, lengthy moments filled with the hubbub of the Greene's breakfast chatter, slipped between my five-year-old sister's current tales of Charge, her imaginary boyfriend. We were having Quaker Oatmeal with milk, brown sugar, a pat of butter, supplemented by our own nutritious staple; day old Liparato's doughnuts and orange juice that Mom had added an extra can of water to, in order that it stretched for all of us. These standard provisions of a Michigan winter breakfast were for us the great taste of mornings in the 1950s.

I recall some serious discussion at the breakfast table that morning. Carole was silent and aloof from the sledding negotiations. I think she was in her, "I

211

am above that sort of foolishness," stage.

I remember the depth of the morning discourse centered on Peg's participation in the sledding. Chip and I were pretty keen about taking our baby sister for this adventure. We had been pulling her by hand and dog without many serious incidents. Oh, she'd get her face full of snow occasionally, but it would just glow all the more from that. We were always careful with her, at least as much as I, at ten and Chip, at six could be. We knew we would have fun and she would, if she got to go.

At least one of the household wasn't too keen on the whole idea to begin with. Mom was pretty formidable and I remember snippets of the talk. Mostly it was, "They might slide under the car, Jerry," and, "What if another car comes along and runs over them."

Surprisingly our counter arguments of "Aw, Mom, Mr. Edwards has been pulling Diane and Robert," and "Gary and Randy went last week and they're still okay," had some effect on Dad.

Dad got up and went over to give Mom a pat on the butt. It might have been a possessive thing with him, but I always admired that about Dad; he liked touching his wife. And she liked him doing that. Good example. He managed to convince Mom, or maybe she just didn't think he would pull us up and down Goddard Drive more than once. How much harm could that really be? For five-year-old Peg, it seemed like it was going to be a wait until next year when you're older event. My baby sister would not go, and herein lays the secret of great negotiation. Clark and Chip were obvious expendables, but pretty little Phoebe Erma Greene, never. Of course Chip and I weren't smart enough to consider that, as our minds were only focused on the imagining of sledding, so we were happy, ignorant of possible sacrifice, but happy. Surprisingly, Dad supported our pleadings and told us all to get bundled up. Of Peg, there was no further discussion. Mom had her say in the matter and that was that.

Chip and I began the wrapping up. No Egyptian monarch was ever so lovingly prepared for embalming. Fruit-of-the-Loom undies and woolen socks, in place; long underwear, is the flap in the back? Check. Flannel shirts and blue jeans with patches on knees and backsides, all done; Snow suits, stocking caps, mittens-with-clips and strings through the coat and Grandma's green woolen scarves. Grandma Phoebe as I recall, knitted everything for us with kindof green or sortof red wool. Oh! We were getting down to the quickening now!

Now Chip has to go pee....

"Geezie-peezie, I knew it! This kid! Of all the lame! Okay. Okay. I didn't mean it. Yes Mom, I know he's my baby brother. I didn't MEAN it, I didn't.

I'm sorrrrrry, I really am."

I had learned at an early age, when my parents demanded contrition, I'd better not fool around. With a younger brother like Chip, I had to practice repentance frequently.

Ok, he's back and I am stifling, but I dare not take anything off for fear of delaying the event any longer. Also, I didn't want to keep Dad waiting. He was notoriously short on patience with us. Who could blame him? Same routine, dressing Chip again, but Mom doesn't have to help me this time.

Finally, put on galoshes that go over shoes; the dull black ones with metal buckles up the front and with room enough to tuck in pant legs. We had patches on our boots, courtesy of Shorty's Gas Station. Dad had patched the inevitable holes with tire patches that you had to light the glue before you applied the patch. We kept tire-patch kits and glue scattered throughout the kitchen drawers to keep up with a never-ending succession of failed bicycle tires, leaky footballs and inner tubes. That was before anybody thought of sniffing for something other than to see if the baby needed to be changed.

Finally, Chip is done! All set! Our nether regions would definitely be maintained at 98.6 degrees or else. We could have withstood the next ice age in those get-ups. We couldn't walk without looking like Boris Karloff in "The Mummy," but that was a minor problem. Outside at last! We were ready!

Open the green front door to the sound of Mom's bells and we are free. Snow that is so pure it squeals when you walk on it, "Screech, screech, screech." Powdery, light as a feather and so white it hurts your eyes to see the contrast between the blanket of snow and the Michigan-blue sky.

"Man is it cold out here!"

Nose-holes closed up at first breath, and the chill took little nips at your lungs.

"Clark Malcolm, pull that scarf up over your mouth," sends us both hopping down the front porch, headed toward the garage before Mom can grab me and do the task. I ran around back and turned Patch loose. First things first.

Walking down the walk to the driveway was always an adventure in the winter, lined with Lake Erie's rocks as it was. We had hauled the lake's stones back home for the driveway and walk for as long as I can remember. The rule was, "sure you can go swimming, fishing, playing down by the lake, etc., as long as you bring home stones." Wagonload, car trunk, beach towels and bushel baskets, all packed with as many stones as possible had contributed to our driveway. It made for pretty treacherous walking, especially in winter, but sure-footed boys on their way to a sledding adventure paid it little mind. Dad is out warming up the blue station wagon. It's funny how so many of my memories revolve around that 1956 Ford. You'd think we never had any other, though I know we did. Almost everything of importance happened to me in that car. Smelly dogs, muskrat pelts, carp that had been speared, rocks from the beach, the list is endless.

Chip and I did have a great sled. It had been a birthday or Christmas gift to one or the other of us. Hadn't been used much, not many hills at the western end of Lake Erie, although we had made attempts to build some out of snow and ice several times. It was a Radio Flyer or American something or other and had red runners that were razor sharp, varnished wood so smooth you would slide off if you didn't concentrate and was it fast! Why, I could get Chip going about a thousand miles an hour all by myself.

We had hooked Patch to harness on that sled several times, with mixed results. She would start out pretty good but soon decide she would much prefer chewing on the sledders and would abandon her role as sled dog. That wasn't really too bad as long as you discounted the effects of frozen dog slobber on exposed surfaces. There weren't all that many open spaces other than breathing holes, but if she couldn't locate cheeks and mouths to wet up, she'd create them by taking mittens and hats whenever possible. What a dog! Yes, oh yes, this time we were ready for some mechanized form of propulsion on that sled. We were after ultimate speed. We were going to fly behind the car!

Pointe aux Peaux's caretaker and sometimes gate guard, Walter Nadeau, had scraped the roads with the old 8N Ford tractor that the subdivision owned. He was always pretty good about taking care of the snow and ice, once he got the snow blade hitched to it. That old tractor just didn't have enough gumption to do a really good job and left two or three inches of snow quickly packed down tight as the cars drove up and down the roads. So much the better, for it quickly became just as hard packed as any Olympic luge run designed and engineered by man. The residents didn't like it very much, but the kids did. There were times when it was packed so hard that we could put on ice skates and have a decent game of hockey right on Goddard Drive.

Out in the garage, Dad had pieced together a not quite credible tow-line made from cast off pieces of rope he or my mother had hoarded. Remember this was the 1950s and people hadn't gotten over having so little during the Depression and World War II. My family saved everything. Pull cords from "before they had re-winder" lawn mowers, the rope used to tie Patch when she was in season, parts of a replaced but still okay swing set ropes were all tied together to keep us far away from the gleaming chrome bumper of the

Ford. We had to stay far enough back so we wouldn't be lost from Dad's eyes in the rear view, far enough so there was time to use feet as extra brakes to stop the sled.

He had lots of instructions for us boys.

"I don't want you weaving back and forth on the road."

"Watch out for other cars."

"Hold on to your brother."

"Keep you legs and feet tucked in."

"Don't be fooling around back there!"

What's this about no fooling around? That's exactly what we wanted to do! How in the world were we going to remember all those rules and have fun too?

At times, parents don't understand that in order to enjoy something, really enjoy it, children can't be encumbered by regulation in any form. No rules. We were dutiful listeners though, appeared attentive because we weren't willing to let any apparent lapse in familial duty spoil this event. The Ford was warmed up and Dad backed it out of the garage to the street, tied the bits and pieces to the rear bumper and we were ready at last.

Chipinthefront, mebehind and Patchalongside, and we're holding on with the anticipation of youngsters about to be propelled down a roller coaster. I can see the snow tires on the car spin a bit as Dad pulls away from the sled, the rope uncoiling as he pulls forward. He's going pretty fast before the rope tightens and as it takes the weight of sled and boys, snaps in two before we are pulled more than three feet. The car diminishes in size as Dad, "who will watch us every second," drives merrily for about two hundred yards before he realized we are sitting on the sled in the middle of the road not going anywhere. I think he noticed only because Patch got his attention by chasing him down and barking. We shouted ourselves hoarse in about fifteen seconds, but he never heard us, until he eventually noticed that he was supposed to have two sons somewhere behind him. So much for the ever-watchful eyes of the parent.

As Dad backed up the car, he did a nice slalom from this side of the road to that, and got out to retie the rope. The piece that had parted was obviously rotted so he took a section out and discarded it before tying it back together. We were still pretty far away from the car, but ever so much closer. I glanced over at our house and could see Mom's disapproving eyes as she watched her beloved male children on a much shorter tether to the station wagon. She disappeared from the window. Looking for the Bag-Balm, no doubt. She may have gone to check that our Sunday suits were clean and pressed for the upcoming funerals. Mom liked to be prepared.

Without pausing for breath, Dad admonished us and went over the rules again. I suspected he was quickly running short for this task. He was also accustomed to sleeping during the day. God, the things we didn't have a clue about in those days. All we ever knew was that he could get mad at us in a heartbeat.

The second time he pulled away slowly and built up speed gradually, but we did go faster. Patch ran along side and tried to get on the sled too. Her repeated charges and attempts to get on the sled threatened to unseat us every time, but we managed to fend her off. The Terry's', the Holler's, Hemry's and Edward's houses moved by in ever increasing blurs and by the time we got to the turn for Ives Street we were flyin'! We were wetted and frosty from Patch too. She thought that she should have benefited from this free ride stuff, but no matter how hard she tried she couldn't manage to fit in between Chip and me. She soon figured it out and just added sound effects to our ride.

What a Dad!! At the turn, the old Ford was sliding and so were we. Dad made the turn, but our momentum kept us going right for the ditch. Something about the laws of motion and it appeared that foot steering the sled wasn't doing much good.

We are gonna crash!! Hot Ziggity!

We came to a jolting stop as the nose of the sled met the frozen, unyielding side of the ditch bank. Snap goes the rope and we were motionless once more. We jumped up quickly to show no permanent damage. Patch jammed us both back to the ground in play, rolling her big body over us and into the shallow ditch. No problem, we weren't hurt, and wouldn't admit it if we had been. This was FUN! The neck-wrenching stop was all part of it. Dad backed up again, checked us both quickly, ordered Patch back toward home and retied the even shorter rope. We were off again (Patch still along side the sled).

Ives Street runs from the gate at the front of the subdivision all the way to Lake Erie before it turns left and becomes Sterling Road, more than a half-mile long. We were much closer to the car because of the rope break, but old Dad was getting the hang of this pullin' stuff. Soon enough we were going faster than before the first wreck, but not fast enough to outrun Patch. She was a definite hazard to sledding. Past Mrs. Lukes', the Whites', up to and speeding by the Girards' house.

Man, are we cookin'!

Dad slowed down to make the turn in plenty of time, but the sled did not. Our legs were all tucked in like Dad said, but other than our galoshes the sled had no brakes.

The tailpipe got lots bigger, but as Dad was watching us this time, he managed to keep ahead of the sled, negotiate the turn and not break the rope. We were off again, this time down Sterling Drive, past the pier, past the three pillars and Dr. Walker's house. I saw Todd Belisle gape at us as we whizzed past his house, all the way to the boat ramp before Dad slowed the car down again.

"This is GREAT, Dad!"

We twisted and tusseled that car-to-sled, umbilical cord through Sterling's turns before we reached Goddard again, but we were getting the hang of newfound speed too. All too soon we were back in front of the house and Mom was standing there making sure there are still two on the sled and neither of us is leaking anything important. I saw Mom tuck the Bag Balm tin into her coat pocket just as we skimmed by.

Dad just honked, we waved dutifully and we went round again, feeling ever more confident, not only in ourselves but Dad's dedication to this fun Saturday as well. Patch decided if she couldn't ride, she'd wait on the porch. No problems that time around, but we were beginning to attract attention. Robert Edwards was almost drooling as we sped by and Chucky White was out standing in front of his house looking jealous. *Their* dads weren't pulling them on sleds. *Ours* was.

I hollered at him, "Like we're gonna stop! No room on this sled, buddy! See you next time around!"

We'd learned to steer this thing pretty well by then and began some of those daring, side to side swerves that we'd been warned against. No problem though, Dad was grinning as he saw us first on this side of the car, then the other. His boys!

Push hard with right foot, go left, hard with left, go right. Why anybody can do this, even Chip.

We kept urging Dad to achieve faster and faster speeds and he accommodated us to our heart's content. I'm sure we weren't doing more that ten or fifteen miles per hour, but it's all relative. We were sure no one had ever been pulled faster. Around that subdivision we went, and Dad sometimes helped the sled swerve by making long controlled curves for us to mimic. We'd figured out where the rough parts were and avoided the patches of pavement, which sometimes appeared, spotty as they were.

After three or four navigations, when we approached our house, we saw Mom leading this pretty, pink swaddled, figure out to the road. Pink snowsuit, white bonnet, white scarf over face, Peg looked like a Hostess Snow Ball topped with a blob of white coconut. I recall her struggles over the mound of snow left by the tractor, her eyes alight as we slowed to a stop. Experience had obviously taught Mom that this sledding adventure was not as dangerous as it first appeared. Mom still appeared wary, but the sight of two uninjured sons after so many times around the neighborhood must have been reassuring. Peg was going sledding.

We'd thought the first set of sledding rules had been excessive, but we had underestimated our mother's ability to think up additional things to tell us not to do. I think most of the time we were sledding Mom had been writing rules down and committing them to memory, for she recited them chapter and verse to us before she relinquished Peg to our keeping. Mom even had a set of rules for Dad to follow, detailed enough to glaze his eyes as well. Mom lined us up; Dad, me, and Chip, according to size. We were all getting orders.

My father knew when to pay attention.

We were made to understand that if anything, "and I mean anything," untoward happened to this angel of a child, Dad and boys should hope for a late thaw on Lake Erie, point the car and sled toward Canada. Write when we got there. If there had been any extra rope left, I'm sure Mom would have devised a foolproof way of tying her baby daughter to the sled, in case of any mishaps.

Off we went, sledding carefully and cautiously until we were well away from the judgmental looks of my mother. Mom's eyes were on us hard as we pulled away and it was just like having to wear a second coat. You knew it was there for your own good, but it sure did hamper your movements. Cautiously, for Dad was receiving those thoughts too, we crept down Goddard, accompanied now by Robert Edwards running alongside. He was not only keeping pace with the sled, but would put on short bursts of speed to pass us while laughing derisively. This was like slow motion, like going backwards, like sledding with Patch, less the slobber. I think Robert's hooting and hollering did the trick.

Boley, as we called him, was no athlete, not by any stretch of the imagination. Whenever he ran, which wasn't often, his stomach continued the motion for at least fifteen seconds after the rest of his body had stopped.

We saw Dad's ears turning red even from our distant vantage point. He motioned to Boley, and demanded that he stop running alongside the car, but to little avail. Finally good ol' Dad couldn't take it any more and he began to speed up faster and faster, leaving our antagonist behind. I glanced at Robert as we sped by and noticed that his belly was still trying to keep up, but his legs had quit. Dad didn't let up on the speed and by the time he got to Ives Street was going too fast to make the sharp turn toward the lake. He eased through the gentle right curve instead, heading for the stone entrance pillars at the front of the subdivision.

These stone pillars were about four feet square, stood about eight feet tall, had held swinging gates at one time and sat next to Mr. Miller's realty office to one side of the entrance. They were as solid as the day they were put up. I thought Dad would come to a stop and we'd just turn around.

Due to the amount of snow that year and the weak engine of the Ford tractor, Walt had been forced to build little mountains of snow alongside the small office whenever that tractor just couldn't push any more. Mr. Miller and our caretaker were good friends and they had an agreement that Walt could pile up snow in front of the small building all winter long, as long as he was careful about the building. I also believe he had some kind of arrangement with the little country store outside the subdivision because he would clean the gas pump and parking area, dragging the snow across the street to build more mountains in front of the small realty office. These mounds of snow continued to grow in size as the winter weather progressed.

Dear Dad, prideful of his sons, made the curve toward the gate, but had not yet slowed down due to the taunting of Boley, so our sled began its entry into the self-satisfying motion known as centrifugal force. The increase in speed was exhilarating! The road blurred as wind and cold made marbles out of our eyes, but our perception of time slowed immeasurably. The pillars appeared to be moving toward us with the speed of an on rushing locomotive and only by sheer will and the application of several sets of galoshes did we clear the entrance. Unfortunately, though it was much too quick to be considered a problem at the time, the sled now headed directly for the mounds of snow outside the gate.

In a heartbeat we were flying. The slope of the snow pile was its own perfect form of a ski jump. Up we went as smoothly as a glider taking off, propelled from the mound of snow! Dad abruptly stopped the car, but nothing stopped us except gravity. We were in actual flight, soaring adjacent to our car, but replaced quickly with the stomach twisting sense of falling. I think of the myriad looks on my father's face as we floated by the driver's window after being launched into space perfectly described the total nature of our flight. I know that I only saw him for a millisecond; however the changes of emotion that colored his face would have done an octopus proud.

Dad's first expression appeared a casual; "Oh, there they are," but turned quickly into; "No, it can't be them," and was followed in rapid succession by;

"Oh, M'God! Are there any cars coming? What am I going to tell their mother? His mouth curled down with the last; "I wonder if Dorothee was kidding about Canada."

Our momentary delight, laced with the fear at being airborne didn't last too long, as three children and a steel runnered sled aren't exactly aerodynamic. The sled came down with a sickening crunch. Three heads played billiards as they cracked together and the sled stopped dead. The rope had swung us around sideways to the car's front end, which was now fortunately stopped. Dad could move quickly when needed and picked us up individually in order of importance.

Peg had hit her head hard enough to momentarily stun her and she was pretty limp as he first lifted her up. It was one of the few times I ever saw my father look uncertain about anything. Peg's silence didn't last long, as she soon realized that she was alive, awake and big time scared. It was also one of the only times I remember her crying as a child. She put out a siren-like scream that emptied Jones's Market of customers and my piano teacher, Mrs. Asyltyne, came rushing to her front door, and she was nearly deaf. I later remember being astonished that Mom didn't hear the wail back at our house. Dad spent a lot of time examining her, totally ignoring Chip and me, until he was well satisfied and her screams had been reduced to the occasional sob and hiccup stage.

He then turned his attention to Chip. Now I loved my brother then and still do, but he was as good a screamer as God ever put on this earth. I was a little surprised that his screams hadn't deafened Dad as soon as he exited the car. What was even more amazing was Dad's ability to completely disregard him during those first moments. If ever there was a kid that needed quieting, it was Chip after the crash. He'd been banged around quite a bit and I recall a nosebleed somewhere in there as well. Dad picked up a handful of snow and began to hold it over his face looking like he was trying to quiet him through the suffocation technique. Fathers do attain some degree of wisdom with practice, although I'm sure Chip didn't think so at the time. He was a handful as Dad scrubbed his face pink, squirmy and loud as ever, but he eventually quieted.

Last but not least, me. I hate to admit it, but that launch had scared the dickens out of me. All well and good to seek speed and thrills, but the reality of hearing Peg's and Chip's screams, seeing dark bruises already beginning to form under Chip's eyes were all too much. I was probably bawling as loud as the others, but being the biggest and last in line, got delayed treatment. I wasn't really hurt, other than my pride. The look on Dad's face was enough to shut me up quickly, but I remember distinctly wanting and not getting some ministrations of my own. I now chalk it up to being the oldest, but I sure did want my Momma.

It didn't take a genius to see the wheels spinning in Dad's head as he was devising some guiltless ending for our misadventure. He spent a great deal of time trying to think and talk his way through a plausible explanation of the events. He coached us all and I remember him trying to convince Peg that she had been in the car with him when it happened, but she wasn't buying that. Her snowsuit was dirty, with spots from Chip's nosebleed splattered on a pink background, and besides she looked pretty bedraggled. She had that "I'm telling Mom" look on her face, and Dad wasn't too happy about that, but what could he do? Chip was still hiccupping occasionally, but the blood had stopped flowing, and I was feeling less sorry for myself. It was time to go home.

The sled was lying on its side by the car and although wounded like the rest of us, still looked like it would work. It almost appeared sorry for the airborne venture, as if contrite for the harm done. Dad picked the sled up and was about to put it in the car when I told him that I would pull Chip and Peg home. He appeared greatly relieved to possibly delay the tongue-lashing he was sure to get. Heck, he was probably glad to get shed of us after all that. He closed the tailgate of the wagon, watched Chip and Peg clamber on the sled and waved out the window of the Ford as he drove slowly toward home.

I had just gotten started, taking the strain of my siblings and sled when we heard the singsong voice of Mrs. Asyltyne calling us over. She'd watched the whole episode through her porch windows and probably thought we had been abandoned. Mrs. Asyltyne was a widow, a retired music teacher, and was in the running for some minor neighborhood saint status. She was tiny and neat, great of bosom, but somehow looked like a sparrow. She made retirement ends meet by teaching the rudiments of piano to all of the dribbling, drooling, scabby-kneed children in the neighborhood. My sister Carole had studied piano and voice with her for years and was becoming an accomplished pianist in her own right. Under her tutelage Carole was also developing what was to become a marvelous singing voice, powerful and pure.

The success with Carole had prompted my mother to enlist her help with me as well, but I'm sure Mrs. Asyltyne thought there wasn't much hope. I recall encouragement from her in the form of "you have a good ear for music, Clark." I didn't know about my ears, but my fingers became spaghetti-like at the mere mention of piano exercises. I continued to go, but dreaded her lessons because she could divine to the second how much time I'd devoted to practice.

Saint that she was, she would just have me begin at the beginning once again. Multiply my awkwardness times ten or twelve and you can figure out much work her inept pupils required. I marveled even then at her patience.

She motioned with an inviting wave and met us at her front door with warm pats and little chirps of condolence and ushered us into her kitchen to "have a cup of hot chocolate and a cookie."

Mrs. Asyltyne sang all of the time. I don't mean singing songs. Her speech was melodic, a soft voice that flowed through the musical scale as she spoke. She Christmas-caroled her way through getting our coats, mittens and hats off, hymned us to the kitchen table and twittered us a soothing melody as she puttered about heating the milk for our hot chocolate. She didn't move very fast, but with the eons of teaching practice and all that experience with children, there wasn't much wasted motion.

She began by spit daubing Peg with her hankie, then progressed to gently washing us up so that by the time the milk was hot and the cookies pulled from the cookie jar, we looked as if we had just stopped by for a visit. She even twisted up her hankie and washed the blood out of Chip's nose. He didn't squirm very much while she was about the task either. She scrubbed the spots off Peg's snowsuit, all the while hypnotizing us with the tune of her voice. We were calmed by her presence, all warm and snug and safe in her kitchen; completely entranced by the special treatment. She played the piano for us while we ate and by the time she finished, we had almost forgotten the episode with the sled. Cookies eaten, cups rinsed, we laughed and giggled our way out the door, situated ourselves to the various tasks of passenger and puller and were on our way home. The magic of the mother, teacher, and woman that day was something so extraordinary, I didn't realize until much later in life the transformation she had orchestrated.

The trip home was uneventful, me pulling my brother and baby sister home, Patch trailing, like I had done so many times before and would do again in a minute if I could get back there. I remember it had started snowing when we were in Mrs. Asyltyne's house, making the world magically quiet and peaceful. I wondered if she had anything to do with the snowflakes and was pretty sure she did. Our spirits and bodies were satisfied, the scare of the adventure was changing into exciting memories, and we were one unit. We were two brothers and a little sister, completely happy to be where and when we were.

Everything was just right.

Chapter 20
Do Right

Even though he lived next door, Tim and I weren't the best of buddies.

Mom was always telling us kids to "love thy neighbor as thyself," but about the best I could for him do was a hearty loathing. Tim was sort of a roly-poly kid who wasn't really interested in Indians or the marsh or much of anything I was. He was mostly a stay around the house boy and seldom got involved with me, unless it was getting me in trouble. Tim also was a bigger tattle-tale than my older sister and Carole was better than most. He had perfected the job of making sure my mother knew every little thing I did and I never saw him happier than when he managed to get me in a fix. When and if I somehow managed to steer clear of self-created problems, Tim had been known to make up some conceivable tale and report the lie. Given all my past recklessness, most stories involving Clark were often taken as fact first and Tim exploited this.

One late summer day everybody was having a great time with the beans from the Catalpa tree. These beans resemble regular green beans except for their size and hardness. They are larger in diameter, grow up to eighteen inches in length and are flexible but tough. They made for the most wonderful throwing and dodging games imaginable. We had two versions of the contest. The short range game allowed ducking while the long range variety required no moving, not even a flinch. Dave and Steve, Chip and I, Boley and Gary were having this spectacular, "everybody against everybody else" short range contest when Tim wanted to get in on the fun, too. We had been slinging them at each other for thirty minutes, laughing and dodging to get out of the way or loudly rubbing the resultant sting when we couldn't. Those hard long beans could leave a mark, but it was all part of the challenge. The object was to hit someone else, all the while watching for some missile heading your way.

I knew letting Tim join in was a mistake even as we told him, "Sure, come on."

The First Rule of this game was no blubbering. Everybody who played knew of the surety of getting hit and played with this understanding. It was kind of like going swimming. If you went in the water you were bound to get wet. Bean chucking equals smarting. Beyond the "Ouch!" or "Yow!" or "Dang!" that went with each score, we played the game with exuberance. Hitting one's target only meant that within a blink the thrower could expect to be dodging the artillery from every other player in the game. The hitter consistently became the hit. The giver continuously became the receiver. It's how the game was played.

Before three minutes had elapsed Tim was crying and ran right in my house to tell my mom. I even tackled him and held him down for a couple of minutes but he kept right on screech after screech. I got Patch to lick his face, but that only made him scream the louder. Our contributions just couldn't keep this pampered baby quiet. I let him up hoping he'd run away and stop on his own. He ran alright. Bawling and yowling, he barged right in and he didn't even knock.

I neglected to give the reasons for rule number one. Kids all knew mothers hear crying children and it doesn't even have to be their kids. Crying might mean telling, if the causer couldn't settle and quiet the crier. Investigation for the source of and reason for the hollering would always put an end to the game. There was another motive for our rule and it had to do with one of Mom's laws, "No throwing the beans at each other." Unfortunately, they were so ideally suited to the game we couldn't resist. Chip and I had been dressed down for slinging them around on any number of occurrences. Once when it happened twice in one day I got sent to my room with the door closed tight.

Mom was probably on her feet by the time Tim pulled open the door. I know everybody else took off for parts unknown as soon as they saw him get to our porch. One minute there were a bunch of warriors, the next instant I was abandoned on the field of battle. Even that rat Chip figured there was wisdom in flight. All the kids in the neighborhood were familiar with my mom and knew how stupid it would be to stick around to see what came next. If I didn't live there I'd have gone into hiding too, but I knew the inevitability of any just rewards I had in store. Better to get it over with now than to wait. Past experience had convinced me that no wrong I did ever went unpunished and

Mom had a memory like an elephant.

Tim followed her out of the house and I met them in the driveway. Tim stood out of reach, hiding behind Mom all the time I was hearing it.

Not crying.

Gloating.

Although he hadn't been in my house for more than fifteen seconds, his small hurt had been replaced with overwhelming delight to see me catch the dickens. Peeking around her with a smirky look on his face, reveling when he heard my sentence. One week grounding. It was the peeking *and* smirking that got to me. If he'd have done one or the other I might have simply taken my restriction. I may have shrugged off his snitching despite losing a week's freedom in the summer, a cost I considered huge. The thought crossed my mind that I might have been set up but I didn't think Tim was that smart.

I found out he was that devious.

My mother made me come inside as part of her edict. When I walked into the living room she added that I was foolish to include Tim in my roughhouse types of play.

"Clark, you know every time he plays with you he ends up crying. I don't understand why you haven't figured out he doesn't have fun the same way you and Chip do. When he cries I have to respond to his tears. If you're going to live next door to him you have to think of another way to amuse yourselves together. You can stay in for a while now. Let him find an alternative to baiting you."

I had an idea myself about baiting.

I managed to glean but few admirable attributes thus far in life, choosing instead to learn most lessons time and again. From my time watching wildlife, I had mastered patience. I knew how to wait. Tim would fail to remember the incident except for the part of my punishment. He'd stroll over to my yard or reach through the lilac bushes to retrieve an errant ball. Something would cause him to overlook the potential for payback he'd created when he complained to my mother.

I wouldn't forget.

I enlisted Chip's help. My baby brother was seven at the time, but he had the same sense of vengeance as I did. We both knew the necessity of payback for some wrong; like telling.

I had to wait three whole days. I saw Tim but pretended to ignore him completely. My apparent indifference led to an inattentive attitude on his part. He was chasing my brother who wasn't under restriction, because Chip was the bait. With my encouragement, he'd grabbed Tim's push-scooter and brought it over to our yard. Chip was good at the luring. He first had to wait until Tim came outside and then act surprised when he was caught in the act. When Chip ran pushing the scooter into our yard Tim followed him right up to the front of our garage.

I cut off his escape route. And got him in a headlock. And Dutch Rubbed him bald. Almost. He started screaming just as soon as I grabbed him but I didn't care. He was blubbering and crying, telling me I'd be sorry when my mom found out. What a baby! I knew upfront my chances of punishment for this were high but the need for payback overshadowed all other thought. Premeditated is the word. I told him if he ever told my mother on me again I'd make him eat grass. From around Patch's dog house. Where she'd pooped. Fresh.

Then I let him up and dared him to go tell my mother. In fact I begged him to. I also told him I wasn't fooling about the grass.

He said I'd be sorry. But he went back home and didn't run in his house to tell. I was satisfied. If his mom didn't know and mine didn't either everything would be just fine. So I wasn't in the least bit sorry at all. I knew my universe was set right once more. I served my seven day restriction, went back to my normal careening about and forgot about the incident.

Until Chip ran in the house four days later and told me he saw Tim hit Patch with a shovel. Patch was just walking behind their garage and he ran out and hit her hard. Hard enough to make her yelp and take off.

When I caught up with Tim, he didn't get any Dutch Rubbing. Nope, this time it was punches, hard as I could mostly right in his fat, blubbery tummy. For real good measure I socked his nose once, too. Then he did have as reason to cry like a baby. I didn't have to tell him why he was getting a licking. He knew and I knew. I saved all my energy to beat him up good. I held him down for the longest time, punching his belly again when I thought he needed it. For emphasis I smeared his bloody snotty nose goop all over his face. I finished up by telling him this would be nothing compared to what would happen if he ever hit my dog again.

Although at first it looked like I was cruising for a bruising of my own when both moms found out, I didn't get in much trouble. Tim's mother was pretty mad when she discovered what Tim had done. She even said he deserved the whipping I gave him. She was right. My mom just shook her head and said she wished we'd get along.

"Fighting doesn't solve anything Clark," she told me.

But Mom was wrong. It sure solved this.

Nobody hits my dog.

Several hours later I was outside playing catch with Chip and Dave Hicks in the field in front of my house. Mom was at the lake with Peg and Carole. When Tim's father got home from work I waved to him but didn't pay any more attention than that. My involvement with his kid was over and done. We went back to playing catch, just tossing the ball back and forth, whiling time.

Dave had just caught a high fly ball I'd thrown, when he said, "Oh, oh. Here comes Tim and his dad."

I turned and looked over my shoulder. Sure enough, Mr. Terry was almost running across the field toward us, hurrying enough so his tie flapped around his collar. Tim had to run to keep up, but he was smiling.

Mr. Terry started right in on me, demanding to know who I thought I was, beating his son up. Tim hid again, this time behind his father. Really grinning this time, savoring every word his father slashed my way. When I tried to tell him what his little baby had done, Mr. Terry just told me to "SHUT UP! KEEP YOUR MOUTH SHUT!" When I did hush and just looked at him, my stupid dumb left eye crossed.

I had a fine view of him and my nose. The double vision of him all mixed up with my nose was too much. I couldn't help it. He looked so funny superimposed on my left nostril. Just like a big nose with a face. I giggled. I didn't mean to, but it just slipped out. If I thought he was angry before it paled to what he acted like now.

"What, you some kind of a smart-ass?" He screamed in my face. "You a little wise ass along with being a bully?"

Mr. Terry grabbed me by one arm and started shaking me. His hand was like a gigantic pincer, squeezing and kneading my arm and I hollered with the harm. When you're eleven years old, adults are not only enormous; their ferocity is a fearsome and electrifying matter. I tried to stay away from all adult anger and men especially when they were furious. He scared the dickens out of me and I started to yell.

Tim thought this was just great. He started jumping up and down and pointing at me.

Tim laughed and hollered, "Get him Daddy!"

Some encouragement was just what the man needed because he grabbed me by both arms. Both hands were digging and bruising my upper arms. He shook me so violently my head whipped forward and backward and my chin bumped my chest with each jangling jerk. He continued to worry me cruelly, back and forth, all the time yelling, hollering, screaming, so mad by now spittle sprayed from his mouth. I was screaming in fright right along with him.

"Smart Ass Little Punk! I'll Whip Your Ass! I'll teach…"

I screamed again and again.

Then Patch bit him.

With a deep snarl she hit him hard from a flat out run. Not one of those bite, step back and see what happens snaps. Patch grabbed his upper thigh and drove him right to his knees. Now it was Mr. Terry's turn to scream and he did a fine job with a high pitched wail that split the air as he toppled over on his side. Tim started running in circles around the melee, waving his arms and adding his screams to his father's.

On his side and still screaming, Mr. Terry flailed at Patch with his fists but she continued to muscle forward. A terrible rumbling in her throat, bent low and shoving, she forced him to stop hitting at her and concentrate more on his shrieking. I'd stopped being scared as soon as Patch grabbed him, but it still took me a few moments to gather myself together enough to call Patch off. When I quieted myself I whistled to get her attention. As soon as I called her name, she turned him loose and trotted back to check me out.

I knelt down and hugged her heavy neck and I could feel the rumbling in her chest. She was even now perched on the sharp edge of violence, still so tense she quivered and trembled hotly despite my arms around her.

Mr. Terry started cussing me once more, screaming louder, frothing spittle now, and using much worse words than before. Patch leaped toward him again but I caught her by the collar. He shrieked when he saw her lunge, but started right in again when I held her back. He was going to *call the police*, he was going to *shoot my dog*, he was going to *sue my father*, he was going to…

I didn't hear anyone come up behind me, but she stood right by my shoulder.

"Bill Terry, *you're* not going to do a damn thing. I heard and saw the entire episode from my yard. If you call the sheriff, I'll tell them how you were man-handling Clark. You could have really hurt him. It's a good thing the dog was here or you would have. You ought to be ashamed of yourself."

Another neighbor, Molly Miller, stood with hands on hips, glorious and glaring down at Mr. Terry.

Molly lived and breathed kitty-corner from our house. This seemed appropriate. She was slinky like a cat. She was flashy and smoked cigarettes stuck in an ebony holder, painted her lips real red and rouged her cheeks. She dyed her hair midnight black and didn't have real eyebrows. She painted hers on with a brush. Molly wore tight black Capri pants and leopard print blouses tied in a knot to show off her belly button. She was loud, brash and I never knew what exciting incident would come alive because of her. She scared the dickens out of me and everybody else in the neighborhood.

I thought then she looked like the Victory Lady picture Grandpa kept in the barn, except for the bare breast.

"What you do need to do is have your wife do something about that dog bite. You're bleeding all over yourself. You ought to get back to your house. *Right now*. Remember what I said about the sheriff, Bill. If they come out here, I'll tell them the whole story."

Molly turned to me.

"You probably need to have Patch checked." When I started to protest, she added, "She might have caught something when she bit him." She snickered and patted the top of Patch's head. "She took him right off his feet. Sort of evened things up quick, didn't she?"

I squeezed Patch tighter, burying my face in her coarse fur, feeling the suspicion and tautness in her yet.

"I'm okay girl. I'm okay."

Molly chortled with laughter now.

"Bill Terry, you are a certified fool. Let boys fix their own problems. Next time you think you can get away with roughing up some child maybe you'll check first to see if their dog is nearby."

Molly bent over and put her face close to Mr. Terry, who was still lying on the ground and she snorted again, softer this time.

"You really are a fool. And you're the bully."

Molly straightened up and spoke to Chip, "You take Dave and go find your mother. You tell her what happened, but ask her to stop by and see me before she does anything else."

And to me, "Bring your dog. You both come to my house until your mother gets here."

Molly chuckled one more time. "You sure don't need any protection, but I want to make certain your mother hears the right story."

Molly and I watched as Mr. Terry struggled to his feet. Patch started growling again when he stood up and I tightened my arms to let her know it was okay. He kept his eyes on Patch the whole time he got up and backed away several steps before he turned to hobble toward his house.

I rose wobbling a little and Molly put her arm over my shoulder.

I spoke softly to Patch, "C'mon girl. Let's go."

But Patch didn't move, wouldn't budge, although I tugged at her collar. At attention, she watched Mr. Terry and Tim walk all the way to their house. She wouldn't turn her head away until they went inside and the door swung closed. I wondered if Mr. Terry knew how lucky he had just been; how Patch targeted his leg instead of other body parts.

I knew how lucky I was because Molly arrived when she did. It never hurt to have an adult on your side. And I had my dog. We were like minded about each other.

Nobody hurts her boy.

Patch had a lot of do-right in her.

She had such a keen sense of fairness and seldom allowed anyone to continue if they chose to ignore her lines. Who the violator was, was of no concern. When Patch decided something was amiss, it was put right as fast as possible. Patch was such a powerful animal that wrongs didn't last long at all.

We were playing football. Just one of those Autumn pick-up games, when the ground is wet and muddy enough so kids *look* like they've been playing football. I'm sure everyone has witnessed dozens, made up of groups of shirt-tails out and patched-jeans boys, all of them wildly reckless in play. Those divided evenly as the numbers allow, no helmets and pads, no tackling around the neck, no points after touchdown games are played over and over by thousands of kids when the leaves start to color. Neighborhood games are not for the faint hearted but reserved for kids with a vitality which exists only between ages seven and twelve.

In the field across from Boley's house we were tackling and running and blocking and Patch was sort of on my side. Patch was extremely good at running. Mostly running off with the football, but we made allowances for her. The goal lines, which were imaginary anyhow, extended circularly for Patch and if she crossed the unseen perimeter in any direction a goal was scored. Patch had a huge head and could grab the fattest part of the football in her mouth without any problem. Of course her carries were always followed by an official time out to wipe the ball off but again these were just part of the allowances. Patch played offense and defense right along with everybody else but she was a heck of a good tackler. I was never able to figure out which she liked best. She wasn't good about waiting for the ball to be snapped and was mostly always off-sides, another modification of rules just for her. Patch played the game more riotously than we did.

It was impossible to put a hand on her when she had the ball, because she

230

dodged and scurried so well. Scored every time. Patch scored when my side had the ball and she scored when the other side was in possession. Even if she didn't get in on the tackle she grabbed the pigskin after every play and we didn't have to call time outs to wipe the ball off. Plus, we had to wait for our laughter to stop. There was plenty of time between plays.

Boley's dad came out to watch the game first and Gary's father came out shortly after. Several more fathers showed up and before long we had a cheering section, coaching staff, referees and line-judges running up and down the field with us. Every one laughed as much as we did when Patch pranced off with the ball.

Before too long the grown-ups decided to join our game but they weren't any better than we were at catching Patch, they just gave up quicker.

Mr. Edwards was playing opposite his son, who happened to be on my team. Mr. Edwards was a big man, about 6'2'' and weighed more than 250 pounds. He had been the Strong Man at our Cub Scout Fair two years ago and to us kids he was a giant. I still laughed when I thought of his skinny legs sticking out of that leopard costume. He drove truck for a living and wasn't home for long periods but when he was here, he played with his kids and us, too. Mr. Edwards constantly seemed to be in a fine mood, with a ready smile and a hello for all of the kids in the neighborhood. I don't recall ever seeing him any other way.

The two men quickly influenced the game. They could get to the ball carrier faster than us kids could because it was easy for them to shove us out of the way. I was the biggest kid on the field at about 75 pounds, although Boley, two years my junior, was catching up to me fast. Mr. Edwards pushed me around like I wasn't even there and so did Gary's father. Mr. Hemry wasn't as big as Boley's dad was but he didn't have to be large to outsize us kids. We were out muscled, out weighed. The men loved every minute. So did we.

Every time Boley got the ball his father would scoop him up like an oversized sack of potatoes and carry him five yards further back than from the scrimmage line where he started. Laughing the entire time as he lugged his kid back. It was fourth or fifth or ninth down and we had about sixty yards to go for a first down. We hadn't been keeping track since the fathers took over. It didn't matter.

The next time Mr. Edwards tackled his son, Boley got some help. Patch grabbed Mr. Edwards by the seat of his jeans and yanked him backwards. Startled, he let go of his son but lost his balance in the process. Patch kept on pulling. Laughing, Mr. Edwards lay on his side and Patch kept backing up.

Tugging and huffing as she dragged him over the muddy field. Mr. Edwards couldn't get up because he was laughing so hard and because Patch had a little momentum. Finally she quit but there was a drag mark on the grass about five feet long. Just as soon as she let go of his jeans she ran around in front of him and gave him one good bark before dashing off to see where Boley had gotten to.

"WOOF!"

The wrong was set right and now she wanted the ball back.

Mr. Edwards sat there a long time. He couldn't stop laughing long enough to find his feet and it was okay with us because we were tired of football.

"WRESTLING!"

As long as he was already down on the ground, we took advantage. Piled right on him. Screaming wildly we ganged up on him. Every one of us. Barking wildly, too.

Did I tell you how good Patch was at wrestling?

Patch was one tough dog.

She'd whipped every dog in our neighborhood twice and most of the dogs in Stoney Pointe too. She wouldn't charge out to bother any animals who ran by or explored areas that she considered in an unmarked "free zone," but those that dared a trespass met a merciless punishment. The only dogs not under Patch's authority were those whose owners kept them tied or fenced in, but because few people kept their dogs restrained, Patch had ample opportunity to establish her standing in the subdivision.

Most families owned at least one dog and some had enough to be called a pack. The Basteins had so many barking and jumping dogs in their yard I was never sure of the count. They lived on Long Road, the one lane dirt rutted, trash lined, gouge that dead-ended at our private stomping grounds in the marsh. Some of their yard was fenced but it was poorly done and wired together in many places to keep it from falling down. The ragged enclosures formed a flimsy and inconsistent barrier, and there were many escapes. Some of Bastein's dogs weren't kept in their fenced yard at all but were free to roam and harass any thing or person they chose. Both those confined in the fence and the unrestricted blustered and barked and bit. When we saw one or two of the Bastein pack loose, Patch and I normally chose to cut through the farmer's field that separated their street and Pointe aux Peaux Road to avoid a scuffle with one of his dogs.

Over the course of several years, in spite of the pain that Patch inflicted on them any number of times, they never learned. Several of Mr. Bastein's pack members had been punctured or lamed by Patch and he didn't like it at all. But Mr. Bastein refused to admit that his dogs jumped or escaped their fence. He also denied their aggressive behavior and would not fix the fence. He had called our house to complain several times but he didn't get much satisfaction. My parents knew Patch and her nature.

That day, we walked Long Road as if it belonged to us. Patch was the only dog I ever saw who could actually gird her loins for battle. Even now, at eight years old, Patch was a fearsome dog if provoked.

Mr. Bastein had acquired another four big lanky hound dogs last summer, ostensibly trained to hunt raccoons. Their baying punctuated many autumn nights and told in mournful voice of some treed creature's plight. I really liked to hear their baleful tones, but that's where my affection for these churlish dogs stopped.

The pack rose in belligerence whenever a stranger and his dog moseyed along in front of their house.

All four male hounds challenged us as we headed into the marsh. Patch and I ignored their ragged barking and rushing feints of attack inside their enclosure. We stayed in the road, eyes front but wary and most of the time this snub would work. Today they were aggressive as never before and the flimsy picket fence was no match for their lunges. Instead of the normal taunting from the driveway, when the fence gave up all pretense of confinement, two of the dogs charged out to the road, baying and snapping their jaws. The other two quickly followed. In ten seconds more I was kicking and hollering at all four dogs as Patch chattered her teeth in defiance. I managed to keep them away for only a few moments, but their attack seemed to go on forever.

In the blink of an eye one of the dogs bit me and I yowled in hurt and fear. Patch stopped being showy as the hound bit and released, then lunged again and grabbed my ankle and held on. I lost my balance and fell in the dirt road, surrounded by dust and dogs, hollering, gasping and choking all at the same time.

Patch struck in an explosion. She grabbed my attacker right below the jaw where the neck meets the skull. Her momentum tore the other dog's teeth away from my ankle and I screamed the louder as her force dragged my leg along with the dog. Her weight drove the dog to the side of the road, but she didn't let up and kept her fury roiling up clouds of dust and dirt. I saw Patch still had my assailant pinned down and wasn't letting up, all the while disregarding the other three darting and biting dogs.

When she finally let go the dog didn't get up. Her muzzle was a riot of bloody slobber and as she whirled away from the dead dog, the blood from her jowls splattered across my shirt and face. I had watched her whip dogs before and enjoyed their tail-tucked retreats I saw when she was finished making her point. She usually listened to my commands and I was able to order her off, to settle her down when I saw fit. This was a Patch I hadn't seen before. Patch grabbed another of the dogs on the upper foreleg and forced him down into the dust, close to where I was still laying. The first dog hadn't an opportunity to make a sound once Patch had it by the throat, but that second dog screamed just like a hurt child.

As soon as the second dog shrieked the other two ran away.

Amid the frightening terrible noise, Patch snarled throatily and didn't let go. I scooted over to the struggle and tried to get her to release the still screaming dog.

"No Patch! No! Back! Back!"

She continued to push-pull the dog's leg, jumping stiff legged as she drove her teeth deeper still. I heard the joint snap, a sharp sound against the roar in Patch's throat. The hound screamed again and went limp, unconscious. I forced my voice to soften enough for Patch to release the second dog and eventually she did, but only to run back to worry the first dog. Patch was still so full of fury and fight. I had to hobble over to get her away from the body of the dead dog. It took continued quiet words to finally get her to look at me.

I knew right off that we had to get away. I was sure glad Mr. Bastein was at work, but I knew his wife had been peering from behind the shabby curtains of their front window. She hadn't even come out when she saw the attack. I dusted my pants off and pulled one jeans leg up to inspect the hurt. Deep puncture wounds laced my ankle. Yup, it was bleeding and it hurt like fire.

We'd had an audience. Mr. and Mrs. Dombroski were watching from their yard across the street. She asked me if I was okay, which surprised me, because I thought she was still mad at me for a snowball last winter when I hit her precious little grandson Danny. Maybe the ferocity of the dogfight or the blood at my exposed ankle softened her heart. I said I was okay but I was going to go home. Mrs. Dombroski said she thought that was a real good idea.

As we started to cross the field, I saw Mom coming my way. Someone obviously called her but they apparently hadn't talked long.

Apron flapping as she hurried, I saw Mom halfway across the field. She was making better time than I was, because my ankle was stiffening up and hobbling along made it hurt with every step.

"Betty Bastein just called me. Are you okay?" she hollered, still far off. "Is Patch all right?"

I hadn't even thought to check Patch for injuries, but I knelt down now and did. She was gory from muzzle to front legs, covered in stiffening redness but I couldn't feel any swelling or see blood except for the front. Patch was still excited though, every muscle quivering tight like she was expecting more problems.

"It's okay girl.

"She's okay, Mom," I said as she walked up. "She was ferocious, Mom! She saved me! There were four against one! Mr. Bastein's dogs attacked us and we weren't doing anything! I think she killed one and messed up another pretty good. Yeah, one got me too."

Mom looked at my ankle and asked me if I could walk the rest of the way home.

"Sure. I'll be okay. Mr. Bastein's gonna be mad though."

She laughed, but it was harsh and held no amusement.

"I'm sure he will. Of course I'm not too happy about his dogs either."

After my ankle was smeared with Bag-Balm and wrapped up, my mother called Mrs. Bastein and I only heard one side of the sometimes loud, excited conversation.

"Betty, hi this is Dorothee."

"Yes, he'll be okay."

"Why were the dogs out?"

"She was just protecting Clark."

"No she's not. I've already told you, she won't let anything hurt him."

"Then he'll have to keep them penned."

"I'm sorry to hear that Betty, but Jim should know better and so should you. Bye."

After she hung up she told me to get Patch inside, in the bathtub and get her washed off.

"Keep her inside when she's cleaned up."

Red water tinged to pink slowly then cleared transparent as it washed off Patch. It took forever to clear the water running down the drain.

I had lots to tell Dad when he got home, but I was concerned about who would pull in the driveway first, he or Mr. Bastein. I was sure glad to see Dad's car be the quickest arrival that evening. He inspected my ankle by unwrapping it to look at the swollen punctures and verify the evidence. He didn't ask any questions past my explanation of the fight. He knew Patch wouldn't have started it. Mr. Bastein wasn't far behind Dad and I just had enough time to get my story laid out before he started pounding on the door.

"Take Patch in your bedroom son and close the door. I'll take care of this."

My father possessed the uncommon ability to expand at chosen times, even though he was a normal five feet seven inches tall. When threatened or angry, or even when he was trying to make a point, he got larger. My brother and I gave him so many reasons to get mad that he walked around big lots of the time. In spite of the many examples of his expansion we were always surprised to see just how big he could get when provoked.

Dad opened the door and Mr. Bastein was standing there with a shotgun in his hand. Dad grew bigger still.

I'd disobeyed my father. After I put Patch in my room I went back to stand in the living room door to watch the proceedings. I wasn't going to let Mr. Bastein freely shout down my dog or me. But Dad didn't need my help.

Mr. Bastein yelled, "I'm gonna shoot that damn dog, Jerry!"

Dad expanded to fill up the doorway and surprisingly now held Mr. Bastein's weapon, because he'd snatched it out of his hands as soon as the man started yelling. Momentarily confused, Mr. Bastein shouted again, but Dad put the shotgun behind him with one hand and fended him off with the other. More loudly than at first, the contention now became one of gun possession.

Finally, my father yelled too. "Jim, you better get back in your car right now. No, you will wait until tomorrow to get it back, and only if and when I think you've calmed down. You and I *are* going to talk about *YOUR* dogs though, and that's a fact."

Two roosters on a porch couldn't have ruffled their feathers any more that the two men did. Mr. Bastein glared at my father for a long time before he moved. My father didn't move a bit. Dad waited until Mr. Bastein turned and stepped off the porch before he closed the door.

"You keep Patch inside tomorrow, son. No rambling about now. You hear me?"

I nodded my assent. The way my ankle hurt, tomorrow wouldn't be a day for much walking anyway.

When Dad got home from work the next day, he and I went over to see Mr. Bastein. Mr. Bastein wasn't smiling when he walked to my father's side of the car. He didn't change the look on his face when Dad handed him his shotgun through the window, but that might have been because Dad still had both shotgun shells in his other hand. I wouldn't have given it back if it had been me but I guessed my father knew what he was doing.

Dad said, "Jim, I'm not going to get out of the car. I don't know what I'd do if I did open the door. You ever come over to my house again with a gun in your hand and I guess you and I will find out. You better pen those dogs. If they ever bite my son or any other of my children, there'll be a lot more than a dog lying in the street."

Mr. Bastein turned red just like my father did. He started to say something but my Dad cut him off.

"No Jim, I don't want you to say a word. I just want you to listen. If you say a word I might have to break the promise I made."

Dad started the car, shifted to reverse and we backed out of the driveway. He told me on the way home to steer clear of Bastein's for a while.

"He really liked those damn dogs, son. You can get to the marsh lots of other ways."

"Okay Dad, I promise. We'll go the other way around." I said, but then asked him. "What'd you promise?"

"Let's just say I promised your mother something. I took you along so I'd keep my word."

Mr. Bastein never really turned loose of his anger. Even a year later, every time he saw Patch, I figured he thought of both his dogs. The one whose leg Patch broke limped around their house for years as a reminder. He threatened again on several occasions to shoot Patch when we walked by, something we had started to do again. He also told me he was going to get a dog that would kill mine. I didn't say anything in return but I never told. He never followed through with either menacing promise. I knew he wouldn't and Mr. Bastein knew he wouldn't either.

I wasn't the only one who thought my Dad got bigger.

Chapter 21
Wild Things

Chip and I wanted a hawk.

Real bad. A falcon would do but they were smaller and had to take undersized prey. I had just finished reading about kings and royalty hunting with these birds of prey and had read the story again for Chip. Falconry, the sport of Kings for centuries, even back in ancient Egypt, with their tales written in hieroglyphs, was my current obsession. We would be falconers, hunting with them for sport, seeing the bird rocket from the sky to snatch an unsuspecting rabbit or grab a pigeon in midair. We would get Mom to sew the accessories, some jesses and a hood for the bird, find a leather glove and be in business. Based on my reading, we knew just how to get our hawk.

Indians needed eagle feathers for headdresses and ornamentation, but they didn't kill eagles to get them. No, they tricked them, grabbed them from camouflaged hiding or light baited nets. Indians plucked a few feathers and returned the birds to fly free again and grow new feathers for the next time. We would modify the Indian techniques to suit our task. We wouldn't pluck their feathers, but we'd keep the hawk. It was simple.

The marsh was home to quite a few hawks. We knew of several jumbled stick nests high in trees along the edges of the marsh. They used the same nest every year, a permanent home. Chip and I often saw them float and circle high above and had sometimes caught a dark blur as they raced down toward their prey. Once I saw one carrying a rabbit or woodchuck back to its nest. There was an eagle's nest behind Marshall's airport, hidden in the woods. The bigger birds floated lazily above the woods but they were big enough to be scary. We knew birds of prey were in the vicinity. We just had to catch one.

First we had to get some bait to attract the keen eyed prey as it soared high.

We had no idea how to catch them with baited nets and the books weren't very clear on that. The bait for the nets was pigeons or doves and we didn't have a clue how to catch them either. No sense in trying to catch a bird in order to catch another bird. No we'd have to stick to ground dwelling bait, something that was easy to catch, a rabbit or squirrel or some mice. Mice should be the easiest to find for we had several in our house despite traps that Mom constantly refreshed with peanut butter and reset to snap shut. Besides, we needed live bait to wiggle and squirm and run for attention attracting. There were hundreds, maybe thousands of mice living in the fields around the house. Dead just would not do for what we had in mind.

The farmer's field behind our house had recently been threshed and harvested of the winter wheat planted last fall, but now sported short stubble and weeds that hadn't yet had enough sunlight to sprout up. A perfect place for us to find field mice and we scoured the field with Patch snuffling for scent. She was an invaluable companion for us. With her excellent nose, which she proved time and again as she tracked and sniffed us out after investigating something that had temporarily separated us. Patch found numerous holes, paused at each, but continued to zigzag around the longer grasses bordering the field looking for the right one. She eventually found one that pleased her, shoved her nose right down to the dirt and snorted.

"Here, here there are mice!" Patch said.

Patch began to dig furiously. Great clods of earth hurtled behind her churning legs. Few dogs equal the earth moving capacity of the Airedale, a breed that could have been used for tunneling or digging to China.

When she located this particular good-mouse-smelling hole, we had to pull her off quick or whatever was down there was doomed. Patch was muscled heavily in the chest and when she wanted to be someplace doing something you didn't want, it was a physical struggle as well as a test of wills. Patch was just as bull-headed as she was strong. All things being balanced according to God's plan, Mom would say. I got her pulled away but Patch was single-minded once on task, lunging back to the mouse nest, trying to resume the dig again and again. It took all I could do to hold her off and if I was going to find out what was down there, she would have to get tied up. I told Chip to stay right there, don't lose sight of the hole while I took Patch back home. It was just a short run to our house.

"Keep your hand over the hole, don't let any get away," I hollered as I dragged Patch toward the house.

By the time I got back, Chip had uncovered the nest, a soft bed of grass and mouse fur. Under a thin covering Chip had discovered mice all right. There were seven almost naked babies now exposed to the sunlight, squirming in the brightness. They were pink all over and sort of translucent. You could almost see right through them and had tiny eyes that weren't open yet. The tiny mice weren't any bigger than the end of my index finger, only an inch long, newborn. These weren't what I had in mind when I thought of catching mice. We needed vigorous grown ones that would run and jump and hop about in order to attract our hawk's attention. These were just lying there, pink and tiny. These would take some growing before they would do anything, in fact quite a bit of raising up. So be it.

"Make do with such things as ye have."

I took off my t-shirt and formed a little nest of my own. We'd take them home for the raising, knowing mice had to grow up quickly. They did everything else that way. Mom would know how to get them to big status.

When we had explained the whole scheme to my mother, she took a look at the baby mice.

"Do you know how much work it's going to be just to keep them alive, boys?" she asked. "These babies can't be more than two or three days old, they're so tiny."

I thought, "Hey, no problem, how hard could it be? They were just mice. If the mother mouse could do it, we could too.

"Okay you two," Mom started, "but once you start this you're going to finish it. No quitting in the middle of it. You've taken them away from the nest; you can't take them back. The momma mouse won't come back. They'd just die."

I think Mom smelled a lesson in boy responsibility here and conveniently disregarded the mouse's ultimate role as bait. She also saw something that she could count on to occupy us both for a long time; keep us out of mischief. Good on two points.

"Come on, I'll show you how they have to be fed."

Mom took my t-shirt nest and we followed her into the kitchen.

"Get some milk and warm it up on the stove. Chip, get me a spool of thread, some of the rug thread from my sewing box."

I did as told. So did Chip. Once the lessons began, particularly since we had asked for help, we knew enough by now to follow instructions exactly. Chip and I had both heard "I thought you wanted to do this. If not, just say so and I'll stop, too," when we allowed our attention to waver.

"Here, let me show you. There aren't any baby bottles small enough for these tiny mouths. You'll have to dip the thread in the milk, see like this," she demonstrated. "Then take the thread and put the drop of milk in front of the mouse's nose. Once they smell the milk, they'll do the rest. Don't put the milk on their noses or they'll drown. Let them move their mouths to the milk. You have to hold it real still."

Sure enough the baby Mom was holding had started to drink from the drop of milk suspended from the thread. Cool. My turn. I practiced the technique under a critical eye. The baby sneezed.

"No, No. You're not listening son. Not on the nose."

"Hey, I didn't do it. The mouse just moved." The baby mouse sneezed again.

Mom told me, "See, I told you Clark, you have to be very careful, these are tiny babies. They don't even have fur yet."

I practiced some more, apparently doing fairly well although the stupid mice kept sticking their noses in the drops.

Mom wiped them off each time and said, "Try again, careful now."

Mom decided Chip was not going to be a wet nurse. She was probably appalled at my slow learning curve and I had ruined Chip's opportunity for feeding the babies. I'd show him later, when Mom went away. We got those seven babies fed and I thought we were through for the day.

"You need to do this every hour and a half or so. These babies will be hungry again quick. Their bellies are real little. Now come on, you've got to make them a nest. They can't stay in your t-shirt lying out. The cats will get them."

This was going to cut into all my stuff, all my other activities, but I was game. Besides, I'd later show Chip and could make him do it instead of me. Mom went in to her bedroom and came back with a shoebox.

"We can fill this with tissue and put it in your room. Poke holes in the lid for air. You'll have to tape the lid shut after you feed them. Tape it good every time or you won't have any mice."

Almost before I knew it the mice scurried around every time I opened the lid to feed them, bumping and ricocheting off the sides of the box. I showed Chip how to feed them and he did okay, I guess. We managed to only drown two of them before they or we got really good at the milk drops. They grew real quick and started to jump toward the open box top trying escape. One managed to make good the leap, and Sun Yat Sen, our Siamese cat nabbed it. Both our cats had been hanging around my bedroom, but were continually foiled by the taped lid. He was gone in a blink, the mouse hanging out of Sun Yat's mouth. There wasn't any catching that cat now. You can't catch a cat if they don't want you to, just ask any kid. We were down to four mice, still plenty for catching the hawk but we'd have to be more careful.

Another mouse leapt, a sacrificial offering to kitty. The babies were bolder and stronger, and Chip and I were running out of patience. Mom thanked us for keeping the cats fed so well, but wondered out loud if that was our original intent. No, it was not. We'd have to get on with the hawk part or we wouldn't have any bait or hawks at this rate. We sure wanted them to be bigger, but couldn't chance any more growing up in a kitty war zone, not with only three left. It was now or risk being mice-less.

Our plan was simple. We would tie some rug thread to a mouse hind-leg and lie down in a field covered with leaves and straw, but not cover the mouse. Lay very still. The frantic jumping and hopping of the mouse would attract a hawk, which will swoop down to catch and eat said mouse. When the hawk grabbed the mouse, the covered up boy will grab the hawk. Wear gloves. Anybody could do this simple task. We were surprised a lot more people didn't have hawks and falcons as pets. We would start a trend. We were sure to be the hit of every show and tell next year in school.

We had a real hard time getting that thread on the mouse. The rodent just would not cooperate. It even bit us. I had terrible trouble getting that little leg to hold still long enough to slip the loop over its foot, but I finally got it.

I was the confident first catcher, who counted on the hawk's keen vision and super sharp hearing and I figured it would take several minutes after getting covered up to attract birds of prey from miles around. Chip would hide in some bushes or reeds nearby to assist if the hawk was really big or vigorous. We were going to catch a hawk for sure. Today.

The wheat straw and weeds that Chip covered me up with itched and had little bugs in it, but the mouse behaved wonderfully. It hopped and ran back and forth and even gave a squeak or two, using very good, very hawk-attractive, mouse type behavior. Peppery dust caused me to sneeze every so often and it was hot under the covering, but I only moved when I couldn't help it. I kept every muscle tensed awaiting the rush of wings I knew was headed my way. Any minute now, any minute now, had to be any minute.

When the sun started its western descent I gave up for the day. The mouse had pooped out long ago and was just huddled motionless on my stomach. Tired from all the dashing about trying to do its job of attracting the hawk, it just laid down. Stopped moving. Gave up. It wasn't such a bad idea.

I was sure that tomorrow, loaded up with a fresh and rested mouse, would be a better day. I actually knew it would be better, because it was Chip's turn under the weeds.

The next day we moved out of the field and closer to the marsh. I pulled fronds from the cattails and laid them across him in a skelter, covering him up good.

"Don't turn loose of the string," I warned.

Chip started out great and I watched from the cattails. On that day we'd moved closer to real wilderness instead of the farmer's field. He lay there for about ten minutes, quietly like he was supposed to. Of a sudden he leaped up with a shriek and started dancing around the field. I first thought he had figured out a new strategy to attract hawks, one I hadn't thought of. I decided against that as soon as he started squirming out of his clothes, trying to strip.

"What now?"

I had to watch Chip every minute, my big brother role and burden. What a dolt. Everybody knows that you can't catch a hawk naked.

I ran over to him and by the time I got there he was screeching. This mouse, instead of doing something attractive, chose to hide in the dark. It searched around until it found the best place. The front of Chip's pants seemed perfect, but Chip wasn't so sure. He shucked off his pants quick like and apparently shucked the mouse right along with them or let go of the tether. I knew I should have tied that thread around his wrist.

"Chip! Geezie-Peezie!"

We headed home, mouse-less. Hawk-less.

We only had two mice left.

Chip and I spent the next week swapping on and off every other day. We didn't lose any more mice, but our hawk still eluded us. Our time in the field shrunk to real short as we came back home more and more discouraged. The camouflage got itchier and scratchier each and every day, almost every second, and those little bugs grew more ferocious, too. We hadn't seen a hawk, not a single speck far off in the sky. We couldn't figure out what was wrong, but something was definitely not going according to plan. Somehow the ownership of a hawk seemed much further away than it did when we started. How had the Indians done this?

Chip and I decided to give it one more day. Despite our failures the technique was sound and we reviewed the account in the book that evening before bed, just in case we missed something. Nope, we were doing it right. This time both of us would get covered up and both of us would hold a tethered mouse. We could cover more territory with two locations even though we risked not having immediate help when the hawk rocketed from the sky. We would risk that part, we reasoned, because neither of us had needed much help so far. Ever the optimists, we thought this dual strategy would not fail us.

We lay still, hardly daring a breath, not wanting to frighten off any hawk hungrily circling above. Although the camouflage limited my vision, I was sure the swept back wings of a bird of prey would cross my eyes any second. My mouse behaved quite well, though Chip later claimed to have problems with his, but we gave up well before the end of the day. Lying in the field for more than a week, we were abused in body and spirit, covered with bug bites and itched constantly from the cattails, leaves and straw we used to cover ourselves. We still didn't have a hawk, either.

I gave up first but Chip was ready by then, too. We decided to free the mice in the marsh as long as we were out there. It would only be a matter of time until they were gone anyhow if we continued to keep them in the house. The odds were with the cats. When we untied their legs, the mice headed off in different directions dodging the plant stems, up and over the uneven dirt. They were giving up. Gratefully, I supposed.

We would try this again, but needed to do something different.

Chip and I turned to go, heading back to home. Maybe next spring we'd climb a tree and rob a nest. Maybe we'd perfect the technique that had failed us. Maybe we'd find out more about the nets. Maybe there was another way.

Maybe a hawk wouldn't come live with us.

Chip shrieked, "Look.... up there!"

Chip pointing well off, way above the marsh and as I followed the direction of his finger, I saw it too.

"Right there!"

A hawk flew at his fingertip. High up a speck, slowly spiraled and dropped, the hawk's flight made fun of us. Circling down but not nearer and we both took off running.

"Let's Go! Let's Go!" We took off toward the dot, wanting to get closer at least.

We ran to where we thought the hawk was circling, running hard until we ran ourselves out, and crouched, hands on knees and panting. It was still circling high up, still far away, and far out of reach. We watched as the hawk spiraled closer, then further away, like a wind blown leaf. We watched it for a long time, mesmerized and gazed upward until our necks hurt. Suddenly, the bird of prey folded its wings, changed into a wingless shape and plummeted. Like a bullet, like a rocket, straight down from the sky, the hawk streaked down toward something we couldn't see.

Chip whispered, "Wow."

Yup, that's what was supposed to happen. That's what should have happened. We just gave up too soon. We swore to each other to do better the next time. We turned again to head home.

Time to go.

By now you know that Patch was good with kids.

She also liked our cats and didn't often chase ones that weren't ours. Even when she did scare them it was sort of half-hearted. She liked most dogs most of the time and all male dogs when she was in heat. She liked big people after introductions. She even liked kids I didn't like. She was better at liking than I was except for one thing.

Patch hated skunks. Black and white was to her a bullfighter's red cape. Our family knew of Patch's hatred very, very, well. More than once she had come back from a marsh excursion drenched in the ordure of skunk. Everyone in North America is familiar with this smell. It is second in smelly awfulness only to the Tasmanian Devil and we didn't worry about them. Many bars of Fels-Naptha soap had shrunk away to nothing trying to diminish that smell. Patch's fur seemed to hold on to the skunk smell with an amazing ability.

That October day was rainy, blustery, cold, one where if you were outside you wished you were in. Any person could tell winter was on its way. As the entire family (Patch included of course) drove the sixty miles to Grandma and Grandpa's farm, I saw the trees had colored long ago and their paint splashes of color were mostly on the ground, piled up in ditches and against fences. I had spent a fair amount of time every fall farm visit raking them into piles and carrying them to the compost pile and garden for Grandma and Grandpa. Grandma had already started putting suet out for the birds, in the backyard birch tree and the pear tree in the front. The storm windows had gone up long ago and the woodpile looked stout enough to see the winter through. Grandpa had hay put in for the horses and corn for the pigs. Every animal and everyone was set for winter. Almost.

The day passed quickly, as days at the farm do and after the chores of raking and hauling, Patch and I went exploring hills and valleys on their sixty acres. We headed back in the late afternoon, damp and cold, but absolutely complete. I think we shared the satisfaction of these treks divided-right-down-the-middle equally. I couldn't wait to get in front of the fireplace and I knew Patch would head for the straw pile in the barn.

I patted her head and told her "no" to the house. Despite being allowed in our house, she was not allowed in Grandma's anymore. Patch had been barred ever since the turkey incident and although everybody, my grandmother included, laughed about it now, the ban remained. Patch understood completely and headed back to the barn. She knew where to go.

I picked up an armful of wood as I went into the house.

"If you want a fire, you have to feed it," Grandpa always said when cold weather arrived. He also said things like "Wood warms you twice, once when you cut, once when you burn," and "Wood in the forest won't help keep you warm."

These were both adages he put to practical application with me by his side.

Mom and Gram worked their usual magic, turned everyday fare into dinners that kings and queens only dream about. Soon, our bellies were full up, and we migrated to other spots. Dad and Grandpa lit pipes and we were wreathed in the fragrance of Cherry blend, my dad's favorite. My grandpa used Prince Albert tobacco, because he was retired and it was cheap. We'd gathered about the fireplace to talk after dinner when Patch, who was supposed to be in the barn, began her, "song of battle."

Patch's voice was one of unmistakable beauty, but frightening too, when in the passion of the hunt or a fight. Her bark voiced deep authority and I had seen big men blanche white, as she made her presence known. When Patch barked everyone looked. It just couldn't be helped. People driving by the house would touch their brakes to see what on earth was making all that noise.

We all ran to windows and doors, pressed our faces to the glass and watched a struggle unfold that would have done the legions of Rome proud. When we first became spectators the fight was still in the "I dare you" mode, but I was sort of surprised at Patch. Even I knew this; you just can't dare a skunk. The posturing quickly progressed to include much more.

I heard Mom say, "Jerry, go chase that skunk away before something bad happens."

I glanced at my father's looks of incredulity and disdain for the request but beyond that my attention was glued to the conflict. A total idiot wouldn't have interfered with what was going on out there. We were all transfixed as if glued to the windows. Patch would feint toward the skunk and the little fellow would let her have it, a full charge in the eyes. Whining and growling from pain, Patch would retreat. She'd paw at her eyes and renew the charge, tearing up the ground as she went, but then stop short.

This prelude went on for some time and the odor of the fray began to reach us, even in the house. Everyone knew it wasn't going to be pretty before it was through. Grandma started running around the house closing storm windows and stuffing rugs under the doors. I couldn't take my eyes off the battle of determination versus chemical warfare. Patch hadn't got in her first licks yet and the smell was already terrible. The skunk changed tactics and charged out to meet Patch on open ground. That was all my dog was waiting for.

She managed one vicious shake, but that only seemed to get the skunk to call up its reserves of disgusting spray. When Patch backed up once more to paw her eyes, the little animal could have used the opportunity to escape, but instead appeared to be admiring his (or her) work. Although staggering around as if she were blind, Patch lunged and grabbed the skunk once more for a head swinging shake. But both animals were getting tired now. Patch was further hampered by her repeated doses of liquid stench. There was a definite lull as both stink'ee and stink'er appeared to be wondering what to do next.

Either the skunk ran out of ammunition or it thought Patch defeated and it turned around and scooted right under the porch. This was a mistake. Patch gathered all the evil intent available and followed the skunk. The wailing and gnashing of teeth that followed was really something to hear. There was barking and squealing and whining and gnashing galore. The howls put up by both of them, even muffled by the porch are still audible to me now, almost forty-five years later.

The poor skunk was simply looking for a cozy place to spend the winter but made the serious miscalculation of traveling close to a dog that would not bear the trespass. Instead of a dignified retreat the skunk chose to attempt defense in the crawl-way beneath Grandpa's porch. It was a quiet refuge for anyone visiting there.

Anyone, excluding skunks, when Patch was defending the territory.

The sounds of war stopped.

Patch didn't quit howling and whining but she crawled back out from under the porch.

"Go get her Jerry!" Mom said.

"Keep that dog away from my house!" Grandma said.

"Goddamn, that stinks!" my grandpa said.

My father didn't say anything. I was worried about my dog because she was staggering around, pawing at her eyes and rubbing her face and muzzle against the ground. She was in pain, but the skunk was dead. Victory!

Mom pushed me outside first. The stench was overwhelming.

Grandpa Teddy was right. My eyes watered immediately and I sure didn't want to but grabbed her collar and headed her to the outside faucet at my mother's pointed directions from the window. Man did this dog smell bad! I

247

almost couldn't get a breath. I didn't want to get a breath. My gag reflexes were all in working order though. Chip joined me, but only after Mom disentangled his arms from around Peg and shoved him out. He immediately began to whine. The smell was so horrid that slow suffocation would have been better. His whines only increased in the few moments he'd been out here. I thought a quick strangle would do just fine for Chip.

The adults still had their faces pressed to the window, but now hard enough to squash their noses flat and they looked funny. After a quick discussion, reinforcements gathered, all laden with Fels-Naptha, scrub brushes and buckets of hot water. Mom and Dad cautiously came outside and met us at the faucet. Their faces were wearing looks that can only be described as scrunched, as if the scrunching would prevent the reek from getting to them. Mom did a quick about face and went back inside to get some clothespins. She had one tightly in place when she came back out and handed one to Dad, Chip and me. Noses pinched together helped some, but the aroma was so heavy you could taste skunk and we talked funny.

Skunk tastes just exactly like it smells. I would pit skunk against the Tasmanian Devil. Any day of the week. Chip kept up the complaints until I wiped my hands on Patch's muzzle and transferred some of the remaining goodness to Chip's mouth. His whining changed to gagging. Dad cuffed me but I didn't care, at least Chip's gagging was muffled.

We scrubbed and soaked, soaked and scrubbed, and got a replacement bar of Fels-Naptha after the first one disappeared in suds. We scoured and drenched and drenched and scoured some more. It was not going away, not coming off. Despite all this lavish attention Patch still stunk of skunk. Grandma, seeing that we would probably burn up their water pump if changes weren't made volunteered her homemade tomato juice as an additional antidote to the skunk's aerosol.

To understand this offering, one must know what the title Grandma indicates. Canning was one of her signature accomplishments. My Grandma put up juices and jams, jellies and vegetables and each fall had a stocked larder to prove it. Her pride and joy were jar after jar of canned tomatoes and tomato juice. One wall of the cellar was devoted to tomato products. There was little that was better in the morning than a glass of her tomato juice. With every glass came an "I did this" look on her face.

She had opened the back door just a crack and spoke to my mother.

"I'm sending Teddy out with some tomato juice, Dot. No Dorothee, don't you come in; he'll bring it out."

None of us might ever get back in that house again. I noticed that Carole and Peg sure weren't bringing it out. I guess we knew who'd be sleeping with Grandma if this scrub up didn't work and we spent the night. I figured the barn would be more crowded than usual.

Grandpa edged out the door with two quart-jars, one in each hand. He set them on the ground by the porch and scurried back to the door. My Grandpa didn't even know how to scurry before this happened. I didn't blame him at all. I really loved Patch, I really did. But I might have traded her for a broken yo-yo then. What we had accomplished so far was to get Patch wet and soapy and she still stank horribly. In addition, all four of us were wet and soapy and now we smelled really, really bad, too. The smell rubbed off. I watched Grandma just crack the door open and give Grandpa a good long sniff before she let him back in.

We used the first two jars on Patch's head where she had borne the brunt of the skunk's attack. We're making progress. All right!!! Now she's wet and soapy and smelly and ...... red. Mom said it was better, but I sure couldn't tell. I was in overload, my sense of smell had been flash fried when I first took Patch by the collar. I smelled so of skunk I could have passed for one. I could have joined in a skunk family reunion and fit right in.

"More juice, Mom!" my mother hollered. "We need more juice!"

I saw Grandma's lips moving as she nodded her head. I didn't know how to read lips, but I'd have bet a million dollars she wasn't saying, "Yes, Dorothee."

Several minutes later Grandpa came out with a half-peck basket, like the one we got peaches and apples in from Albers' Orchard, right there in Manchester. There were six quart-jars this time and every one looked like it had lip print on the lid, but I could have been mistaken. Was Grandma kissing them goodbye? No, of course not. We used them on Patch and each other. I took off my clothespin. Hey, it was getting better. I had been worried for the last twenty minutes or so, because my nose had gone numb and I wasn't sure if it was from the smell or being pinched.

"More juice!" Mom hollered again. "We need more juice!"

The wait for re-supply was longer this time and my mother was getting impatient.

"Clark, go up to the house and see what's taking so long," she commanded.

I had no sooner set my right foot on the first step when I was stopped by Grandma Phoebe.

"You stay right there Clock and we'll hand it out. Don't you dare come any closer than you are."

"More juice, Mom!" Mom shrieked. "We need more juice, Mom! It's starting to come off!"

We ended up using so much of Grandma's juice that she refused to give us more and instead sent out her canned tomatoes. Grandpa probably had something to do with that. Any breakfast I ever saw him eat was accompanied by a glass of tomato juice. If I remember correctly we used 26 quarts of tomato something getting the smell off reasonably well for the dog and ourselves. The actual number of quart jars is lost in family lore but of two things I am certain: Patch was forever banished from the farm. The ride home was memorable.

Patch still smelled bad, even outside, and there was a stiff wind blowing. I had to stay with her while Mom and Dad packed the family up. Mom brought out an old towel for me to dry off a bit, but it wasn't Grandma's good linen. I had to hold Patch so she wouldn't go check on the skunk to make sure it was still dead. She would do things like that. Most of the smell was gone from us; but only because people didn't have as much hair as Patch. I could still smell skunk when I sniffed arms and sleeves. I was going to have a tough time in school on Monday if this didn't get better by a bunch.

Mom went out to the station wagon and pinned a blanket between the middle seat and the back. Chip and I got into the car first, sitting with Patch behind the back seat.

When Dad closed the back end we hollered, "Dad, don't! Can't breathe!"

He opened it back up quick enough, but my urp reflex was kicking back in, and I think Chip passed out. I needed air. Dad tried it again, but with the back window rolled down this time. The smell was still bad, but as long as I had my head out the window or if Patch did, I managed. We couldn't do the same thing at the same time. Her inside, me with head out, was okay. Me inside, her with head out, was okay, too. Any other combination was insufferable.

Carole started complaining before she got halfway to the car and Mom had draped something with perfume on it over Peg's head but the good scent doesn't penetrate into the back. That was the only time I ever recall my grandparents refusing to come outside and wave goodbye as we drove away.

The Greene family sure didn't pile in the car. On that occasion we crept. The doors were opened cautiously and the sound of sniffs abounded. Everyone's first reaction was of drawing heads back out of the door. We weren't out of the driveway yet, not even warmed up by the heater or occupants and the car reeked.

When we did get going, it was all the more horrible. Even with the all the windows down so that Dad remained conscious and everyone else could breathe, it was very bad. Carole threatened to hold her breath in the back seat and I said I'd help her and Peg began making funny noises too. As the car got warmer, the stench changed. Warm skunk was more terrible than cold. It got worse despite the open windows and by the time we got home Chip and I about froze to death. I had a terrible time with Patch who only wanted her nose to quit burning and had to wrestle her to lay down the whole way and she was still wet from the baths. It wasn't long before she gave me half her wet, wanting to share. No one besides Carole and my Dad talked much on the way and all they did was complain. Everyone else was trying to minimize breathing requirements.

We did set a record for piling out when we pulled in the driveway.

My father was extremely angry over the resident smell in the car and said it was going to get fumigated by me. My dog, her smell, my responsibility. Mom helped me scrub the back end of the station wagon over and over again, but it did only small good except for under-crowding. People stopped riding to church in our car.

The car still retained the evidence of Patch and the skunk when my father got in a wreck and totaled it.

Grandma wasn't the only one who stayed mad at Patch for the episode.

My father seemed displeased with Patch from then on. I didn't realize then it was a general decline, because it was difficult to see the change, and he wasn't overtly mean or cruel, but rather seemed to become more distant than usual.

With my brother and sisters.

With my dog.

And with me.

I suppose, because my powers of observation may have been on equal with a tree stump, it took me some time to recognize his withdrawal. I didn't know it then, but it wasn't Patch he was mad at.

My father was mad at everything.

Never a stunning conversationalist, he wrapped himself in newspaper and book so completely that he took up space in the room but left voids in the family. When my father did speak it was mainly to give us kids something to do or complain about some thing we'd already done. Patch seemed to be an additional target and if it hadn't been for Mom, my dog might have lived outside from that time on. He complained about Patch's affection for his big vinyl chair, he griped about her laying by the dinner table, he grumbled about her very presence when we were in the living room as a family after dinner and continued to bear some unknown grudge even after the Ford station wagon was junked out after the accident.

That winter was particularly difficult because the weather, while not a complete deterrent to outdoor activities, did mean that we spent more time than usual in the house. Contrary to popular belief and our parent's view that healthy youngsters played outside, even the Greene kids came in to get warmed up occasionally. When we came in, Patch came in. In our house after cold weather arrived, we had a fire every day.

Our living room was central to the house and central to the room was the fireplace. Made and mortared of multicolored field stone, stained ebony by countless smoky fires, we kept a brass covered wood-box on one side and the fireplace tools on the other. Directly over the full width mantle was a ship's picture and directly under the mantle was Patch. Chip and I kept the wood box filled, but that's where our log handling ended. When he was home, Dad took it from there.

My father took inordinate ownership of maintaining the fire, bordering on the ridiculous. Some ancestral remembering of provider for the family perhaps, but he took umbrage when anyone even put wood on the flames. His displeasure when we kids or even Mom stole the duty radiated from him in waves and on one occasion, my father snatched the split logs from Chip's hands when he was about to add fuel to the fire. It all seems so silly now, but my father was the keeper of the flame.

Patch was the only one brave enough to dispute space around the fireplace and she claimed the spot immediately in front. Single minded as she was, Patch hogged the heat. Disregarding her perfectly suited to winter and heavy coat, Patch was happiest from October through March if she had her nose just as close as doggily possible to the fire.

Right in my father's way.

At least that's what he claimed.

He foot herded Patch away from the hearth at each refueling and the shoves were usually accompanied with complaints.

"YOUR dog, Clark... Geeze. Get that dog outta here!"

Patch got up without protest and she never really caused an inconvenience longer than ten seconds, but my father took exception to her just being there, as if her position was a personal affront to him and prevented his self-appointed duty.

While my father helped with cutting wood and the transportation to bring it home, once it got to the driveway, it all belonged to me. From the age of ten,

I split and stacked every piece of wood we burned until Chip turned the same age and was old enough to help. It was a chore that started in September and went through until March because my father insisted on having two full cords, four feet by eight feet each, split and stacked before the extra heat was needed. Seldom was the fall weekend that didn't see me working with sledge hammer and wedges in the space between our house and driveway. I'm sure if he'd have thought of a way for me to do the cutting and carrying I'd have had that responsibility as well, but I wasn't driving yet. I really didn't mind. I actually liked the work and at a young age learned to admire the sight of a wood-pile ready for winter.

I didn't care much for the way he pushed Patch out of the way, even when she wasn't really obstructing anything more than heat. Surprising even myself, I had begun to determine best ways to accomplish tasks which were a source of annoyance to him. I got Patch to move.

Bringing an old blanket into the living room took some convincing of Mom, but she saw the wisdom as clearly as did I. So did my dog.

Once Patch was given a spot of her own, she stayed strictly within the confines of the frayed edges. With the blanket off to one side, even my father couldn't continue his bluster if it weren't actually true. He did examine Patch's location each time he approached the wood-box to make sure she hadn't scooted closer and she always raised her head when he did put on a log or two, but she'd learned well. When he wasn't home Patch resumed her rightful spot front and center, under the mantle, but got up, moved to her proper location and feigned obedience whenever she heard him say hello.

Just like the rest of the family.

Chapter 22

Through the Ice

January was bitter cold, registering -10 degrees on our inside/ outside porch thermometer.

It was the eighth or ninth day of below zero temperatures and we had a fire in the fireplace every minute, day and night. My father got up in the night to stoke the fire and to check on the electric heater under the house we used to keep the water from freezing. So far both had worked well. It was toasty in the living room every morning and the water was still running when we brushed our teeth. It was so cold Jefferson School cancelled classes several days in a row. Winter snows were expected to be problematic, but this cold was really unwelcome and we couldn't wait for it to leave. We still had a good supply of wood and would make it through the winter just fine if the heater for the water pipes didn't give up the ghost.

Lake Erie was frozen as far as the eye could see, even right to the shore, with no open water anywhere. Ed Brown was planning on ice fishing and told of ice almost three feet thick when he stopped by to tell the tale. Ice so thick he had worn out by the time he got a hole through it. He came back without fishing, laughing that the ice had frozen all the fishing right out of him. There were lots of shanties out on the ice and lots of cars too. Nothing would plunge through the thick layer anymore this year, though Harley's father had a car plunge through the ice just before Christmas. Fortunately the car broke through close to shore, only into about two feet of water and Daniels' big wrecker had been able to pull it back to dry land.

We watched as Ed Daniels walked a cable out to the car and had to reach way under the water to get the cable attached. That big wrecker was sure powerful, when it started pulling the car toward shore, it broke the ice as the car moved closer. The ice broke the taillights and dented the trunk on the car too. Harley said his mother hollered at his dad every day for a week after that stunt.

Johnny was down from Detroit that week. His father was concerned about the cold weather and came down for a long weekend to check on their house, something they didn't do often in the winter. Johnny and I would make the most of no school, paying slight attention to winter's worst.

We dressed for winter, knew how to wrap up so tingling ears and white spotted cheeks were pretty rare, though every once in a while winter would fool us. Chip and I had both been stung with frost bite a few times, with our fingers going numb from the cold. You just knew they would really wake you up as they thawed. I got a good pair of leather insulated mittens as a gift the previous Christmas and they were warm as toast. They even had a strap to tighten the mittens around my wrists preventing snow and cold from creeping in unawares. We would need to prevent all creeping in this weather. It was cold.

It had been a windy night, keening in the windows, poking to find a place to get in, picking up snow from the ground and throwing it further still. The wind came right off the lake picking up all the snow there, sweeping the ice clean and piling drifts against houses and trees. Our backyard was four feet deep in places, the snow curling off the roof peaks to land cold and thick at the doorstep. We had Patch inside during this bitter weather. Even her thick fur couldn't keep out this cold and we would have had to dig our way to her doghouse for food and water every day. In this cold her water bowl froze so quickly it was just better all around to keep her inside. When it was time for her to tend to business, she'd woof at the door telling us. Despite her urgency, she wouldn't leave the back porch until one of us accompanied her off the porch. She trained us early that during the winter at least she wanted company when she had to go out. We got fresh air every time she did.

This particular cold snap had done much more than freshen the air. It was so cold outside that if you breathed through your nose the little hairs froze way up in there and stung. If you breathed open-mouthed, your throat felt like it was on fire, raw quickly from the sub-zero air. We didn't blame Patch for wanting someone to be with her, nobody thought much of this weather. "Misery loves company" was a saying known by dogs too. She kept her necessaries to a minimum and we did too. We did "Paper, Scissors, Rock" to see who had to get more firewood, then contests to keep track of their speed. If you set a new speed record, you got to skip getting wood the next time. Nobody wanted to be outside in this weather.

Not unless there was something important for us to do.

Johnny called me early in the morning and said he'd heard the ice grinding up with great cracks and rumblings during last night's wind. Their house was much closer to the lake than ours, he could see the grass of the lakeside park, and when he looked out this morning he could see great hills and piles of ice.

"Get dressed and come on over," Johnny said. "We'll go take a look at the ice."

He added "from the shore" just a little louder for his mother's benefit. When opportunities for ice exploration arose we took advantage quickly, they had a strong magic for us every time the lake ice pushed up.

When the winter wind blew across a frozen Lake Erie from the north and east, great heaps of pale blue ice would stack up at the shore. Some winters the ice thought to leave the lake entirely, slowly and steadily pushing across the road more than 100 feet from the water's edge. It sounded like a dull, metallic clanking of armored vehicles, cracking again and again under its own weight as it moved forward. The growling and roaring of the ice as it pushed everything out of its way was menacing, almost alive.

Chip and I got suited up under Mom's watchful eyes. She didn't want her children coming back frostbitten and she also knew how quickly it could happen in this weather. She wanted to be sure her children were prepared well enough and covered in all the necessary places. She did not try to dissuade us from the lake. Unless there was imminent danger, like that from lighted dynamite or a charging rogue elephant, Mom mostly let us do these kinds of things. Whether from her knowledge of some predestination for us or her philosophy of letting us learn our own lessons, we mostly determined our own course. Since none of us had been seriously maimed or worse, it seemed like good strategy so far.

Patch wasn't so sure about going out in this weather, but she got into the spirit of the trek once she was outside for a while, wagging her usual happiness at being with her boys. Pretty soon she was dashing back and forth, barking loudly, throwing clouds of snow into the air like a puppy at play. We seldom trimmed Patch's shaggy coat, we thought she looked better wooly and her heavy coat was certainly more suited for this cold. This snow wasn't good for snowballs, it was much too cold to pack well and so I couldn't pelt Chip on the way, one part of his training I really enjoyed. There were a few paybacks for putting up with little brothers. The snow sounded like sneakers on wood squealing with every step as we walked the road to Johnny's. The wind was still coming off the lake, stinging our exposed cheeks and quickly turned them red. I told Chip I'd meet him at Johnny's and ran back to our house for the ski masks we scoffed at when Mom told us to take them. She was right and said as much when I grabbed them both off the hall tree.

By the time we got to Johnny's house we were warmed up from the heavy clothes and exertion of fighting the wind. We had become accustomed to the cold air, were ready for the ice castles and ready to discover caverns and forts created just for us. I put Chip's ski mask on him as we walked and followed with my own. We could have been mistaken for bank robbers but Johnny and his mother knew we were on our way. The mother network existed for just such as this. If kids didn't quickly show up someplace they were going, their mothers would know to call the bloodhounds out. Johnny was outside and ready. He had to be outside once he got dressed for winter. Once enclosed in winter wear, you had about two minutes to get to the cold before you passed out from heat stroke.

"You boys stay off the ice," his mother warned.

Patch had frosted over already, her muzzle white with ice and the mouth holes and nose holes in our ski masks glistened the same way. The moisture from breathing froze almost instantly in this weather, forming extra dimensions to Patch's muzzle and our winter gear. I checked her feet for ice forming between the toes but she was okay.

Even from a distance the lake was a wonderland of ice, abstract shapes jutting out and up, buttresses of thick and broken ice balanced high. Adjacent to the three pillars where the bank was sloped more gently, the ice had already reached the road, more than thirty yards distant. The wind had been strong enough in the night to push the ice into a layer several feet thick at the road already. We heard the ice still grinding against itself, snapping with loud cracks and pops up and down the beach. The blocks varied in thickness. Some were more than two feet thick, and so large and heavy we couldn't lift them. We shoved some of them across the frozen road, clearing the chunks that had started to cross the pavement. Walter wouldn't be able to move these. We were vain of our strength and pushed the road clean of ice, even though Chip and I knew we couldn't tell at dinner. I had not figured how to tell my folks about something good I had done without appearing in their eyes to brag. I had heard "not of good works, lest any man should boast," enough to make me puke.

We walked down by the pier, which was really just a concrete form jutting out forty feet into the lake, but to us the pier was a pathway toward the unknown kingdom of the frozen lake. The ice was massed particularly high here, jumbled hard up against the crumbling concrete. The pier had withstood ice on more than this occasion and we knew it would again. The men who built it had done a good job and regardless of the icy battering, it was still sound and solid. The ice had pushed and cracked fiercely here, completely burying the very end of the pier where it was lower to the water. We would check these mounds out. Oh yeah.

This spot was perfect. The mountains of ice were immense and beckoning, with fantastic blue openings scattered around their edges.

"Jeezie, they're huge!" I said. "Look how big!"

We strode out like lords returning. That's just what we were, knights returning from a quest, King Arthur back from the Crusades, claiming our cold castles. By far colder. This might have been the coldest place on earth and we felt it. No matter how we ran or moved, our toes and fingers were seeking equality with the weather.

The large ice pieces were slick and smooth on one side, glassy, but with snow frozen and stuck on the other, like cake icing. We kicked them hard to make sure the stack was solid and crawled inside one large cavern, way back. Patch crawled in behind us when we disappeared from sight, wondering just where in the heck we were going. The space was about six feet square. There was room for all three to sit upright, with a great ice slab for our roof, jammed and held up by other columns and walls of ice to form our room. Inside everything was translucent blue, even us. The outside light filtering through the ice gave everything a glow, another world's look. We stayed as long as we could, thirty minutes or so, until chattering teeth and shivering told us to get. Had it not been for the growing cold we would have stayed longer.

We needed to get warm and crawled back out to the cloudy sky. Johnny's house was the closest place where we could warm up. Maybe we'd come back. These ice masses were just great. Chip and Patch headed toward the shore but Johnny and I decided to cut across the ice, really shivering with the cold and we broke into a run, just wanting to get to Johnny's quick. We were about half way between the pier and the three pillars when Johnny and I both broke through the ice with a crack.

"Gol Dang it! Sheep's-foot!"

I still mostly saved my cuss words for under the breath. I was always convinced Mom would either be close by or could somehow hear despite the distance.

The water was so cold it stole my breath. The water wasn't terribly deep this close to shore but it was deep enough to wet us way past the belt line. It didn't have to be real deep. The frigid lake water made shallow unimportant.

Our feet hit the rocky bottom and although they didn't stay there long, it was long enough to get wet and shockingly cold.

When the ice moved in the night the wedges of ice stuck together at angles leaving open water between several piles. The winter's intense cold quickly froze the newly exposed water over and blowing snow had finished the illusion of safe, thick ice. Johnny and I had run straight across the sheet ice, but we didn't run far. It wouldn't have supported even one of us, let alone both. We both tried to leap back out of the water, scrabbling for purchase on the remaining ice, but it took long moments to break through the thinner ice in order to reach the thick portions. I managed to heave myself back on the safety of stable ice, but Johnny couldn't get a grip. I sat down and extended my hands for him. He was waterlogged, heavy, and frantic, hollering with the cold and fear. It took every bit of our strength just to hang on to one another. After another, seeming forever, struggle, I pulled him out as well. We lay back, panting with the exertion, but not for long. Johnny jumped up first.

"C'mon! C'mon! We gotta get!" he screamed.

I tried to get up, but I needed his help. My pants had quickly frozen tight to the lake's icy surface. We both laughed at the tearing sound when he pulled me up, but the laughs hid a real fear. With the plunge and with the frenzied struggles to get out of the water, we were both wet through to the neck. Big trouble.

Chip and Patch had taken a different route and so veered closer to the shore and missed the thin ice. I hollered at Chip to stay where he was. I was sure glad this wasn't happening to him. I would be in enough trouble as it was. I wouldn't have wanted Chip in this mix.

Johnny and I both recognized the need to get home, get dry and warm. The water had been bad enough and the wind was equally bad. We were quite far from his house and even further from mine. Our pants, shirts and coats were frozen stiff and my skin burned like a flame. We had to get. Right away.

"Run!"

We had been out of the water now just a few moments, and our rigid clothing was only a hint of what we'd quickly be without some warmth. We didn't need any hints. We knew we were just moments away from some serious frostbite.

"Run!"

We took off with stiff legged gaits, unable to bend our legs without great difficulty.

"Run!"

With the soaked long johns and jeans our legs were encased in about a half inch of ice and the clothes chafed terribly when we moved.

"Run!"

It felt just as if my legs were roasting, scorching and burning over every speck of flesh.

"Run!"

Chip and Patch caught up to us once we reached the shore. Once we'd scrambled over the rocks he kept telling us how much trouble we were going to be in.

"You're gonna really catch it," he laughed.

If I could have grabbed him we would see who caught what, but right now I had to get to Johnny's. I probably couldn't have caught him. Chip's pants weren't frozen stiff. We kept running.

Johnny turned into his driveway, lurching toward the door.

"Come on!" he shouted. "Come on!"

His mother would be furious. She was sure to chew out both of us. Why I kept going, why I didn't follow Johnny up the driveway when we got there I don't know, but I didn't.

I should have stopped but even though his mother hollered at me when she saw Johnny, "Get in here! Get in here right NOW!"

I didn't. I was going home. Maybe I thought I needed some attention I couldn't get at Johnny's. Maybe I thought she'd call my mother and I'd be in even more trouble for not going home first. It was only a few hundred yards more and my legs were numbing up now, so had stopped hurting pretty much anyhow. My legs were still working okay but they were funny, kind of numb but burning, and still stiff. I was certain the clothes were rubbing raw spots all over me. I sure felt that way and I knew first hand what freezing your balls off meant.

Though they'd been running alongside me since we passed by Johnny's house, Chip and Patch ran ahead. Chip to tell on me probably. He was really good at telling and should be; he practiced every chance he got. He'd be setting me up to catch it good. I knew only too well what it would be. There'd be the devil and Mom to pay for this. I knew which I'd choose if I had a choice. It wouldn't start with "M."

Mom was waiting with towels at the door. I knew she would be, just knew she would, but there weren't any I told you so's, there wasn't a dirty look or disapproval anywhere to be found on the porch. Chip was disappointed, but Peg just looked on as Mom tugged and pulled the frozen clothing off me. It hurt

260

coming off even more than it did staying on and Mom told Carole to turn up the heat and stood me on the hot air register to thaw out before she tried anymore taking off stuff. Once stripped to my skivvies she started rubbing my legs with the towels, but had to stop. My legs were burned by the cold and had turned bright red like a burn, and furthermore, felt just like a burn. The warm air from the register felt oh so fine and my legs soon started to feel much better.

I sat on the small brown chair, waiting to catch that old devil. Waiting for the hammer to drop. Still expecting a real Q&A session, I sat on the heat with my head down. I ran through all the scenarios: trust, obedience, common sense, not taking chances, not putting my brother at risk, I should know better, and more besides. I had heard them before, chapter and verse, always as chapter and verse. I even knew what order they would be in starting with trust, always a big one for my folks, ending with I should know better. It came, as I knew it must.

My mother stood in the doorway until I raised my eyes to hers. "So, before you fell in, did you boys have any fun?"

Chapter 23
Collecting

I wanted a paper route.

But what I really wanted was the money. I never seemed to have much, despite having an allowance paid every week. That quarter didn't go very far, unless I wanted a pocket full of two-for-a-penny candy. What I needed was some frivolity and some big money to go along with it. Dollars. I had been given several dollar bills, with George Washington's tight-lipped face staring out, which were neatly tucked into birthday cards from Grandmas and Grandpas. They still spent fast, one at a time. The movies in Monroe cost twenty-five cents, and you had to spend a dime for a soda and another dime for a box of popcorn. Birthdays only came around once a year, so I obviously didn't get to see many movies. Once I had a five-dollar bill from Grandma I.G. but I had to spend it on underwear and socks. Mom said I had to have something to show Gram when she came back from Florida in the summer. I doubted that I would ever show my Grandma my underwear but my parents never lost an opportunity to clothe their kids.

Do kids on bikes still deliver the newspapers anymore?

The papers are mostly mailed out today, I think, but in those days someone placed them house by house, family by family so people had something to read after dinner. The news stories were scary: Khrushchev pounding his shoe on the table, school drills of hiding under desks, pictures in the Saturday Evening Post of ICBM's, poised and ready to launch. But everybody wanted to read about these things.

Pastor Johns' promise of eternal Hell and brimstone damnation for the unsaved topped my list of scary. He always closed his sermons by telling his congregation to make sure they were ready to go. Despite lip service to the contrary, I wasn't sure I had figured out yet what that meant. I wasn't ready to go anywhere and I suspected lots of other people weren't either.

It was the spring of 1959, and having turned twelve the previous December, I had reached the age required to have a paper route. The first obstacle to overcome was finding one that was available, and the rural area that I lived in didn't provide many opportunities. I had it on good authority that there was a chance to take over one in the summer, to allow the existing carrier to spend his vacation in the pursuit of summer-time stuff.

I asked our paperboy if he was interested in getting rid of the route.

Apparently he needed the money during the remainder of the school year. He said, "No, but ask me after school is out."

I made sure he remembered that I was interested. John was one year ahead of me in school, but two years in age because I'd started school early. "All things work to those that believe" became my motto during the last part of the school year. I'm sure I made a nuisance of myself, but I was determined to get that route and to make *something* of myself. I spent a good deal of time telling John about all the fun I had planned for the summer, how sweet the sound of the word vacation and anything else that came to mind to support my cause. He listened to me tell of the good times planned at the beach and then lamented about the fact that his summers had been full for two years of delivering papers. I was sure that he was weakening.

It apparently worked, because well before school was out, he came over to my house and told me of his plan to "sell" me his route and the rules that accompanied the job.

"Twenty-five dollars and it's yours," he said.

Well, that pretty much ruled out the idea of a paper route for me. In 1959, that was a terrible amount of money to a twelve-year-old. I didn't think that there was that much money in my father's pocket and couldn't believe that I could ever have that sum. John, being ages older, saw the look of dismay and astonishment on my face, then told me of his grand scheme: After serving an apprenticeship for two weeks, during which I would receive no money, none, I could have the route, providing I paid him the amount of $2.50 from my profits each week. Ten weeks, almost the whole summer.

Okay.

The profits part had a real nice sound to it.

I could do this, supposing now that I had convinced John, I could also talk my parents into it. They probably wouldn't be quite so easy, although they would understand the money part. I would soon be exactly where I wanted to be. In our side yard John and I shook hands. Sealed the deal. Of course, without Mom and Dad's approval it was still unofficial. But at that instant in my mind, I had become an honest to goodness, bonafide paperboy. I would have to register with the newspaper, but John told me that this would be a mere formality. John told me to meet him at the corner grocery at 3:30 the next afternoon when the papers would be delivered from town. He would show me the route.

Sitting at the dinner table that night, as was our custom after dinner, we had a "family news and information" time and I proudly announced that I was going to be an additional breadwinner in the house. I had convinced myself that an announcement was more grownup than asking permission. The reactions I received were something that I had anticipated, but I was still quite startled.

"I don't know son, it's a big responsibility."

"Are you sure?"

"How long will you keep it?"

"I'm not helping."

Their responses went around the table faster than a dish of unwanted vegetables. Mom and Dad were dubious as I tried to explain my burning desire to become independently wealthy. I was sure though and fired by that once in a lifetime twelve-year-old enthusiasm, and could hardly wait for the next day. I made countless promises that evening, all centering on the fact that I knew I was old enough to handle any amount of responsibility. I was twelve after all. For Pete's sake already.

After my father got home from his midnight shift at Ford's, Mom called the paper to make arrangements. She took me into Monroe the next morning. A parent's signature was required and there was some sort of swearing in thing I had to do. The Monroe Evening News building took up more than half a city block and you could hear the noise of the presses when Mom parked the car in front. As a new paperboy, I would get a tour to help impress me with the paper's importance. The title on the door said Circulation Manager. He shook my hand just like I was grownup, but proceeded to question me like I was in trouble.

"Why do you think you're paperboy material?"

Grin.

"Can the paper trust you?"

Nod.

"Will you deliver the papers on time?"

Nod, nod.

He ended with, "You will be responsible for any money shortfalls every week."

He towered over me during my interview and I must have answered fairly well, although I remember him looking for some confirmation from Mom every time I spoke. I sure felt like I'd been grilled, almost as well as by a parent, but I must have been acceptable.

He thought I would do.

He went to a big gray metal cabinet behind his desk and took out my paperboy kit. A heavy, white canvas bag marked "The Monroe Evening News," with a shoulder strap, was handed to me with a solemn nod. I took it as if it were the Holy Grail. This was my badge of authority and my license. He also gave me a paper punch and a change device. These were my sword and my shield. Yeah! Should I kneel?

The coin changer had places for nickels, dimes and quarters that could be counted one, two, three quick, out with a flick of your thumb. He went on to explain that all the equipment was just on loan from the paper and if I was to quit I would have to turn the things back in or I would have to pay for them. I saw him look at my mother and she nodded in agreement too. I signed my name and Mom signed hers, an official contract now, with "The Monroe Evening News" at the top. Once that was through, the man motioned for us to follow him and said we were going on the tour.

This was the first real factory I had ever been in and I was fascinated. The noises were sort of whiskery, soft clickety, clackety, clickety, hum and buzz, and there was a long, long, long strip of paper moving by so fast that you couldn't read the words on it. He explained about two and three color presses and how many papers were printed every day. He showed us the place where the papers were cut and folded, a jumble of mechanical arm and knives, slicing and creasing until the newspapers fell neatly in a row. I smelled the sharp pungency of ink. We passed doors that were marked "Editor" and "Newsroom" but we didn't go in. He showed us the Layout Room where he said people put the pieces of the paper together until it was completed. He said they got national news off the "wire" from the cities of Detroit, Chicago, Los Angeles and New York, but the only thing I equated that with was a wire strung between two tin cans. I was pretty sure that's not what he meant. We walked to a door marked "EXIT" marked in red and he shook my hand again.

"Do a good job for *The Paper* son," he said as he held the door open for Mom and me.

I said that I would. Man, was I pumped! Now, I was a paperboy. I was entrusted with "The Paper." The ride home was full of Mom statements and Clark promises. I crossed my heart so many times there were groves in my chest by the time we pulled into our driveway.

I was at Jones's Market, the corner store, around noon the following afternoon, even though the papers weren't due until much later. This gave me plenty of chances to brag to all the kids. Mr. Jones told me that I needed to get the papers quickly, he didn't want them lying around in the front of the store too long. He also told me that the paper's deliveryman would put them inside when it rained or snowed. He was concerned that they would block the aisle when inside. I told Mr. Jones that *my* papers would never even hit the ground. I'd be there waiting to catch them. He looked doubtful.

The first day I was to help happened to be a Thursday, the normal collection day. John knew this route forward and backward. This would be an excellent way of introducing me to the customers that made up the route. John showed up much later, well after 3:30, and began to show me some of the tricks that go along with having a route. He laughed at my care with the paper bag and said it wouldn't stay white for long.

"Here's how to fold the paper so you can throw it."

Got it.

"Here's how you tie the paper bag so it hangs off the handle bars of the bike and doesn't get caught in the spokes."

Yeah.

"You have to punch the cards of the customers to indicate payment for the week's paper."

Okay.

"Make them find their cards."

Yup.

John briefed me to the horrors of each Thursday collection, but I paid them little mind as we set out to the first house. I was quietly in the background during that afternoon's delivery, smiling as I was presented as the new paperboy. Quite a few doors weren't answered, several people told John to come back tomorrow, while others gave him two quarters and said, "Keep the change."

Wow, I hadn't even thought of tips! I had had the weekly profits figured out right after John and I shook hands. Eighty-four customers at five cents profit per week. Four dollars and twenty cents, of course it would be less the $2.50 to John for ten weeks. One dollar and seventy cents would be all mine and soon enough everything would be. Tips! I had an opportunity for even more money!

But Thursday John kept all the money.

The papers were right on time the next day, and I had to scurry home to change clothes before I started out with John. As soon as I got back to the store I started folding the papers while I waited for John. And waited. And waited.

John never showed up on Friday. I waited for more than two hours, sitting in front of the store before I went back home with the paper-bag full of my neatly folded papers. I sure was discouraged, and even though I knew full well what I should do, I was afraid to do it by myself.

My father was up. He normally went to bed right after getting home from work in the morning and was up for the day between 3:00 and 4:00 in the afternoon.

Waiting for his paper.

I told him John hadn't shown up and I protested that I didn't know the route well enough to do it all by myself. My father's face turned smoky, grim and glaring. I told him I didn't even have a list of customers' names. His face turned even more steely. I said I couldn't be expected to do this on my own after only one day's training. His face turned darker still, but was now tinged with red and he began to give me "what for."

"Why are you here?"

"John didn't show up."

"So what?"

"I don't know the route good enough."

"That's a bunch of crap. You just do it."

"I can't Dad."

"You're bygod going to. Whose paper route is it?"

"Mine."

"Who wanted the route in the first place?"

"Me."

"Who promised your mother and me promise after promise after promise that you would take care of your customers?"

"Me."

"If the papers don't get delivered, who is to blame?"

"Me."

"Where's my paper?"

Instead of answering the last question, I walked out on the porch. He trailed behind me, not finished, but before he said anything more I handed him his newspaper. I headed back out the door and grabbed my paper bag on the way out.

My job.

"This better not happen again!" followed me out the door.

His words kept following me, all the way back to Jones's Market, all the way around the route that day.

My job.

I sure hoped I remembered where all the customers were. I hoped I knew the right place to put their papers. I hoped I remembered who hadn't been home or didn't have the money yesterday. I hoped Mrs. Holler's dog was put away. I hoped my father liked his paper.

I hoped.

In 1959 we had an official baseball team from Pointe aux Peaux Farms.

There was a league of sorts. Stony Pointe, Grand Beach, and Detroit Beach all had teams, too. Fathers in each area had gotten together and formed the league, assumed the responsibilities of transportation to and from the different beaches, paid for and kept the equipment, bats ands balls, catcher's chest protector, mask, catcher's glove and kneepads and the bases. Because there were only four teams we didn't play every week. During the summer, even though we weren't playing "regulation" games that particular weekend, we practiced virtually every day. That year was the first and last year for organized baseball at Pointe aux Peaux.

Johnny and I alternated pitching and catching duties to round out this loose knit group. Johnny could really throw the ball. I relied mostly on control when I was pitching, but he just reared back and threw the ball hard. I was slightly scared of being the catcher when he pitched, but he and I were the only ones who could do both. We worked well together that way, but the palm of my left hand hurt for three days after catching him for seven innings. He didn't have a curve, but the fastball he threw moved around a lot and it seemed that I caught as many balls on the rebound from the chest protector as I did directly from his hand.

We had official practices on Tuesdays and Fridays because on those days there was almost always a father available to coach and prevent the practices from disintegrating into "3 fly balls, 6 grounders," or just tossing the ball around. My father would be there whenever he could, but he was working selling insurance now and that meant afternoons and evenings when customers were at home were some of his busiest times.

Between him, Mr. White, Mr. Marshall, Mr. Edwards, Mr. Girard, Mr. Belisle and Mr. Hemry we had lots of coaching help. Ed Brown didn't have any sons and drove a truck for a living but came over to watch and help whenever he could. Mr. Edwards drove truck too, and when he wasn't on the road he was at the ball diamond. He never knew when he was going to be home, but when he was, he coached and watched us play ball. Mr. Hemry was the best coach we had. He wasn't the nicest coach, but he knew a lot about the game and how it was supposed to be played. He could be pretty harsh for a bunch of ten to twelve year olds, but he taught us everything we needed to know to be a competitive team of boys.

"Get down on that ball! Look at it, LOOK at it! Keep the bat off your shoulder, and step into the ball," he hollered.

He taught us how to catch with two hands and run toward ground balls so that you could throw the base runner out sooner. He chided us when we missed easy ones and praised us when we got the hard ones. He put us through practices of ground balls to all positions, then throw to first. He hit ground balls and line drives, double play. He showed how to "cut off" a throw from the outfield and put the man out at home. He told us to always be aware of where the ball was. I was to wish that one of us paid a little more attention to that one before the summer was through.

Bob Girard was our batting coach. He could hit a ball farther than any man I had ever seen. Mr. Girard played softball in a men's league, fast pitch ball. He hit the ball consistently across the road bordering left field. On several occasions he would bounce one off of the roof of the house on the other side of the street. He could hit. He taught us timing. He taught us that home runs don't win games, base hits do.

That was pretty funny coming from such a long ball hitter, but he told us, "Boys, just learn how to hit the ball first, the home runs will come later."

We all wanted the biggest bat possible, but he helped us see the wisdom of choosing the right one for our size. We learned how to hit the ball and Johnny and Pete were our strongest hitters, although I could plink out a base hit pretty well.

We had played several games already, with only moderate success and were scheduled to play Stoney Pointe the next weekend. We practiced hard during those two weeks, honing the skills we had developed. Bud Hemry worked with us extra during those two weeks. Stoney Pointe was the beach just across the road, in the same area. Everyone was a friend with everyone else, but when we were playing ball, all friendships were put aside. They became our archrivals and we knew that the winner would have considerable stature, at least until the next meeting.

These ball games were major community events. Mothers in sundresses, boys in short pants, little girls in pinafores and people without children came to watch the afternoon games. Dads with boys playing, dads without boys, retired people of all shapes and sizes and ages came to watch us play. The teams each had a bench made of one long plank stuck in three iron posts cemented in the ground on both sides of the diamond, but there were no other benches or bleachers so people brought blankets or folding chairs. Trees bordered the chain link backstop for those who wanted some shade and there was another one adjacent to third base about five feet from the road. Numerous in-play, pop-up, or foul balls were claimed by the tree instead of someone's mitt. Every once in a while someone would forget the tree was there and have a collision as they chased after a ball.

Games were afternoon contests and parents showed up for almost every game. It took something serious for a kid's personal cheering section not to be there. There would sometimes be more than a hundred people watching the games. Because the roads bordering the baseball field ran parallel to first and third baselines at a distance of only about 25 feet, the spectators were often seated without regard to the "in play" areas. Smaller kids had to be carefully watched, but they were mostly kept under pretty good control.

There were lots of young kids running loose that day. Their mom's or dad's attention was somewhere else or the parents were indifferent to the behavior and may not have even been there. Those kids were interested in the game for just about the first inning, but not much after that. It wasn't long before they were running back and forth behind the backstop, weaving in and out of people in chairs and families on blankets. Several times one or another of the resident parents would grab one of them by the arm and settle them down, but it wasn't long before they were at it again.

The day had turned out beautifully, with the skies blue and full of cottony clouds. It was hot, but not too and we just knew we were going to beat Stoney Pointe's pants off. How could we not? Their team showed up straggling over in twos and threes. No one drove from the other beach as it was close enough to walk. It was some time before they got organized enough to start: warming up, getting equipment out, getting parents and brothers and sisters situated so that everyone could see.

Soon enough, however, our umpire that day, Ed Brown called, "Play ball!"

Johnny was pitching and I was catching, but I don't remember much else about the game. I don't remember who won or who lost, what inning it was or who was up to bat. I don't remember what time it was or who the base runners were. I remember we didn't finish the game.

The only play I remember was; a man on first, a man on second. When the next batter just ticked the ball, it ended up about three feet in front of home plate and just sat there. Piece of cake. I lunged forward from my crouch and grabbed the ball barehanded.

The runner on second base took off to beat the forced out. I picked up the ball and whipped it to third base. That runner was the play and I had a clear throw to put him out, and I had a good arm. Chucky White was playing third base. As soon as I let go of the ball, I was horrified to see Chucky's attention was on two little boys running around the third base area.

I remember people in the crowd hollering to the batter, "Run!" The coach yelled at the batter, "Run! Run!" and he screamed again at the base runners, "Run!"

That was my introduction to life in slow motion. I could see the red stitching rotate slowly around the circumference of the ball. I watched the path of the ball as gravity vainly tried to pull it to the earth. I watched the ball as it headed true and hard and quick toward third base. I watched everything. I had plenty of time to holler, ages to act; I had decades to let him know.

I screamed, "Chucky, LOOK OUT!"

He didn't hear me over the yells of the crowd. His attention from the two boys didn't waver and it was over in a split second. There was a terrible, sickening *THWACK*, a hollow, empty, sad kind of sound, as the ball hit Chuck just below the left temple. He went down without a sound and folded up like the bones were gone from his body. Like I had just shot him.

Like he was dead.

I thought he was.

Everything went from slow motion to a still life photograph; all motion came to a complete stop. The kid running from second to third base stopped midway between and the coaches stopped yelling. People stopped cheering and hollering. People stopped talking, and those little kids playing around by third base froze in mid-stride. The ball was still at Chuck's side and the whole world just stopped. I had grown roots that sank deep into the ground.

Until Mrs. White screamed.

The few minutes that followed were a real blur, but I heard Ed Brown holler at Pete Soncrant to run over to his house across the street and call the sheriff. There was no such thing as 911 or cell phones in the 1950s and I saw Pete take off like a rocket. Everyone ran to third base and jostled and pushed for good position. Everyone was screaming and hollering and staring down at Chucky's crumpled body. His mother sat down and pulled his head into her lap and I could see that he was bleeding from the left eye and ear as well as his nose and mouth. There was a lot of blood and it soon colored the front of her dress. Someone soon thought enough to wet down a T-shirt or towel from a cooler and hand it to Mrs. White and I saw her place it on her son's head. I thought I saw his chest move before I burst into tears, but I wasn't sure. The movement might have been wishful thinking.

I started walking, but didn't realize it until I found myself going past second base toward right field. I was sick in my heart and soul and just knew Chucky was going to die. I remember wondering why I couldn't have held on to the ball until he looked at me. How could I have done that? I wondered why God didn't make the ball miss him. How could God let it happen? I thought I might be a killer. Chucky was my friend and....

I was tackled from behind with enough impact to knock my breath away and shove my face into the grass and dirt of the ball field. Mr. White had charged after me and knocked me to the ground. With a scream he blindsided my face into the dirt. I gasped for breath as much from the surprise as from the impact but couldn't quite catch up with the breathing. I didn't know what the heck had happened.

He was sitting or kneeling on my back, and in his fury, was hitting and slapping the back of my head and calling me goddamnyoustupidboy, goddamnyoustupidboy, goddamnyoustupidboy, over and over and over.

His violence didn't really register on me. The grass was warm on my face and smelled good, and I don't recall being hurt by his flailing. I was still so overwhelmed by the sight of Chucky lying by third base for my mind to register anything more than the grass. I don't know how long he pummeled and cursed me before someone pulled him off me. I'm not even sure I recognized it when the weight was suddenly gone and nobody was slapping at me any more. I rolled over on my back but didn't try to get up. All I could think about was Chucky and sat up only when I heard the siren of the sheriff's car.

Somebody else was hollering close by, but I didn't know who it was at first. I looked up at the commotion next to me. Ed Brown had his arms wrapped around Mr. White in a bear hug from behind and was yelling, "SettletheHelldown, Chuck, SettletheHelldown!" He umpired more than a ballgame that day and was now taking care of a real infraction. He was much bigger than Chucky's dad and had lifted him off his feet to put some distance between him and me.

Back by third the deputy chased everybody, "Back! Everybody back away,

I said! Now! C'mon, now!"

The deputy knelt down to take a look at Chucky, but from my spot in right field, it still didn't look like Chucky had moved a muscle. I knew he was dead. I saw the deputy put his fingers to Chucky's throat. He put his ear by Chucky's mouth and just turned his head and nodded slowly at Mrs. White. He raised himself up, put his hands on his thighs and turned nodding and saying something to the group of people huddled around Chucky's body. The ones in front turned and relayed the message to those behind.

A couple of minutes later (it seemed infinitely longer), I heard the wails of another siren and an orange and white ambulance roared up and two guys jumped out. One of them pulled a bag off the front seat and sprinted toward the knot of people who hadn't got "Back!" very well at all, but they parted again quick enough when he hollered at them too. The passage closed up behind him as he reached third base. The other attendant ran to the back of the van and grabbed a stretcher; its legs unfolded as he pulled it out.

He shoved it through the crowd too; all the while telling people again, "Get back! Move now!" He knelt in the dirt by Chucky's still inert body.

The attendants carefully stretched Chucky out straight after putting a foam rubber collar around his neck. They rolled him gently to his right side, slid a plywood board with hand-holes and straps under his back, rolled him carefully back over and strapped him in place. The attendants hoisted the board on to the stretcher and tied that down too before pushing the stretcher back toward the ambulance.

My father had originally run over to Chucky by third base, but when he noticed the hubbub out in right field he dashed out to meet the two men. I was sitting up by now and Ed had walked the still shouting man about twenty feet away from me when my father reached them.

After about a ten second consultation, he ran over to me and asked, "Clark, you okay son? What did he do? What did he do to you? Chucky's gonna be okay, son."

I just nodded. I really didn't know what had happened with Mr. White and besides, I didn't want to talk. He reached down and took my chin in his hand and looked at me for a long time before turning away and going back to where Mr. Brown still held Chucky's dad securely from behind.

He wasn't struggling against the bear hug anymore. Mr. Brown soon released his hold on him. I watched my father begin fairly calmly (for him) to talk to both of the men. He listened to Ed Brown and Mr. White but one of them was a lot louder. Mr. White began gesturing wildly toward the ball diamond and back at me, pivoting back and forth, back and forth, getting loud enough for me to hear another goddamnstupidboy, before my father did anything.

I saw my father's face turn red, really bright, something I was familiar enough with. He raised his right index finger to the tip of Mr. White's nose, took another step forward so their faces were really close, and said something I couldn't hear. Mr. White took a quick step back away from him, looked over in my direction once, back at the still pointed finger, then turned and walked back toward the ball diamond. I wasn't to find out until years later what was said, and my father wasn't the one who told me.

Mr. White got back to the ball diamond in time to get into the back of the ambulance with Chucky, his mother and the attendant. Off they sped, kids and dogs chasing the ambulance as it turned the corner to head to St. Mary's Mercy Hospital in Monroe, more than twenty minutes away. Someone must have pointed me out, for the deputy sheriff walked out to where my father and Ed Brown were talking. I was still sitting in right field, my forearms on my knees, and my head buried just as deep as it would go. I would have been perfectly happy to stay there till nightfall, or until next year. It didn't matter.

Johnny had walked out by this time and hunkered down in front of me, but I still didn't feel like talking. He reached out to put his hand on my shoulder. I was crying yet, my breath catching in hitches and had never learned to talk when I was sobbing. That always managed to infuriate my father, whenever my "tail was on the line," but Johnny scooted around until he was by my side and then put his arm over my shoulder. We just sat there, me sick at what I had done, him there to be my friend. My mother had been busy calming kids down, and keeping Mrs. White on the safe side of hysteria, and helping the sheriff's deputy maintain crowd control. She came over and put her hand on my head. Mom knew somehow that I didn't want to talk yet.

When you're twelve, despite a sincere wish not to admit it, there is still nothing better than best friends and mothers.

None of us were strangers to hurts and bumps and bruises. We had skinned knees, and had Band-Aids applied to cuts with Mercurochrome and Bag-Balm. Hydrogen peroxide had been poured over lots and lots of places to keep marsh germs out of cuts. We operated in the knowledge that hurts went away eventually. I wasn't even a stranger to death. We had butchered rabbits to stock our freezer with cheap meat. I had helped with slaughtering and plucking chickens at home and watched pigs being killed at the farm. I had discovered a dead body floating in Lake Erie one year and my Uncle Dave had been killed in the Korean War. But this, this was my fault. I'd caused this. If not for me, this wouldn't have happened. This was a lot different.

The deputy and my father walked over to where Johnny and I sat in the grass, but Mom inserted herself between us and the deputy. He asked several questions I don't remember and I shook or nodded my head the best that I could. I still had my head down on my arms and I sure didn't want to talk. Still crying. He seemed satisfied with the head movement, probably because Mom or my father supplied some words every time I shook my head "no" or nodded "yes."

Dad pointed our house out, just visible from the ball field and I heard him give our address, 6169 on Goddard, "right over there" and our phone number, CHerry-1-6574. The deputy wrote it all down and turned back toward his squad car. When I finally looked, the crowd of people was still gathered tightly around the ball diamond, but the ball players of both teams had gathered up the equipment and stuffed it in the duffle bags. This game was over.

I was still wearing the shin-pads and chest protector.

Mom gently pulled me to my feet saying, "Come on son, let's go home."

I was shaky on my feet so Johnny knelt behind me and unclasped the elastic straps of the shin-pads and loosed the bow that held on my chest protector. I shrugged out of the protector and handed it to Johnny.

He took the equipment and headed back toward the diamond with, "I'll be over later. He's gonna be okay, you'll see."

My mother took my hand and we turned to go, Chip and Peg following along. Halfway across the ball field, Dad caught up and took my other hand. I didn't like to acknowledge it but I was still just a kid.

The rest of the afternoon was pretty much a haze. It turned out to be the only day I can remember that I was allowed to mope and nobody gave me the dickens. In fact conversation with me was out of bounds. I heard my Dad tell everyone else to "just let him be for a while."

We didn't find out anything about Chucky until late that night when one of the neighbors called Mom to give her the news. I was worn out with the drama and uncertainty of the day and had gone to bed while it was still light, early evening. I was still awake when I heard Mom tell Johnny to come back the next day, that I had already gone to bed, but he snuck around by my window and tapped on it. When I went to the window I just stood there while he said not to worry and he'd see me tomorrow. I didn't sleep much that night and saw the moon make the journey from one bedroom window to the next. I was achy all over, but knew for sure I wasn't hurting any more than Chucky was. I wondered if he was still alive.

The next morning, Sunday, the news from last night was better than I dared hope, but still serious.

He was alive!

Chucky remained unconscious through the night and x-rays had revealed a badly fractured skull and jaw. He had a severe concussion, was in intensive care and couldn't have any visitors. The doctors were anxious about him, but no more so than this family. Updates would be waited for nervously and I had to relive the entire episode at breakfast, as Mom and Dad insisted on a recounting of what had happened from my viewpoint. I disliked the re-telling just as much as the event and was glad when it was time to get ready for Sunday school and church.

There was another crowd gathered around the front door of the church. I had to fight my way through questioning kids. I was sticking close to my parents this day. I let my parents run interference for me and I let Chip tell the gory details. The word of the incident had spread fast throughout the community and the pastor opened services with a prayer for Chucky in particular and the White family in general. This was unusual, in that their family had never been to Stoney Point Baptist Church and was Catholic to boot. The Baptists didn't pray for other faiths unless it was to "Save Their Poor Misguided Souls From Damnation." The Sunday school teacher even used the event for her lesson.

"Everyone needs to be prepared, we can never know what was going to happen. I'll bet that poor little boy never thought this could happen to him. We can never know when God might call us. Are you saved?"

I couldn't believe she said anything about it! I was pretty mad at God just then. I figured if He called me, I'd pretend I didn't hear the summons. I got up, walked out of the class and sat in the car until church was through. It was hot in the car, but I kept the windows rolled up as a barrier to any wandering questioner. The wait for church to end was horrible, because in my mind I was back on the ball-field. I re-heard my yell and saw the ball strike his head over and over again, like a skipping record. When Mom got to the car, she asked me why I'd left Sunday School, but I don't think she expected an answer. I didn't give her one.

Soon after we sat down to eat dinner, we were interrupted by the jangle of the telephone. Mom spent a lot of time on the phone and sat in the kitchen a good while after hanging up. All conversation had stopped at the table until she came back.

"Chucky is awake! He regained consciousness early this morning," Mom said, "Praise the Lord."

She went on to tell us that his face was swollen lopsided and horribly discolored. His jaw had been wired back together and the concussion was severe. He would be in the hospital for observation several more days until the swelling went down, but it looked like he was going to be okay.

I asked Mom if we could go visit him and was surprised when she said, "I think we'll just give everybody a few days, son."

Johnny came over in the afternoon and we wandered down to the beach, to spend time talking about everything except the day before. His brother Tommy followed along waving a branch that he'd pulled from a luckless tree.

Soon enough it was time again for evening services at church, but I had thought to skip it, being intentionally late and hoped they would go without me. My parents drove down by the lake, I thought to pick up their errant son, and Johnny and I walked up to my Dad's open window. Both parents accepted the answer of "fooling around," when he asked us what we were doing, despite his hating that response normally. We were both surprised when Dad said I didn't have to go this evening, but that I was to be home before dark, even if they weren't. Johnny and I piddled around down by the lake until we wore our arms out throwing stones and when the light began to fail Johnny and Tommy cut off to the right and I headed to our house. I went straight to bed and didn't hear the family come in after church. I'd find out more about Chucky tomorrow.

I delivered the evening newspaper and on Monday there was a small article about Saturday's incident but it was cold and clinical. We hadn't received any more updates from the hospital, but I was sure we'd find out something from someone. Chucky's grandparents were customers on my route, so I'd stop there first and ask. I always knew them as "old" Mr. and Mrs. White. They went back to the city every two weeks or so to check up on their city home, and normally spent several weeks there as well, so I wasn't surprised when there was a note on the door telling me to stop their paper. The note had a nickel and two pennies scotch-taped to it for that day's copy.

I knew they would call me when they were back although I wondered why they were leaving while their grandson was still in the hospital. I made a mental note to call the paper to decrease the number of papers they delivered or I would have to pay for their papers myself. I continued my deliveries, riding my bike quickly with Patch running alongside. Every once in a while she would dart off on dog business, to chase this or that, sniff this new smell. She always caught back up, always seemed to know where I would be when she thought enough time had elapsed. I hurried through the next section of my route, in anticipation of hearing something when I got to their house.

The note on their door said the same thing, but there was no money. Surely they weren't going back to the city while their son was still hospitalized.

Maybe he was home already, a miracle! Oh boy, home! I had to see him!

I knocked on the side door and when I didn't get an immediate answer, went around to the front. Heck, I wanted to know. I knocked several times at the front, still got no answer and went back to the side door and really banged hard. I could hear the radio or television noise coming from the house and thought they might not have heard me. Mr. White snatched the door open so hard the blinds fell off the inside door. I still didn't realize what had happened between he and I on Saturday or maybe I just felt I deserved whatever it had been. I don't know what I thought. I started to ask how Chucky was, but Mr. White interrupted immediately.

"Whadd'ya want?" he spat down at me.

"How's Chucky? Mom said we could go visit as soon as he can have visitors," I asked as I backed away from the door. His face was a scowl. The man was still… something.

"What-do-you-want?" he bit again at each word.

I thought I'd told him what I wanted already.

"How's Chucky?"

No response.

"I got the note, are you going back to the city? Is Chucky okay?" I changed the subject. "When are you coming back?"

He didn't answer me but stepped out the door and walked down the steps. I backed up a little farther, but he kept following me down the drive as I backed up, retreating. I remembered Mom saying something about giving everybody some time. Okay, I'd come back later. Mr. White got close enough to me to grab my arm and he jerked me close to his hot breath. He didn't say anything more, but concentrated on squeezing my arm until he got it just right.

"Oww! Let go!"

Then I heard a deep, serious growl at my side and a pressure on my leg.

Patch was right there and was showing an insight that I couldn't imagine or hadn't wanted to believe. She had her nose scrunched up tight and she curled her lips to show her teeth and her seriousness. She growled again.

This wasn't play.

Mr. White looked at her and let go of my arm real slowly, but only after giving it another long, hard squeeze, one more intended to hurt. It did.

He turned around without a word and started back to the house, but turned

278

at the door and hollered back at me, "I don't want your goddamnpaper anymore!"

He yelled again as he stuck his head back around the edge of the screen door, "Don't you come around here!"

I was speechless. I just stood there, not knowing what to do or how to do it. I remained motionless for long minutes.

He'd slammed the door before I realized that he owed me for today's paper. It would now be considered left over and I'd have to pay for it. I'd gotten over my astonishment and was pretty mad by now. He'd deliberately hurt my arm and would have continued if not for my dog. Patch was here, as good as having Dad. I went back up to the door and knocked lightly, with Patch standing alongside so close we were touching. When the door was torn open for a second time, Patch began to growl immediately. Mr. White closed the door to a crack.

This time I stood my ground.

Mr. White started to ask, "What…?"

I interrupted him. "You owe me for today's paper, Mr. White. You were my customer and I can't cancel it until tomorrow. You'll have to pay for it."

He dug in his pocket, threw a dime to the ground and slammed the door.

I left his three cents on the doorstep.

That was the last conversation I had with any of the Whites. They still came out to the beach, but Chucky wasn't allowed to "associate" with me. He never played ball with us again and the only thing I could do was wave if I saw him. His parents and grandparents never again took the paper, never spoke to me, and never forgave me for that Saturday afternoon.

If he only knew one thing… I didn't forgive me either.

Chapter 24

It's All a Dance

Patch preferred variety.

We were after bunny rabbits on an October day in 1959. Patch was not a trained hunting dog, unless you count the hours of roaming she and I spent together in search of something that might be called prey.

I might set out with specifics in mind but Patch chose a more non-prejudicial approach when on the trail. I would want pheasant whereas she selected whatever came first. I could have promised my mother a rabbit or two for dinner even as Patch's thoughts approached a deer or a woodchuck or even something with fins. It always made for mysterious fillings of my game bag as well as unexpected menus at the dinner table. That is, when we were fortunate enough to bring home more than prickly burrs. While I would never label Patch as indifferent when we were hunting, her exuberance sometimes got in the way of taking anything more than mosquito bites from the field.

Mom had started a stew with freezer and garden contents only to find that the combination wouldn't feed more than half of us. When I got home from school she'd already changed the supper plans to macaroni and cheese, a dish gooey and not always welcome at our house. We'd have the stew tomorrow night after the hunters of the family came back loaded down with fresh meat.

I hunted with an old Stevens 12 gauge single shot I inherited from Mom. I always had a hard time envisioning Mom shooting anything with the gun, but she insisted that she had hunted with her brothers plenty of times when she was younger. Judging from the condition it was in when I got it, plenty of something had left it nicked and dinged enough to have been in World War II. It was all mine though, presented as "it's yours now son, you're old enough" and I loved that old shotgun. I was allowed to take two shells when I went hunting, a strict adherence to some family rule or tradition and I knew to have a pair of dead animals if the casings were empty when I came home.

"Do not tell me you missed one," Mom would say if the bounty was scant.

When I hunted the expectation was to do more than have a good time, although fun was okay too. The goal of providing food didn't lessen my enjoyment. I wasn't required to be some grim faced slaughterer, nothing ever as severe as that, but my parents' unstated anticipation was that any expenditure of money must provide more worth than the cost in dollars. Shotgun shells cost money means bring home food if you use one. My father and grandfathers both were strict teachers in the field and I had paid close attention. I had to. There were tests afterwards. I had to pass them all with no mistakes before graduating to my shotgun. I was taught never to shoot for the sake of the noise and I didn't even think of wasting ammunition.

I was always convinced that if I shot at nothing, something eatable would appear in the next instant, but then I'd be out of ammo. I'd have to come home empty handed. In addition to everything else, I enjoyed the small admirations given me when I did bring food to the table. I invariably looked forward to more. In spite of her cavalier attitude regarding which prey to follow, Patch and I were chiefly serious on the hunt.

We hunted the ditch rows bordering a farmer's fields adjacent to the marsh with no success. Patch smelled lots of somethings, but nothing appeared while she snuffed and snorted through the grass and brambles. One advantage to having a heavily coated dog was that she went everywhere. Maybe it was her nature that said no cover was too severe and I never saw her shy away from following a trail, no matter where it led. Her enthusiasm hadn't gained us anything so far, but she soon caught something in the airs. Instantly we were both running flat out towards the woods and just as quick I was way behind. In complete disregard of her nine years, Patch could still turn on the speed when she wanted to.

Just as I broke into the edge of the wood I saw what Patch had scented. A doe and her last spring's fawn were feeding on the acorns underneath a huge oak about fifty yards from the edge of the field. I was surprised to see the littler one and mother because this was past the time when the does drove off their fawns in preparation of the next generation. This fawn may have been a late birth. Possibly it wasn't even her offspring, and the pair might have been just feeding together. At first it looked like they were ganging up on my dog and I readied myself to shoot the large doe.

Instead, under the oak my dog and both deer were playing a game. Well,

Patch was fooling around but I think the deer were serious.

The soft dirt under the reaching branches of the tree was pockmarked from the deer's pawing through the fallen leaves for acorns. The bower the oak created was a hundred feet or more in diameter and Patch and I had hunted here for squirrels even though she always scared them away. The canopy and big tree trunk offered us a resting place or shelter from a shower on many occasions. It always smelled wet underneath the shade, moist and cool like a basement. This was a favorite spot, not exactly hallowed but a place Patch and I came for quiet or to lick some wound of boyhood spirit. The trunk was so big around that Chip and Dave and Steve and I couldn't touch fingers when we tried. I had seen deer sign here before, the disturbed earth, scat and some of the rubbed off velvet of a buck's antlers but had never seen even a white tailed withdrawal from this spot. Deer in southern Michigan were wary and I had only ever seen a few. Mostly they set eyes on us first and the flag of a distant tail was only a recollection.

However, these two animals were not about to give up their dining area. I would have thought they would have flown at the first sound of Patch lumbering through the leaves, but they were still there when I got within a few feet of the tree's outmost branches. I stood behind a smaller tree and watched.

When I first got in position Patch was in a high back end crouch, just like she would do when she played with Chip and me. Forelegs outstretched, her head low to the ground, she would fake a movement, then repeat until one of us, didn't matter who, moved too far. The game was made up of mini stand-offs that were interrupted only when boy or dog would more than twitch. When these stalemates were broken all parties had to break into wild aimless rushes, until one or the other players froze again, quivering until the next mad dash sprang forth. When Patch played this contest with us, the game could go on for minutes or hours before breaking off. It could be picked up again without any notice of resumption but we always knew when the sport began. The wriggling of her upturned rump was just like a starting pistol.

The deer might not have known the rules first off, but they caught on quickly. The grown doe charged head down at Patch, who eluded her like a toreador as the deer danced by. When the doe spun to face the dog again, her hooves threw little clods of dirt into the air and she waited, poised until courage or some signal demanded another rush. Both deer played this feinting and charging game with Patch. First one and then the other teased my crafty and fearless dog. I watched, fascinated with this animal ballet, until Patch began to get tired. The deer had the advantage of a breather when one substituted for the other, but Patch had been on her own so far. The deer were panting with open mouths but Patch was really tired and she slowed down enough that the doe made contact. The impact wasn't hard enough to hurt Patch but the doe grazed her hind end during the last few moments of competition. I stepped out from my hiding place and took a few steps toward the trio. Patch at first looked pretty miffed with me for not already joining the game.

I thought my appearance would signal game's end, but when Patch looked at me, the big doe saw her chance to score. In slow motion I saw her charge again, but Patch's attention was on me, glad that her partner was here to join in. The competition had taken on new meaning and her behind waggled back and forth as she imagined a now even-sided match. I swung the shotgun up to firing position, and readied for an easy target even though my shells were loaded with #6 pellets, pretty light pellets for a deer. I was only fifteen feet away from the deer, and couldn't have missed. From this distance, even with the light load, the shot would surely be fatal. There would be lots of meat to put in the freezer.

I just didn't have the heart to end the game that way. Instead I lowered the barrel and discharged the Stevens into the ground, blasting a hole two feet in front of me. Both deer just seemed to vanish. One went one way, while the other tore off in a flash of broken field running marked by white flashes.

Patch rose from her crouch, sat there and watched them run away and turned her head to catch a glimpse of both.

She was pretty glad the game was through, came over to me and we walked to the base of the tree together. She plopped between two exposed roots and I broke the shotgun to remove the spent shell, tucking it into a pocket. I didn't reload. There wouldn't be a need for any more ammunition today. Patch needed a rest.

I poured her some water from the canteen I carried, liking the feel of her tongue as she lapped the water from my hand.

My dog, my friend. My me.

Her panting slowed and I tangled my fingers in her coat, so close we were surrounded by one another. There wasn't any hurry, macaroni and cheese tasted just fine reheated. We stayed under that canopy for a long time, past the drop of twilight before we started back to home.

I fed and watered my dancing warrior of a dog and waited while she ate before I went in. Mom would be displeased that I hadn't shown up for dinner, but she'd love the tale of why.

I went through our dinner-time routine when I got home.

"I'm starving!" I called as I came through the door.

"Nice to meet you, Starving!" five voices crowed in unison. It was a terrible joke but we said it to one another at least three times a week.

They had waited dinner even though Chip claimed to be dying from want of food and my father always liked to eat on time. Mom had just covered the casserole back up and kept it hot in the oven.

"We'll wait," her edict came as Peg laid out the dinner plates and silverware.

When Patch and I got home that evening, my mother was disappointed with the empty game bag, but once I started to tell her the story her face took on an air of amazement. She stopped me before I told much of it.

"You need to wait and tell this story at dinner tonight. First time stories are best. Peg's already got the table set."

As always, Patch got to lay by my chair that night as I told my family about her game of tag. Every time I said "Patch" during the story, she sat up for emphasis. I had to tell the chasing sequences two or three times before the family let me stop. After I finished Dad said Patch was lucky the deer didn't hurt her.

"A hundred and fifty pound deer could have you know. I can't imagine what got into those two deer," he said. "Even with no horns they're strong and dangerous. I'm surprised you didn't shoot one of them."

My father didn't mention the wasted shotgun shell, although I knew he would have liked the venison. I didn't argue with him about the risk we took, but he was wrong. I think everybody else at the table knew he was wrong too, especially Chip. I saw the magical game those three had played and God himself wouldn't have dared to interrupt that little contest.

"If you could only have seen her Dad," I thought, "then you'd know."

My mother was the mother for more kids than just us.

While none of us ever felt a lack of love in my parents' home there were lots of times when we suffered from a lack of space. My mother cared for other children frequently. On two other occasions it was for teacher's kids during the school year, but this episode spilled over into summer. The overpopulation of our house would never be any more true than in 1959 and 1960, when we shared our beds, space, clothes and food with two extra hordes of children.

Our family's six members were often supplemented by as many kids and as many 'lost' adults as Mom felt she could lead to the Lord. We never knew who (or even what) would be at the breakfast or dinner table. Many were the mornings when we would stumble from our bedrooms to find a Dave or Randy, a Wanda or Frieda lying in tangled bedclothes on the pulled out davenport in the living room. It usually meant that the Cheerios or oatmeal would be divided into smaller portions or that school shirt selection could be limited and sometimes required that we share toothbrush and comb. We kept folding chairs stacked in the dining room corner next to the piano, just in case someone dropped by, whether avoiding the law of parent or county or just staying out.

Our dining room table had extra leaves to expand so we didn't leave the table with bruised elbows and ribs from the newcomer's eating habits. We once had a troubled youth, sponsored by some church in another city that stayed one or two nights. He stole my father's coin collection and his wallet and disappeared. That episode slowed Mom's efforts at populating heaven for a while but soon enough we were rubbing elbows again with enough sinners to satisfy anybody. The road to salvation was oft times as difficult for the savers as it was for the unsaved.

My father never made a great deal of money. Repeatedly his temper got smack in the path of advancement and he would feel belittled by the work. Dad always seemed to be in the shadow of his father, a dark place that he couldn't see well enough to escape. Grandpa's successes were a burden my father couldn't bear. Our family was so often on the cusp of assistance that both Mom and Dad had gone to respective parents for help with any number of deficiencies. Whether inflation ran rampant during our growing up or Dad's niche remained hidden from him, we always needed more money. Mom tried to help and took babysitting jobs.

Mom normally got paid a dollar a day per *family*. Sometimes she did the job for charity. The number of children didn't matter to anyone else but us.

Summer school meant extra income for teachers and so meant five dollars a week for each troop. When Carole left for college right after high school graduation we had more room. With Mom's magic math this meant there was now space for five more children. Three from one family and two from another invaded our lives with all the subtlety of Genghis Kahn. They weren't spending the nights but the freight that got unloaded on their behalf belied the fact: Toys, clothes, bicycles, wagons, bottles, diapers, salves, creams and powders stacked up inside the door when the families discharged their loads. It took my mother weeks to create spaces for their baggage.

We were resigned to these guests' arrival however dissimilar they were to us. With them unfortunately came their foreign germs and before long we caught what they had. Their hacking coughs found new territory in our chests, their runny noses snuck into ours with regularity. Like drinking the water in Mexico something bad would happen whenever new kids came to stay.

I particularly had been celebrating Carole's departure for college. Her vacancy was one of my major milestones. No more constant battles over dishes in the kitchen, no more having to deal with her overlong stays in the bathroom or constant bickering. My joy wasn't allowed to last long, although I inherited the upstairs attic bedroom. Upstairs provided sanctuary but in order to get to there I had to run a gauntlet of underfoot kids that didn't belong here.

My mother had slowly also begun a period when she described God in the dichromatic colors of black and white. Black was for a sinner, white for someone bound for the Promised Land. Her faith wasn't new but her religious fervor was climbing toward treacherous heights. The five extra bodies, lack of money and Mom's growing reliance on the Lord to solve every problem drove the wedge deep enough to split anyone right down the middle.

Mom became a member of the pray with, pray for, pray on, pray about, pray long and pray hard, washed in the Blood of the Lamb, Everybody is bound for Hell, Baptist School of salvation. We were affiliated with the Southern Baptists and for years I thought that meant they joined in secession with the rest of the Confederacy, but found out they really believed that EVERYTHING which wasn't in the Bible would condemn your soul. That's what Mom believed, too. Belonging to the Southern Baptist really meant that these Christians held small hope that many people would gain salvation.

I was fairly sure their references included me.

Chapter 25

Food and Table

Patch could turn up or disappear with a cloak of invisibility.
One minute she wasn't with me and then "POOF" she was standing right in front of me.

Patch was sort of like my mother.

Patch spent most of her time by my side but never missed an opportunity to investigate some mystery or touch up her standing among the neighborhood dogs she'd spotted. Her ability to catch up once she'd solved the mystery or said her hellos was uncanny. She may have tracked me or maybe she possessed some extraordinary method to divine my location. Even after being tied when I left to go to the corner store or sent back home from beach or road, she'd pick up the trail and appear, wondering what I was up to. What ever the talent, Patch could find me whenever she chose.

When I was growing up, we children had few outside, store-bought activities. We were expected to create our own entertainment. There weren't video arcades, weren't music stores, weren't theme restaurants and Mom probably wouldn't have allowed us to go anyway. School and church functions were okay of course, but our rural setting didn't include many prospects to go to Monroe for movies or bowling or park picnics. Coupled with Mom's insistence that her children's social activities be strictly limited to supervised events, we just didn't get many opportunities to get out.

School was the big tempter. We didn't even have a high school in our community yet but I'd heard about many schoolmates' older siblings enjoying the good things of life. These kids talked of street dances, or the new attraction of a McDonald's hamburger joint, north in the big city of Trenton, the A&W drive-in on Monroe Street, sock hops after football and basketball games at

Monroe High School. American Bandstand was NOT allowed in our house but I'd heard about it's learning and jiggling potential from my buddies. Although I was loath to admit these interests to my parents for fear of planting the seed of being worldly in Mom's brain, I was attracted.

We did have a skating rink.

It had a bad reputation, though no one could tell me why.

But the first time we went it was with the church group, a radical move on Mom's part because heretofore our association with whatever secret and terrible activities went on under its cloak of semi-darkness were strictly forbidden to us. Our church banded together with others of our ilk to organize and reserve the rink for a party. Posters saying *Baptist Holy-Roller Skating Party* were put up at church and school. Despite being mortified to be associated with a group of people who so blatantly boasted of their religious fanaticism, I went but I didn't admit it in advance at school. Recorded hymns were blasted from the loudspeakers and if you weren't saved and couldn't prove it you didn't get in. Prayer before, during and after with a special call to salvation. As bad as it seems, one of the pastors invited us to "skate right up to Jesus" and declare our liberation from Hell. I cowered during the whole evening, worried that some other sinner or schoolmate would peek through the glass doors and see me with these uncompromising Baptists but two good things happened.

I learned to roller-skate.

And the visit loosed my mother's reins.

Mom must have felt some Holy clung to the rafters and remained after the first visit. Now that Dixie Skateland had been blessed by the presence of the Holy Ghost, it was okay. Even association with the sinners who normally went there wouldn't be strong enough to pull the Greene children away from Jesus. Mom went with me the first two times just to make sure Beelzebub wasn't skating but after the first time the new horizons were open.

I exploited the new freedom. Since acquiring the paper route, I was expected to contribute to the family coffers. This was not an unusual request or circumstance, most actual earnings at our house required tithing to God and the family. 10% for God, 40% for Family, the rest is the earner's. I had my own money and was allowed to put it to whatever use I chose. I went roller-skating every time I could scrape up the small amount required. My weekly get to keep money hovered around the $2.00 mark, a fairly large sum in the early sixties.

Often one or the other of my folks would drop me off on a Friday evening or Saturday afternoon after I'd finished delivering the newspapers. Sometimes another teen was going and I'd catch a ride with them, sometimes I'd just plain hitchhike the two or so miles to the rink and infrequently I walked the distance. I wanted to skate and never waited long whatever the transportation, including my grandfather's pronounced method of shank's mare.

This time I was getting picked up at Jones's Store. I didn't notice Patch until Stan's father pulled up for me alongside the subdivision gates. I don't even think she was there until he stopped the car but she may have been in secret observation the whole time.

"Go home," I ordered and pointed for emphasis. "Go on home, girl."

Patch knew this command. Although her order list wasn't extensive she was well accustomed to all voice directives. She knew the meaning of every single gesture and word, but sometimes appeared as if she didn't think we were serious. She turned to go.

I watched for only a few moments before I clambered into the back seat of the car and looked once over my shoulder as we pulled away. Stan's father suffered from the same impatience as did mine and I didn't want to keep him waiting. Patch was headed back down Goddard toward home. I knew someone would bring her in when she signaled her arrival at the back door.

She never got there.

Instead she doubled back and tracked me.

Of course I was oblivious to this for some time. For an hour or so I was lost in the music and whirling, glittering from a mirrored ball, lights of Dixie Skateland. Skating with someone (some slight interest in girls by now, another reason to come) or speeding around when "Fast Skate" was announced on the PA system. I had learned to skate well and could race or skate doubles with my arm tucked around a girl's waist as well as I needed.

I became aware of a disturbance at the doors to the building but didn't pay any more than cursory attention. By the second or third circuit after my initial notice, more and more kids were gathering, creating a din of laughter that vied with the music for loudness. Then I saw her.

Actually she saw me, because she came out on the rink in her hunt.

It took a long time to get to me because she had to say hello to every one of her new friends while they were skating. Bouncing and barking, chasing and romping, I honestly believe she sniffed every other person there. Patch was having a great game of it, scooting around the rink with the crowd of skaters, stopping to crouch but then leaping away as some new "rabbit" whizzed by. Some kids started a game of tag with Patch and she played that game with fervor. When someone would pat her, off she went in pursuit until someone else playfully slapped her rump, then "Away!" in an opposite direction. Everybody thought it was hilarious.

Except Jim, the son of the owner and the manager of the rink. He didn't start out mad although he kept asking over the loudspeaker who let the dog in and who it belonged to. He only got angry after Patch couldn't be corralled and put back out. She was having too much fun to let anyone get in the way of her enjoyment.

Even me. She completely ignored my summons. There were way too many new kids to play with.

Jim began chasing Patch around the rink.

She thought it was just a variation of the game of tag. The kids thought it was more entertaining than their game. Patch couldn't get good traction on the slick surface of the skating area but she was still more than a match for anyone on roller-skates. Ducking and dodging were right up her alley, having been perfected through hours of the game with her real "children." Just as it seemed she had no place to go, she'd scoot, nails scrabbling, with hind legs tucked in, out from the clutch of the manager. Everybody except Jim was thoroughly enjoying this new game of Gotcha, Patch especially.

All good things must come to an end.

When Jim couldn't catch her, couldn't even come close, he stopped the music and announced over the loudspeakers; "ONE OF YOU KIDS BETTER GET THAT GODDAMN DOG OR I'M CALLING THE SHERRIF."

There was a scattering of "Boos!" then silence.

Someone must have told Jim that Patch belonged to me because he skated up and asked if "That Goddamn Dog" was mine.

"Yeah, I guess she is."

"Well, you and your dog can get the Hell out." He pointed to the door.

"I didn't let her in," I defended her. "She's not hurting anything. Everybody's laughing at her and playing with her. She won't hurt anybody."

"Out! Now!"

"Whheeet!" I whistled. "C'mon girl, let's go home."

Patch came to me reluctantly. She was still having so much fun. She barked once sharply. *"Why has everyone stopped? What happened to the pretty music? How come we're not playing any more?"*

Jim escorted us to the bench where I removed my rented skates and handed them to him. He turned them in to the skate rental counter with my tag, got my shoes and handed them to me, and after I put them on then walked us both to the door.

290

"Don't be bringing that dog again if you want to keep skating here."

"She must have followed me," I said. "I didn't bring her and I didn't let her in. Besides, she didn't hurt anything."

"No dogs. If she comes again, you're out!"

"Okay." I reached down, patting her flank. "Time to go girl."

As Patch and I walked on the side of the road toward Pointe aux Peaux, we turned down several rides when people stopped to offer. The hike home, all two miles of it under the autumn moon, was too spectacular to miss and she'd had such a great time. I had, too.

We talked the whole way home.

Just ask anybody. Mr. Yost was benevolent.

All the people at church knew Mr. Yost was generous and Mr. Yost was good. Mr. Yost also took advantage of cheap labor. He gave me a job three weeks before Thanksgiving working Saturdays. I would earn extra money for Christmas presents, money in addition to the few paper route dollars I made every week. I would be able to afford real presents for my family and for Sharon, a girl I liked in the ninth grade.

All I had to do was pluck turkeys.

"Report to the big shed with all the fans right up front." Mr. Yost said. "My brother will show you what to do."

The Yost Turkey Farm was located in Newport only seven or eight miles from Pointe aux Peaux. We used to attend the same church with Mr. Yost, who, along with my father, was a deacon. Beyond collecting the offerings, I never understood what the deacons did, except shush loud little boys during Sunday service.

Many people in the community liked fresh, not frozen turkeys for their holiday dinners, and my family was no exception. We got a big, fresh, farm-raised, newly plucked, fat, tom turkey from Mr. Yost every Thanksgiving. We would this year too, but there'd be a difference. I was plucking ours for sure in addition to the ones I would earn a dime for. A dime for every turkey I plucked. Why I'd be rich in no time.

I'd get Chip and Peg to fill in for me on my paper route. This was always easy to do; they were Greene kids and after big money just like me. I promised them twenty-five cents apiece for Saturday deliveries.

I showed up the first Saturday expecting to butcher and pluck the birds by hand. There was the shed with steam billowing out from the fans. That had to be the one. At the door of the low shed I could see the turkey pens on the other side of their farm, full of cackling dirty white birds. The pens were attached to low sheds on one side. It looked as if there wasn't room for the birds to move; they were packed in the wire enclosures so tight it was a sea of white with red heads. There were thousands of them and the noise was constant in the distance like a low gurgle. Mr. Yost's brother, who didn't go to church at all, met me when I went through the door to the foremost low shed.

"You here to pluck?" he asked me.

Something heavy grabbed the back of my throat. I was busy fighting my gag reflex at the moment but managed to nod. Gah! Gluh! Damn, what was the smell?

I stuck out my hand in greeting but he had already turned away. Dammit, what was this smell? I hesitantly followed him over to one of eight big white machines that had steam pouring out all over them. The hot smell in the shed was heavy with moisture and a sharp bite of ammonia, like a sauna gone sour with neglect. There were lights hanging from the exposed ceiling joists with large metal shades which dripped dirty water drops onto a floor that was in more need of a scrubbing than any I had ever seen. The walkways were framed wooden slats set on the concrete floor that were wet and slick, with scummy small feathers laying and sticking and coating everything. The stink was sickening; a reek of turkey crap mixed with the odor of wet feathers, damp and gummy and instantly coated my nose and throat.

There were people busy at several of the machines and we went over to watch a man in an apron and gloves, who was busy at the whirring machine.

"Here, see that foot switch?" he asked me.

I nodded and he went on.

"That controls the scrub drum and the hot water, too. When you grab one of those turkeys off the rack over there, you hold it under that spray right there. See it?"

He pointed. I nodded again.

"You hold the turkey's legs in one hand and ruffle the feathers backwards as you hold it under that water jet, just like he's doing."

I watched trying to take this all in. The front of the man's apron was covered in turkey....

"Shit," Mr. Yost's brother finished the thought for me. "When you push the bodies on the scrub drum to get the feathers off, it just pushes the shit right out of them," he laughed. "That's what the aprons are for."

"There's aprons and rubber gloves over there. You've got to wear both. That water is scalding hot. It will take the hide off you quick. Don't use gloves that have holes in them, you'll get boiled hands before you know it. Got it so far?"

My nose got a cramp from holding my face scrunched up.

He must have noticed my look and laughed again, "You get used to the smell."

His laughs didn't sound like any I heard around the dinner table, more of a cough, as if to rid his mouth of the taste. That's what it was! The smell was stomach-turning and so pasty, it was in my mouth, coating my tongue. Glah!

Got what, what had he said just then? I didn't want to appear inattentive.

Nod.

Nod.

I nodded again, but wasn't sure about the foot switch.

"Water or drum?" For sure I forgot the middle part.

"Now when the bird's wet, still hot and you're still holding the feet that way, you hold it against the scrub drum. You've got to keep turning it so you don't scrub the hide off it. People like their turkeys with the skin on. You got to keep your hands away from the scrub drum too or you'll wear a hole in your gloves. Got it?"

Nod.

As the man held the bird's body under the hot spray, the billows of steam smelled even more putrid. My clothes were already damp with the steam and I'd only been here ten minutes.

Nod.

Nod.

Nod. I kept nodding, hoping the movement would hide the fact I hadn't understood much of anything past aprons and gloves, and that I was seriously considering adding some vomit to the floor. The thought that no one would ever know quelled my nausea.

"Now when most all the feathers are off, take one wing and pull it out to get those feathers, then the other. Do the same thing with the legs. Be careful with your hands, we ain't going to buy you a bunch of gloves if you ruin them. Got it?"

Nod. Nod. Nod.

"When you're all done slide it right down that chute where them women will gut it and pull the pinfeathers out. Rinse it off before you slide it down. Don't hold the bird under the water long either, you'll cook it. And don't be going down there to bother them women. They won't be able to keep up as it is. Careful you don't jam that turkey in them brushes too far either, we'll have to sell it as dog food and the machine will blow the fuses. Got it?"

Nod. Nod. Nod. Nod.

293

"Get to it, then. We got 2500 turkeys to do every day before Thanksgiving. Nobody gets to leave before they're all done either. I ain't staying to finish up or clean up after any of you."

I nodded some more even though he wasn't asking questions. He didn't seem to notice. Did people know what their turkeys went through before they put them on the table? This plucking process must be the best-kept secret on the planet. The plucking shed had to be somebody's secret, too.

I went over to the rack that held the aprons and gloves. The aprons were brown rubber-covered, long enough to drag the floor, and stiff enough to make walking difficult. No one had bothered to wash these off before they hung them up. The black rubber gloves were stiff from the repeated contact with scalding water and I had to look through the whole pile before I found a right hand and a left hand glove that weren't torn or worn through.

Okay, I'm ready now.

Give me a turkey.

The turkeys hung upside down on large metal racks with wheels by metal hooks that held their feet. Their wings hung outstretched like immense grimy butterflies. I grabbed one of them and turned to my station, tentatively stepping on the foot switch. The billows of steam from the hot water spray were immediate. I couldn't see a thing.

"Why don't they turn the fans on and get rid of the steam?" I shouted at the guy next to me.

"Shit, they been shorted out since I been plucking. I been a'doing it two years now. The steam killed them fans." He laughed. "You'll get used to it."

The spinning bristles almost grabbed the big body out of my hands and I quickly pulled it back toward my waist.

Spurt!

Yup, that's what the aprons were for. Green and white turkey dung slid down the apron. These turkeys carried lots of muck around with 'em. I had to keep pulling the turkey back against the drag of the rotating brushes. The feathers came off all right. Flying everywhere, they stuck to me, the gloves, to the apron.

"You got to get the feathers off better!" I jumped when Mr. Yost's brother hollered in my ear.

Nod.

I steadied into a drill: grab a turkey by the legs, hold it under the water spray, twist and turn till it's steaming and soaked, push one side to the brushes till the feathers fly and then the other, pull one wing out, other wing too, do the same with each leg. Rinse and slide, down the chute to make the counter click. The last part was very important. That's how I got paid.

I started to get the hang of it by the time I got to the fourth turkey.

Oh yeah. The smell wasn't so bad either, why I could barely smell anything.

My nose was stuffed, plugged up tight in rebellion. I needed some tissue, or a handkerchief to blow into then realized it was better on my senses this way. It was ever so much better with them stopped up. Why, soon I didn't even mind the turkey crap on my apron. Much. The racks of headless turkeys to be plucked kept coming and coming. There were always turkeys to be plucked, cadavers waiting upside down to be stripped. Whenever I got close to the end of one rack, somebody shoved another one in behind it. The feathers lay in soggy masses all around my machine. I had to scoot them out of the way with my feet, off the wood mat I was standing on.

That Saturday did not fly by, bird by bird. It went on forever. The counter on the chute from my machine said 183 when Mr. Yost's brother said it was time to clean up.

He also said, "You're going to have to pick it up a Hellofalot more than that."

The clean up consisted of kind of washing the machines, sort of raking the gluey feathers into piles to be shoveled up and almost doing a good job. We did something like rinsing the floor down, but the drains were blocked with feathers and the water lay in pools of frothy scum. It was dark outside the dirty windows. The big clock read 9:30 and had Allore's Funeral Parlor written under the hands.

A guy named Larry from Detroit Beach gave me a ride home. He'd attended school with my older sister at Monroe High and drove his own car, a jalopy. The '47 Chevrolet smoked like a trash fire but it got me to my house. He said he would pick me up next Saturday if I wanted him to.

"Yeah, sure. Thanks for the ride," I replied grateful and tired.

It was just before 10 o'clock that night, the end of a long, long day that began at 7 am. I carried the eighteen dollars and change in my pocket, proud despite having been told to "pick it up" the next time. I didn't have a chance to wave my $10 and $5 and three $1 bills around before I was rushed into the bathroom. Nobody in the house cared about anything I brought home except the smell.

"Son, you stink! Get outside! You get those clothes off, and put them in this paper bag. Close up the bag when you're done and set it on the back porch. Get in that tub and scrub good. Church in the morning, you know. We're all going to bed. How was it? You really smell bad, Clark," Mom finished.

She didn't wait to hear. I didn't really feel like going over it anyhow.

Patch, on the other hand thought I smelled great. She thought I had finally gotten the scent masking thing down perfectly. I kept shoving her away and finally had to put her in my room so I could get cleaned up.

I was glad to note that the family had finished baths several hours ago. That meant the water filling the bathtub was pristine and steamy and hot, something I didn't get very often. A bath all of my own, no sharing the space and water with Chip, no hurrying so Dad would get my once used water while it was still warm. I felt privileged. As I waited for the tub to fill, the steamy water loosened my sinuses and I blew my nose but didn't look at the results. I had seen the coating in that shed. My imagination sufficed.

I doubt I ever enjoyed a soak as much as I did that one, though by the time I got clean the water wasn't. I had to rinse off with the shower, even though the water was now cold. I'd used every hot molecule for the bath.

Every family member the next morning told me they could still smell wet feathers. They all told me two and three times. Chip and Peg scooted their chairs as far away as they could, held their noses and made faces until Dad told them "Enough!" and "Eat your breakfast!"

They were right. I still smelled pretty bad. If I didn't have to sit with me, I wouldn't either.

Nonetheless, I was eager to get back the next weekend. I received a few odd looks on Monday in school, but because I scrubbed myself in another bath Sunday night knew I smelled a whole lot better. I wore enough Old Spice and Vitalis to hide rotten eggs, and by Tuesday I had mostly forgotten the stench. I would have plenty of time for recall soon enough.

Larry picked me up Saturday early so he could get a cup of coffee at the Newport Inn. I had one, too and he told me not to take everything so serious when I told him what Mr. Yost's brother said to me. Larry said he was a prick and wait until I had met the nephew, who thought he was the boss of everybody.

"Fug 'em. Just ignore him," Larry told me. "Have a little fun, take a break a little. As big a prick as he is, he needs all of us to pluck those Goddamnturkeys. If he hollers too much, tell him you're gonna quit. He'll stop his crap real quick."

I listened carefully to his profane wisdom. Since I rarely heard that kind of language, his experienced sounding advice should probably be followed.

This Saturday was a repeat of the first although I was better running that machine, with the big spinning brushes. After a while, my mind stopped thinking about what to do and I watched fascinated as my hands did it anyway. Lift, spray, scrub and turn, scrub and turn, slide. Grab another. Lift, spray, scrub and turn, scrub and turn, slide. Grab another. And on and on and on.

I started noticing other things, the talk and laughter of the women and girls as they finished the pinfeathers and gutted the birds. The seven other people hollered and laughed at each other, told dirty jokes and teased as they slipped between machines. Larry and another kid I didn't know were tossing a carcass back and forth playing turkey football, swapping machines and hooting until Mr. Yost's brother told them to quit it.

"OOOOWWWW!! SonofaBitch!"

My left glove was suddenly full of blistering water. Not watching the turkey, enjoying the game they were playing I shoved the turkey under the spray far enough to get the open cuff under the liquid stream. I flicked my glove off with a jerk, but the almost boiling water was already raising blisters across the back of my hand and wrist.

"Dammit!"

That burned like fire. Nobody but the guy next to me saw what happened.

"Go down by them women," he hissed. "They got some salve for your hand. Hurry up 'fore he sees you."

He pointed to the end of the shed where the women were. I didn't need to ask who "he" was.

I got some ointment from the women and it did make the burns feel better but the blisters got bigger immediately. One of the women slipped a new glove over my left hand and handed me a new right one, too.

"Here, these new ones are softer, you just get back there before he comes. He won't like you down here and he won't like the new gloves if he sees them."

They were talking about the same "he" as the guy next to me was.

I got back to work. But I was paying lots of attention now. My hand hurt enough to focus my brain to the task at hand. Every time I grabbed one of the turkey wings or legs to pull it out I could feel the blisters on the back of my hand pop and ooze. Every time one broke the burning changed to another position. New ones formed up, because the oozing and squishing continued.

My concentration was intense. This machine was dangerous. No, the machine wasn't dangerous. I was dangerous if I wasn't deliberate in my work. That would not happen again. The liquid feeling in my glove was almost pleasant now, still burning some, but the turkeys were waiting and I was picking it up a Hellofalot! I wasn't going to take my glove off, not until we were through for the day. And then not until Mr. Yost's brother was somewhere else.

Lift, spray, scrub and turn, scrub and turn, slide. Grab another. Lift, spray, scrub and turn, scrub and turn, slide. Grab another. Lift, spray, scrub and turn, scrub and turn, slide. Grab another. Lift, spray, scrub and turn, scrub and turn, slide. Grab another. Endlessly.

My counter read 286, *and* I was wounded.

I heard the same exclamations of disgust when I walked in the house that night, but got the same enthusiastic greeting from Patch. Some things never change. Patch was always glad to see me and now she had a new reason. Mom drew her breath in quick when she saw my hand, a bright red from wrist to fingers, and smeared my hand with Bag-Balm and wrapped it before she retreated from the smell.

"Did you tell Mr. Yost?"

When I shook my head no, she turned to go.

"That's a bad burn, Clark. Be careful."

I put my gauze-covered mitt in a plastic bag before I took a bath. My clothes went into another "put it on the porch outside" bag.

Every smelly comment was a repeat at the breakfast table Sunday morning. Monday was no better. I didn't think the Old Spice covered the disgusting odor as well on this Monday. Maybe the smell accumulated. Sharon had something else to do, someone else she sat with at lunch instead of me. I noticed that she didn't come to my locker between classes, either.

I had one more Saturday to go. One more Saturday night of wrinkled noses and Sunday morning's chair scooting. I didn't care. I'd made almost fifty bucks already, the most money I'd ever had.

Everybody was in a good mood that last Saturday before Thanksgiving. Although some worked through the week, many of the workers were just like me and only showed up on Saturdays. But nobody worked on Sundays, even with the need to get all the turkeys done before Thanksgiving. Mr. Yost's church standing might be jeopardized because Sundays were for the Lord and the Family. First and last. Most businesses were closed on Sundays. One grocery store in Monroe, part of a national chain was open on Sundays, but aside from some gas stations, nothing else. Mom said they were owned by heathens and we believed her.

Lift, spray, scrub and turn, scrub and turn, slide. Grab another. Lift, spray, scrub and turn, scrub and turn, slide. Grab another. Lift, spray, scrub and turn, scrub and turn, slide. Grab another. Lift, spray, scrub and turn, scrub and turn, slide. Grab another. Without end.

Someone wanted to play soccer or hockey so we had a combination game with one of the turkeys. The plucked birds skimmed really well on the slimy floor and slid back and forth between the players. The day was full of banter, no one was serious, but everybody was intensely doing the work, despite the laughter. The naked birds stacked up at the women's tables. At the machines we were really moving, the turkeys flew down the chutes, faster than they could have with feathered wings. When all the racks were empty, and the machine operators helped finish up the birds piled in front of the women. We had to gut, scrape out the chest and stomach cavity, clean the heart and liver, split the gizzard and wrap everything up in a piece of paper. The birds got rinsed, wiped off and shoved into a plastic bag for weighing. We were ready for cleanup at 6 o'clock, the fastest we had ever completed the day's quota of 2500.

My counter read 319. My Hellofalot! Almost $32 in one day. Riches!

We swept and cleaned with a speedy vengeance, though not any better than we had previously done, just lots faster because everybody wanted to go home. There, the place looked just like it did when I first started and it smelled exactly the same. Nasty. Perfect.

I'd tasted that plucking, gutting, shitting shed continually and wanted no more of that place. My hand was still raw from the burn and would remain that way for some weeks. I never again looked at a turkey the same way. They would always be associated with this evil smelling place. I'd had enough of Mr. Yost's benevolence, his brother and enough turkeys, but he asked me to come back after Thanksgiving to get more birds ready for Christmas.

When he handed me our "free" turkey I said "No" for one and "Thanks" for the other. There would be no more plucking in my future.

However, during those last two Saturdays, I found that people could have fun while they worked. In spite of horrible working conditions, they laughed and teased one another enough to make up for what we were doing. The money was great, I had another $31.90 for Christmas, but I decided right there and then that anything including turkeys was a thing of the past.

I spent almost all the money on Christmas presents that year. I got everyone in the family something much nicer than the usual dollar or two we kids had spent in the past. I felt pretty good about spending the money on my family. I even purchased a big bone from the butcher shop for Patch. There were lots of grins and smiles when the "to's" got something marked 'Merry Christmas from Clark.' I bought Sharon a bracelet from Penney's, and she really liked it, but her liking of me didn't extend much past January.

The presents didn't smell like hot, wet, turkeys to anyone but me.

Chapter 26
Sinners All

The paths I trod didn't often include girls as traveling companions.
My life was full up with boy things: sports, scouts, wondering how I got into this or that mess, how I would get out of it, Patch and my paper-route. Although I met frequently with girls at the intersections marked school dances, sock-hops, skating rink, or church and summer beaches, girls remained a peripheral influence of how fast or slow the scenery went by. The winter of 1960-61 would change that forever and journey's end provided me with a generous helping of deep and lasting sorrow. During the snows and cold of that season I walked alongside one girl who continued to occupy my thoughts long after the path ended.

There were a number of girls my own age scattered throughout Pointe aux Peaux and Stoney Pointe. Diane, Tanya, Sharon, Karen, Agnes, the twins Marleen and Josephine, Kaye and Cassandra were girls that I had secretly liked or loved from kindergarten through my current ninth grade. My dreams included visions of several older women my sister Carole's age. Darleen and Mary were ignorant of my very existence and thus available for undiscovered and hidden-from-my-bedroom stares when they came for visits.

I knew something about girls regardless of the hasty glances or hurried meetings. Girls were mostly smarter and a few weren't shy about showing it, though some could be just shy. They smelled a whole lot better than the boys I fought with at recess or wrestled and ran with in gym class. They were smoother and softer than boys were and were prone to behind-their-hands giggling. Boys laughed with open-mouthed guffaws and hoots even when there wasn't anything funny. Girls never did. Some had already developed slim waists, long, even slimmer legs and breasts where breasts were supposed to go. I liked what I saw but mostly I still watched from afar.

Earlier that fall I began spending some time with Cassandra Worall. She allowed only her mother to use that name and insisted on being called Sandy by her friends. She was a year younger than I, but regardless of the chasm that can exist between different grades in school, we were close friends. We had known each other for years, when we met, she riding the same bus to kindergarten that I rode to first grade. Sandy normally went to school with me but during much of the last year had spent a lot of time being ill, sometimes staying in the hospital or just staying home. I had volunteered to gather up and bring her schoolwork to her whenever she couldn't come to school.

To my absolute amazement, I had also been allowed to attend church several times with Sandy and her parents. They were Catholics and went to the Catholic Church in Newport, on Newport Road. When I asked permission to go, I only got approval after a lengthy discourse by my mother regarding the Catholic religion. She told me not to be taken in by the pageantry and what she termed idolatry of their church. I heard about "Holy Water" and their worship of Mary, who was only a vehicle for Jesus, just an ordinary woman chosen by God. Mom told me that few Catholics would ever see heaven because they believed that their priests could forgive their sins. Mom said it was all utter nonsense. The Catholics were bound for Hell and Damnation.

It was a simple task for me to accomplish, although it sometimes seemed strange to revisit my old junior high school building, more strange to be with the little kids. I had moved to the brand new high school building beginning that fall, graduating in ways I hadn't yet recognized. Technically, Sandy and I didn't go to school together any more though we still rode the same bus, morning and afternoon. During lunch hour each day I walked across the field to the Junior High building and picked up her new work from the office and handed in the work that she had completed from the previous assignments. Like many girls she was smart and took her schooling seriously. I aspired to be the kind of student Sandy was, although my aspirations were hidden, a good secret to both teachers and to myself.

The chore quickly became more than just a duty to perform or a task that I had to do. I looked forward to stopping by every day when I delivered their newspaper and Sandy's schoolwork on the way around my paper route. I kept her notebooks tucked safely in my newspaper bag with the everyday adult news, knowing that the stop by her house would break the monotony of routine for me and the routine of confinement for her. Her mother always insisted that I deliver the schoolbooks and papers to Sandy personally. Sandy's mother delivered me to Sandy's bedroom door every time I stopped.

Sandy was a pretty girl, sweet in disposition, blonde and blue-eyed. Her bedroom was perfectly suited to her, with pink bed-ruffles and curtains, stuffed animals, put-away dolls that kept watch over her and a dressing table that held powders and pictures. It looked like she had more frills and toys than my sisters did even though I only got to look into their room from the doorway. Despite her mother's insistence that Sandy stay in bed she always looked like she was ready to go somewhere. I always liked how Sandy smelled, little girlish good with a hint of roses and honey.

She had her own television on a table and a telephone by her bed because her mother had been pretty good at keeping her confined. It took some time for me to get accustomed to visiting in her bedroom, as if this was foreign land because I was never allowed in Carole's room, always denied entrance, off limits.

I never got over the sense that I was visiting royalty when I went in to see Sandy, but the reason she was in bed was that she had a heart murmur and got short of breath easily. She wasn't in bed on a whim, but because that was where doctors insisted she stay while they figured out what to do. Her illness hadn't affected her disposition or her happiness; it seemed nothing could do that. Sandy liked everyone and everyone included me.

Mom told me how proud she was that I was being such a good friend. She also gave me little clues about Sandy's illness.

"Her heart is weak. The doctors hear a murmur. Her heart could stop at any time."

I said she was getting better any time Mom broached the subject.

Sandy's mother didn't talk about it at all. Mostly her mother cried, but Sandra was always smiling, so I would smile, too.

Because her house was situated along the first part of my paper route I usually didn't stay long when I delivered her homework. I'd spend a few minutes if there were verbal instructions I needed to relay or interpret or if we just needed to chat. I still had more than an hour's trek before my last customer had their paper, but I often came back. More days than not when I finished up, I'd go home and open my front door, sling my now empty paper-bag in behind the door and holler.

"I'm going to Sandy's for a while. Homework."

That last word, homework, always won approval for the trip. I could occasionally skip chores if I had schoolwork to do. I'm sure my mother figured that if I would be studying, it was okay with her.

Sandy and I used the time to study but we also talked to reinforce our bonds of friendship and talk our way through fears, both hers and mine. I'd recount unknown-to-her high school stories, of how we went to different classes every hour, speeding along the way with bells that told us how late we were. I made her laugh with descriptions of teachers, who had been holding hands with whom, trivial things mostly, but to us, life's important facets.

Our relationship strengthened when we entered an area of confidences that neither of us had experienced before.

In November, Sandy told me that her parents were talking with a special heart surgeon about an operation that might help her heart. I wasn't to tell anyone that I knew this confidential bit of information, but Sandy was pretty sure that she would have the operation.

Some day.

Sandy had a birthday in December, two weeks after my own. I had just turned fourteen, and she would turn thirteen. She seemed inordinately pleased with her soon-to-be teenage status and couldn't wait for the day to get there. I asked her what she wanted for her birthday and she said a new heart and she laughed when she said it. I laughed only because Sandy laughed. By that time, she had influenced me into an acceptance about her medical problems that I fell short of believing in completely. I didn't see anything funny in her remark. Sandy's birthday party was an event for the whole neighborhood. I had money from my paper route and my sister Carole went shopping with me for a present.

Her mother repeatedly said, "Cassandra is an angel that came just before Christmas."

I could really relate to that because I knew an angel who came on Christmas, too, my baby sister. I knew two angels, Sandy and Peg, one since she got on the bus and the other since my father carried her through the front door.

Sandy's party on December 14 was pretty subdued. No that's not right, we kids were pretty subdued. Her mother insisted, to Sandy's embarrassment, that there would be none of the usual screaming and running about at this party. We were mostly getting past that childish behavior stuff anyhow. There was cake with vanilla and chocolate and strawberry ice cream and party hats and the favors that unrolled with a squeak when you blew on them.

Sandy whispered, "Thank you, it's just what I wanted" with every package she opened. She got lots of things that teenage girls get. I bought her a birthstone and silver angel pin. I looked for a new heart but I couldn't find one.

Sandy did look like an angel, but a very tired angel in the glow of the candles.

We all helped blow out the birthday candles with her, thirteen of them, one for each year. I decided at that party that I was in love with Sandy. It didn't matter that she was a year younger than me. Next year we would be in high school together and I would walk her to classes. When the party was winding down Mrs. Worall asked me to stay.

After the others were gone, Mrs. Worall took Sandy and me into their front room. We sat on the couch with Sandy between her mother and me. Mr. Worall was there too, although he hadn't been at home for the party. Mrs. Worall held Sandy's hands and I wanted to also, but didn't know if it would be allowed. Her father told me of their decision for Cassandra to go ahead and have a heart operation. Both parents went on to explain that Sandy had a hole in her heart, it leaked and made her get tired the way she did, which was the secret I kept tucked away. Mrs. Worall went on to say that the operation was dangerous, but the doctors were worried now about the hole getting bigger. Sandy could die if something didn't happen.

Wow, this was serious. Mom's hints came to mind. Somehow this seemed much more real. Sandy was in the middle of a life and death struggle. I hadn't been paying near enough attention, not even close.

"When?" I asked.

"In January, toward the end of the month," Mr. Worall said. "She's going to a hospital in Detroit where there is a good heart surgeon. The surgeon thinks there's a pretty good chance that Sandy will be just fine. We know that God will watch over her and we pray every night about her recovery. God won't let anything happen to our angel."

When he went on to say that the odds were 50/50, I recall that I didn't think those weren't very good odds. Like flipping a coin. Who could tell what kind of outcome there would be? Nobody could tell what would happen, but I kept my thoughts inside.

However, it sure sounded like they were talking to the same God I did. How good was Mom's information, I wondered?

I continued to bring Sandy her homework before and after Christmas and the New Year. Her father carried her to the enclosed porch several times and we drank the hot chocolate her mother brought us until Sandy got tired. We had both enjoyed the holidays and I spent extra time with her, just friends watching the snowfall or the ice break up on the lake through the front porch windows of their house. We breathed on the windows and wrote our names in the frost but didn't draw a heart around them.

After a big snow, Sandy sat inside on the porch and watched as I built her a snowman complete with coal eyes and mouth, a carrot nose, and a top hat and scarf. I told her the snowman would keep her company when I went home at night or had to deliver my papers. She was delighted with the gift and clapped her hands and laughed in appreciation. She named him Malcolm but only after I made her promise not to tell anyone it was my middle name. He stood sentinel everyday until she went to the hospital and waited for her to come home with a fixed heart.

Sandy wasn't nervous about the upcoming operation but her mother was nervous enough for everybody. Sandy said her mother would want to go through with the operation one day, the next day she would say no they weren't. Mrs. Worall's jitters wore off on everybody except Sandy. To my eyes and mind she remained calm about the whole proceeding. She laughed and joked about having to catch up on lots of schoolwork after the operation. I told her I would help, that all she needed to do was get better.

The day before Sandy went into the hospital I cut school. I went to the bus stop like usual but I walked back down toward the lake and circled around to Sandy's instead of getting on the bus. It was still half dark, so I wasn't too worried about discovery, but I really didn't care if anyone saw me. I stood and looked at their house a long time before I went up. Their kitchen lights were on so I walked up and softly knocked on the kitchen door. Mr. and Mrs. Worall were surprised to see me that early in the morning because they thought I was coming over after school. I said I was sorry for being there that early, but I wanted to spend more time with Sandy before she went to the hospital. I said it just didn't seem important to go to school. Somehow they understood and opened the door to let me in.

With a smile and a glance, Sandy's mother asked me if I wanted cup of coffee.

"Sure," I said, though I still didn't drink it at home.

"Cassandra is still asleep," Mrs. Worall said. "I mustn't wake her yet, she needs to sleep a while longer."

I told her I didn't mind waiting if they didn't mind having me there. I didn't say anything and just wanted to be there even though there wasn't much I could do. I sat and looked at my coffee, not trying conversation, probably not even thinking. Sandy's mother looked weary, worn and run down low. I was, too, but I couldn't figure out why.

Mr. Worall said he had to go take care of a few things at his office this morning. They would be spending the next several days in Detroit while Sandy was checked and prepared for the operation, and afterward, too. He stood to go, then turned around and shook my hand.

"Thank you, Clark," he whispered. "I probably won't see you again before we take Cassandra to Detroit. Thank you for caring for my daughter."

I said that his daughter was my special friend and I meant it. He smiled with his lips, but the smile didn't extend to the rest of his face. His eyes were red and worried and sort of far away. It was all I could do to choke back my tears. I needed to hold it together. I was afraid of crying and not being able to stop. I kept thinking of the odds. I thought her father was, too.

Sandy got up later in the morning and we spent the entire day together. I can't remember one single thing her mother said or what Sandy and I talked about. We may have listened to 45's on the record player or we may have watched the television in her room or maybe we read a book to one another. I do remember that Sandy took a nap about noon and while she slept her mother and I looked through her baby book. She'd looked like an angel in every one of her pictures, although I'd kid her about the bare-nitchey ones.

After Sandy woke up, I stayed a while longer. Her mother sat on the bed and brushed Sandy's hair for a long time after she woke up.

She looked really pretty, really beautiful, and I told her just how nice she looked. She liked that, and I was glad she did.

Three o'clock. It was time for me to go, but I sure didn't want to. I had made it the whole day without being discovered. It wouldn't do for me to nix it at this point. I had the paper to deliver and I needed get home to change clothes.

Sandy's mother said she had something to do and she would meet me at the back door. It was time for me to say goodbye. I held Sandy's hands for a long time, not knowing what to say or even if I should speak. I looked at her a long time, fixing her face in my mind. I think I cried a little despite trying really hard not to. I gave her a hug, held on to her until I was embarrassed and said I'd see her when she got back home. There wasn't anything left for me to say. She told me not to worry, that everything would work out fine. I kissed her on the forehead and again on the lips with true feelings of affection. I turned to look at her lying on the bed when I got to the door.

She smiled and waved, "Bye Clark. I'll be home in a few days."

"Okay," I said, "See you later."

Her mother met me at the kitchen door to say goodbye. She gave me a long soft embrace and said thanks for being such a friend to her daughter. I told her I really liked her daughter, that she was a special friend. I told her that nothing bad could happen to Sandy. She looked at me a long time as if trying to figure out who this was, this boy who came in the dark morning. I told her thanks for letting me cut school today and she started crying. I spent several more minutes telling Sandy's mother that everything would work out fine, and that Sandy would be okay, although I wasn't so sure. Her mother wouldn't let me go and kept her head tucked into my shoulder crying. I finally took her arms from around my shoulders, went out the door and walked home. On the way around my route I asked God over and over and over again to take care of my friend during her operation and hoped the message got through.

Two days later, someone, maybe my father, told me Cassandra's heart ruptured during the operation. I thought mine might, too.

Patch and I walked down by the lake. Patch understood and kept herself pressed against me the whole time. We were quite alone until after dark when my dad found us and walked us home.

I put off going to "view" her until Mom insisted it was my responsibility to go. My family went to the funeral parlor on the last day and I went with them. Sandy's father shook my hand and asked me to help carry the casket. Her mother couldn't even look at me when I embraced her. Her mother was inconsolable and had been hospitalized for several days before the funeral. She looked like she should still be hospitalized. I couldn't bear to look at my friend in a casket, but I did it. Unlike what others said, Sandy didn't look like she was sleeping.

This was not my friend, not the Sandy I knew. Sandy was cute and pink and happy and alive. This looked waxy and false and dead.

There were only three people in this whole room who knew what had happened, what had been lost and one of them was standing in my shoes. I had to get away from all those other people. I waited for my parents, sitting outside on the front steps of the funeral parlor watching traffic, but not seeing one damn thing. This was for shit. I couldn't believe this had happened. Sandy told me she'd see me when she got home and this wasn't home. I needed to be someplace else, anywhere except here. I sure hadn't expected this. I didn't like this at all. One day we were talking, another day she would never say anything to me again.

I thought of asking God what had happened, but couldn't form the thoughts. He hadn't responded to my prayers before, why would He want to talk now? Besides, I didn't think I could be civil.

On the way home Mom said she thought we should talk about this. I told her to talk all she wanted, but just not to me. I don't recall that we ever did.

I was a pallbearer at Sandy's funeral. Billy and I were the only kids to help carry the casket into the St. Charles Church in Newport. The rest of the pallbearers were adults, but I sure as Hell wasn't. It was a long way to carry my friend. I didn't care about the distance and was just glad to be following behind someone because I couldn't see anything through the tears. I appreciated the pageantry of the funeral service, the priest's robes and the incense and the Latin liturgy. It seemed an appropriate way to honor someone special who had died.

I couldn't help thinking that Mom had said Catholics weren't going to heaven.

"Priests cannot forgive sins," Mom had said. "Only Jesus."

As I threw a handful of dirt on Sandy's casket I knew better.

Mom wasn't right.

Mom wasn't even close.

Sandy was already an angel. Everybody who knew her said so.

We had a visitor who stopped by after Sandy's death and he stayed so long it caused some serious rifts in the family's fabric.

At first the get-togethers were short but grew longer every time he showed up and everybody was getting real tired of the jerk. Mom was always inviting some poor lost soul(s) home for a rebuild and usually her applications of care and concern worked. We all had become inured to the challenges of having these people in our house, thinking it would just be a matter of time before both parents turned him toward the light, but not this one. This guy was really different and even Mom was having a struggle with him. I think my father gave up and just wanted him out of the house. Pretty much everybody gave up on him except Patch.

I was beyond help.

School had started and ninth grade was helping me kick my own butt right after the first introduction. I entered a phase that school and teachers and learning and trying were not part of my program. I didn't like going, I didn't like my instructors and I knew there was something better for me to be doing. I didn't know what it was but I wasn't letting anyone else tell me either. I wandered. I moped. I screwed around.

The teachers weren't pleased, but I didn't care. Mom and Dad weren't pleased and I didn't care about that either. In fact there was little I did care about, certainly school was way down the list. Mom and Dad weren't the ones who had to put up with those stupid teachers and as a matter of fact I thought my folks might be stupid for making me go. My first report card sent my mother and father running into the enemy's camp and suddenly there was open conflict at home and at school. I was on restriction, grounded, no television, no reading except for schoolwork. Get your butt home from the paper route and crack the schoolbooks. Don't think about asking because the answer is "No."

I cut school. Dad was working, of course, and Mom was babysitting for the Newsome's so there was no one on patrol. When I got off the bus at school, I frequently just walked back down Williams Road and hoofed it back home where Patch would do her wiggle-bottom greeting when she saw me. There was nobody to stop my absenteeism. I wrote my own school excuses, devised fantastic reasons for my absences and signed my mother's name. I lied and lied and lied to everyone, but mostly to myself. When the school's truant officer came to the house, I was in open defiance. Of everything.

For some years now I was silently growing suspicious, more and more questioning of my parents' professions of faith. An avid reader, I secretly got copies of the Koran and the Talmud from the county library, which drew apprehensive looks from the librarian.

"For a report," I said as I satisfied her glares.

I read about witchcraft and dark arts and the Inquisition and Stalin's purges and used the same reason for them at the desk. I looked and searched and grew more lost with every page I turned. There was no map for this path.

I refused to go to church and battled about it every Sunday. If they insisted, I tried to ruin the service for everyone else, by feigning sleep with loud snores or singing deliberately off-key to the hymns. One Sunday I stashed a sheet in the trunk of the car. Between Sunday school and church, I draped myself with it for a toga and put the crown of thorny black locust branches I secretly made on my head. I pushed the crown down hard enough to make my forehead bleed. Perfect! That solved the church requirement for a long time. The Baptists didn't think "Clark as Christ" was funny at all. I knew those people were stupid. Their lack of humor convinced me even more that I didn't want anything to do with them.

My parents should have committed me. If there would have been "Tough Love" that may have worked but I doubt anything could have made much of an impression. I was now big enough to physically resist my father's attempts to give me a whipping and blackly impervious to Mom's pleadings and "what have I done wrongs."

I just plain didn't give a damn. I was ashamed of myself but not enough to change. I liked the notoriety more than I felt the disgrace I had wrapped around myself.

I chose to fight every step of the way.

Bedrooms were designated study areas in our house but I was soon studying in the dining room. In public so I could be watched, but public didn't bother me one bit. I had perfected looking but not seeing, a blank slate that I defied everybody to write on and I sat for hours with open textbooks and didn't read a thing. I'd be damned if I would let anything penetrate this mind. My teachers conferred with me, then retreated to my folks, who withdrew further still to our pastor, but I was the one losing ground. It's a wonder my parents didn't sneak in at night and smother me with a pillow. My school grades kept pace, neck and neck with my attitude, racing to see which one could reach the bottom first. It was a tie.

Relatives tried to rescue me but I slapped away or ignored every proffered hand each time they reached them out. Again and again. My Grandpa Teddy said he was worried about me but wouldn't say more and Grandma Phoebe was just plain mad. I was "wasting myself" and she wouldn't squander her efforts. If I wouldn't open my eyes, she wouldn't waste her time trying to help me see.

"It's better for him to fall down hard enough to crack his skull wide open," she said. "He's got to want to do….*something*, sooner or later."

Grandpa Clark and Grandma Grace came to our house and he shook me up, rattled me around and I just let him, limp, a big, bitter filled scarecrow. Maybe I still had some respect or maybe I didn't care about even that. My Grandma Grace was a psychologist and dealt with troubled youth in Detroit and postponed her regular counseling to stay with us for several days, vainly talking with me. Nothing worked.

My folks made an appointment with a psychiatrist, this one at the "nut house" in Ypsilanti. The Michigan State Mental Hospital. The only reason I went is because they said they would call the police and have me locked up if I didn't go. I went, but I had a real hard time deciding which choice I wanted. The only part of the interview I enjoyed was when the doctor asked me to describe my feelings.

"Lackadaisical." I replied, trying to impress her with the big word. She needed to know she was dealing with a well read and superior being.

When I gave her my indifferent and apathetic explanation I finished the thought with, "what the Hell do *you* think it means?"

That ended that interview. Fine with me, just fine.

I refused to see anything until one of my teachers said she was glad I was enjoying her class so much. What? This class? Why, this was the worst of the worst. This was the stupidest class I had ever been in and they had all been stupid. She was stupid, the school was stupid and the school was stupid for hiring her, and furthermore that was a stupid thing to say. Every word battered the inside of my head like a gong, but she didn't hear a sound. Of course, she would have had to be a mind reader to get the message. Even if she had ESP she would have only read the word stupid. The word fit in my skull perfectly.

Miss Mathis sort of laughed when she said I must really like the class because I was certainly going to come back next year and do it again.

"Huh?"

I knew kids who had been "held back." I knew kids who flunked. I even knew a kid who was still in fourth grade and he was my age, fourteen. The question was not whether I was bright enough, the question now became whether or not I wanted to carry the stigma of doing a year over. Gee, I never thought of that.... I could flunk. I would flunk. I was flunking right now. Oh, oh. I thought of the kids who would be leaving me behind.

They'd talk about. They'd laugh at. They'd think less of. Me.

How Miss Mathis got through, I don't know. Maybe the flippancy of her laugh told me I wasn't able to see the mess I was creating, or perhaps it was her disbelief that I could be that stupid. The laugh landed in the perfect place to germinate and grow. There wasn't anything else in my head to prevent its repeating. I heard the little merriment again and again for the next few days, until I finally got it. I needed to fix this.

I could only hope to repair the chaos I had created. No, the right word wasn't hope. I would have to *work* to repair the damage. I knew how to work. I had just neglected the skills. Maybe I could fix this. I saw the bemused look on my teacher's face, and I heard her giggle. That sight and sound took their places in my brain. I struggled, I really struggled, but with the added picture in my mind of spending an extra year, maybe my adult life in the tenth grade, even growing old there, I started to make small progresses.

Catching up is much more difficult than staying abreast.

You have to spend a lot more energy when you're alone, not running with the pack.

It's harder to chop wood with a dull axe. And I had learned that, years ago.

Maybe I was stupid.

Fortunately, my teachers were great. My parents were better still. It took so much of their patience and assistance for me to pick up the cadence. I'm surprised they helped at all. I had to drop a class in order to have an extra study period. My teachers came to the study hall and worked right along with me. Mom or Dad helped me at night after dinner while Patch lay at my feet. I studied, but was really far behind. A guy named Despair was right there looking over my shoulder and he wasn't helping me study. I did extra credit until my teachers ran out of ideas for me to accomplish yet I was still far back. The grade average necessary to pass me into the 10th grade was in question almost right up until the final exams. I all but didn't make it, and came so close to failure that I still get queasy when I think of my deliberate attempts at self-destruction. When I got my final grades no one was more surprised than I.

I went to the flame many times before I figured out it was hot. I singed myself time and again, and on this last approach I almost burst into flames. I wasn't completely fixed yet but I was better.

Mom praised the Lord, but I still wasn't talking to Him.

I should have done penance for the all problems I caused, but instead I reveled in my regained freedom. I celebrated getting off of all those restrictions, and then disregarded the thoughts that started the mess in the first place. I hadn't yet grown smart enough to thank everyone for the help.

I'd been in Dutch so much lately I should have had an accent.

Occasionally there were flashes of brilliance, but they didn't occur very often. I was bored with school, although I never admitted it out loud. My teachers all said I was smart, but my father said I was a smart aleck, smart ass and smart mouth. He was probably the more correct.

I still took care of my paper route and still did my chores, but I stopped being a participant other than with blank stares and deliberate defiance. I struggled with the authority of my folks, my well-earned reputation of indifference at school and rebelled against the struggles of my parents to help me See the Light. In order to minimize their judgmental words and looks and completely against their wishes, Patch and I spent even more time away, in our marsh. Mom and Dad had rightfully stopped giving me the freedoms I was so accustomed to. With permission. Without permission. But that didn't matter much.

I'd stopped asking.

Once we got inside Fermi's perimeter fencing, there was virtually no one who could find us if we chose to avoid discovery. I'd learned my woodcraft well, could stay out indefinitely, could successfully trap small game, and wasn't bothered by weathers of any sort. Our trails were faint, our campsites well hidden, and we moved about with almost complete impunity. Even though my folks enlisted Chip's help in trying to bring me home, it produced small result. He found me only if I let him. While the security force that patrolled the vastness of the nuclear facility was equipped with radios and trucks, they seldom managed to get the briefest glimpse of us. Their uniformed numbers and even the extensive gravel roads couldn't cover the area well enough to deny us the pleasure of our ramblings. Mostly we hid out, but it was all a game and we always won.

I loved the autumn woods. The annual winding down of summer always seemed the most significant and dramatic. To me, the rustle of falling leaves, squirrels hurrying to get the last acorn or the puttering of raccoons preparing for winter were as lovely a music as ever conceived. This fall was the best I'd had back here in a long time. Normally I had to share my woods during hunting season, but Fermi's construction had put an end to everyone's use but mine.

I continued to withdraw from my place in the family in most ways. The problem was me.

It was snowing when Patch and I picked up my papers on a December day just before Christmas at Jones's Market.

In fact, it had been snowing the whole day through, but it was nothing unusual. Light, lacy flakes piled up on top of an already established blanket. The sky was leaden and dark with the promise of a good snowfall. There might not be school tomorrow. Oh Boy! Wintertime in Michigan was often interspersed with school closings, icy streets and snowdrifts. I recall more than one occasion when we could step onto the roof over my parent's bedroom from the top of the snow that had drifted up next to the windows. It looked like the winter of 1960-61 would be another of those cold seasons full up with snow to hinder and hamper. Adults, my father in particular didn't care for the snow but children would be delighted with any days away from school.

My father had purchased a brand new car last fall, one of only two new cars he ever owned when I was younger. A 1960 Volkswagen, a small blue car that hardly suited our family of six, but that he needed for the gas mileage it provided. "Thirty-two miles per gallon!" He boasted. As an insurance agent with a collection route to make for those customers who paid their premiums monthly, Dad was always on the road, sometimes logging more than the astronomical amount of ten thousand miles a month. Had it not been for the car we purchased from my grandparents, a 1950 Dodge, someone would have had to stay home when family excursions came about. Most times I tried hard to make sure it was me.

The Volkswagen, which my father insisted we pronounce "Volks-vagen" was an unusual car to see on the road in 1960, and not many people owned or drove them. For many people World War II was a recent memory and it was a German built car, sometimes seen in old newsreels depicting Hitler's madness. Grandpa Clark in particular sarcastically commented, "Goddamn Kraut car" every time he saw the car. This was even more unusual in that Grandpa's grandfather was German and had come to this country as a lumberman to take advantage of the Michigan timber being harvested in the upper part of the state.

My father fiercely defended the car to everyone with "it will go when others won't," "never been stuck," "the darned thing even floats," always ending with a recount of his latest mileage economy figures. He kept track of the figures religiously and recounted mpg to the family virtually every time he filled the tank. The car's impressive, miles per gallon statistics, could not be matched by the guzzling monsters Detroit was producing at that time.

My father would always laugh when he said, "It doesn't go fast, but I pass everyone by at the gas station."

He loved that car vigorously.

I was dressed for the winter weather; I wasn't foolish about the seasons in this part of Michigan. I had witnessed too many storms blowing across the lake from Canada dumping heavy snow and freezing trees hard enough to split their limbs. Long underwear, heavy flannel shirt covered by a sweater, thick gloves, woolen socks doubled up, a Navy cap pulled down to keep ears warm and a lined coat kept me warm despite the bite of the increasing wind. I could do my route in about 1½ hours start to finish on non-collection days, but more time was necessary when roads were snowy and icy. There was enough snow on the roads already to make my bike hard to pedal, so I asked the storeowner to watch it. I would pick it up when I was finished.

He said, "Nobody will bother it."

I did know people in our area didn't have to lock things up or be concerned about theft in the early 60's. It seems naive and almost unbelievable today, but it just wasn't an issue in our neighborhood. We never locked our garage, seldom locked our house, except when we were away for extended periods and kids left their stuff lying around unfettered all the time.

It would take me double the normal time to walk my paper route, three plus hours, but I had walked it before and would again as long as the route was in Michigan and there was a season called winter. I believed in the same credo as the U.S. Mail and delivered in spite of the weather and was proud of the consistency of my paper delivery. The wind was blowing out of the north so the walk down Pointe aux Peaux Road was tough before I turned onto Long

Road, blowing hard enough to make the snow almost horizontally by now and my eyes blurred from the cold. I kept thinking, "No school tomorrow, no school tomorrow," in singsong thoughts. Long Road was just like its name implies and I had to walk almost all the way to its end, because my only three customers all lived a few yards from the sign that said "ROAD ENDS" at the marsh canal. It was a half-mile up and a half-mile back, a good slog even during nice weather. I had four customers in the summer, but the old couple at the very end of the road went back to Detroit each winter. I walked a mile every day for weekly profit of fifteen cents, but it was part of the job.

By the time I got back to Pointe aux Peaux Road, turned toward Moody's house and cut across Walt's yard to my street, the storm had already laid about another foot of snow down for my enjoyment. With the wind the snowdrifts were twice that and more, growing and piling up quickly. Three, four, five, six, seven more houses and I could warm up at home, something I frequently did during really cold days. Patch took up her thawing position in front of the fireplace. I took the heat register just inside the front door, and perched over the warm air, thawing fingers, feet and face before I headed back out to finish. At my house I still had more than two-thirds of the route to go, but fortified with a good dose of the heat had been able to last long enough until finished.

My mother was weather observant.

"Your father can drive you around when he gets home, it looks pretty nasty out there," Mom said. "You wait. Do you want me to drive you?"

"No Mom, that's okay. It's not so bad."

Who knew when my father would get home? He often didn't get in until seven or eight o'clock from his insurance route. I didn't want to be delivering papers in the middle of the night. Who could tell how bad the snow would be by then? I told my mother again I would be okay, bundled myself back up and slung the paper bag across my shoulder. She looked like she wanted to make me wait but that wouldn't have been in keeping with her methods of operation. She liked her children to make their own decisions about everything except God. She just knew that with healthy doses of God and Jesus, every other decision would be the right one. Ha!

Patch stayed home. Always smarter than I was.

The rest of the trip through my subdivision wasn't too bad. The houses with their hedges and trees blocked the wind, although every time I came to a vacant lot I had to lean into the wind. At Sterling Road, fronting Lake Erie, the wind became an enemy cutting and slashing at exposed face parts and wrists. This was bitter and the snow hadn't let up at all, building plumes of snow into drifts and continuing to pile up in the wind. Mrs. Walker looked horrified when she saw me through the window as I put their paper inside the storm door.

She asked and told me in the same breath. "What are you doing out in this? You come right in here and get warm. You must be freezing, its –10 out there!"

I was freezing and I did come in, thawing and dripping all over their foyer as the snow melted. Both boys, Pete and Richie came down from their rooms and we talked about going out on the ice tomorrow, there sure wouldn't be any school. Ha, ha!

Their mother went in and called my house to let my mother know where I was, and I heard her say, "I'll tell him to wait."

She came back in to tell me my mother would be here in a few minutes to pick me up.

"You're not going anywhere in this weather young man," she said with mother authority.

Ten minutes later the phone rang and she came back to the front door where I had just about finished soaking their carpet.

"Your mother can't get out of the driveway. I looked out the window and I don't think I could either. Do you think you can get home okay?"

I had just celebrated a fourteenth birthday and may not have been the brightest bulb in the house. What boy is until they reach about thirty? Smart I was, but my wisdom was mostly of the tiny size. I tended to gain wisdom SLOWLY and then only after some sort of lesson (or two, or three, or four) and hadn't gathered this one in yet. After all, I was outside in a terrible blizzard and refused to recognize its real dangers. I certainly knew better.

I was smart enough to appear compliant in the face of a Supreme Being though. Besides, I figured that the storm had already done the worst and most that it could do. Hey, I still had papers to deliver… this was my job.

I wasn't going to let any Mother conspiracy stop me from finishing, late though I was. I had never taken this long to finish up. It was already past seven and I wasn't done. It had turned full dark by now and there were no streetlights in our neighborhood. I figured I could just slip around the back of their house as if to appear heading home and then head toward Stoney Pointe peninsula to finish up my route. Another hour or so and I'd be done and I wouldn't have to hear the "Responsibility" speech from my father. Anything would be better than a lecture. I got them often enough as it was.

I said to her, "Sure, it's just down the street and across the ball field. I'll be fine."

I circled undetected around the back of their house just like I knew I could.

All my Indian training hadn't been for naught. I could sneak with the best of them, although I believed now any self-respecting Red Man would have been in his wigwam wrapped in several buffalo hides. I had about twenty customers on the peninsula and the walk was just short of two miles to circle the Pointe. I could do this. I was going to do this. I was doing it. The drifts on the road were getting worse and I had to thread my way around them when I could, plow through when they were covering the whole road. By the time I got out to the peninsula's tip, where the road looped back around on itself the snow was 2½ feet deep in the road. The going was really slowing down.

I had really struggled to get past the last ten houses before I headed back to the other side. The peninsula was a finger jutting out into the frozen lake and the wind picked up and dumped the snow in the first available place, right where I was. I was getting tired from the constant battle of the biting wind, flexing fingers and toes constantly to regain some feeling. Only half way more and I would be through.

I suddenly found myself getting nice and warm.

"All right!" I told myself. "A thaw, right in the middle of a blizzard." I didn't think this odd, not a bit. I was getting sleepy too, but that didn't register. I just knew that I had to get these blinking papers delivered. Heck, I was halfway through with the peninsula, almost home now, almost home, but I needed a breather.

I sat down, with my back to a tree trunk. I'd only rest a bit.

The distinctive sound of the Volkswagen's engine only just penetrated to my brain. I remember sort of, almost thinking, "Who's got a VW out here? I'll have to tell my father there's another one in the neighborhood."

My father and the car that wouldn't get stuck, would go anywhere and got great gas mileage, 32 miles per gallon, pulled up alongside me on the road.

He asked, "Want some help son?"

When I didn't answer him he jumped out of the car and grabbed hold of my shoulders and gave me a shake.

"What're you... hi Dad... doing here out? I'm sorry done, be a minute in home."

He didn't wait for me to slur any more words together, but walked me around to the passenger side, opened the door and sat me down. I dreamt he said, "Put your legs in son."

But I didn't, couldn't, hey, I was happy just like I was. He had to lift my legs up and swing me around to face the front of the car before he could close the door.

317

One thing that certainly wasn't great about the early Volkswagen was its heater. A person would have been better served to hold their hands over a match than to gather any heat from those air-cooled engines. I didn't care about German engineering faults right then, of course, but my father was worried. That little car sped toward home, going as fast as he could get it to go, engine screaming the whole way.

He drove wildly, swerving and hitting drifts to explode up over the hood of the car and talking loudly, almost screaming, the whole way.

"Don't go to sleep, Clark."

"Don't go to sleep, Clark."

"Don't go to sleep, Clark."

"Hey, I'm trying to go to sleep here!" Over and over, the words kept interrupting me, and kept me awake.

My father wasn't a big man, but he somehow managed to get me in the house, carrying me despite the fact I now outweighed him. Pushing, insisting, and shoving. Mom was there too with caring hands and worried looks. Carole, Chip and Peg too, wide-eyed wondering what was happening.

I dreamt I heard my mother say, "What? Oh my God, Jerry.... GET HIM IN THIS HOUSE!"

"What's the matter with him?" someone's voice asked.

"Carole, get Chip and Peg out of here, right now," an answer floated back.

Who were these people? Who was Carole?

Boy, what a weird dream.

"Where's my dog?"

Mom answered only the last question, "In the bathroom, out of the way."

I allowed more pushing and shoving, then undressing and rubbing. Whatever they wanted to do was okay with me. Dad stripped off my boots and socks in front of the fireplace. He unbuttoned his shirt and took both of my bare feet and shoved them under his armpits, while Mom applied a warmed up dishcloth to the half-dollar sized white spots on my cheeks and tucked it around my head to warm my ears. She gently massaged my hands, each one, each finger, in turn right hand, left hand, right hand, left hand, until I recognized all too well that I had hands again. I had forgotten them right along with ears and cheeks and feet.

I was frost bit all over.

I heard Mom say, "I don't see anything turning black, Jerry. Thank God for that."

"Ouch, ouch, ouch, OW, OW, OW!!'

318

There, I was fully awake now, not sleepy and if this burning, tingling, burning, hurting, doesn't go away I may never sleep again. Feels just like fingers are burning, ears flaming, toes being roasted, toasted and cooked.

"That's good, it means the feeling's coming back. Good, that's good." my father said.

I thought, *You might think this is good, but these toes and fingers aren't hanging off you like burnt wieners on a grill.*

I allowed myself an out loud, "Dammit, they hurt, sooooo bad!"

Neither parent said anything, so I tried another. The second cuss earned me a Mom's "hush now, that won't make it feel better."

It actually did, I felt a whole lot better, but I quit cussing. Mom did more rubbing and brought pans of just warm water for my hands and feet, which still burned, like a really, really hot cup of cocoa that I couldn't put down. The washcloth over my face remained warm from the fire. Carole, Chip and Peg came over to peek, and I said I was okay. The tingling and burning went on and on and on and I started to get drowsy despite the pain.

Somehow, I got wrapped up in one of the wool army blankets from the cedar chest. I smelled mothballs and cedar and firewood and warm. Strange and toasty things were happening, sort of drifting, just like walking around the peninsula. I was getting sleepy in front of the fire, but it must have been okay now because nobody was saying, "Don't go to sleep Clark, don't go to sleep, Clark."

Someone let Patch out of the bathroom, because I could smell dog. She lay down between the fire and me, hogging the heat, but I didn't care.

Just before I faded to full sleep I heard my father say, "I'll be right back, Dorothee. It looks like there are nine more papers to deliver. Come on, Carole, you can run them up."

I thought I heard the bells tinkle softly on the front door.

I found out later that it was Patch who forced the issue. My folks had figured that I had just holed up at one of my friend's home, although they weren't too pleased that I hadn't called. Patch became wild in the house, something she had never done before, pawing and whining at the door. Dad came looking after he'd had his fill of Patch's noisy concern and he couldn't get her to quiet.

Winter sports in our neighborhoods were just as fervent an undertaking as anything else we kids did.

Every once in a while one of the fathers pulled kids on sleds around the streets with his car. During one cold snap Mom flooded our side yard and we had an ice rink all our own but mostly we skated on the lake and in the marshes. We ice skated for fun, had tremendous snowball wars from behind snow walled forts, built various snow figures and played hockey. The hockey games were just pick-up types with teams divided as evenly as the numbers allowed. No one really kept score but many was the Saturday afternoon that we bashed and checked one another under the guise of a hockey game.

Jim called me last night.

"Let's play hockey tomorrow."

A hockey game behind O'Dell's house in the marsh, a big deal for me to be invited into the clique of older kids from Stoney Pointe. Must have something to do with my fearless play or speed on skates.

"Get there early, we'll have to clean the snow off the ice." Jim said.

Oh, that's what it was. They wanted my help in shoveling the area so a hockey game could be played without snowdrifts on defense. Oh well, if I wanted to play, it was a way onto the ice with these guys.

Despite going to school with the teens my age that lived in Stoney Pointe, with the exception of Bernie, I hadn't formed many close friend relationships with any of them. Bernie was a close friend. We were only separated by a few months in age and saw eye to eye on most everything. In fact we had been in and out of enough scrapes together to be termed brothers. But if I had to categorize the other guy associations at all, I would say they were wary. Under a bright light some could be downright antagonistic and aggressive. Thus far I had managed to elude any serious damage due to Dad's long ago boxing lessons and lots of practice. Unfortunately all the "no clear winner" declarations only fueled several unresolved fires between neighborhood camps. Being accepted by kids of whom my mother might not approve was an additional attraction, due in some perverse way to the specter of her disapproval. The opportunity to play was just too great to pass up.

Jim was just a year ahead of me in school but almost two years in age. Having turned 14 last month, I thought myself ready to play hockey with the big boys but that wasn't the game I ended up with. The age difference between my 14 and his 16 was enormous and I didn't see the gap. Nonetheless, he and I were friendlier than just nodding a greeting at school. In fact he and I had been in a tenuous spot with some older guys from Detroit at the beach last summer and we had come out of it together just fine. I asked Jim if he had called Bernie to play. He said Bernie would be there, so I didn't bother to call him.

January's Saturday morning was crystal cold and I dressed for a long day on the ice, woolen mittens covered with leather ones and a scarf across my mouth, long undies with jeans, a heavy flannel shirt and sweater under my farmer style denim coat and two pair of extra socks. I knew there'd be a fire built in the marsh for hand warming but feet are a priority. Once your feet are cold in freezing temperatures, it is a known fact that they will remain frigid until you have been back in your house for a full hour. "An ounce of prevention…" my mother would say. I carried my hockey stick, and brown and black skates hung round my neck by the knotted laces. I snatched our snow shovel from the garage just in case and had a pair of sandwiches for lunch from Mom in my coat pocket. I whistled for Patch and she reluctantly followed me out for the walk to the far off marsh.

Although Patch, soon now to be twelve years old was first unwilling, I still seldom left her home when I went tramping about. For one thing I refused to admit her advancing years and secondly I knew she'd get into the trip once her bones got moving. I really liked her by my side, now as always she was my companion. It sounds so simple to say now but where I was, Patch would be also. Wanting her company plus the primary fact she'd be at the door whining to go find me if I did leave her insured her company. Saturdays were a day off work for my father and he would only put up with that sort of nonsense from her for just a short while before he had somebody tie her outside. If she was going to be cold, she might as well be cold with me. True to form, by the time we got out of our subdivision she was nose to ground excited in her hunt for something interesting.

Jim and Dennis were the only ones there when I arrived and they had already started clearing the drifting snow from the playing area. They already had a fire going on a jut of land sticking into the frozen ice. I got my skates laced up by the fire and when I went out on the ice Patch stayed to guard the flames. "Good Girl." I was glad to have brought my own shovel and I started out at the end opposite their workspace after shouting and waving a "Hey Jim! Hey Dennis!" They both waved but kept on pushing snow to the edges. There was still a lot of snow to clear.

The hockey area was laid out in a space about 100 square yards of open ice ringed irregularly with cattails frozen and sticking up like jackstraws. Somebody had made goal nets of a sort, out of scrap lumber that had by now frozen into semi permanent places. The field's edges were marked on all sides by previously shoveled piles of snow and it wasn't hard to push the shovel in the light snow. The hummocks with small trees where they had built the fire were about thirty yards from one of the longer sides of the playing area and the bare trees and cattails cut some of the wind, but it was pretty brisk out on the ice. The idea of the fire was brilliant and when my fingers began to tingle I joined Jim and Dennis to warm them up.

"Who's going to play?" I asked.

As they ticked them off, I was glad they hadn't mentioned the name of one boy my sister's age, four years older than me. Bill and I hadn't seen the same side of the street together for a long time, ever since I'd entered junior high school. I didn't know why then and I don't recall a single incident that could have lit the fire, but the dislike was there. I just avoided him. When we three had warmed up a bit, we got some help when two brothers showed up. Ted was a year older than me, but Rick and I were in the same grade and we all went to Jefferson, but we didn't really chum about together. Same bus, same school, different planet.

They each had brought shovels and between the five of us the ice was cleared by the time our fingers were prickling again. Now all we had to do was wait until the rest of the players showed up. We left our skates on and picked up branches for the fire while we waited. Patch had done a good job and no one had bothered the fire while we were clearing the hockey area. After all the work was done Harley, Pete, Andy and Ronnie got there. They laughed and said thanks. Everybody except Bernie had shown up. We had enough for five on a side though because Bill (of all the guys at the beach who could have) showed up to fill Bernie's slot.

The rules were simple. One guy plays goalie and everybody takes a turn. No face offs. No referee. Side scored on brings the puck back out. No lifting the puck off the ice with slap shots. No high sticking. Checking is okay.

It was probably the checking that started it. The no high sticking rule may have had something to do with it too. These guys played serious hockey. If you didn't make body contact while you were skating it was because you weren't playing in the game and having the puck had nothing to do with body contact. Bill outweighed me by thirty pounds so you know who came out on top whenever he checked me. His superior weight didn't stop me from trying though and I tried to give better than I got but all I did was make him mad. Back and forth on the ice we chased, passing and checking and shooting with complete ferocity. Each team scored a couple of goals before we took a break to warm up by the fire.

Back on the ice it was my turn at goal, a pretty boring job when the whirling slashing skates and wind-milling sticks were at the other end on the ice. When they were in front of my goal it was a chaotic contest. We played for about another thirty minutes before Bill broke free with the puck and slapped a shot high off the ice that hit me in the center of my chest just under the chin. The only pads we wore were shirts and coats, almost no protection from that black missile. It was just the same as getting hit with a big rock. It hurt like fire.

"Dang, watch that crap!" I hollered at him. "No gosh dang slap shots!"

Bill just snickered at me and the puck and players streaked off toward the other goal to score. Bill got the puck again when his side started out and he slapped another shot high up but it sailed past my head. I came out on the ice at him, mad with my stick upraised but Harley skated between us to tell me he was just messing around and I let it go at that. I didn't consider it messing around at all. Somebody's teeth (mine if this kept up) could get knocked out. That's what the rule was for. Keep the puck on the ice. We took a break by the fire, warming hands but I was cooling off.

The conversation and banter was just as you might expect from a group of teenage boys. We ragged on one another, calling stupid names out to the one nearest or someone who had just scored one on you. This game picked up intensity as if the competition didn't stop when we took a break from hockey. Instead, it had become a contest called "let's pick on the kid from Pointe aux Peaux," Bill leading and everybody joined in. To my dismay everybody included my "sort of" friend, Jim. I didn't like to but I put up with the names. "Sticks and Stones." They were just kids running off their mouths, feeding on one another's stupidity but I didn't know how to react to their sudden antagonistic attitudes. I never instigated problems. I was taught not to start trouble.

I was also taught never to walk away if there was an issue requiring resolution. But never be the source. There was never reason enough to do so. I had helped a few instigators see the light on occasion but not when faced with so many at once. I thought it might be time to go but they weren't done playing.

I was vastly outnumbered and I might not have been the brightest kid but Mr. and Mrs. Greene didn't raise a fool. When Bill decided more emphasis was needed, I knew it had passed the time to go. The boy-pack thought of another game called "throw Clark's shoes out on the ice." I got shoved around a bit when I got up from the fire but I managed to get back on the ice and away from the boys, ignoring their taunts. After skating out to get my shoes I called Patch and skated well down the ice to change out of my skates. I glanced over my shoulder but they were still at the fire though their sneers followed me past another spit of jutting land. I skated around to the other side, out of their sight and sat down to change. I hurried as much as I could, wanting to get a bit of distance, to be on my home ground of Pointe aux Peaux but I wasn't fast enough. With perfect timing for me to be stocking footed the mob skimmed around the small peninsula. They decided to play a variation of the shoes game with my skates.

One of my inheritances from the Greene side of the family was a fine temper. Mom didn't think it was so fine but my Grandpa Greene had it and so did my father so at least I was keeping up the family tradition. Today, discretion had so far owned the loudest voice but it was fading dimmer and dimmer. I was getting more than a bit mad with this crap and when they saw the way I looked they knew they had me. I told the bunch I wasn't looking for any trouble, but they needed to back off just a bit and I'd go home.

Bill laughed that I didn't have to look.

"You got plenty right here, a** h***!"

The leader was Bill. My intuition about him was correct. He had initiated changing the bantering game to one of deliberate meanness. When he grabbed one of my skates and threw it sliding across the ice with a laugh and snatched the other out of my hand, I forgot about the numbers of boys surrounding me. I snatched my hockey stick from the bank. Swinging it like a scythe from the ground up I cracked him right on the side of his head. He went down stunned on one knee holding his hand to his smashed and bleeding ear. I knew I should run but it wouldn't have mattered, I'd never have made it. I was at the ice's edge with just socks on, not much use for traction. That group would have caught me. One of them grabbed me from behind while Bill got to his feet.

"You're f***** now Greene!" He screamed in my face as he wound up and punched me in the stomach. "You shou'da kept you're F******* A** to home!"

Several took turns hitting me, mostly punching the breath out of me until I didn't have legs steady enough to stand. During the slugging session I had been fairly quiet save for the grunts and groans that escaped when they hit me. I knew I didn't have any friends close by and screaming for help wouldn't do any good. I might even have not wanted them to hear me holler out in pain or fear. Ronnie, the kid who was holding me let me slide to the ice and they began kicking.

When they started lashing out with their ice-skates my silence vanished. My heavy clothing helped cushion the ice skates' impact, but the blade tips hurt like hell. They got worked up pretty good and I did too, screaming the same language back at them. As soon as I started screaming I got help.

Patch muscled her way inside the circle of kicking boys and started snapping and barking and whirling first at one kid or another. One of the guys grabbed for the hockey stick that I had laid down but I got to it first and sent it sliding over the ice out of anyone's reach.

Patch's voice had lost none of its vigor with time and she was still such an imposing animal that the boys began backing away.

"RUGH! RUGH!"

Snapping! Gnashing!

"RUGH! RUGH! RUGH!"

Graying at the muzzle and back didn't mean old that day. She was still big and right now she was frenzied, quickly approaching out of control. Several of the boys tried to kick her as well and at least two of them were bitten for the effort. Nobody tried anymore kicks. Patch stayed right in front, head down low, and pivoting side to side, on the attack, daring someone to "come get some." The boys skated backwards and Patch herded them about fifty feet from where I had now scrambled to my feet. One of the boys, Rick, didn't skate backwards as fast as the rest of the guys, sort of a forward straggler because nobody took their eyes off Patch. He didn't notice he was alone until it was too late, but Patch did. When Rick was separated from his pack, Patch grabbed one of his pant-legs and pulled him off his skates with the lunge.

When he was on his back on the ice, Patch darted up to crouch low, within inches of his face. Her mouth half open, lips pulled back high, muzzle snarled taut, she growled long and low down with such menace I was immediately worried for him. She stayed low, her snout no more than six inches away from his face, daring the now terrified boy to move. I told Rick to be real still and he didn't so much as twitch. None of the gang of boys did either. Rick froze still just like the ice and nobody was throwing any more names around.

The only one talking was Patch.

"Watch him, girl." But I didn't need to say it. There was *only* that boy as far as Patch was concerned.

I left Rick there while I went and got my hockey stick and skates out on the ice. I left him there the whole time it took to put my boots back on, with Patch still crouched low, her growl one of imminent peril to the teen. Patch hadn't moved a muscle while I got myself put back together.

Neither had Rick.

I walked fifty or sixty feet away and turned around.

One of the knot of guys hollered, "Call her off! Let him up!"

As soon as I whistled she whirled away and trotted back to me. I saw Rick sit up on the ice but he didn't get up on his skates. I wasn't the only one who lost the use of their legs today. I wondered if he peed his pants. I would have. I knelt down and put my face alongside hers savoring the absoluteness of her.

She whined a little to say, *"Let's get home."*

I nodded and said, "In a minute girl."

I held her close feeling her drop the rage, settling her soul and body.

"Well girl," I whispered. "You did it again. One more time."

She licked my face for reassurance and I gave her a good long hug before I got to my feet. When I looked back up Rick was still sitting on the ice but was now surrounded by the rest of the group. I observed them for what seemed the longest time though it was only several moments. Wouldn't do to turn my back quite yet and I watched them until somebody pulled Rick to his feet and they all skated back to the fire. I knew I'd have to pay close attention to that group for a long time.

We started toward home, but when Patch and I had walked as far as Orleans' store she went over and lay down by a tree just off the road and put her head on her front legs. I went over and sat down by her, put my hands on her flank and felt the weariness in her.

"You okay girl?"

She whined a little in her throat in answer and raised her head.

"Sure you are. What a dog you are. Good girl Patch, good girl."

We sat quiet a while, both lost somewhere back there on the icy marsh. What a day. When I stood back up she did too but I noticed a little wobble to her legs when she was up.

"You okay girl?" I repeated and she sank back down on her haunches.

She was wondering about this as well and whined again.

I threw my skates and stick to the ground and knelt down to look her fully on. I held her head in both hands and saw something.... age? No, that's not it. Can't be.

I rose back up and called to her, "C'mon girl, let's get home to the fire."

When she didn't follow I stooped down and put my head under her stomach and lifted her up, legs draping over my shoulders. I could feel the warmth and life of her just like ten thousands of nights sleeping in my bed. She felt so good, so much my partner. I shifted her around and reached up to stroke her strong neck. She grabbed my hand in her mouth, firm strong jaws saying something I could hear more plainly than words. A reassurance for us both, *"I'm okay. Just tired."*

My dog.

Her boy.

"My turn to help now, girl. Okay?"

Chapter 27

Still On Duty

We were going to get a new septic tank.

This summer, in 1961, after more than ten years of putting up with a soggy bad smelling backyard spot in the summer and a discolored ice rink in the winter, my parents decided to get the old construction replaced. The original tank and field were directly behind the dining room, a smelly impetus for spending the money. Many dinners were perfumed by the odor from the inefficient system when the wind was blowing just right. My father and I had dug up the clay tiles connecting house to tank and tank to field several times getting rid of the tree roots attracted by the continuous supply of moisture and fertilizer. When the system was built many years ago the idea of a maple tree outside the back door was a great idea. The tree still was a great idea, now more than sixty feet tall and shade producing for us and for Patch, who had her doghouse under the great branches. It was a disobedient tree however and continued to clog the effluent piping adding to the problem of backed up drains and poor seepage.

My father contracted with some man he knew, a friend who did this "on the side," meaning that he had a regular job, too. They would only do the work on the weekends when he and his crew weren't working at their weekday occupations. They would do all of the work, digging up the side yard for the leech field and the cavity for the new tank plus the installation of new components before they disconnected our old unit. Wouldn't be any loss of use that way and because the schedule could be altered to fit the personal needs of the workers, my father was going to save some significant money.

They had a small bulldozer and a backhoe to do the digging the first Saturday. The new drainage field would have to go in the side yard, a new location to avoid any future incursions of tree roots. Mom stood out by her side yard flowers armed with a shovel to make sure they all survived the earth moving during the dozer work. Chip and I watched with glee as she shooed the big machine away from her precious tulips and daffodils. The racket produced during the excavation prevented anybody from hearing, and made hand signals necessary. Waving the shovel to get the operator's attention, she pointed to her flowers and shook her head. The operator had obvious past experience with gardeners, so he cheerfully nodded and covered them up anyway. That's why Mom had the shovel.

We had to keep Patch tied up the whole day. She didn't like the machinery or the noise. She didn't like the men who were running the big stuff either. She barked and growled, pawing the earth like an enraged bull every time the backhoe took another scoop or the bulldozer came into view. She would have attacked the yellow monsters if she weren't tied. We couldn't get her to calm down and my father had to swear to the crew she couldn't get loose.

Patch must have thought that they carried shovels and picks and rakes (weapons?) around with them and they were strangers (good or bad, who knew?) to boot.

We went through all the necessary introductions with them and Patch but she was still wary and let them know of her distrust, growling when they crossed some imaginary boundary.

Patch was getting older and her 84 dog years were catching up with her, though I wouldn't admit it. Her tight brown and black curls had lots of gray in them, her muzzle and face in particular. She liked to lay in front of the fireplace in cold weather even more than usual and usual was always a lot to begin with. She didn't run as fast or as far, had to be more convinced that there was some high adventure before she joined in. She and I still enjoyed the walks at the beach, still loved the sights, smells and sounds of the marsh, we just didn't get to those places as often. When we did get to our spots the stays weren't as long either. She didn't wait for me at the bus stop any longer, because I got off the bus at the gas station to go to work after school.

I was in high school now, with sports and studies, roller-skating and sock-hops taking up lots of my time. I was also working at a gas station up on Dixie Highway and Pointe aux Peaux Road, three hours after school everyday and a whole day on Saturday. I was making a dollar an hour and closed up the station at six pm. The owner, Marvin "Shorty" Vore, was teaching me to work on cars, something he was very good at and I hoped to be too. The money was great. I made more than $20 every week and contributed half of my earnings in keeping with family rules.

Chip had taken over my paper route so that he could make some big money of his own.

The changes in Patch came so slowly I ignored them.

Although Patch had passed her prime, she was still an awesome animal, having lost none of her bulk. Patch had a head I could not reach across with thumb and little finger spread outstretched and she could fit the fat part of a football in her mouth without opening her jaws all the way. She was even now heavy in the chest and hindquarters, still muscled up big. Notwithstanding her advancing age, strangers still approached cautiously. Rightfully so, she was yet in charge of her household.

Still the yard-boss.

That first Saturday brought great accomplishment to our new septic system. The men worked steadily all day, not stopping until after I got home in the evening, well past six o'clock. The excavation for the field bed was done, the hole for the new tank almost complete. The three men came to the front door before they left. The men would spread gravel and start laying the tile in the field bed tomorrow and they would complete the hole and set the new tank too.

When Mom heard that they were working on Sunday, she raced out to offer them all salvation before my father could stop her, but the workers just laughed politely saying they would make up the church time later. They had work to do. I thought of interjecting the "Not of good works" piece, but knew Mom's disproval of Sunday work so I kept my mouth closed. I wasn't always foolish enough to run off at the mouth. I knew from church where one Salvation lay, but I was also convinced that Mom gave another. Her saving capabilities rivaled any offered by Jesus.

All three men showed up before we went to church. I had not yet convinced Shorty to open his station on Sunday, but I was working on it. I figured if I *had* to work, if my boss demanded it, I might get special dispensation even though the Baptists didn't offer it. But until I persuaded Shorty to open for an extra day, I would attend church. I needed the benedictions of my mother more so than those of the Lord.

When we got back from church we were surprised at the inactivity. Although their trucks were parked in the field across from the house and we heard the backhoe idling in the back yard, we didn't see anyone working. The pile of gravel had been delivered while we were away, but it still needed to be spread and the red clay tile was still banded together in stacks on four pallets. What was happening?

As soon as the car doors slammed shut, the men began hollering in the back yard.

"Hey, can you hear us? Hey, come get this dog! Hey!"

All three men were shouting.

I ran around the back of the house and at the outside water faucet sat the three men. They had their backs to the wall of the house, leaning up against the stucco plaster. Patch was loose and lying about three feet in front of them with her head outstretched on her front paws. When she saw me, she growled. Not at me. At the men. When they stood up she growled louder, telling them and me she had captives. I could see her chain broken and dangling from her collar. I called her to me and she sat at my side still watching.

My dad came around the house too and the men began to tell their story. They thought to take a break about 10 o'clock, get some water from the outside faucet, smoke a cigarette before going back to work. When all three were at the faucet Patch had pulled hard enough to pop a worn link in her lead. When they heard the chain snap and her growl, they just stood there for the longest time, not moving, knowing she would eventually go away. She didn't go away.

When that tactic didn't work, the men thought to try to scare her away. This tactic too wasn't good. Much worse.

When they went, "YAAHHH!" at Patch, she went "RAHG! RAGH! RAHG!" at them.

Patch might be getting old, but you couldn't tell by her bark. She was scarier than they were. One of the men said he thought she was going to attack him. She got down real low to the ground growling and clicking her teeth together in anger. He said he could imagine her teeth clicking on him like that and tried to calm her down, talking nice. She did calm down, but renewed her serious growls every time one of them tried to walk away.

The only way they could get her to relax was to sit down. When they sat down, she lay down. When they tried to get up and walk away, she got up too. When she got up she started growling and clicking her teeth together. All three guys said this is what got to them, the teeth clicking like castanets. They sat. Patch sat. They got up. Patch got up. The teeth convinced them. Simple.

They decided to just wait for us to get back from church. They weren't making any headway with Patch. When they gave up trying different diplomacies it was approaching noon, and Patch had already kept them captive for close to two hours. It couldn't be that much longer now they thought.

They obviously weren't Baptists.

By the time we finished goodbye handshakes and hugs, the "God Bless

You, Go, and Sin No More" from the pastor as we walked out and standing around looking Holy we didn't get home until almost 1 pm.

Once we got back home, it became a joke on them. It didn't matter that they had lost so much time. They weren't mad. They understood that Patch was only doing her job. They laughed about it now. Three men were impressed by her ownership, understood they had crossed some invisible line of demarcation. It was a line once crossed that they were unable to retreat back the way they had started. Their fate lay in other hands. Paws, that is. Teeth, that is. They laughed at themselves because they'd allowed themselves to be bullied by my dog. When I pulled back Patch's lips and they got a close look at her teeth, they didn't think they had been bullied. Instead, they congratulated themselves on how smart they were.

"Hey, would you look at those teeth!" said one.

Patch growled just a little, but the petting and attention the men gave her when I held her collar quickly cured her suspicion of the workers. By the time everyone was finished telling and laughing the story through, Patch was their friend for life. They finished up Sunday's work with barely a glance from her.

When they came back the next weekend to finish the job she didn't even bark. Nothing like a little intimate contact to set aside differences.

At dinner that Sunday night, normally a quick affair, my mother made sure everyone knew what we'd really seen when we got home from church.

"Your dog was a vehicle for the Lord today, Clark. Those men didn't get to work during church anyway. See what happens when you disobey one of God's commandments?"

And here I just thought she was a heck of a dog.

Patch began a new hunting strategy that fall.

I began to take Patch with me to the gas station every Saturday. While I washed windshields, checked oil, pumped gas, ran service calls and helped in the garage, Patch guarded the heat. She was just as good at greeting people who came inside the building as Shorty and I but even more personal in her hellos. Most of the folks who purchased gasoline or had their cars serviced at this local station lived at the beach. The few who didn't know her from our ramblings were quickly sniffed and declared okay by her short tail's wriggling.

Patch's position by the stove was right in everyone's way but it didn't seem to bother the customers. I knew she didn't mind their steps over or detours around to the counter. Within two weekends she looked at home with the accessories of the service station. Name-brand metal cans of engine oil and bottles of bulk-oil, windshield washer solution, a rack of fan-belts, the cash register, a key grinding machine, tires and Patch, all on display. People came in to pay for their gasoline and petted my dog.

At first I had a hard time keeping her out of the service area. Shorty's was a full service station; he tuned cars, rebuilt transmissions and engines, sold and repaired tires and would even fix body damage and paint cars. He was attempting to show me the intricacies of working on automobiles but had his hands full enough without Patch underfoot. When Patch would get cooked sufficiently she'd wander out into the garage to get in on whatever action was happening. Her twelve-year-old habit of being by my side was difficult to modify and during the first few weekends she helped me change oil or repair flat tires. When Shorty tripped over her one day as he changed oil she was banished to the front room.

I don't think Patch really minded the exclusion. She had reached an age where her best work was done in front of the heat. She protected and defended and downright hogged the station's stove just as well as she did our fireplace at home. By the time winter really arrived everyone who wanted to warm their hands had to get her permission but again I don't think people found fault. Most of the beach's people were aware of Patch's place in local lore. I cannot recall one instance when a friend or neighbor didn't take the time to say hello to her. Other people, strangers to the area or those not accustomed to a big dog weren't allowed to become quite so familiar.

One Saturday, as Shorty continued to delegate ever-increasing duties to me, I was removing a transmission from a car. Shorty was running the gas pumps and counter while I fumbled my way through his Transmission Removal 101. He'd come into the garage every so often under the pretense of making sure I was moving forward and doing the job correctly. He was also probably checking to make sure something hadn't fallen and crushed the life out of me. The fact of my employment hinged on my ability to help him and up to this point even I had doubts regarding my ability to demonstrate any mechanical skills. Shorty wasn't big on praise. He didn't have to be. He was long on criticism. His comments regarding my contributions were made up of "you did what?," "how could you?" and "I don't believe it." There wasn't much room for positive comments.

I heard the ding-ding of the bell signal a car's arrival at the gas pumps but being busy with the transmission, beyond the sound I didn't pay any more attention. I heard the additional bell on the front room's door above the whirr of the exhaust fan in the garage, too. After a few moments I heard the front door bell again and then a loud screech of tires as some car sped away.

Shorty laughed from the office.

"Clark, come in here a minute. You gotta hear this. Come here."

I scooted out from underneath the car I was working on. By the time I got to the office area Shorty was on the phone.

"Shorty Vore here. At Dixie and Pointe aux Peaux. That's right."

"I think someone was going to rob me."

"No, they didn't."

"Damnedest thing. One guy came in. Didn't want gas. Said he wanted cigarettes. Noticed my helper's big dog laying on the floor. Looked around a bit more but then didn't know what kind of cigarettes he wanted. Funny. He looked at the dog again and then just walked out the door and he and his buddy took off. Squealing their tires."

"Two guys in a ragged old Chevy. White guys. '51 sedan. Black with a green right fender. Lots of rust. No, couldn't get the tag number. They headed toward Newport."

"Thanks, sheriff. Yeah, if I see them again I'll call. Thanks."

Shorty hung up and went over to Patch and squatted next to her. He gave her a few pats and ruffled the fur on her head, a huge demonstration of affection for someone like Shorty.

"I think she scared them off. He couldn't stop looking at her. I think that guy was gonna rob me but changed his mind."

I gave her some pats myself after I knelt down but I don't believe Patch knew the reason Shorty was petting her. I don't think she recognized what had happened because I felt no tenseness in her body as I stroked her flanks. Just the sight of her had been enough if those guys had been up to no good. From that day forward Shorty was convinced of Patch's preventive role in a robbery attempt but neither of us ever knew for sure. He never heard from the sheriff and never saw the car again that he told me.

Patch had the run of the place again. She could go into the garage, she could hog all the heat, could do whatever she wanted, whenever she wanted as far as Shorty was concerned.

Patch made impressions on most people she met.

My father left us early in the year.

Gone, right before the end of January in 1962. Quit the job. Quit the family. Quit the life and quit the church. Just didn't come back home one day and took his paycheck with him. We were busted-ass flat.

If I could have talked to him before he left I might have asked to go too. Mom's climb toward new pinnacles of the Lord was only matched by her view that I was falling headfirst once again into the fiery lake of Hell. I think she believed she was in a race with the Devil for me and she wasn't about to let one of her children be taken as the hindmost. I got Jesus jammed, crammed and slammed at me every waking moment and I was convinced she was staying up late at night to pray extra on top of the daylight stuff. I was so fed up with the packed full sanctity of our house I could have run off myself.

Instead I stuck around and secretly took a perverse pleasure that all Mom's praying hadn't kept my father at home. It sure as heck wasn't paying our bills either.

No one was paying much toward our living expenses.

Mom made twenty dollars per week from babysitting two sets of kids and I made about thirty dollars at the gas station. Chip and Peg both delivered the *Monroe Evening News* now and earned four or so dollars from the paper route. If you think fifty dollars is small change now, you should have seen it then divided between one adult and three kids. Even in 1962 this total wasn't enough to do much of anything. People came over to pray and fortunately brought food along with their Bibles. I joined in the prayers as an expression of family solidarity. Our living room was encamped by hordes of Christian soldiers and they all had their loins girded for battle. Wave after wave of do-gooders did so much good they were sure of a place in heaven, but I would have been glad for them to go immediately.

We went on county assistance three days after my father drove away. People from local agencies probed and prodded us to find any hidden loot so we didn't get something we didn't deserve. Mom went to the bank that held the mortgage and pleaded with them when she got the notice that my father hadn't made payments in several months. We got boxes of plastic-wrapped processed cheese, cartons of powdered milk and cellophane bags of cornflakes, stamped "U.S GOVERNMENT," big enough to feed the thousands of starving Chinese we'd heard about all these years.

Even Patch wouldn't eat the processed cheese. Remember she ate cat poop.

I got sick of powdered milk the first time I tasted it.

Mom cried every night. Chip withdrew from the hubbub in silence, but Peg cried right along with Mom.

I got sick of all that, too.

By the time spring first peeked at Michigan in 1963, I'd had plenty of the humiliation that went with county assistance, continual prayer meetings in our living room, Grandma Phoebe's visits and hoping someone didn't recognize an article of my clothing their parents donated last month.

Fifteen months after he left, my father came back. One day he was just there with an old beat up Ford that he parked in the driveway. Out of work. Out of the church. Out of money.

When I walked in after closing the gas station one evening, he was sitting in his chair. He did put down the newspaper or book he was reading and rose to meet me, but all he said was hello and sank back into chair. He was back into the life, into the family. Same routine.

Mom pretended nothing ever happened. Mom opened her arms and her heart back up to my father. Chip and Peg were a bit more standoffish and Peg may never have put him back in the same place of her heart.

He and I had more serious problems.

Mom forbade us to ask Dad anything about the elapsed time. We couldn't ask him, "Where've you been? What'd you do? Why'd you go?"

I just wanted to ask if he was staying, but I didn't.

Dad had treated us just like he treated most of the jobs he held when we were growing up. During my childhood he had at least a dozen different jobs, none of which were suitable either for income or his nature. He showed every smart-ass boss, after smart-ass boss what he thought of them. Walked, stormed, stalked, or stomped off in a huff and did not let the door hit him in the ass on the way out.

Now he wanted to just start again.

I didn't have any real difficulty with his attempt. I was actually very relieved to see him home again and could see a definite uplift in Mom's spirits, but I did have serious issues with the pretense of memory lapse, as well as his demanding nature and deliberate attempts at confrontation with someone he saw as a threat to his authority.

Me.

I had provided as much support as I could and probably hadn't done the greatest job, but at least I'd tried every day. I surrendered any and all money I earned and attempted to make up for his absence. I'd cut grass, raked leaves, painted shutters, shoveled snow and went door to door throughout all three subdivisions trying to find some work that would bring extra money into the house. Chip and Peg hunted ways to make a few dollars beyond the paper route as well. There weren't many moments that didn't include school and work during the year and three months Dad was gone. I'm sorry to say it was beyond my 16 years to act as if nothing had happened.

My father spent the next several weeks reasserting his position as head of the house. Mom was so happy to have him back she let him think anything he wanted, but it didn't look as if he was too interested in finding work. Safely ensconced again in his chair and her bed, he didn't seem interested in much of anything except making sure his children knew their proper place. We were at odds almost from the start.

It began with his demands for the money I earned, in spite of the fact he knew I automatically gave it to Mom every time I got paid. He insisted I hand it to *him*, making it a show of obedience to demonstrate to me and the rest of the family how much control he still wielded. The second week he was back I rebelled, ignoring his outstretched hand and gave the folded bills to Mom.

"I told you, I take care of the money in this house!"

He snatched the money from Mom's hand and pushed me away with his shoulder.

I backed away, reluctant to let such a deliberately defiant and foolish act on my part to escalate into a show of his making. While he'd been gone, to my delight and his surprise, I got bigger still. I was much bigger than he was now, but I wasn't trying to make my size and weight advantage any part of the confrontation. I was well acquainted with the history of his temper and I enjoyed it when he directed it at my adversaries. But when I was in his sights, I still feared him. Passivity was certainly the best path. Maybe he'd mistake it for blind obedience.

For the next two months or more he and I dodged one another with only one or two small conflicts. Even these were limited to cold stares. This may have been the only time when the Greene house was occupied and silent at the same time.

I was very surprised when Mom said she wanted me to go to Bible Camp, but I shouldn't have been. The atmosphere was so poor with my father and me in the same house, it's a wonder anyone could get a full breath. I didn't talk to him and he didn't talk to me. He didn't say much of anything to anyone except Mom. I was more than happy with his silence. I despised the manner with which he treated me and Chip and Peg, but at least with his silence I didn't have to deal with his speeches. It wasn't really Mom's idea that I go. He wanted me out of the house and where the money came from for camp I had no idea, but someone sure scraped it together.

To give everyone a breather from the tension I agreed to go.

Chapter 28

Just Like Always

Patch changed last winter.

Overnight she seemed to stiffen, slow and shrink. At first I was dumfounded at her transformation, and absolutely refused to accept her decline. This was the friend who had run by my side for more than thirteen years. She was so much an expectation of my life. Now she seldom ventured anywhere especially during the cold of January, when I just barely could get her to brave the snows. Patch was reluctant even for the necessities of life and I had to struggle to get her outside every night before bed. Nighttime was now the most time we saw one another except for Sundays. I had been working at the gas station every day after school and all of Saturday now. Work and the social choices I made during high school limited the amount of time I had left for her, but she never seemed to mind. Patch mostly liked to lay in front of the fireplace so much now that Mom put a large flat pillow for her to lay on. She looked slightly miffed at everyone when spring arrived and we stopped building a fire for her.

Patch forgave my absences every night when I did get home. Her knowledge of the now was ever so much better than mine and her rear end swinging welcome was evidence of her glad tidings. Before I got my coat off, she would be doing her little four step routine for me, a delight at my return. I think her continued puppyish behavior may have had something to do with my failure to acknowledge her decline.

I sure didn't want to go on this summer Bible Camp excursion although it meant spending two weeks with a new girlfriend, Mitzi. Firstly, Patch had a small stroke several weeks previous to the onset of summer, and while she seemed okay now, I was concerned. Equally important to my reluctance,

Center Lake Bible Camp was patrolled by the most suspicious Baptists on the face of the planet.

Now with Dad back home and at odds with me, I agreed, but I dreaded the trip until the day I left.

My sister Peg said she'd take good care of Patch and that's the only reason I went.

Two weeks had gone when our pastor pulled up at our house to drop me off after camp.

Standing on the front porch, Peg hurried to me as soon as pastor's car pulled into the driveway. When she rushed to meet me before I even got the door open, I read the disaster on her face.

"It's Patch, she's bad again," Peg whispered.

She slipped her arm around my waist and started quick walking me into the house.

"Clark, Patch is really sick this time," Peg started to weep. "I've been sitting with her now for two days. I think she's going to die. Hurry. You need to get in there right away. She's been waiting for you. Even your Patch can't wait much longer."

Chip and Mom were waiting just inside the door and they three escorted me to the bathroom. Before she opened the door Mom gathered her brood in an encompassing embrace.

"Clark, look at me," Mom pleaded. "Don't excite her. She's not good, son. She's not good at all."

I turned from face to face, using their teary condolence like a crutch. I couldn't think of what to do. My mouth was as numb as the rest of me. I didn't have words. I didn't have thoughts and I never wanted to not do something so much as I didn't want to open that bathroom door. Everyone was weeping uncontrollably now, me so much I couldn't find the courage or the door knob.

Patch got me started. Just like always.

"Woof."

But she said it soft and thread-like, only a whisper.

"You'd better get in here," Patch rumbled now. *"You come when I call you."*

"We've made her a bed next to the sink," Mom soothed. "Your brother and sister haven't left her side since she turned worse two days ago. She's had another stroke."

A sharper bark now but still faint.

"Rrrrgh!"

Impatient to get started. Just like always.

Patch lay on several rugs spread over some pillows in the corner of the bathroom. Her sides were heaving with each breath and she struggled to raise her head when I swung the door open.

A deep whine as she sees me. Talking now. Just like always.

"Rmmmgh."

"You'll get better girl."

Her shaggy head raised further, brown eyes more alive with me in them. She tried to wag her rear end but it was beyond her.

"It's okay girl."

I knelt next to her. In honest prayer now.

"We'll get past this. You'll be okay."

Just like always.

Patch whined and struggled to get up. As if she were embarrassed for me to see her like this, she quivered up enough to get her forelegs under her. I used the opening to sit down next to the bedding, scooting under and gathering her big head in my lap. Peg and Chip both crouched down in my abandoned spot, each reaching to touch and caress my dog and me. I runneled my hands down her flank, fingers spread to furrow in her kinky, graying fur. I curled my fingers through her rough coat, feeling for her strength, touching desperately for some sign of the never-ending and monstrous vitality I knew so well. But her fur felt loose and deflated, like a week old balloon.

"Rmmmgh."

"I'm sorry I'm late, girl. I'm right here now."

I lifted her head off my lap, turning it to look her full on and bending down to lay my face to hers. Feeling the feel of her. Smelling her. Wanting to turn it all back, start all over again. Sobs raked, torn from my throat and along with the cries, something sharp slashed the heart right out of me. Her brown eyes lifted to mine as I held her big head and another rumble from her settled in my brain.

"Rmmmgh, rrrgh."

"I'm not going any where girl. I'm not going anywhere at all. I'm not leaving."

My sister bent down to lay her head next to Patch's muzzle and draped one arm over me. The other Peg rested on my dog, connecting us together, offering me the only possible balm that existed at that moment. Patch whined low in her throat and relaxed. I asked everybody to let me be with her alone.

"We need to do this on our own, Mom. Chip? Peg? Please?"

My family wanted to stay but allowed my plea. Except for tear filled hugs and kisses Patch and I were on our own.

Just like always.

I left her only long enough for my family to take care of their necessities before bed. I sat awake holding her massive head in my lap, talking back and forth through the night. Running trails, tracking animals and one another, we visited each and every place we'd claimed and owned. Her breathing was steady and calm, not like we'd been running flat out at all. I was the only one who was trying to catch my breath.

I dozed beside my Patch.

Just before dawn, Patch gently grabbed my left hand in her mouth and slipped away.

Running far ahead of her boy.

Just like always.

I sat with her for long moments afterward, and as the night first turned to dawn, went in and shook first Chip and then Peg awake. Patch was such a huge part of their lives. They must be allowed to partake of this farewell.

"Chip, c'mon. Patch died about an hour ago. I need your help with this." I was weeping, hitching my breath in quiet rasps and couldn't stop. Chip was awake in an instant, almost as if he'd been awake the whole night.

"Peg, wake up. Patch is gone." Peg woke quickly and started to cry softly, consciously aware that this must be an only Greene children task. No outsiders on this trip, not even parents.

Mom later said she heard us go.

We went to the garage and got a shovel and I rigged a twine to tie it to my shoulder. Peg quietly pulled the big slat-sided wagon around to the back door, over the stones in the walkway between the garage and the house. I told them to wait and crept back into the bathroom and shrouded the blankets around Patch and hoisted her in my arms. She was still an armful, heavy, limp and still just as much as I could handle. Footing the back door open I stood for just a moment, settling my partner comfortably in my arms, talking to my dog.

"C'mon girl. Let's go."

"Help me lay her in," I whispered.

All three of us gentled her body into the wagon. Tucking her in with blankets, reverently touching her, but sad and reluctant with the task. No talk now, only tears and memories.

We trundled the wagon across the field to the road, away from the house and remembered aloud.

"Remember Puppy, the baby bunny? She sure loved that rabbit."

"Those guys digging the septic tank. It was so funny."

"When she bit Mr. Terry? That was scary."

"I remember when I used to ride her all over the house."

We all knew where we were going and how we were getting there. It took about an hour because we took the long way, but we relived a lifetime during the walk. Down by the lake, where Patch rolled in fish and we all gave her baths. Long Road; where every one of us was escorted by Patch on the paper-route. Retracing steps and adventures, right to where I'd watched troubles fly away, all swirled up with laughs and growls, Mom's calls from the back porch and the wonder of a dog named Patch. Right where Patch, Chip and I watched Fermi's security guards hunt in vain, time and time again. Right where everything important was.

We ended up when we pulled the wagon out to the point of the short peninsula at the end of Long Road.

"I want to hold her. To make sure she's going to be okay without us," Peg whispered.

I lifted Patch out of the wagon and lay her on Peg's lap. Chip and I did the digging.

"It has to be deep. We're going to put her standing upright. Not lying down. I want her to be looking out over the marsh," I told Chip and Peg between sobs.

The tears were on us all in a flood and it took me a long time to get it out.

"I read somewhere that gypsies are buried standing. That's how it has to be with Patch. She'd want to be ready for whatever is out there."

Chip and I dug a long time through the tree root laced dirt and Peg held Patch's big bulk the whole time we worked, talking to my dog, bathing Patch with her tears. We had a hard time propping her big body upright in the hole but we somehow managed it together. We draped the blankets over her and laid the dirt around her by hand. Nothing so crude as a shovel full would do for this warrior. We scooted and scooped the crumbled earth around the shrouded body of my dog, patting it softly under and around. All three of us were filthy by the time we'd finished putting her body where she'd want it most. Where she'd been the most at home.

When we were through, there weren't words to say, just silent feelings interlaced with a terrible sadness. We all struggled to stay upright and if we hadn't been supporting one another, our hearts couldn't have done it on their own. We each knelt and smoothed the mound of dirt a final time. Her gravesite didn't need a marker.

The marsh knew everything there was to say about my dog.

And I've wished every day for more than forty years it had happened that way. It was supposed to end just like that.

I didn't get the chance to say good bye before Patch left.

Two weeks gone.

Our pastor dropped me off at the house and my father came out when he heard the car. Nobody else. My father made everybody else stay inside while he told me. He was in such a hurry to get it done he didn't even say hello.

Instead he declared, "Patch got worse while you were at camp so I took her out by the Catalpa tree and shot her to put her out of her misery. I dug a hole and had her lay down in it and I shot her in the head. She didn't feel a thing."

And he pointed.

A lifetime gone.

Oh no you didn't. This is some sort of terrible lie, I thought.

My father followed me, trailing as I walked out to the tree. Dogging my footsteps, wanting and needing to see the result. There by a mound of earth, he tried to put his arm around me and with the act he pulled another trigger.

I asked him just who gave him the right to shoot my dog, "MY DOG! YOU NEED TO GET THE HELL AWAY FROM ME RIGHT NOW! NOW!" But I only screamed in my mind.

I shrugged off his arm, horrified by his touch and warned him coldly, "You had no right. She wasn't your dog. How could you have done that to her? To me? Please, won't you *please* get away from me."

But he wouldn't let it go. He had to justify himself.

"Patch had another stroke and couldn't get up, couldn't control her bowels, she could only lie on her rug. I did what needed doing."

What he didn't tell me was that he'd dragged Peg out of the bathroom too when he picked up my Patch to carry her outside. Peg wouldn't let go of his leg. Screaming, pleading, begging him to wait, to stop, to put down Clark's dog, NO! NO, YOU CAN'T!, as he twisted away.

What he didn't tell me about was my brother. How twelve-year-old Chip had fought him literally until my father wrestled him down and subdued him. How my father shoved him to the ground, holding him there until Chip gave in to my father. How Chip even then ran to the bathroom and locked the door so Dad couldn't get to her.

He never said anything about my mother either. How he made her cry and kept right on. Hers was the voice most pleading, the most insistent for him to wait until I got back. The voice he ignored right to the very end.

He said not a word about him pounding on the bathroom door. Hammering until it appeared it would shatter and Chip was frightened by his rage so much he unlocked it. He said nothing about commanding, "Enough is enough," when he carried my dog out the door.

He didn't think to tell me those items.

My baby sister did. Peg told me everything.

My father had found one more way to show me and everyone else who the boss was. I knew of my father's tyranny and his need for deference from the family. I recognized years ago how much hatred he had for people who didn't agree with his decisions. He did this to assert who was in control. Just like he always did when anyone butted heads with him.

Standing next to the tree, he kept on and on and on.

"No you did not. You didn't even come close to doing the right thing. I can tell you all the right things you could've done and they would have started by coming to get me from Center Lake," I continued to shout. "You bastard. You weren't the one to do this. I can't believe you did it. You killed *my* dog. She was not yours. You might just as well as shot me. You really need to get away from me before I do something I can't help."

Mom and Chip and Peg came out to stand alongside the mound underneath the catalpa tree. All of them gathered around me with Peg and Chip the closest, offering their arms of solace. Mom reached around Peg and put her hand on my shoulder. Tendering their touches, some of my family offered the silence I needed. My father started all over again for his audience and I started to bawl, huge sobs just falling out of me.

"Mom, won't you please get him away from me? Please? Get him away from me!"

My mother managed to do what my pleadings and near hysteria could not. "Come on Jerry, come on you two, let's leave your brother alone for a while."

I sat under the Catalpa tree for a long time, long enough for both Mom and Peg to walk back out and see if I was okay. I just waved them away, couldn't speak with the choke that had lodged somewhere between my heart and my throat. I just didn't have any faith in my voice. For a time I was numbed by the enormity of this huge hole in my heart and I had cried myself out before the thought came. I'd returned home in the early afternoon and it took me several hours to realize how futile was this grave.

I didn't say goodbye to anyone although I saw Chip standing at the back door. My heart hadn't allowed the thought and I walked Pointe aux Peaux

Road down to the lake to find the courage for a farewell. I heard the click of her toenails on the pavement just like the other countless tic-tic-tics on this road. The lake was flat, calm, not a ripple moved on that summer day. Everything looked the same here, even though I'd left it behind for long months.

A dead fish lay washed up above the waterline. An errant thought that I wouldn't have to worry about Patch baths anymore brought new tears to my eyes. At the rocky ledge where Ralph and I were once scared out of our wits, I sat down, dangling my feet over the water. I saw the imprints of fossilized clamshells in the small pools of water and trailed my fingers though the wetness. Patch wasn't here. I might have seen a paw print pointing north but it must have been my imagination, for when I looked closer it was just the shadow in the ledge. I heard something far off, but it was so slight a whisper I thought I'd imagined that, too. I looked over my shoulder, back toward Long Road. Maybe there.

I walked the dusty road alone, past Goltowskis', past Dombrowskis' and stood in front of the Basteins'. Right there she was in such an awesome fury. I still shuddered when I thought of her ferocity the day she protected me from those dogs' attack. This was the first day I ever walked here without having a choice of companionship. Puppies or weather or tether were the only preventions then. This was very different. My feet kicked little dusts off the road and I looked here, eyes downcast, for her track, some evidence of Patch passing this way. When I got to the end of Long Road I ignored the NO TRESSPASSING sign that warned of other ownership.

Just like always.

Patch and I had possessed every step of this area. No matter whose name was on the register, this ground had been staked out for years. Before Fermi even thought about another use it had been completely mapped in our minds and hearts. I walked down the beach until I saw the small stream that fell into the lake. I crawled under the security fence and cut across into the heart of the marsh. I knew then where I was going and I found the faint and overgrown trail as if I'd been here yesterday.

Another soft murmur, perhaps just a little louder this time.

Our old camp looked terrible, abandoned in a shamble with the lean-to fallen in and canvas moldy when I lifted a corner. A mouse family fled in the dying sunlight when the tarp was lifted and I carefully put it back, sorry to have disturbed their home. The grass had grown long in our absence this year, no sign now of the scraping and scuffing of a dog and young boy. I didn't feel too young right now anyway. I sat with my back against a tree looking into the marsh and woods, being still as a stone while I waited. The sounds of the marsh that had been quieted by my invasion came back so slowly. Softly. Red-winged blackbird's call, dragonfly wings buzzing, cicada and grasshopper legs. I heard the mice squeak as they reclaimed their territory.

It was so quiet.

My fingers trailed in the stubbly grass next to the fallen down shelter. In a fold of the fallen canvas, I discovered a cast away burr with tan fur still attached. A careless remnant of an idle boy and dog's visit.

I traced the fur across my cheek. I could smell something like dog when I held it to my nose. Patch had an amazing attraction of burrs and the thought of my fingers as they separated one from the other came back with a freshet of tears. But I needed to be quiet.

There was the noise again.

I shushed my tears to hear the better.

The sun settled further beneath the treetops, bringing long shadows and night. Darkness also brought mosquitoes and I gathered wood for a fire. In the ring of stones, once I got it burning, I piled the flames with green wood for help with the bugs. I stared into the fire, hearing the snap and spit of the branches mix with the night buzz of crickets and blend with frog croak harmony. I'd heard this symphony a hundred times before, but listening alone sure was different. I heard sounds of lonesome and abandoned in the hum of the marsh. I understood sadness as I had never felt before.

Patch wasn't here. Patch was gone and I hadn't been allowed to say goodbye.

I cursed everything I could think of that evening, spitting out places and names. I especially damned my father. I went back through a second and third time, enjoying the bitter taste and just to be sure I gave everything its due. Using my arm for a pillow, I lay down in Patch's favorite spot, where she'd kept me and another dozen boys under her watchful eyes. Just before I cried myself to sleep I heard that rumor of a sound again, but the weariness that fell on me wouldn't allow me to move.

The mosquitoes ate me up that night. I felt better with the sacrifice.

Something woke me up.

Another stirring.

Some noise. Some passage.

The new day wasn't full yet, but it was time to go. I'd held the prickly burr remnant in my hand the whole night, mashing it flat in dreams. I knew where I had to go.

I ran flat out, as hard and as long and as fast as I could go, pushing, pushing until there wasn't anything left except the thought of getting there. I hurtled across the marsh edge, splashing every step, damn the clothes, damn the shoes, damn it all. Into the north edge of the woods, drawn to the path once more by something just ahead of me by a step, I followed the rumor of sound around the small pond, reached the second woods and turned onto another of the indelible trails. I could have done them blind and never missed a turn.

I knew when I got there.

This was the place.

The oak tree looked just the same, huge and in full summer leaf, spread out to shade the day just dawning. I put my foot in the same knothole I'd used before and climbed up just like I should have.

Up high in the branches I watched the dance again, over and over and over and over, but that time Patch didn't get tired. I heard every sound, every pant of dog and deer and every crackle of every leaf as they trampled up their theater. I remembered which way both deer ran. I smelled Patch's hot breath as we rested in the shade and felt of her drink from my hand.

This was the place. I'd wait a while longer.

I woke up to a sky gone dusk, darkening again, and heard sounds once more as I lowered from the tree. I looked over my shoulder into the deep of the wood but Patch wouldn't have been there. She'd be here, where she belonged.

She *was* with me. But for now, it would be the last time. I wouldn't come back here without her.

I crept out of the woods. Deep night now and the moon sliver had sidled into the sky.

Probably need to get home, I thought.

Mom might start to worry if I didn't turn up pretty soon, but I sure wasn't looking forward to seeing my father. I walked down Pointe aux Peaux Road from the opposite direction I'd started. Walking past the store, past the stone pillars of the subdivision until I got even with our house again. I finished up exactly where I began and peered back toward the marsh. Way off I heard Patch again, but this time loud and clear and strong like always, but only once more. Nothing else.

We'd made our rounds, she and I, checked every step of the property, the circuit was complete. Patch would wait for me to catch up one more time, just like she'd always done. I know right where she'll be and I'm going to meet her there. She'll be waiting.

Just like always.

Printed in the United States
49725LVS00005B/1-51